Encyclopaedia of Information Technology and Communication Science

Encyclopaedia of Information Technology and Communication Science

Volume 2

David Park

ANMOL PUBLICATIONS PVT. LTD.
NEW DELHI - 110 002 (INDIA)

ANMOL PUBLICATIONS PVT. LTD.

H.O.: 4374/4B, Ansari Road, Darya Ganj,
New Delhi - 110 002 (India)

B.O.: No. 1015, Ist Main Road, BSK IIIrd Stage
IIIrd Phase, IIIrd Block,
Bangalore - 560 085 (India)
Visit us at: www.anmolpublication.com

Encyclopaedia of Information Technology and Communication Science

First Published, 2007

ISBN 978-81-261-3374-1 (Set)

PRINTED IN INDIA

Printed at Mehra Offset Press Delhi.

Contents

Preface

In today's world communication science and information technology are rapidly growing fields of study, research and development that is cutting across many traditional boundaries. This encyclopaedia titled "Encyclopaedia of Information Technology and Communication Science" is really very unique in terms of coverage, scope, elaboration, usefulness and futuristic perspective. It will provide readers with a user-friendly approach towards acquainting themselves with various select traditional and newly emerging fields of world communication science and information technology. Everyday we see that these sciences and technologies have varied fields of study, which are always growing. To understand the applications and usefulness of these sciences, we need to explain at least one of its fields, such as Multimedia, for example. Multimedia science is a relatively new discipline, and there is currently no consensus on a precise definition of what this science actually is.

Information as a concept bears a diversity of meanings, from everyday usage to technical settings. Generally speaking, the concept of information is closely related to notions of constraint, communication, control, data, form, instruction, knowledge, meaning, mental stimulus, pattern, perception, and representation. Many people speak about the Information Age as the advent of the Knowledge Age or knowledge society, the information society, and information technologies, and even though informatics, information science and computer science are often in the spotlight, the word "information" is often used without careful consideration of the various meanings it has acquired. As with other industrial processes, commercial IT has moved in all respects from a custom, craft-based industry where the product was tailored to fit the customer; to multi-use components taken off the shelf to find the best-fit in any situation. Mass-production has greatly reduced costs and IT is available to the smallest company or one-man band — or school-kid. LEO was hardware tailored for a single client. Today, Intel Pentium and compatible chips are standard and become parts of other components which are combined as needed. One individual change of note was the freeing of computers and removable storage from protected, air-filtered environments. Microsoft and IBM at various times have been influential enough to impose order on IT and the resultant standardisations allowed specialist software to flourish.

Software is available off the shelf: apart from Microsoft Office or IBM Lotus Notes, there are also specialist packages for payroll and personnel management, account maintenance and customer management, to name a few. These are highly specialised and intricate components of larger environments, but they rely upon common conventions and interfaces. Data storage has also standardised. Relational databases are developed by different suppliers to common formats and conventions. Common file formats can be shared by large main-frames and desk-top personal computers, allowing online, real-time input and validation. In parallel, software development has fragmented. There are still specialist technicians, but these increasingly use standardised methodologies where outcomes are predictable and accessible. At the other end of the scale, any office manager can dabble in spreadsheets or databases and obtain acceptable results.

This encyclopaedia titled "Encyclopaedia of Information Technology and Communication Science" is of great contemporary relevance. It will serve as a reference book on the said subject and tends to acquaint readers with both in-depth and extensive knowledge of the subject concerned. This "Encyclopaedia of Information Technology and Communication Science" is a unique initiative to provide the most comprehensive coverage to the subject area in question. This encyclopedia mainly focuses on the following areas: Introduction to Information Technology & Communication Science; Multimedia Information Graphics, Design & Printing; Computer Programming and Hardware Systems; Internet, E-mail, Network System and Computer Security; Music Science and Technology; Audio Visual Technology, Photography and Design; Elements of Advanced Communication System; Mobile Phone and Mobile Computing; and Speech Recoginition Tools and Technologies.

—Editor

5

Music Science and Technology

Wave Shapes and Spectral Content

The shape of a wave is directly related to its spectral content, or the particular frequencies, amplitudes and phases of its components. Spectral content is the primary factor in our perception of timbre or *tone color.* We are familiar with the fact that white light, when properly refracted, can be broken down into component colors, as in the rainbow. So too with a complex sound wave, which is the composite shape of multiple frequencies.

So far, we have made several references to sine waves, so called because they follow the plotted shape of the mathematical sine function. A perfect sine wave or its cosine cousin will produce a single frequency known as the fundamental. Once any deviation is introduced into the sinus shape (but not its basic period), other frequencies, known as harmonic partials are produced. Partials are any additional frequencies but are not necessarily harmonic. Harmonics or harmonic partials are integer (whole number) multiples of the fundamental frequency (*f*) (1*f*, 2*f*, 3*f*, 4*f*...). Overtones are the harmonics *above* the fundamental. For convention's sake, we usually refer to the fundamental as partial #1. The first few harmonic partials are the fundamental frequency, 8ve above, perfect fifth, 2 8ves above, 2 8ves + major 3rd, 2 8ves + major 5th as pictured below for the pitch 'A.' After the 8th partial, the pitches begin to grow ever closer and do not necessarily correspond to equal-tempered pitches, as shown in the chart. In fact, even the fifths and thirds are slightly off their equal-tempered frequencies. You may note that the first few pitches correspond to the harmonic nodes of a violin (or any vibrating) string.

Phase

Phase denotes the particular point in the cycle of a waveform, measured as an angle in degrees. It is normally not an audible characteristic of a single wave (but can be when we using very low-frequency waves as controls in synthesis). It is a very important factor in the interaction of one wave with another, either acoustically or electronically. The Flash example below traces a sine wave by plotting the height of the tip of a spoke (or radius) of a rotating wheel (y-axis) against time (x-axis). The height of the spoke-tip corresponds to the waveforms relative amplitude, here plotted between an imaginary +1 to -1. To measure the phase angle, we start with the reference of the spoke pointing completly to the right and refer to that as 0°, with a relative height or amplitude of 0 as well. A the wheel rotates couterclockwise, the sine wave reaches its peak positive amplitude when the spoke has traveled 90° from its starting point (click on the 90° button), with a relative amplitude of +1. At 180° from the starting point, the amplitude of the sine wave has returned to 0 (click on the 180° button). At 270°, the sine wave reaches its peak negative amplitude of -1 (click on the 270° button) and then returns to 0 as it returns to its starting point of 360° or 0°. Another common sinusoidal waveform used in synthesis or measurement is the cosine wave, which is exactly the same shape as a sine wave and would sound exactly the same all by itself, but is distinguished by the fact that it's cycle begins 90° out of phase to a sine wave, or at +1.

Resonance

There is much more to what makes an instrument sound like a particular instrument, or your voice sound like your voice and not your neighbors, besides the spectral envelope of the excitation source. One such element is resonance. If you have ever stretched a string across a cardboard box and plucked it, you likely noticed the resultant timbre did not sound like a fine acoustic guitar. That is because cardboard boxes do not have the same resonating characteristics as both the material and shape of a guitar body. When a guitar string is plucked, it vibrates and creates a rich spectrum of harmonic partials. The string itself is called the excitation source. The disturbed air molecules cause the guitar body to vibrate through sympathetic vibrations. The larger vibrating surface area creates higher amplitudes by causing more substantially more air to move.

The guitar body does not *proportionately* amplify all of the frequencies of the string. Instead, some frequencies are amplified more than others. This quality is called *resonance*. Unless instruments are able to change their shape with each note, most exhibit a complex of many resonant frequencies that do not change, or are fixed—the specific complex of resonances are called formants and those that do not change are called fixed formants. When different frequencies are applied to these fixed resonances, some partials may be excited more than others—this is part of what gives instruments both their overall tone quality and also their registral characteristics i.e. they have noticeably different tone qualities playing low pitches than playing high ones, since *differing partials of their spectra are being enhanced*. Cellists are familiar with a 'wolf tone,' which is a particular pitch in which there are virtually no lower partials resonated, creating an unpleasant 'dead' result (when purchasing an instrument, cellists look for ones where the wolf tone falls in between equal-tempered pitches). Digital samplers can change pitch by simply speeding up or slowing down the replay rate of a recorded sound to change its pitch—however, if we took the lowest 'C' Steinway grand piano sample and transposed it up 4 octaves, the result would be much more akin to a cheap honky-tonk instrument, since the true acoustic effect would have been to transpose all of the fixed resonances of the Steinway. 'Alvin and the Chipmunks' made a living by such transposition. We use formants everyday—they are the *vowel sounds* we produce when speaking. Our vocal cords are the excitation source, but they don't change shape for each vowel—instead we change the shape of our oral cavity, which (along with our sinuses) create a specific complex of resonances resulting in an 'A', 'O', 'U' etc. Unlike instrumental fixed formants, when we produce diphthongs (vowels that morph from one into another ('ai-yo', 'oo-ee'), we smoothly change the shape of our oral cavity and hence the resonating characteristics. Later on, when we study synthesis, we will discuss resonant filters that allow us to enhance or reduce certain specific frequency areas of a signal. Tubes of various diameters and lengths also have easy-to-calculate resonating frequencies as demonstrated by blowing across the opening of a bottle. Whether the tube is open on both ends or closed on one end or cylindrical or conical in shape will also effect the resonant frequency. The vibrating air column set up in such 'resonators' also produce standing waves, discussed in the next chapter. See the Hyperphysics air column reference below for further study. The entire woodwind and brass family of acoustic instruments produce sound in this method. Recently, physical modeling synthesis software has made use of the resonator principles to recreate similar phenomena with software without the physical restrictions of the real world—for example, a program might model a 200'-long flute.

Reflection

Sound waves reflect off of objects the same way billiard balls bounce off the bumpers of a pool table—*the angle of incidence equals the angle of reflection.* A sound wave hitting a flat wall at 45° will reflect off it at 45.

Flash Example of Reflection Here

The reflected wave can interfere with the incident (original) wave, producing the constructive and destructive interference mentioned above—it can increase its amplitude or, with phase cancellation, decrease its amplitude. In a typical listening environment, we are hearing sounds that have reflected off numerous objects and surfaces, with the reflections themselves interfering with other reflections. Just as color is determined by which frequencies of light are reflected or not, the 'color' or acoustic characteristics of a particular listening environment is determined by the angles and materials the sound may reflect off. Different materials reflect some frequencies more efficiently than others, due to their roughness or absobancy characteristics. The acoustic foam at the end of our studio, for example, does not reflect higher frequencies very efficiently, but has little effect on particularly low frequencies (we need a 'bass trap' for that). The distance both the incident sound and the reflected sounds must travel is another key element in the characterstics of an acoustic environment, since the incident sound typically reflects off many surfaces at differing distances from the listener, thereby striking the ears at differing times.

Reverberation (Reverb)

The sound waves that reach the listener's ear directly from the sound source is often referred to as the direct sound. These waves reach the listeners ears first in most acoustic environments. The first reflected sounds to reach a listener's ears are called early reflections. Since they travel a longer path, the amount of time it takes the first reflected sounds to reach our ears give us clues as to the size and nature of the listening environment. Because the reflected sound may continue to bounce off of many surfaces, a continuous stream of sound fuses into a single entity, which continues after the original sound ceases. The stream of continuing sound is called reverberation. *The rate of build-up of echo density is proportional to the square root of the volume of the room.*

Picture Here

The time-domain and frequency-domain reverb characteristics of an environment can be represented by its impulse response, which is equivalent to subtracting the original sound from its reverb and storing it. Combining digital sound files with an impulse response file in a process call convolution will result in something equivalent to playing the sound in that hall. Many high-end digital reverb units have stored impulse responses from famous concert halls. Later, we will see how digital filters are also measured by their impulse responses.

Because of the inverse-square law described above, reverberated sounds will eventually lose enough energy and drop below the level of perception. The amount of time a sound takes to die away is called the reverb time. A standard measurement of an environment's reverb time is the amount of time required for a sound to fade to -60 dB. Concert halls will normally have much longer reverb times than small rooms, but maybe not as much as tunnels. Rooms with lots of reverb are called 'wet' and those without are called 'dry.' The nature of both reverb time and characteristics of which frequencies will die away before others keeps acoustic designers up at night. Special chambers for acoustic research and recording of special sound examples are called anechoic chambers (an=no echoic=echoes), which should have reverb times of 0.

Diffusion, often a setting on reverb units, refers to higher frequencies spreading and dying out more quickly than lower frequencies, something we use as an aural cue to the size of a space. A football field will have a higher degree of diffusion than a small studio. Humidity plays a large factor in diffusion as well.

Almost all studios have either hardware or software reverb units. The controls are usually reverb time (how long will it take the reflections to completely die away, a pre-delay, which determine when the first early reflection will be heard, filters which allow the user to tune the acoustic characteristics of the imaginary environment and diffusion, which determines how much more quickly the higher frequencies will die away. Reflections from surfaces that stand out from normal reverberation levels are called echoes. An echo of prominent amplitude, close in time to the original sound may be referred to as a slapback echo. Concert halls with a *focusing* flat back stage wall may produce slapback echoes with sharp loud sounds, such as percussion.

Standing Waves

A particular pattern of constructive and destructive interference is called a standing wave, which is essential to the way string instruments produce sound, but very undesirable in the listening environment of an electronic studio. The characteristic mode of vibration of a string with one fixed end is the standing wave pattern. In a normal reflection of a sound wave from a hard surface, the phase of the reflected wave is not changed. With a wave induced in a string with a fixed end, the wave reflects from the fixed end out of phase with the incident wave, creating patterns of constructive interfere at certain resonant frequencies. Nodes and antinodes on the resultant string correspond the points of minimum (node) and maximum (antinode) vibrations. Air columns in both closed and open tubes also exhibit standing wave properties. In this case, the nodes and antinodes refer to the minimum (node) and maximum (antinode) pressure in the tube. Woodwind instruments are examples of half- or quarter wave resonators that produce multiple standing waves—the differences are whether the tube is open at both ends (flute, including the embouchure hole) or closed at one end, such as the oboe or clarinet.

Standing waves in rooms can cause certain resonant frequencies to either be unduly enhanced (nodes) or completely disappear (antinodes). For that reason, it is always a good idea to listen to your work from a few different spots in the studio, since we have not completely eliminated our standing wave potential.

Working of Ear

This chapter begins our study of psychoacoustics, or how the human body and mind *perceive* the physics of sound discussed above. Obviously, our primary organ used to sense sound is the ear (although sitting next to a subwoofer at a rock concert might convince you otherwise). The structure of the ear can be divided into three main parts: the outer ear or pinna, the middle ear and the inner ear. The outer structure of the ear is responsible, in part, for helping us to place the original location of a sound, be it ahead or behind, above or below us. It also helps to funnel and focus sound waves on their way to the middle ear and auditory canal. The middle ear contains the auditory canal, which terminates in the eardrum, or tympanic membrane. Attached to the other side of the eardrum, in a small space of air, are three tiny bones or ossicles, the *malleus, incus and stapes* (or hammer, anvil and stirrup) which then attach to a fluid-filled structure called the cochlea of the inner ear at a point called the oval window. It is in the cochlea that the vibrations transmitted from the eardrum through the tiny bones are converted into electrical impulses sent along the auditory nerve to the brain. The inner ear, which is surrounded by bone, also contains semicircular canals, which function more for purposes of equilibrium than hearing. One of the difficulties above is determining a universal threshold of pain is that the chain of ossicles can be stiffened or muted by a contraction of the stapedius muscle. This provides a form of protection against loud sustained sounds, but not of sharp, sudden ones, such as a gunshot. This reflex is far less efficient in older people, which along with differing tastes, may explain their lower tolerance to louder music as well as an increased risk level for hearing loss. The most fascinating aspect of perception takes place in an area of the cochlea called the basilar membrane. The cochlea is a tapered tube, which circles around itself like the scroll on a violin. The basilar membrane divides the tube lengthwise into two fluid-filled canals, which are joined at the tapered end. The ossicles transmit the vibration to the cochlea where they attach at the oval window. The resultant waves travel down the basilar membrane where they are "sensed" by the approximately 16-20,000 hair cells (cilia) attached to it which poke up from a third canal called the organ of Corti. It is the organ of Corti that transforms the stimulated hair cells into nerve impulses. Because of the tapered design of the cochlea, waveforms traveling down the basilar membrane peak in amplitude at differing spots along the way according to their frequency. Higher frequencies peak out at a shorter distance down the tube than lower frequencies. The hair cells at that peak point give us a sense of that particular frequency—it is thought that a single musical pitch is perceived by 10-12 hair cells. Due the tapered shape of the cochlea, the distance between pitches follows the same logarithmic distance as our perception of pitch i.e. the placement of octaves are equidistant. This arrangement is responsible for the fact that a higher frequency can mask or hide a lower one, but a lower one can mask a higher on.

Perceiving Pitch

Pitch is our perceptual interpretation of *frequency*. As mentioned, ideal human hearing ranges from 20 to 20,000 Hz, yet we have our greatest sensitivity to frequencies which lie within 200 to 2000 Hz, which takes up two-thirds of the distance on the basilar membrane. One proof of this is the "just noticeable difference" or JND. The JND is the smallest change in frequency of a single sine tone that is perceptible by the average listener. Most studies place is around 3% in the 100 Hz range, but only 0.5% in the 2000 Hz range. One might extrapolate that a bass player has more liberty to play out of tune than a violinist In general, we perceive pitch logarithmically in relation to frequency. The formula for successive semitones is a frequency ratio of 1:12th Root of 2 or 1:1.05946. Every doubling in Hz is perceived as an equivalent octave. It is thought that because a doublings of frequency causes a response at equal distance on the basilar membrane, we hear octaves as related. In fact, because of the logarithmic spacing of pitch placement on the membrane it can be extrapolated that we perceive differences in pitches not as differences frequency, but as the ratio of pitches separating them or musical intervals (which are ratios of frequencies and not linear differences). So A220 to A440 is perceived as the "same" interval as A440 to A880, even though one pair has a difference of 220 Hz and the other a difference of 440 Hz. View a chart of frequency vs. pitch here.

Loudness

Loudness is the way in which we perceive amplitude. As mentioned above, a particular change in amplitude is not necessarily perceived as being a proportionate change in loudness. That is because our perception of loudness is influenced by both the frequency and timbre of a sound. The 'just noticeable difference' or JND for amplitude, i.e. the minimal perceptible change in amplitude, varies by the starting amplitude and frequency, but in general ranges between 0.2 and 0.4 dB.

The most famous, well-used measurement for plotting our perception of loudness against the frequency of tones is the Fletcher-Munson curve(s) of equal loudness, published in 1933. The graphs were updated in 1956 by D.W. Robinson and R.S. Dadson. The purpose of the graph is to show that for humans to consider two pitches equally loud, the amount of energy necessary to produce the tone at one frequency may be completely different than at another. The multiple lines also show that the energy/frequency differences are steeper at lower intensity levels and flatten out at extremely high intensities.

F-M GRAPH HERE—Until Permission is Received, Please Click on Hyperphysics->Equal Loudness

The "loudness button" on a stereo amplifier is intended to boost bass frequencies at lower volume levels where the curve is the steepest. In viewing the graph, it immediately becomes apparent that much more acoustic energy is required in the lower frequencies to create sounds of equal loudness to those in higher frequencies—with a minimum around 4000 Hz, some additional energy is also required for equal loudness at higher frequencies. You do not buy a 500 watt amplifier for frequencies in the 5000 kHz range, but your might for equally loud bass in the 20-100 Hz range.

Most natural and instrumental sounds have the majority of their acoustic energy in the lower portion of their spectra—this naturally follows the way we hear. Certain synthesis methods, such as frequency modulation (FM) are prone to creating energy equally distributed across the spectrum, and so sound weighted toward the higher frequencies to us. Above, there was mention of "weighted" methods of dB measurement that were more closely related to the way in which we hear. The most widely used is the 'A'-weighted or dBA scale, which *rolls off* or progressively filters out lower frequencies and so creates a measurement in which all audible frequencies are treated equally for sounds of approximately 40 dB.

Timbre

Our perception of timbre or tone quality seems most closely related to the physical phenomena of unfolding partials in the spectrum of a sound, called the spectral envelope. It is what allows us to distinguish between two different instruments playing the same note at the same amplitude. What we expect of familiar sounds, say of a piano note, are certain characteristics that change over time. If one were to chop off the attack of a piano note and hear the remainder, it may not sound very piano-like to us at all. As mentioned above, classical studies of timbre were written in the 19th Century first by Helmholtz in his book *On the Sensations of Tone,* in which the overall envelope, which *enveloped* a complex waveform, comprised the basis for our tonal judgment. A more accurate picture was created by Fourier in which he stated that all complex waves can be expressed as a sum of one or more sine waves. We say sounds with stronger upper partials sound "brighter" and those with weaker higher partials sound "duller." More natural spectra will roll off with varying slopes with higher frequencies. Computer music is capable of creating any rolloff desired, and so harmonic sounds that have equal energy in their upper partial compared to their lower one are often characterized as being "buzzy." Noise with equally strong higher-frequency components is characterized as being more "hissy."

Other aspects of timbre include vibrato (most important) and tremolo (less important). Violins have very narrow formants (or resonating frequencies), and the addition of vibrato may push a tone in and ou of a peak formant region, making for a very dynamic sound. This is further tempered by our perception of the complex of formants for a particular sound or instrument regardless of its register, so that, although somewhat different a low clarinet note may still be considered related to a much higher one. The art of orchestration depends heavily on the ability of a composer to mix the spectra of numerous instruments, not necessarily playing the same pitch or octave doubling, and create a single timbral entity, perhaps unheard before. Most wind players are familiar with the slang term *floboe,* referring to the frequent octave doubling of melodic lines by a flute and oboe in Classic symphonies. Some studies have indicated it takes at least 60 ms. to recognize the timbre of a sound. It has also been hypothesized that we hear differences in tones up to the 30th partial (recall how closely related in pitch higher partials become). Temporal relationships also form an aspect of timbre. Though highly influence by the intervallic distance between pitches, if a series of tones is played rapidly enough, they will merge into a single timbre in a process called fusion. With sufficient reverberation, even disparate tones can fuse; Stockhausen used this principle in Studie II to create *mixtures* of sine tones played thought a reverb to create unique timbres.

Finally, instruments do not radiate their spectra equally in all directions (see the excellent diagram of the radiation pattern of a cello in Huber-Runstein, pg. 37), making it tricky to mic such instruments and gather their full tonal qualities.

Localization

Localization refers to our ability to place a sound source in space. We use a number of audible cues for this purpose. One such cue is the *interaural time difference* or ITD. This refers to the difference in time it take a sound to reach one ear compared to the other. Sounds located directly in front of or behind us will reach both ear simultaneously. If the angle of the source is moved until the difference is greater than 20 microseconds (millionths of a second), a difference in location can be perceived. As a source moves more directly to one side of your head or the other, our ability to discriminate its location using the ITD method diminishes somewhat.

A second mechanism, called the *interaural intensity difference* or IID uses the difference in amplitude caused by the head physically masking sounds coming from one side or the other. Because lower frequencies with longer wavelengths refract more easily around objects, this mechanism is more effective for higher frequencies. The shape of the pinna (outer ear flap) also filters frequencies depending on their angle of incidence. The pinna is also responsible for our ability to place sounds in the vertical plane using this filtering mechanism. Try folding your ear flap over and see how well you can still place sounds. Sound waves reflecting off the shoulder also provide some location cues. All of these mechanisms are ineffective below approximately 270 Hz, as witnessed by the often out-of-the-way placement of subwoofers in surround sound setups.

A phenomenon to keep in mind when placing loudspeakers is the precedence effect, in which a listener receiving the same signal from multiple speakers will place it at the closest speaker and not in between unless the time difference between the signals is less than a millisecond. This is why you should try to sit in a central location at an electronic music concert! In judging the apparent size of an acoustic space, the aural cues depend on many factors, including the time elapsed from hearing the source sound to hearing the earliest reflections, the onset of reverberation, the intensity and duration of reverberation, diffusion of high frequencies and the resonant frequencies of the reverberation. With multi-channel sound and control over artificial reverb, many interesting and novel spatial effects can be created.

Digital Audio

The principles which underlie almost all digital audio applications and devices, be they digital synthesis, sampling, digital recording or CD or iPod playback are based on the basic concepts which follow in this chapter. New forms of playback, file formats, compression and storage of data are all changing on a seemingly daily basis, but the underlying mechanisms for converting real-world sound into digital values, manipulating those data and finally converting them back into real-world sound has not varied much since Max Mathews developed MUSIC I in 1957 at Bell Labs.

The theoretical framework that enabled musical pioneers such as Max Mathews to develop his digital audio programs stretches back over a century. For the brevity of this introduction, a mention of the groundbreaking theoretical work done at Bell Labs in the mid-20th century is worth noting. Bell Labs was concerned with transmitting larger amounts of voice data over existing telephone lines than could normally be sent with analog transmissions, due to bandwidth restrictions. Many of the developments pertaining to computer music where directly related to work on this topic. Module 4 will explore the implications of the Nyquist Theorem on the limitations of digital audio.

First presented by Harry Nyquist, a Swedish-born physicist in *Certain Topics in Telegraph Transmission Theory* (Trans. AIEE, vol. 47, pp. 617-644, Apr. 1928), he laid out the principles for sampling analog signals at even intervals of time and at twice the rate of the highest frequency so they could be transmitted over telephone lines as 'digital' signals, even though the technology to do so did not exist at the time—part of this work is now known as the Nyquist Theorem. Nyquist worked for AT&T, then Bell Labs. Twenty years later, Claude Shannon, mathematician and early computer scientist, also working at Bells Labs and then M.I.T., developed a proof for the Nyquist theory (thereby making it a theorem)*. The importance of their work to information theory, computing, networks and digital audio cannot be understated. For example, the same data stream theory used in high-speed networking, known as T-1 lines is the same technology used in higher-end Digidesign Pro Tools systems today (TDM or time division multiplexing). A widely used method for encoding and decoding binary data, such as that used in digital audio, pulse code modulation or PCM was also developed early on at Bell Labs, attributed to John R. Pierce, a brilliant engineer in many fields, including computer music, and others.

Competing claims for the title of the world's first computer music program exist. Not to offend our good friends down under, a mention of Geoff Hill, who programmed the CSIR MkI developed in Sydney (credited as being among the first stored program digital computer, later known as the CSIRAC) to play the Colonel Bogey March in 1951 is in order, as this seems to be the first instance of programmed computer-generated music this author can find, primitive as it may have been. For a history of the musical contributions of CSIRAC.

Consuming Music Together

Listening to, buying and interacting around music is an immensely important part of everyday life and a key part of the cultural material through which social action is constructed and organised (e.g. DeNora, 1986, 2000; Hargreaves and North, 1997,

1999; Cohen, 1993; Crozier, 1997). Music can make us feel happy or sad, relaxed or energetic, it can highlight special occasions or evoke valuable memories. Music is a rich part of our environment - providing cues for structuring activity and creating appropriate atmospheres and ambience. Music also plays a role in our social lives - talking about, displaying, swapping and sharing music are all ways through which we express who we are and interact with others (e.g. Brown et al, 2001; Willis; 1978; Frith, 1978).

The way we consume music is not simply about listening but involves the waysit becomes integrated into our personal and social lives. This is very much determined by the technologies through which we experience it: how music is distributed, rendered, purchased, organised, shared, chosen, listened to, interacted with and repurposed. This relationship between technology and the ways people consume music in their everyday lives can be illustrated by looking at some keytechnical shifts over the years and how they created new and interesting social phenomena around music consumption. A notable example here is home taping technology. At the time of its introduction, this technology was seen as a threat to the music industry in terms of replacing actual music purchases. Social Research has shown, however, that the effect of home taping on consumption was much more complex providing a means by which friends could swap and share music. Such behaviour was socially rich, providing a vehicle for conversation, identity management and tokens of affection and gift giving. A second notable example, also based on tape technology was the hugley influential Sony Walkman. Through this process of miniaturisation of music delivery, the Walkman allowed music to be consumed in new places such as the car and urban environments. As a consequence music consumption could now accompany, a whole host of new activities under new social circumstances (e.g. Bull, 2000; du Gay and Hall, 1997).

Yet technical shifts over recent years have disrupted existing music practices and created new social phenomena around music and its consumption. Parallels with the above examples can be seen in more recent technological advances, namely peer-to-peer online file sharing applications (e.g. Napster, Gnutella) and the hugely successful iPod. While in some respects, these new digital alternatives afford some common social and behavioural phenomena with their historical counterparts, there are also significant new behaviours and social consequences of their new digital capabilities. For example, with peer-to peer applications such as Napster, the sheer scale of the Network over which music is shared can have a tendency to remove some of the social aspects of the music sharing seen with swapping tapes among friends. Likewise, a simple increase in storage capacity afforded by the iPod over the Walkman allows entire music collections to be carried around with a person. Not only does this change listening behaviour and circumstances, it also affords the social value of the portable device as a projection of a person's musical identity.

The aim of the current book is to explore the impact of technology on the way people consume music within the context of their everyday lives. In particular, the concern of the book is to emphasise the social and collaborative behaviours and values that occur around music consumption. It seeks to understand the role of technology within these practices: how technology shapes these practices and in turn how these practices shape new technology. While, there has been much pioneering work in the social sciences around the social circumstances and values under which music is consumed (e.g. DeNora, 2000; Hargreaves and North, 1999), these have, with a few notable exceptions (e.g. Bull, 2000), not been so concerned with the techological components of these practices. Likewise, many discussions of new technological possibilities for music consumption have not attempted to couch their descriptions with reference to the intricate details of social practice outlined by the social sciences. The current ungrounded debate in the music industry around music piracy and copyright theft stem from the lack of careful attention to social practices in relation to new music technology. There is a narrow concern for music consumers as passive audiences for distributed music rather than thinking of consumers as active users of music.

With this in mind, the current book brings together the work of key researchers from both the social, and computing sciences, documenting in detail how music technologies are currently used and the complex practices which have arisen around music listening. The book goes beyond reporting on current social practices of music consumption to explore what new technologies can be built, and the potential new social and collaborative possibilities these may bring. Accordingly, this book combines studying current practice, with the design of technologies for new practices. It contains both lessons from the present, and the technologies that will likely be important in the future. By combining the careful study of social situations with the design of new technologies in this way, the book bridges two different research approaches who have much to gain from each other. Bringing technology design to social research can focus research by the need to test findings in the form of specific technologies. In turn, bringing social research to technology design can prove to be a powerful motivator for new design concepts, as well as grounding technology in real life practices and needs. As the chapters in this book show, the combination of social science work with technology design can break important ground in both designing technology and understanding the social world.

We begin the book with a chapter by Tia DeNora. DeNora's work is an important starting point for the book in that it introduces some of the key ways in which music "gets into" our daily lives and experiences. Music, DeNora argues, is a key resource in the formation of a social reality; a resource from which social, cognitive and emotional structures are created through people's everyday activities as social beings. Understanding the ways music plays a role in the formation of our everyday social experiences is key to exploring technologically mediated musical experiences. In this respect, DeNora's chapter lays some of the important foundations of social understanding around music that pervades many of the discussions of new technologies elsewhere in the book. Drawing on three actual examples of music experiences in everyday life (listening to a song on the radio; an aerobics class; and an in-store shopping experience), she sets out to demonstrate the key theme of the chapter, namely that music, via its emotional effects, is a condition of action in real time. It is part of a conglomorate of features (e.g. actors, time, space, acts of engagement, social conditions and the material spatial environment) that produce social events. Drawing on a musical metaphor, different ways in which the social effects of music are manifest are presented as variations on the main theme. One such variation is that music, as part of the aesthetic of social spaces, suggests or encourages appropriate actions or roles we might play in these spaces. It is part of the way people make sense of a place. Another variation is the way music triggers memory and that remembering is key to the process of musical occasioning. That is, music is not simply paired with memories but, rather, music is seen as a fundamental part of the thing being remembered as well as a fundamental part of means 'through' which the remembering is done. Music is used to structure situational ambience and emotion; to get people in a particular mood and to convey social meaning to other social beings. Further music is a considered as technology of the self. The extent to which people comfortably or uncomfortably inhabit a musically configured space, and the actions through which this is conveyed, highlight characteristics of the self and others. Music, then, becomes a resource for the identity work that people do on a daily basis. New music technologies, and the new modes of distribution and use they bring, shift the ways in which some of these social and emotional activities and experiences can be realised. This inevitably raises many new questions and it is these which we are beginning to explore through the social-technical investigations presented here in this collection.

The next section of the book tackles the issue of music sharing, a particularly salient topic in recent years with the rise of on-line file sharing applications, such as Gnutella, Kazzaa and Napster. The chapter by Brown and Sellen opens the section with a critical look at the rhetoric surrounding the industry debate about on-line file sharing and its impact on the music industry. Much of the rhetoric, in particular that from representatives of the music industry, has been infused with negative value judgements in relation to music sharing behaviour. Use of terms such as "piracy" and "copyright theft" leave in no doubt the moral message the industry is trying to communicate. The moral values found in this rhetoric, though, seem at odds with those found in the everyday copying behaviour of ordinary people. Brown and Sellen argue that this the industry rhetoric stifiles sensible consideration of the issues around copying issues. Brown and Sellen take a step back to understand how music sharing behaviour fits into the broader context of music consumption behaviour, such as listening, buying, owning and collecting. Exploring the pragmatics of music sharing, the authors explore how conventional music sharing is something which is embedded in social practices. For example, Brown and Sellen discuss how music is played in social spaces where friends come together. The music that accompanies these social gatherings is, as DeNora would argue, a resource for social "occasioning" in the way it is chosen, listened to and discussed. Music become a vehicle through which tastes and values are understood, discussed and evaluated. Music tastes are a resource for understanding and portraying the identity of friends within these networks.

It is not unsurprising, then, that the majority of music sharing takes place inexisiting social networks. As discussed in the following chapter, sharing among existing social networks is an important reason for the success of the iPod. It also helps understand the importance of collecting music because of the way it comes to represent something of the self and the group. With this, an important feature of these collections is how they come to be displayed to others, this act of display being bound up with the impression management work that gets done among friends. Likewise, the actual exchange of music between friends becomes rich with social meaning, ritual and reciprocty (cf. Taylor and Harper, 2002). It embodies key aspects of the relationship between the giver and the receiver and demonstrate, for example, the givers knowledge of music and awareness of the receivers taste and circumstances (indeed much of this social element of music sharing is lost in the relatively anonymous large scale online music sharing applications). What Brown and Sellen argue is that ownership and sharing of legitimate and copied material takes place within the context of particular social values and meanings. It is only through this level of understanding that can we engage in a sensible debate about on-line file sharing practices, music piracy and different ways that music can be distributed and purchased legitimately.

The second chapter builds on similar arguments but with a different technology, namley Tunes and, in particular, the ability of iTunes to share music on local networks. With iTunes, Voida et al. argue that the 'person' (which Brown and Sellen claim is lost in the large scale peer-to-peer file sharing applications) is returned to the centre of the music sharing experience. Unlike previous file sharing technologies, the sharing of music files in iTunes does not involve them being copied across machines. Rather they are streamed from one computer to another on a particular subnetwork. This unique position of Tunes within the spectrum of music sharing possibilities enables new social effects to be created. It is these which Voida and her colleagues unpack in their study of the everyday practices of musicsharing in the workplace using Tunes. By displaying individuals' music collections and making them visible to others, Tunes becomes an resource for impression management and other social acts such as those outlined in DeNora's work. People not only use it to make judgements about other users but are acutely aware that they too are being judged by others.

This chapter highlight people's behavioural changes that occur in the knowledge that they can be viewed and judged. For example, people were seen to rip more CDs to their iTunes to create "representative" collections. A critical aspect of this impression management comes from the fact that iTunes only shares music across a subnetwork. What this means is that the members on this subnetwork are likely to meet in real life, and to share membership of real world social and organisational entities. In contrast to other online communities where identities can be entirely fabricated, the subnetworks have social meaning reflected in the real world. In this regard, Voida notes, for example, how the presence of a departmental manager on the subnetwork, creates an impetus for refining identities as portrayed through play lists and online names. The chapter goes on to argue that this relationship between the online and offline networks is important enough that problems are caused when the mapping between them is not perfect – for example, when a departmental member finds they are on a different subnetwork from their colleagues.

The streaming of music rather than copying also lends itself to particular frustrations, for example when a colleagues machine is switched off. This also makes the ritual hand over of music a slightly different proposition in iTunes than it is with the more tangible exchange associated with, for example, compilation tapes. Voida nevertheless points to some additional behaviours to which social and emotional significance is attached and which approximates to some of the gift giving type behaviour associate with music sharing, e.g. bringing in CDs and ripping them to iTunes especially because someone "special" on the network wants to listen them.

In the next section, the book examines issues concerning choosing music. Given some of the social consequences that music brings about and the social meaning it can convey, the control over music weilds significant social and economic power to those who possess it. Different technologies allocate this control across parties in different ways in particular social settings. This distribution of control over music in public spaces is explored in Chapter 5 by O'Hara and colleagues. They look at key stakeholders in a public café/bar setting and their different reasons for wanting to control the musical aesthetic of that space. For the owners of that space and those who work there, music is used to differentiate different periods of the day and fit comfortably with the kinds of social activity appropriate for these periods. Likewise, through the choice of music and its properties (e.g. volume) they are able to maintain a certain amount of social control over the group of people who go there (e.g., playing a cheesy tune at the end of the evening being used to encourage people to leave). However, by keeping all the control over music with the owners of the space, the patros of the café bar are left unempowered. They are passive consumers of the music that is played for them.

O'Hara et al. attempt to explore the importance of music choice for both parties in these public settings by altering the distribution of choice and noting the social effects. They do this by introducing Jukola, a digital jukebox that allows the patrons of the bar to collectively nominate and vote on what music should get played from the bar's music collection using hand held computer on the tabletops. Introducing such technology inevitably created a certain amount of tension among the owners and workers of the space since it removed some of their ability to maintain social control and manage identity through music choice. However by empowering the patrons of the space, it created new possibilities for social action through musicchoice. Choice of music was something which became discussed and negotiated and this becames the basis for the for doing identity work, shared reminiscing, communication of power relations and 'doing friendship' through playful games around the choice. What is highlighted by the chapter is the importance of thinking about music choice in process terms rather than simply outcome terms. The introduction of the technology does more than just improve the musical outcome to reflect more closely the tastes of the patrons. Rather, it changes the whole process of choice in the sense that the end consumers become actively involved in the choice. It is through the conversation and negotiation leading up to the choice that much of the valuable social meaning and value of music is embodied.

In Crossen and Budzik present their Flytrap recommendation system. Digital technologies for purchasing and listening to music have provided an important source of data that can be used for socially grounded music choice and recommendations. Data mining techniques employed across groups of people can help derive patterns in listening and purchasing behaviour and relationships between songs and music genres that simply would not be available through reflection and introspection. The aim of the Flytrap system is to use such patterns to select music in public settings that reflect the shared preferences of groups of people in this setting.

Like the pioneering Music FX system (McCarthy, and Anagnost, 1998) from which it's inspiration is derived, Flytrap uses active badges to identify who is in a particular public space and on the basis of their respective listening profiles, calculates the preferred tracks to be played. However, the Flytrap system has some key differences from Music FX both in intent and design. In particular the aim of Flytrap system is not just to create a more enjoyable music outcome that matches the tastes of the group. Rather, it aims to provide a musical "common ground" that can be used to promote social interaction among its participants. This aim has particular implications for the construction of the algorithm used to calculate the appropriate music. It is also the reason why they explored different ways for people to visualise how a choice was derived from the preferences of people present in the space. This makes more explicit to the users of the system, the links between music and actual people - again highlighting the social importance of music and identity. This contrasts with other systems such as Music FX which, in some senses, were designed to make these things disappear. The Flytrap system also derives its Introduction and Overview information from the actual listening habits of people. The system has an agent attached to the media players of individuals' computers. This is important for a number of reasons. First is that there is no burden on the users to create their musical profiles. Rather it is something that is derived automatically in the background. Second, it allows for a much richer set of information to be derived that relate to the context of listening habits and which can be used in a more sophisticated group preference calculation. This "automation" of choice raises some important questions and the need for a balanced approach to the design of these systems. For example, as with the chapter on Tunes and later chapter on tunA, there are concerns with how the public and private are managed. Making things visible has both pros and cons according to particular circumstances. Flytrap, in making individual preferences visible to others is no exception to this concern. Likewise, there is debate raised about the extent to which automation can fully be achieved given the complexity of social and contextual factors that influence music choice. So while the Flytrap system has the potential to extract a richer and richer set of circumstantial factors that could facilitate automation, the authors also highlight that there comes a point where some mediated human intervention should also be given.

Given the cultural significance of portable music technologies over the years, notably the Walkman and most recently the iPod, the next section of the book is devoted to mobile music. The section starts with a piece by Michael Bull, who in Chapter 7 explores the culture of mobile music listening through perhaps the most significant music technology of recent years, namely the Apple iPod. While these mobile music devices are generally characterised and understood as personal stereos, Bull argues that the behaviours surrounding them are deeply social. These devices allowing music listening practices to be immersed in a whole host of new social spaces and situations, altering the way people relate to their surroundings (the aesthetic dimension of relational experience) and to other people within those surroundings (the moral dimension of relational experience). These mobile listening devices then, through the strategies used to control music in public places, become a means by which our sense of the social becomes, mediated, managed and understood. To illustrate this, Bull presents a Taxonomy of control strategies seen in the use of personal stereos and explores the social consequences thereof. For example, headphones are used as an implicit "do not disturb" sign. Likewise, listening to personal stereos in public affords a certain amount of "civil disattention"(Goffman, 1971) by allowing what Bull calls a non-reciprocal gazing – an important concern, in particular for women who wish to avoid the unwanted gazes of others.

While Bull acknowledges the social context of personal stereo use as not being something peculiar to the new crop of "MP3" players, he highlights that their new functionalities provide new means by which music can be controlled in public spaces. He discusses how features such as flexile playlist creation or shuffle play, as well as the large storage capacity, dramatically alter the consumption of music and audoury aestheticisation of experience in public spaces. In addition, because of its huge storage capacity, the iPod becomes an embodiment of people's musical identity which they can then carry around with them. They become something that can be browsed by others with whom one is interacting, again with important social consequences. Indeed, this even allows them to be used as the basis for "iPod clubs" in which people use their own particular iPods to provide the entertainment for a particular social occasion. This leads on to the other key feature of Bull's chapter, namley the collective listening behaviours that occur with the iPod. Bull highlights how particular features of the iPod make it more likely than it's Walkman predecessors, to be used as a collective listening device in shared spaces such as the home or the car. Accompanying these collective possibilities are a range of new social issues such as power and control that were not so apparent in consumption behaviour surrounding traditional personal stereo use. For example, who controls the iPod when there are passengers in the car or when more than one person is listening to it in the home. These become important considerations for how these devices should be conceived and how they might come to be designed in the future.

The collective use of portable music devices is picked up in Chapter 8. In this chapter, Bassoli and her Media Lab colleagues present the tunA system, a mobile peer-to-peer application for proximity based music sharing. The work builds on the notion of music consumption as a social experience, drawing on, for example, observations of shared Walkman use (as described in the work of Michael Bull) and the social motivations underlying the success of certain on-line music sharing applications. While Bull's work highlights the sometimes subtle and implicit aspects of "personal stereo" use, Bassoli's tunA system seeks to more explicitly support the social and collective in a reconceptualised walkman design. Essentially the device is an MP3 player with wireless networking capabilities. When other tunA devices come into range it is possible to share the music profiles on these other devices. Playlists on the other devices in range can be viewed, music from one device can be streamed to another for synchronous listening, and tracks on other devices can be bookmarked as a reminder. On top of this the devices also have the ability to message between each other such that people can have text based conversation. In this respect, the music becomes a conversation key (Sachs, 1992) for people providing them with a socially important resource for initiating communication with coproximate others. Such technical capabilities raise all sorts of intriguing social opposabilities and concerns. These devices, much more than personal stereos become a resource for identity understanding as well as identity presentation. The music carried around with you can longer be understood simply in terms of what people want to listen to. Its visibility to others mean that it becomes something to be carefully managed in terms of what gets presented to particular people under what circumstances. As with the discussion of Tunes presented earlier, this visibility has potentially both positive and negative social consequences that need to be carefully managed. For example, what might be regarded as a positive projection of identity in one set of circumstance, may in another set of circumstances be an invasion of privacy and security concern. The chapter goes on to explore issues such as these through a small scale user trial of the system.

Ostergren and Juhlin in chapter 9 discuss music listening in the car. The work described in the chapter draws again on key observations in the work of Michael Bull (2001). First, that music listening is a key part of the aesthetic experience of driving and something which "binds together the disparate threads of much urban movement" and which makes interesting the otherwise mundane places that people travel through. The second, is that while driving is often in many ways a solitary activity, in traffic, much of this is an accompanied solitude. In traffic, drivers are aware of the presence of other drivers around them, taking an interest in what they look like and what they are doing. These brief social encounters with other drivers in traffic are a place where judgements about each other are exchanged on very limited information, such as what they look like, the car they are driving, etc. For Ostergren and Juhlin, the car driver is a modern day flaneur.

With these observations in mind, they set out to create a more social experience around the music that people listen too in their cars. They present their SoundPryer concept, a collaborative car stereo which, like the tunA concept described in the previous chapter, moves away from the notion of music listening as a solitary experience within the bubble that is the car. Sound Pryer allows both local play asin a traditional car stereo but also remote play in which the device picks up local broadcasts from other Sound Pryer users. The system is deployed on a PDA and uses MANET technology to provide a cost free broadband exchange using the inbuilt wireless transmitters the PDAs contain. The range of this wireless technology is limited. This, though, is regarded by the authors as an advantage as it emphasises the importance of physical proximity in the shared musical experience as opposed to something that is removed from space and the possibility of seeing people with whom you are sharing music. This shared musical experience comes either from listening in to the music of passing Sound Pryer users or by being listened to by passing Sound Pryer users. Both of these types of experience immerse people within a social interaction along the lines of the brief traffic encounters described in the work of Michael Bull (2001). Importantly in Sound Pryer, the interface presents some representation of the car that provides some means of identifying the music played with a particular car. This allows people to use the system for identity work seen in other systems presented in the book. In the fieldwork they present of the system in use, people were seen to look round for the source car from which the remote music was being broadcast. Likewise, as modern day flaneurs they would also smile at passing drivers if they felt that driver was listening into their music. Doing identification work through shared music consumption is thus considered to be an experience enjoyed from both sides – from the listener and the one being listened to.

In this next section we take a look at music and dance, As well as the collective nature of dance in relation to music, the section explores the associated fan cultures and communities that surround music consumption through dance. It does this from the perspective of some very different technologies. In, Chapter 10, Jacob Smith, takes a look at music video games and their fan culture, focussing most explicitly on the dance simulation games, Dance Dance Revolution (DDR) and ParaParaParadise. With DDR consoles in arcades, players choose a song to dance to. The machine then plays the song along with a series of dance moves in the form of arrows on the screen which direct the player to touch the corresponding dance pads with their feet. This activity must be done in time with the music. As the player interacts with the music through the dance, the machine responds to the performance with cheers and boos and associated terms of encouragement or derision.. In this sense the game creates a heightened sense of interaction with the music. An important feature of this interaction with the music through dance is that the body becomes a spectacle. Being played in arcades, these are public settings where the body spectacle typically attracts an audience. That the performance is public changes the way music is consumed in much the same way that kareoke changed music consumption through the publicity of its performance (Drew, 2001). For Smith, this public performance in arcades becomes an important part of the development of the fan culture around DDR, a fundamental social part of music consumption practices. Local DDR clubs get together compete against each other in tournaments. Particular kudos is given to performers in these tournaments who learn the moves in reverse specifically so that they can turn around to "dance for the crowd" rather than the machine.

Alongside the fan culture that is built up through these localised in situ activities, Smith also examines the role of the Internet in the creation of a more global fan culture around DDR. Fans, for example, are able to discuss the peculiar brand of Japanese Hip Hop that is unique to DDR, the uniqueness of which is an important part of the whole DDR experience, fan identity and sense of community. Fans are also able to discuss their favourite songs online, swap the songs and search for DDR rarities. The web sites also feature videos of tournaments that allow people to follow the fortunes of their particular teams and star performers. In this respect, the chapter argues that the Web has mainstreamed fandom making it much more readily available to people. The chapter goes on to explore some interesting gender issues associated with fan cultures that arise through the types of dance encouraged by the charateristics of particular interaction devices. With DDR, the dance pads encourage a very physical and athletic style of dance that has created a sometimes macho community and culture – in particular, as seen in the competitive nature of DDR tournaments. This is contrasted with the much more restrained Para Para dance of ParaParaParadise in which the player interacts with the game via infrared sensors responding to choreographed hand movements. As a consequence, the nature of the dance is much less competitive resulting in a more open and less competitive online community. What Smith demonstrates in this chapter, then, is how such music games provide new ways for bodies to interact with pre-recorded music and how this can become a significant and powerful factor for the formation of community and performance of identity. The discussion of music, dance and community continues in Chapter 11 by Karneza Moore. In this chapter, Moore offers a socio-technical perspective on "clubbers", dance music consumption and contemporary "clubbing" culture. The focus of this socio-technical analysis is not on the technologies that one might typically associate with dance music/club culture (e.g. DJ Decks).

Rather, she explores a seemingly much more mundane technology and the role it plays in the organisation of dance music consumption practices, namely the mobile phone. Of particular interest here is that in contrast to many of the other technologies presented in this book, the mobile phone has, at first glance, a somewhat indirect relationship to music consumption practice. However, this importantly broadens the way we think about technologies in relation to collaorative music consumption. In Moore's analysis of club culture, then, the phone is positioned as a technology that is inextricably bound up in the social and collaborative experiences of dance music consumption; a technology that is both a creator and enabler of dance community activities. The aim is to move our understanding beyond the simple notion that clubbing is just a "group of people coming together to listen to music at a set time and place." The organisational practices of dance music consumption are something which extend to contexts and settings pre and post club and into "real life". It is only by examining these practices across these broader settings that we can come to understand the social and emotional significance of mobile phones for dance clubbers. Such an understanding, Moore argues, can play an important role in the design of new mobile applications and services in the domain of dance music consumption.

Bearing in mind the above discussion, Moore presents key examples of mobilephone use within clubbing culture. First is the role of the mobile phone in the procurement of illegal substances prior to going into a club. The consumption of illegal substances goes hand-in-hand with the consumption of dance music. As illegal substances, though, there is inevitably risk associated with these procurement practices. Key here is the mobile phone and its relationship to the perception and management of risks associated with this procurement of illegal drugs. Second, is the use of the mobile phones in the organisation of clubbing nights out. While this may not appear something unique to dance music culture there are specific practices of this organisation that are. For example, the rounding up of randoms" as well as "real life" friends is an important feature of the open culture of organising clubbers nights out. The mobile phone also brings a certain fluidity and mutability to the arrangements which paradoxically is both a source of feelings of freedom as well as anxiety that arrangements will fall through (especially in combination with illegal substance use). Within the club, the mobile phone provides the means to maintain group bonds within the club itself. Text messages are used to bring disparate party members together when a good tune comes on as well as to manage the wellbeing of friends through particular phases of substance use. Through these findings, then, Moore presents a more grounded notion of clubbing culture and community as mediated though mundane technologies that actually relate to the real world practices and values of clubbers.

Staying with the dance music and the nightclub, the next chapter considers a somewhat different technology. In Chpater 12, Cliff presents an automatic DJ system called hpDJ in which collections of dance music are sequenced and seamlessly mixed by a computer. The mix that is output from the system is presented as a single continuous audio file that can be played in a nightclub of people or through a media device such as an iPod. Our concerns here are with the use of the system within a nightclub setting. Sequencing is of course a very social concern in that the ordering of music is used to transport a group of people through various emotional and physical states. There is also an important social relationship between the DJ and audience, with the DJ using "white of the eyes" feedack from the audience to fine tune what is played and when. While Cliff respects these social concern, he argues that there are key features of the task that are mechanistic and which therefore make it ripe for automation. He also argues that there are alternative ways to derive feedback from the audience using sensor technologies from which social and behavioural judgements can be made. The social nature of dance can be "summarised" through patterns of sensor technology output. With this in mind he presents extensions to the core hpDJ system, that use a variety of sensor technologies to determine ongoing crowd response to an automated sequence of music. This feedback is used to determine ongoing sequencing. Some of these technologies passively sense features of the environment or audience; others depend on an explicit technology mediated response from the audience such as a button-press vote. In this respect, the crowd determines the sequencing collaboratively as well as potentially composes completely new remixes collaboratively. Cliff raises many interesting issues about copyright, authorship and ownership that come about due to the new and explicit relationships between the audience and the ongoing musical composition. It is these issues that we turn to in the final section of the book.

The final section on Consumption as Production opens with a chapter by Atau Tanaka. In Chapter 13, Tanaka describes how new technological infrastructures for creating, rendering and distributing music, change the way that music can be consumed and appreciated. Accordingly the relationship between producer and consumer must shift. A key part of Tanaka's work centres around the notion of idiomatic writing. That is, people write music that specifically suits the particular charactersitics of the instrument on which it is to be performed, or the acoustical properties of where it is going to be performed (e.g. a Cathedral). Tanaka's claim is that while idiomatic writing practices have been employed in relation to instruments and spaces, they have not really been applied to particular properties of the new technologies for rendering and distribution of music. Take for example, network music performances in which music is performed not just for a local audience but also to be consumed by an audience of people over the Internet. Transmission delays and losses in quality are typical characteristics of music via this medium that traditionally have proved a frustration to many musicians. The argument of the chapter, however, is that such characteristics are an inherent property of the medium which need to be embraced in more idiomatic composition.

The basic tenet of idiomatic writing becomes of particular interest here when Tanaka introduces technological possibilities for end user participation. In the MP3q system, for example, the listeners mix multiple music streams using an abstract graphical text interface, as well as contribute their own sounds. The musical piece starts off as an empty shell but is evolved by the participation of the listeners who add their own contributions as the base material for the piece. The point here is that the original author has to give up a certain level of control over the piece. The composition for them lies in the creation of the "open system" which listeners can contribute to. The production process changes by virtue of the interactive possibilities for the end consumer.

Tanaka's broader aim then is to find the "musical voice" idiomatic to the democratic network and create architectures for collective musical processes that blur the boundaries between production and consumption. With this in mind he presents his Malleable Mobile Music System in which people collectively listen to a familiar piece of music via their respective portable music players. The music is remixed on the fly according to the movements and gestures of the listeners as they move around an urban environment. The music is sensitive to the social dynamic of the listeners. In this respect, music pieces are no longer seen simply as a deterministic products to be downloaded and consumed. Rather, they are better viewed as structures of possibility, to be completed only at render time with the active participation of the listeners.

The relationship between content producers and consumers is further explored in the final chapter by Dillon. Once again the rhetoric of the music industry surrounding copyright laws are called into question, this time within the context of contemporary sampling culture in music making. Within this culture, music is not simply consumed as an end product but rather is appropriated and repurposed in the creation of new music. The everyday practices of music consumption within this sampling culture do not fit neatly within the music industry's model of copyright and piracy. This has led to the formation of the Creative Commons Movement (CCM) which recognises the link between music distribution and creation through the repurposing of distributed content. This link is manifest in the CCM's more flexible licensing arrangements associated with distributed materials that allow them to be appropriated within the sampling culture. As with Brown and Sellen's efforts to inform music industry rhetoric, Dillon argues that an exploration of everyday music repurposing practices is necessary to inform the debate. Towards this goal, she presents some research looking at the everyday collaborative music creation practices of school children. As with O'Hara's distinction between process and outcome described in Chapter 5, Dillon argues that creativity cannot be understood by simply looking at the outcome product. Rather, to understand what is really happening, it is necessary to look at the process of music creativity. The process Dillon presents is a collaborative one. This collaboration is a social process; a negotiation that provides an opportunity for many of the social values of music to be manifest. Through one's orientation to particular samples, their associated cultural references, and how one makes these visible in their repurposing, much social meaning can be expressed.

Dillon continues the explorations of collaborative music creation and content repurposing with a discussion of Interconnected Music Networks. These allow distributed groups of people to collectively repurpose material in the creation of new music. Much of the work in this area has been criticised for its tendencies towards high art rather than appealing to a broader audience. Dillon however, highlights some exceptions, namely the Beatbug Network and F@ust Music Online. Again it is the social aspects of these processes that the chapter draws out. With the F@ust system for example, users input their preferences for musical content to be repurposed. These preferences become a common ground scaffolding on which strangers are brought together online to collaborate creatively in producing new music through the reproposing of mutually understood published content.

Through her examples, then, Dillon shows how the new technological possibilities for accessing, downloading, sharing, composing and co-constructing music on-the-fly mean we need to rethink our approach to the consumption of published music. The music industry, she claims, should recognise the social, creative and political power of computer networks in the ways people can and will be able to consume music in the future. Rather than becoming entrenched in existing approaches to consumption, the industry should understand and embrace the new practices and opportunities that technologies are bringing in a way that suits both consumers and producers and the evolving relationship between them.

The collection of chapters presented here is not intended to provide a comprehensive account of social and collaborative music consumption practices as mediated through particular technologies. Rather, the attempt is to consolidate some important examples of research effort and the diverse perspectives they represent. Without this consolidation, it remains difficult to assimilate these diverse perspectives and, as such, many important issues get overlooked by the respective social and technical camps. By drawing the perspectives together, we hope to raise questions and highlight issues that help us think more critically about the social shaping of music consumption technologies and the technological shaping of social practices surrounding music consumption.

Musical Instrument Digital Interface: An Introduction

MIDI, or the Musical Instrument Digital Interface, is a means by which computers and musical instruments can communicate. It's a language that allows you to give instructions to a computer that it will then send to the synthesizer on your sound card, or to any other MIDI devices that you may have available. MIDI is a great way to work with music and has very powerful capabilities that will appeal to users of all levels. There are lots of unfamiliar terms and concepts in the MIDI language, though, and it's easy to get frustrated if you don't have a grasp of some basic ideas. The first section of this guide will help you understand what MIDI is and teach you what it can do for you.

MIDI was born in the early 1980's when electronic instrument makers, primarily in the US and Japan, recognized that their instruments must be able to talk to one another. After the details were worked out, manufacturers soon began to include electronic circuitry in their equipment that allowed them to understand the instructions MIDI used. Before long, nearly every instrument maker in the world had adopted the standard, and though there have been refinements and modifications to MIDI along the way, even the earliest MIDI instruments are still capable enough to be used today. Since its adoption, MIDI has dramatically changed the way music is created, performed and recorded.

MIDI is a universally accepted standard for communicating information about a musical performance by digital means. It encompasses both a hardware and software component, and though it could be used for sending information about many other things, such as the control of lighting in a theater, or even to control your coffee maker, it was developed to transmit instructions about music. Like a music score, on which notes and other symbols are placed, a MIDI transmission carries instructions that must be acted on by some device that can make sound. While a clarinet or guitar player will interpret a written music score and produce the sound required, it is most likely a synthesizer or drum machine that will react to MIDI information. Fortunately for us, a complete set of these instructions can be captured and stored by a computer, and several types of music software can be used to edit and alter them. If the information is sent to several different MIDI devices, an entire electronic orchestra can be at the musician's disposal. MIDI does not (except in rare cases) actually transmit sound electronically; you couldn't connect a MIDI cable to a loudspeaker and expect to hear anything (you'd probably damage both your speakers and your ears if you tried!). Instead, it is the sound-producing capabilities of the synthesizer, whether it's on a sound card in your computer or a stand-alone device, that will create the sound you hear. A MIDI transmission consists of a series of signals, called bits for binary digits, that pass through a MIDI cable. These signals are electrical impulses, some strong, some weak, that represent the 1s and 0s that make up the language of computers (any device that wants to send or receive MIDI data must be equipped with a microprocessor, the "brains" of every computer). When the impulses reach their destination, for example a synthesizer, the operating system of the synthesizer interprets them as a series of instructions that usually result in the production of a sound. This sound must be amplified, so the synthesizer will typically be connected to an amplifier or mixer.

The bits in the MIDI transmission move at a fairly high rate of speed, 31,250 per second to be exact, and are transmitted in a serial manner, meaning one after another. (A parallel transmission contains a number of signals that pass at the same time). Every bit does not represent a different note or event, however. Bits are grouped into strings of 10 to create MIDI messages, each of which conveys important information about some musical event. (Individual MIDI messages are actually eight bits or one byte long, though when messages are being transmitted, two extra bits, called the stop and start bits, are added to the beginning and end of the byte, hence the 10 bit length of most events.)

Some MIDI messages detail specific aspects of a musical performance: what notes should be heard; how loud they should be; what type of sound (trumpet, drum, flute) should play the notes, etc.; while others are more general in nature. Together, MIDI messages represent an entire language of musical actions, and can be used to convey all the details of a complete symphony or a simple hymn.

In order to communicate in the language of MIDI, a device should be able to send and receive MIDI information, though many common devices are created to do primarily one or the other. A sound card in a computer, for example, must be given instructions that are generated by some other source; it cannot create any MIDI messages on its own. Similarly, certain electronic instruments known as tone or sound modules, are also only able to respond to messages generated from the "outside." By contrast, a class of instruments called keyboard controllers are intended for transmitting MIDI data only, and have no way to make sound. Whatever their capabilities, all MIDI devices must contain a microprocessor, which is a computer chip that deciphers and acts upon MIDI messages, as well as physical connections called Ports, for sending and receiving data.

One of the great capabilities of MIDI is its ability to transmit messages to different electronic musical instruments at the same time. Each instrument can distinguish which messages are for it because the messages contain channel information, which acts like an address or shipping label for the message. These MIDI channels are not physically separated, i.e., they are not transmitted on separate strands of wire. Rather, the different channel numbers (1-16) are contained in the beginning of the MIDI message, and determine whether an instrument or device will respond to that message. In this way, messages can be directed to certain devices, while other devices, which might also be receiving the information, will ignore them. Most newer instruments can be programmed to respond to any one or even all MIDI channels. Because of this, the user has extensive control over how different instruments react to the information that they receive.

There are certain classes of messages called system messages that don't use a channel, since they are intended for all devices connected to the MIDI chain. Messages that deal with tuning or timing information are in this category. Therè are also other cases where individual messages do not need their own channel label, for example when all the notes of a melody are to played by a certain instrument on the same channel. In this case, a channel designation can be set at the beginning of the melodic sequence and used for all messages in that series.

MIDI messages are the language of MIDI; they are the words MIDI uses in a transmission to communicate the information that must pass from a source to a destination. There are many types of MIDI messages, though they all fall into two categories: channel messages and system messages. Channel messages are those that carry specific channel information, such as those described above. These include messages such as what note an instrument should play (called a Note Message), and Program Change messages, which tell the instrument what sound it should make while playing the note. System messages, as described above, are either intended for all the instruments currently connected to the transmitting device, or are meant to convey information to a specific instrument that is general in nature and doesn't represent specific details of a performance.

Most messages consist of at least two bytes. The first byte is called the status byte, which tells the receiving device what type of message it is. Basically, it identifies the message and prepares the device for a response. MIDI uses the numbers between 128 and 255 for this part of the message. What follows is the actual data the device needs; these bytes are called data bytes. They represent the details of the message; the values the instrument will use to perform its task. MIDI uses the numbers 0 to 127 for data bytes. Some messages use only one data byte, others need two, while some need none at all. We'll look at a few common messages to see what type of information they contain.

Perhaps the most basic of all messages is the pair called Note On and Note Off. A Note On message is transmitted when a key is pressed on a keyboard, and a Note Off is transmitted when it is released. When a synthesizer receives a Note On message, it looks immediately for additional information, specifically, a data byte that details what note it should play and another that specifies how loud it should play it. MIDI has only 128 different numbers for designating pitch and loudness (or velocity) levels, so immediately after the Note On message is sent, a data byte representing a number between 0 and 127 will appear for the Note Number, followed by another that specifies the velocity level for that note. The note will continue to play until the Note Off message is received, and it too must contain note and velocity numbers. Note and velocity details must be included with the Note Off message because it is possible that a synthesizer will be playing several notes when the Note Off is received. If it received the Note Off without a specific Note number, it wouldn't know which note to stop playing. The Velocity number that appears with the Note Off is not quite as important; in fact, some synthesizers simply ignore it. Nevertheless, it will be sent as part of the data. The Note On / Note Off combination constitutes the most common pair of messages in any MIDI transmission, though there are many other parts of the transmission.

When a synthesizer is first turned on, it will load one of its sounds into its RAM (random access memory) and prepare itself to receive note messages. These sounds are permanently stored in the synthesizer's ROM (read only memory) and are, in essence, individual computer programs that tell the device how to create the required sound. When the computer is directed to load a new sound, it must change the program it is currently running so it will be ready to play notes using the new tone. Hence, the MIDI message that tells the device what sound to make is called a Program Change message. Program Changes are followed by a single data byte.

MIDI devices use two different numbering schemes to catalog their programs, either 0-127 or 1-128, and it is important to know which scheme the different devices you will be using employ. A recent standardization of this numbering scheme, called the General MIDI specification, states that the numbers will run from 1-128, and also specifies which sounds will have what numbers. We'll take a closer look at General MIDI at the end of this section. Control Change messages are used to represent some change in the status of a physical control on a device. These controls are the foot pedals, volume sliders, modulation wheels, and similar peripherals found on most electronic instruments. Some control messages act like simple on and off switches; for example, the sustain pedal on a synthesizer can only be down or up, so a single status byte can be used to specify which state the pedal is in, and no data byte is needed. Other controls are continuously changing and need to be represented by more detailed data called continuous controller data. For example, if you move the pitch wheel on a synthesizer very slowly from its resting position to one extreme up or down, MIDI transmits data representing the wheel's position at numerous points along its path. In this case, the data must be very high in resolution, so 14-bit (2-byte) messages are used. This provides a total of 16,384 values to track the movement of the wheel.

Controller data can be used for many different functions in MIDI, even multiple functions at the same time. For this reason, the different controller data streams are numbered from 0 to 127. Some of these controller numbers have become standardized to control certain tasks, for example, controller 10 (often abbreviated cc 10) is most often used for panning between left and right speakers, while controller seven (cc 7) is typically used for volume changes. Many synthesizers allow the user to change the effect controller data will have. When this is possible, any controller could theoretically be used to control any aspect of a sound that changes over time.

One final category of MIDI messages is called system messages. There are several types of system messages, but they all share the characteristic of transmitting information without a channel assignment. As a result, all instruments that receive messages of this type would act upon them, though one particular type of system message, called system exclusive, is intended for communicating only with a device or devices made by a specific manufacturer. System exclusive is often used when a musician wants to transmit large amounts of data to a specific synthesizer or receive data from the device. Because all major instrument makers have an ID number (#7 for Kurzweil devices, #67 for Yamaha, etc.), a message can be "addressed" to one device and all other receiving instruments will see it, but ignore it. For example, all the instructions specifying how a synthesizer makes it sounds could be "dumped" from the device and stored on a computer. Users could then trade custom libraries of sounds, or reload all the original factory settings if their equipment's memory were wiped out. Moreover, a whole new setup of sounds could be sent by a computer just before actual note data was transmitted, thereby getting the instrument properly configured before the music starts.

Other system messages include timing messages, which provide information about the tempo of the music; and Song Position messages, which indicate where a recorded MIDI sequence should begin playback. These last messages are particularly useful with synthesizers that contain built-in sequencing capabilities.

Before General MIDI (GM) was popularized, there was no consistency in the way manufacturers numbered the sounds in their instruments, so that on one device program #1 might be a piano, while on another, it might be a flute. Because MIDI data files (or sequences) often contain program change instructions, i.e., the actual specifications for which sound an instrument should use to perform each layer of the music, it was unlikely that music created for one synthesizer would sound correct when performed by another. With the adoption of General MIDI, files that use its numbering scheme are now "portable," meaning they will sound identical, or nearly so, when played by different instruments. This assumes, of course, that the instruments conform to the GM specification.

In addition to a standardized assignment of program change numbers, General MIDI includes several other guidelines, the most important of which is the use of Channel 10 for drum sounds. It also provides a Drum Map, which is the fixed assignment of certain drums sounds to specific MIDI note numbers. For example, sending middle C, MIDI note #60, will trigger a high bongo sound on the receiving General MIDI instrument. A "C" one octave below, note #48, will produce a Hi-Mid tom, and so on. This mapping scheme provides yet another layer of standardization, thereby insuring that MIDI sequences can be transported among different studios and desktop systems around the world.

Different MIDI devices have different capabilities and functions. We'll look closely at the various options on a traditional synthesizer first, then explore some of the other options that are found on different types of instruments. When you first look at a synthesizer, you are likely to see a piano-style keyboard, one or more rows of buttons and perhaps. Inside the synthesizer are the sound-producing components, the actual brains of the unit, that respond to messages received when a key is pressed on the keyboard or when a MIDI message is sent from some other source. The keyboard part of the unit is called a controller, which is a term used for any MIDI device that can initiate an action. There are other types of controllers, including those in the form of a guitar (guitar controllers), drum machines (drum controllers), and even those that look and work like wind instruments (wind controllers). It's possible to buy a controller that does not include the capability to make any sound, and it's just as easy to buy the sound producing components alone, which are devices commonly known as tone or sound modules. In essence, the devices we commonly refer to as "synthesizers" are actually tone modules with integrated keyboard controllers attached.

Keyboard synthesizers are by far the most common MIDI devices, although the tone modules included with nearly all sound cards for the PC are also extremely common. Like any device that wants to join into a MIDI conversation, synthesizers are equipped with the proper connectors that allow MIDI information to pass in, and sometimes out. These connectors, called MIDI ports, are usually grouped in threes: MIDI In, MIDI Out and MIDI Thru. A standard arrangement of the Ports on the back of a synthesizer, and also shows the end of a MIDI cable, which connects the sending and receiving devices. Unlike single ended audio plugs (guitar cords and stereo RCA plugs), MIDI cables and Ports use a 5 pin DIN connection. The MIDI communication does not have to be two-way; for example the MIDI input of device one can be connected to the MIDI Out of device two, but not vice versa. The MIDI Thru port is used to relay the information that is sent to a device on to yet another unit without altering it in any way. By using this port, many MIDI instruments can be chained together, allowing a single controller to transmit to numerous different sound-producing devices simultaneously.

To connect a MIDI synthesizer to a computer, the computer must have a MIDI interface, which typically contains the same three MIDI ports described above. Like the synthesizer, the MIDI interface converts the electrical signals it receives to the proper format needed by the computer. The MIDI interface might be a separate card that installs into a free PC expansion card slot; it could be a stand-alone, external unit that attaches to the PC's parallel or serial port; or it might be an integrated part of a sound card. Some sound cards use proprietary connectors for their MIDI hookup and require an optional MIDI adapter for connections to external MIDI units. On the Macintosh, the interface is almost always external, and typically connects to either the modem or printer port.

Keyboard and other MIDI controllers share many common features. Most have the ability to detect how hard a key was pressed. This feature, called Velocity Sensitivity, is used to determine a note's loudness, or amplitude. Like other controllers, a keyboard controller typically works by constantly watching the position of every key on the keyboard. An optical sensor is used to determine whether a key is up in its at-rest position, or down. Then, whenever a key is pressed, the instrument knows exactly how long it takes for the key to go down, and it assigns a value to that note by measuring the time it took to go from its starting point to the bottom of the keyboard. This value is called velocity, meaning "speed," but actually determines how loud the note will be played. An instrument that has the ability to measure this speed is said to be velocity sensitive.

Synthesizers and tone modules have many other features, including the ability to play many notes at once. This capability, called polyphony (for "many sounds"), usually ranges from eight notes, up to a maximum of 32, or in rare cases, 64. (Musicians usually use the term Voices when describing the polyphonic capabilities of an instrument, so "8-voice polyphonic" means the device can play eight notes at once.) When a device receives a new message after it has already reached its maximum, it must decide how to allocate its resources. For example, it might choose to drop the oldest note it is playing, or maybe it would drop the lowest or softest note. Some instruments will just ignore the new note that puts it over the top. In a professional synthesizer, this allocation might be programmable by the user, though in many cases it is fixed by the manufacturer. It's important to keep in mind that certain sounds on a tone module might use up more than one voice. For example, even a simple flute sound could require two notes (or voices) of the available polyphony, while a complex, evolving sound, such as those often intended for use as movie soundtrack backgrounds, might require four or more voices. Playing a four note chord using a sound that requires 4 voices could, in theory, use the entire polyphonic capability of a 16-voice synthesizer. Other sounds, such as drum sounds, typically use only a single note of polyphony, and are not likely to be needed for playing chords!

When a synthesizer can make more than one type of sound at the same time, it is called multitimbral. This term comes from the French word timbre (pronounced "tam-ber"), which means tone or sound color. If a synthesizer can make the sound of a trumpet, flute, clarinet and oboe simultaneously, it is clearly multitimbral. How many different timbres can be used at once is a significant factor in determining the usefulness of a tone module for one's music; for example if you plan to write your next symphony using a single synthesizer, you should be sure it is at least 16-part multitimbral and has 24 or more voices of polyphony. For choral music, four-part multitimbral and 8-voice polyphony might be adequate, but obviously the more the merrier.

One final basic feature of a MIDI device is its ability to respond to instructions on several different MIDI channels at once. This subject was mentioned earlier, but to review, MIDI can keep all the different layers of a musical performance separate from one another by transmitting each layer on its own channel, so an instrument should be able to handle the full "bandwidth" of a MIDI transmission, which is 16 different channels. Most instruments allow the user to set the Reception Mode of a MIDI device, which determines how it will respond to the messages it receives. The most common (and useful!) Reception Mode is called OMNI OFF \ POLY, which tells the device to distinguish what channel messages are on (OMNI OFF), and play back several notes at once if requested to do so (POLY, from polyphonic). Many older synths were limited to other reception modes, which kept them from distinguishing the different channels of a transmission. For example, if OMNI were ON, the device might play all messages without regard for their channel status. In nearly all recent devices, Reception Mode is selectable, though OMNI OFF/POLY is by far the most common Mode in use today.

Most synthesizers have the ability to assign one sound to play over part of the keyboard, and another sound to play over the rest. This is called keyboard splitting or zoning, and would allow you, for example, to play a bass guitar sound with the left hand on the low notes, and a piano sound with the right hand on the high notes. Synthesizers, by the way, typically offer keyboards that range from as few as four octaves, or forty-eight notes, to full, traditional piano lengths of just over seven octaves, or eighty-eight notes.

There is a wide range of programming options available on synthesizers today, but most have capabilities that allow the user to design sounds with great precision. Normally, you can layer different sounds, combining a flute with a cymbal for example, or merging the beginning portion of a trumpet with the sustaining segment of a cello. Numerous filters are also typically available, which, like the tone controls on a stereo system, let you raise or lower a sound's treble or bass response. Another useful programming feature is an envelope generator. Because natural sounds do not remain static throughout their duration-the piano, for example, begins to fade away or decay immediately after a note is struck-these generators allow the user to change the way a sound evolves over time. Normally, the characteristic that changes most is the sound's amplitude (loudness), but envelopes might also be applied to the sound's pitch or even timbre. The shape of the envelope is usually alterable, which allows the user to determine how long it takes for the sound to move through each of its "segments." In the example below, the sound will move gradually to its peak level during the attack segment, get a bit softer during the decay, maintain a steady level over the sustain segment, then slowly fade during the release. Samplers

Samplers are electronic devices that allow you to record audio, manipulate it, and play it back using MIDI commands. In effect, they allow the entire range of acoustic sounds to be employed in a musical composition. Under the control of MIDI messages, dog barks, train whistles, car horns and more can be integrated alongside violins and guitars, but samplers can be used for a lot more than just sound effects. Because of their extensive capabilities, samplers are used to create entire original compositions, using exacting reproductions of traditional instruments. Composers can preview their orchestral works and arrangers can listen to elaborate horn arrangements before committing the music to notation. In addition to these tasks, an entire musical style has evolved that uses samplers to store short phrases from existing recordings that are then used as the basis for entirely new musical compositions. While some of these capabilities are possible using traditional synthesizers, samplers expand the musician's palette of sounds enormously.

All samplers contain sample RAM that is used to hold digital recordings while the sampler processes them and plays them back. The amount of RAM determines the total length of recording time available to the unit. For example, if a sampler were to record sound using the quality of a commercial CD, it would require just over 10 MEGS (10,000,000 bytes) of RAM to hold just one minute of stereo or two minutes of monophonic sound. Many professional samplers contain hard disk drives for more permanent storage of recordings, while some also include floppy drives for moving sounds into and out of the unit. Besides the standard audio outputs used to record and playback, some samplers provide direct digital connections so sound can be moved back and forth to a digital tape recorder (DAT) or computer.

Among the many features of most samplers, one particular favorite is looping. This function allows the sampler to play repeatedly a short segment of sound. Using looping, small recordings can be played back for long periods of time, saving RAM and storage resources. When a sound loops, it merely plays through to the end, then restarts at the beginning or at some other point while the key is being held down. Looping works particularly well with string and wind sounds, but some sounds cannot be sustained; drum hits and other short sounds with sharp attacks, for example, simply do not loop well.

Among the other techniques samplers provide are filtering; crossfading, in which one sound fades out while another fades in; and pitch shifting, where the original pitch of a sampled sound is raised or lowered. Pitch shifting is very useful when you need to change or transpose the pitch of a sound, perhaps to change the key of your music. Unfortunately, after a certain amount of shifting in either direction, the sound will no longer resemble the original. It is very common for a sampler to use a technique known as multisampling, in which the original sound is recorded at numerous different pitch levels, and each individual sample is assigned to playback over a different range of the keyboard. In this way, no single sample has to be shifted beyond a small amount.

Samplers provide numerous other manipulation techniques, some of which will be mentioned in the section on digital audio. These include time compression/expansion, which is the ability to stretch or shrink sounds without changing their pitch; amplitude modulation, a technique used to change the sample's amplitude (loudness) at a variable rate; and playing back a sound in reverse. In all, samplers offer versatile options to the musician for shaping and crafting their music.

One final MIDI device is the drum machine and a related instrument, the drum controller. The drum machine, one of the most common of all MIDI peripherals, typically contains buttons or "pads" for playing drum sounds "live," and internal software to generate or store MIDI data. The sounds in the drum machine are most often sampled drums, i.e., digital recordings of actual acoustic drums. Unlike a sampler, you can rarely add your own sounds to such devices; instead you are limited to playback of the internal sounds, perhaps with some minor alterations.

While the buttons on a typical drum machine can be used to play the instrument in "real-time," you can also record any pattern of button presses right into the device. When requested, the drum machine will then play back the patterns you've created. In this way, one can create elaborate drum parts "note by note," then play them back repeatedly and at any tempo required. Drum machines also typically include preset patterns, providing very realistic drum parts that musicians who don't play the instrument can use in their own productions. Unfortunately, many of these patterns sound "canned," and their overuse has created somewhat of a backlash against this type of device. Creative drum programming by capable musicians can, however, produce excellent results. While the vast majority of MIDI music emanates from keyboard controllers and synthesizers, instrument makers have come to realize that many other instrumentalists would like to share in the joy of MIDI. For this reason, various types of guitar and wind controllers have been created to provide a familiar performance interface for players of these instruments. While they typically produce no sound on their own, these instruments can be connected to tone modules or samplers, which then generate sound under their control.

Shaped and performed like traditional six string guitars, MIDI guitars contain small sensors that detect the player's finger position on the strings, as well as the amount of pressure applied to the string by the pick. Most can also track movements of the string and convert this bending into continuous controller data. Some guitar controllers even allow the user to assign a different MIDI channel to every string, thereby offering the ability to play up to six different sounds on the receiving device simultaneously. Wind controllers can easily detect which keys have been closed by the player, but must make far more difficult measurements of the amount of air pressure passing through the device's mouthpiece. Typically, a sensor in the mouthpiece is used for such measurements, and over the years, the accuracy of wind controllers has improved dramatically. Because a single MIDI note can be used to generate an entire chord, (if the receiving synthesizer is so programmed), musicians who have spent most of their lives playing monophonic (single note) instruments, now have the ability to play elaborate, chordal textures.

One final controlling device is the pitch-to-MIDI converter. This somewhat uncommon device is attached to a traditional acoustic wind instrument such as a saxophone or trumpet and converts the acoustic tones the instrument generates into MIDI notes.

The Pitch-to-MIDI converter offers perhaps the best of both worlds, in that a musician can use his or her favorite instrument to create a performance that combines "natural" and synthetic sounds. Unfortunately, the conversion is not always accurate, and these devices still must undergo some refinements before they will be completely reliable. Nevertheless, converters are becoming more common, and offer musicians including singers tremendous expressive qualities in a MIDI performance.

There are many categories of MIDI software available. Perhaps the most common is the MIDI sequencer, which is a type of program that can record, edit and playback MIDI data. Sequencers, which originally were often found as stand-alone hardware devices, have very powerful capabilities to transform MIDI information, and today represent a very complex and mature category of software. Sequencers share many basic features, and allow the user to put the strength of a personal computer to the task of making music.

Like a multi-track tape recorder, sequencers most often arrange multiple layers of MIDI information into tracks. Each track represents an independent melody or part of the music. The number of tracks in a sequencer can range from as few as sixteen in an entry-level program, to hundreds, or even thousands in others. Each track can be used to hold any type of MIDI data, and there is no single standard for how this information should be arranged. Rather, the best sequencers give the user a high degree of flexibility in organizing the various types of information their music requires.

The main screen of a popular Windows-based sequencer, Cakewalk Pro Audio(TM). The first sixteen tracks are shown here, but different screen resolutions would allow you to see more or fewer at once on your own monitor. Each track is assigned to a specific MIDI channel, though you can see that several of the tracks have the same setting. This indicates that the events on all of these tracks will go to the same destination. Most sequencers allow you to put information for several channels on the same track, though this could make editing the information somewhat more difficult.

Sequencers typically provide different ways to view and edit your data, and it's important to understand the function of each of a program's work areas. Usually, one will find a Piano Roll view, where individual or small groups of notes can be altered; a Track Overview, where entire measures or even whole tracks can be manipulated; a Notation or Staff view, where the music is represented using standard music notation; and an Event View, which is a text-based list of all the events in one or more tracks. The editing options that such programs provide are numerous and vary greatly among programs, but typically, one can cut, copy and paste data, as well as apply extensive modifications to the music, such as raising or lowering the pitch and volume characteristics, and expanding or compressing the amount of time a section takes to playback.

Some programs also provides features that can assist the user with the operation of his/her MIDI hardware. It is not uncommon to find sequencers that will list all the different sounds in your synthesizer, allowing you to work with specific names rather than the less familiar patch numbers. Some will also import or export system exclusive (Sysx) data to a synthesizer, meaning you can load an entire setup of sounds before the first note is played. While they don't offer all the editing capabilities of full-blown patch editors (discussed later), these patch librarian features are very useful, especially in settings where there are two or more MIDI devices.

Overall, sequencers are the most common of all MIDI software programs, and provide tremendous power that can be applied to the production of music. Another category of MIDI software is the notation, or transcription program. Because standard notation remains the most common way to represent music, an entire market has been established for programs that let musicians work "the old fashioned way." Typically, these programs provide huge libraries of musical symbols that can be entered onto the page to produce professional looking scores. Some even allow the user to create new symbols. Sophisticated page layout features, often comparable to high-end desktop publishing programs, are also included in the more advanced notation software, and all programs of this type offer printing options.

Most programs allow "point and click" entry as well as real-time transcription from a MIDI keyboard. With real-time entry, musicians can play their music directly into the program and see it appear instantly on screen as notation. Once the notes are recorded, numerous editing capabilities, such as the cut, copy and paste features of a word processor, are available. Other editing functions needed by musicians, such as the ability to shift or "transpose" the music up or down are also commonly found.

Because of the complexity of many of today's synthesizers, an entire software niche has developed to facilitate the control of such devices from a computer. Patch editors typically display all of a synthesizer's programming controls on one or two computer screens, allowing the user to "see into" the synthesizer and control it directly from the computer keyboard. Rather than spend many minutes pushing buttons, trying to locate a particular screen within the synthesizer's own display, the patch editor lays all the device's parameters before the user, and allows him or her to make extensive changes with the sweep of the mouse or press of a few keys. Changes made on the computer screen are typically sent immediately to the device, making it possible to preview them before any permanent changes are made.

Stand-alone librarian programs, or those usually included with the patch editor, simply store all the device's sounds and make them available for quick searching or sorting. Typically, a librarian will request a "dump" from the device via Sysx, then show the user the sounds currently available on the instrument. This listing can then be stored on a computer and reloaded into the device if needed. Not only are the names of the patches stored, but also the specifications as to how the sounds are created. In other words, if the internal memory of a synthesizer were wiped out, the librarian could send a list of the original factory programs back to the synthesizer and return it to its original status.

Librarians are also commonly employed when users owning the same equipment wish to share programs they have created. Simply load the sounds into the librarian and save them on a floppy disk, then transport them to another computer anywhere in the world.

An interesting trend in MIDI software today is the appearance of integrated programs that combine many of the features of the programs listed above. Like their counterpart in the business world, the "desktop suite," these integrated programs offer professional sequencing, notation, patch librarian, and in some cases, digital audio functions in an all-in-one environment. This trend shows tremendous promise, and has far-reaching implications for the user. It will be exciting to see how far it develops.

Digital Audio: An Introduction

One of the most exciting developments in desktop music in recent years is the ability to work with digital audio on a home PC. Long the province of research institutions and recording studios, digital audio editing software has become nearly commonplace on the desktop, and is now among the most accessible and powerful types of computer software available. Recording, editing, and playing digital audio on a home computer gives the user considerable power to design and produce new sounds, and to edit and craft one's own music with great precision. Digital audio can be a highly technical and elusive concept though, and we'll try to make the terms and concepts perfectly clear.

Digital audio is a numeric representation of sound; it is sound stored as numbers. In order to understand what the numbers mean, we need to review some of the basic principles of acoustics, the study of sound.

Sound is produced when molecules in the air are disturbed by some type of motion produced by a vibrating body. This body, which might be a guitar string, human vocal cord or garbage can, is set into motion because energy is applied to it. The guitar string is struck by a pick or finger, while the garbage can is hit perhaps by a hammer, but the basic result is the same: they both begin to vibrate. The rate and amount of vibration is critical to our perception of the sound. If it is not fast enough or strong enough, we won't hear it. But if the vibration occurs at least twenty times a second and the molecules in the air are moved enough (a more difficult phenomena to measure), then we will hear sound. To understand the process better, let's take a closer look at a guitar string.

When the pick hits the string, the entire string moves back and forth at a certain rate of speed. This speed is called the frequency of the vibration. Because a single back and forth motion is called a cycle, we use a measure of frequency called cycles per second, or cps. This measure is also known as hertz, abbreviated Hz. Like that of other bodies, the frequency of the string is often very fast, so it is useful to use the abbreviation kHz to measure frequency in thousands of vibrations per second. A frequency of 2 kHz then, signifies a frequency of 2,000 cycles per second, meaning the string goes through its back and forth motion 2,000 times per second. The actual distance the string moves is called its displacement, and is proportional to how hard we pluck it. The actual measurement used for this distance is not particularly important for our purposes, but we will often refer to the amplitude or strength of the vibration.

As the string moves, it displaces the molecules around it in a wave-like pattern, i.e., while the string moves back and forth, the molecules also move back and forth. The movement of the molecules is propagated in the air; individual molecules bump against molecules next to them, which in turn bump their neighbors, etc., until the molecules next to our ears are set in motion. At the end of the chain, these molecules move our eardrum in a pattern analogous to the original string movement, and we hear the sound. This pattern of motion, which is an air pressure wave, can be represented in many ways, for example as a mathematical formula, or graphically as a waveform. Below shows the movement of the string over time: the segment marked "A" represents the string as it is pulled back by the pick; "B" shows it moving back towards its resting point, "C" represents the string moving through the resting point and onward to its outer limit; then "D" has it moving back towards the point of rest. This pattern repeats continuously under the friction of the molecules in the air gradually slows the string down to a stop. In order for us to hear the string tone, the pattern must repeat at least twenty times per second. This threshold, 20 cps, is the lower limit of human hearing.

If this back and forth motion were the only phenomena involved in creating a sound, then all stringed instruments would probably sound much the same. We know this is not true, of course, and alas, the laws of physics are not quite so simple. In fact, the string vibrates not only at its entire length, but at one-half its length, one-third, one-fourth, one-fifth, etc. These additional vibrations occur at a rate faster than the original vibration, (known as the fundamental frequency), but are usually weaker in strength. Our ear doesn't hear each vibration individually however. If it if did, we would hear a multi-note chord every time a single note were played. Rather, all these vibrations are added together to form a complex or composite waveform that our ear perceives as a single tone

This composite waveform still doesn't account for the uniqueness of the sound of different instruments, as there is one more major factor in determining the quality of the tone we hear. This is the resonator. The resonator in the case of the guitar is the big block of hollow wood that the string is attached, i.e., the guitar body. This has a major impact on the sound we perceive when a guitar is played as it actually enhances some of the vibrations produced by the string and diminishes or attenuates others. The ultimate effect of all the vibrations occurring simultaneously, being altered by the resonator, adds up to the sound we know as guitar.

So what has all this got to do with digital audio? What is it we need to record from all of this motion in the air? It is the strength of the composite pressure wave created by all the vibrations that we must measure very accurately and very often. That is the basic principle behind digital audio. When a microphone records a guitar playing, a small membrane in the mic (called the diaphragm) is set into motion in a pattern identical to the guitar wave's own pattern. The diaphragm moves back and forth, creating an electrical current that is sent through a cable. The voltages in the cable are also "alternating" in strength at a very rapid rate: strong, weaker, weak, strong again. When the cable arrives at our measuring device, called an analog to digital (A/D) converter, the device measures how strong the signal is at every instant and sends a numeric value to a storage device, probably the hard drive in your computer. The A/D converter, along with its counterpart, the digital to analog (D/A) converter that turns the numbers back into voltages, is typically found as a component of your sound card, or as a stand-alone device.

There are several important aspects of this measuring process that we need to discuss. First is the rate at which we choose to examine the signal coming into the converter. It is a known fact of physics that we must measure or sample the signal at a rate twice as fast as the highest frequency we wish to capture. Let's say we are trying to record a moderately high note on a violin. Let's also assume that the fundamental frequency of this tone repeats 440 times per second (the note would be an "A," of course), and that we want to capture all vibrations up to five times the rate of the fundamental, or 2,200 cycles per second. To capture all the components of this note and convert the resulting sound into numbers, we would have to measure it 4,400 times per second.

But humans can hear tones that occur at rates well up into the tens of thousands of times per second, so our system must be capable of much better than that! In theory, we might want to capture an extremely high sound, for example one that actually contains a frequency component of 20,000 cps. In that case, our measurements must occur 40,000 times per second, which in fact, would allow us to capture every possible sound that any human might be able to hear. Because of some complex laws that digital audio obeys however, we use a rate of 44,100 measurements or "snapshots" of a sound per second in our professional equipment. This sampling rate, abbreviated 44.1 kHz (44.1 kilohertz) is one aspect of what we call CD-quality recording, as it is the same rate that commercial CDs use. Other common sampling rates are 11kHz, 22kHz, and for some professional equipment, 48kHz.

The other important issue is how accurate our measuring system will be. Will we have 20 different values to select from for each measurement? How about 200 or 2,000? How accurately do we need to represent the incredible variety of fluctuations in a pressure wave? Think about the different types of time pieces you know about. If your digital watch shows you minutes and seconds, that's adequate for most purposes. If you are doing scientific measurements of time, then you might need more accuracy, perhaps minutes, seconds, tenths, hundredths and even thousandths of seconds. Soundwaves actually encompass an infinite range of strengths, but we must draw the line somewhere, or else we would need gigantic hard drives just to store the information for a short amount of sound. The music industry has settled on a system that provides 65,536 different values to assign to the amplitude (strength) of a waveform at any given instant. In a certain sense, that number represents a compromise, as we will definitely not capture every possible value that the amplitude can take. However, our ears can live with that compromise, and in any event, using a more sophisticated measuring system is simply not worth the extra cost in computing and storage resources.

Obviously you are wondering, "Why in the world did they choose 65,536?" The answer is simply because it is 216, that is, 2 to the 16th power (2 multiplied by itself sixteen times). This is the largest number we can express in the binary numbering system if we use 16 bits, or 16 places. Recall from your high school math that the binary numbering system uses only two digits, 0 and 1, and that this is what computers use as well. A string of sixteen 1's in the binary system produces the number 65,535 in decimal, and a string of 16 0's is, of course the decimal number 0. So from 0 through 65,535 we have 65,536 different numbers that we can express using 16 bits. Computers actually think in terms of 8 digit strings, which you will remember are called bytes. Therefore, if we use numbers that are two bytes long to represent every different value in our system, we have the total range described above. One byte, or a string of 8 bits, would allow us to represent the numbers 0 through 255, and MIDI is quite happy with that range, but there is so much more detail in the digital audio world that our system must be far more sophisticated.

If you've followed the discussion up until now, you should have a pretty good idea of what is on a compact disc. It's a massive amount of numbers, each two bytes long, that represent the fluctuating amplitude of the pressure wave in front of the microphone that made the recording. No matter if the sound was an orchestra, a guitar or a car horn, the CD simply contains measurements for the pattern of motion produced by that sound. We can use our hard drives to record the information in the same form as that on a CD, or if we wish, we can use a somewhat less accurate representation. For example, if we choose not to capture the data as accurately as the CD, we might only use eight bits, or one byte, for each amplitude value. Such a measuring system has only what we call 8-bit accuracy or resolution. This will have a significant impact on the quality of our representation, but it may be adequate for the purpose at hand. Or we might wish to look at the sound and take a measurement only every eleven or twenty-two thousands times a second, i.e., an 11k or 22 kHz sampling rate, realizing that we will miss some detail, in particular the high end (upper frequencies) in the sound. In truth, that rate may be good enough to represent certain types of sound, for example the frequencies produced by the human voice are much lower than those produced by a cymbal, so we might be able to get the whole picture by looking at the voice at a lower rate. The decision regarding how accurate we need to be will be determined by the material we are recording and the amount of storage space we have available to hold the recording. These choices are usually made from within our audio software, so perhaps it's time to turn or attention to the PC.

There are several common varieties of software used to manipulate digital audio data on a computer. The most popular is wave editing software, which is often included as part of the software packaged with sound cards. This type of software allows someone to work with a graphic representation of sound, the waveform, and cut, copy and paste it with the ease of a word processor. The software also typically includes a number of editing features that allow additional processing of the material; this processing can be used to create special effects, such as dogs barking backwards, and gun shots being stretched to one hundred times their length. Features of this type fall into the category of signal processing, or digital signal processing (DSP) functions. Professional versions of waveform editors often cost several hundred dollars, but offer the user tremendous flexibility in the type of manipulations they can perform. By the way, on the IBM-compatible platform, digital audio files are typically called Wave files and carry the extension, .WAV. On the Macintosh, the standard audio file type is the AIFF file.

Usually, wave editing software can accommodate no more than a single, stereo file, though a new category, called multi-track software, lets the user work with several stereo files at once. After being manipulated and edited, these files are mixed together into a single composite stereo file that is sent to the left and right channel outputs of a sound card. In many cases, the multi-track software doesn't offer a full range of editing options; most often it is the signal processing functions that are omitted, but the ability to mix many different layers of audio is very appealing.

One other type of editing software is used with dedicated hard-disk recording systems. These professional products are very sophisticated, and often very expensive. Their key advantage is that they provide extensive editing capabilities, such as those needed to make commercial audio recordings, and often include storage devices devoted to holding large amounts of high quality audio. They also provide multiple tracks of digital audio, in some cases up to ten or even twelve simultaneous tracks on a single PC, as well as multiple audio outputs. This makes them well suited for the production of radio and television commercials, where a vocal narration, sound effects and music soundtrack are often combined.

Far less expensive than the dedicated hardware described above are the massively popular sound cards found in nearly every PC today. Much of the success of these products can be attributed to the fact that IBM-compatible computers never enjoyed the quality of sound production that the Macintosh(TM) had from its inception. When card maker Creative Labs reached the consumer with its industry standard Sound Blaster(TM) card, they found a huge untapped market that is now quite saturated with products.

Sound cards typically serve several important functions. First, they contain a synthesizer that uses either frequency modulation (FM) synthesis to produce sound, or that stores actual recorded audio data in wavetables for use in playback. FM is a somewhat dated method of synthesis that uses one or more wave(s), called the modulator, to alter the frequency and amplitude of another, called the carrier. The range of sounds that can be produced is limited, though often adequate for simple sound effects or other game sounds. While the FM-style card has nearly disappeared from the market, most software manufacturers must include support for it in their products because of the vast number of cards that are still installed in computers.

Nearly all newer cards use the preferable wavetable approach because it provides far more realistic sound. Wavetables are digital recordings that exist in some type of compressed form in the card's ROM (read only memory). These sounds can never be erased, but can be altered in numerous ways as they playback. For example, a trumpet sound could be reversed, or a piano could be layered with a snare drum. Depending upon the programmability provided by the manufacturer, this type of card can be quite flexible in the sounds it makes. Most wavetable cards, regardless of their manufacturer, offer a General MIDI soundset, which makes them compatible with many popular multimedia programs. Despite what their ads may claim, sound cards vary tremendously in quality, even those that use the same playback method. Magazine reviews and roundups are a good source of information for evaluating a card's characteristics.

Most cards also contain a MIDI interface for MIDI input and output, plus the digital to analog (D/A) and analog to digital (A/D) converters described above. While all MIDI interfaces are essentially created equal, there can be major differences among the converters on these cards. Many cards claim "CD Quality Sound," which simply means they can record and playback audio at a sampling rate of 44.1 kHz using 16-bit resolution. Unfortunately, the personal computer was not originally intended to be a musical instrument, and the high level of electronic activity inside its case can cause interference problems with some cards. With properly built cards, these problems can be avoided, and most users won't experience any difficulties.

MIDI and digital audio have coexisted in separate worlds until very recently. Now, using an entirely new class of software, we have the potential to work with both types of data within a single program. This new category, called simply, integrated MIDI and Digital audio software, solves many of the most nagging problems desktop musicians have had for years. The capabilities it offers greatly facilitate the integration of "real world" audio with the "virtual" world of MIDI tracks. Before we discuss this software, let's look at the way things used to work. Here's how musicians combined audio and MIDI in the past.

For many years, in home and professional music studios around the world, musicians have employed elaborate and somewhat complex means to join live audio with MIDI music. Guitarists, vocalists, drummers and others have used different synchronization techniques to mix their live playing with the music produced by their MIDI software. Typically, a musician would record live audio onto a tape recorder, then use the tape recorder to send information to the computer which told it when to start and stop playing. In this way, the music on the tape and the sequenced music could be perfectly aligned.

The information sent by the tape recorder in this case is known as SMPTE time code, and is actually an audio signal recorded (or "striped") on the tape. SMPTE (pronounced "simp-tee") serves as a timing reference for both the tape and the computer running the MIDI software. In essence, this code tells the software "what time it is," i.e., where into the music it should be. If a MIDI drum part must start exactly one minute after the music on the tape recorder begins, then the sequencer will watch the time pass from the beginning of the tape (time 00:00), until it reaches time 01:00, at which point it begins to play. Sequencers can jump instantly to any time point that's required, so the sequencer will simply wait for its "cue" then start playing.

SMPTE, which stands for the Society of Motion Picture and Television Engineers, was initially created by the NASA space agency for use with its tracking stations. It provided an absolute timing reference that allowed the agency to keep track of when transmissions occurred. Like a digital clock, SMPTE works on a 24 hour cycle, and the precision it provides is considerable: a normal SMPTE time represents hours, minutes, seconds, and "frames,. The "frames" designation is important to the television and movie industry for tracking time in film and video productions. A frame in television occurs 30 times a second, while in film it represents an interval of 1/24th or 1/25th of a second, so SMPTE can measure time quite accurately. Because most professional video equipment is SMPTE-compatible, musicians creating audio for video productions can also use it to synchronize their music with the various types of video equipment they commonly work with. When scoring for films, it is an invaluable way for the composer to know exactly when a sound effect or music cue must begin and end.

Rather than deal with the intricacies of SMPTE, today's musician can work with integrated software to combine audio and MIDI tracks with great precision. New programs like Cakewalk Pro Audio represent digital audio data in the same form as

MIDI data, and allow the user to manipulate the two with ease. Once audio files are recorded onto disk, they can be aligned for playback along with the MIDI information, and what's more, numerous tracks of audio can be performed simultaneously. If synchronization with an external device is needed, the entire project can still be controlled by that device. Thus, the best features of multi-track audio software can now be found integrated with the advanced options of MIDI sequencers.

The number of audio tracks that can be mixed together in an integrated program, or in a stand-alone audio editor for that matter, is very much a function of the computer hardware being used for the task. In the IBM world, the processor (CPU) speed, access or "seek" time of the hard drive, and available system RAM are among the key components to evaluate. In the early years of desktop multimedia, software leader Microsoft produced a "multimedia" specification that described the minimal requirements for work of this type. That spec has been modified to keep up with enhancements in today's computers, and has, as of this writing, reached "Level III" status. This calls for a computer with a Pentium 75 MHz or better processor, at least 8 MEGS of RAM, a 540 MEG hard drive, a quad-speed CD-ROM player, a sound card that uses wavetable synthesis, and a video card that is MPEG 1 (a form of compression) compliant. Keep in mind that any component of a system can slow the process: a fast CPU with an inadequate hard drive can bring a system to its knees, for example. It's important that all the pieces of the system are well balanced and in good working order.

Here's a tip to keep in mind: one of the easiest and most effective tasks you can do to prepare your system for recording or playing audio is defragmenting your hard drive. A fragmented drive contains pieces of files spread over different physical locations, and makes the job of streaming data to and from that disk very difficult. Use one of the cleanup programs, such as defrag, which comes with your operating system, before making recordings. Also if possible, devote a separate drive partition to digital audio. When you first setup your computer, you can create partitions easily using DOS's fdisk program, but later, you'll have to backup your drive and reformat it.

We hope you've enjoyed this initial presentation of the ins and outs of desktop music and that it will encourage you to experiment on your own. Much of today's software is very powerful, though manufacturers have done a good job in making it easy to use, and you've got many hours of pleasure and excitement to look forward to. Of course the more you can learn about desktop music, the more you will get out of your equipment, so keep your eyes on the numerous books and magazines devoted to the subject, and consider subscribing to some of the multimedia newsgroups on the Internet. There's a whole world of music waiting for you, right on your desktop.

High Technology, Individual Copyrights and Music

The impact of technology on the production of Ghanaian music, along with the music's associated values and aesthetics, has two different aspects. Firstly, there are the direct positive and negative effects of hi-technology (videos, computer studios, synthesizers and drum machines) upon Ghanaian popular music. Secondly, there is the indirect effect of technology on music production in Ghana through the introduction of copyright regulations.

Copyright itself is a product of Western printing and electronic inventions, combined with the Western individualistic ethos applied to the arts. Although the idea of individually owned artistic or intellectual property is fruitful in practical terms when applied to contemporary commercial Ghanaian music (i.e. it yields royalties for the author), problems arise when this European-derived notion is applied to the collectively-created and orally-transmitted folkloric music of Ghana. Unlike that of the West, folkloric music in Ghana is very much alive and evolving.

The dualistic schism between mind and matter of the 17th century French philosopher Descartes has been regarded analytically — since Ryle's critique in the 1950s — as bearing the problem of 'the ghost in the machine'. For the modern urbanized world this also describes the existential state of alienation and anomie often found among those living in a completely technological environment. This environment includes the contemporary soundscape and musical practices that have been transformed by modern recording and mass communication techniques.

I have been running a recording studio in Ghana since 1982 and have noticed a number of technical changes that have dramatically affected local popular music-making. These have resulted in many recording artists and performers becoming lost in the musical machine. The number of tracks in a recording studio has increased to the nearly infinite number available from digital computer systems. This makes overdubbing the order of the day, whereby a single musical technician can provide all of a song's instrumentation. So musicians on stage interacting with a live audience have been superseded by electronic mediation, mobile discos (spinners), videos, television and lip-synching, i.e. television musicians miming to pre-recorded work. Another change that began in the late 1980s is the replacement of drummers by drum machines, horn sections by single keyboard players and guitars by synthesizers. In some cases the entire instrumentation of a band is provided by one electronic instrument, such as the Yamaha computerized keyboard.

Before turning to some of the negative aspects of these technical developments, consider six advantages. Firstly, they make things cheaper for a composer to record, since only a few musicians are needed — in some productions just one musician is sufficient. Secondly, the drumulator and other metronomic-like machines impose rhythmic discipline on the recording session. Thirdly, electronic gadgets provide an instrumental background that has a hi-tech and international flavor. Fourthly, electronics help to democratize music by making it easy for everyone, even those without musical skills, to become budding pop stars. Fifthly, given purely analytical motivations, the computer is useful for studying the minute details of complex rhythms, (such as local cross-rhythms), since standard notation is often not precise enough to deal with the tiny spaces between the quavers. Finally, computers are useful for composers making preliminary sketches of their musical works.

Now we turn to some of the main problems for musicians and composers when machines replace performers. Firstly, there is a loss of African content. If one listens to local pop music on Ghanaian FM radio today, one hears mostly vernacular love lyrics sung over a synthesized background, with no local rhythmic content and with no relation between the song melody and the tonal movement of the language. One result is that although this music is patronized by Ghanaian youth, it is not exportable — for no one abroad wants to hear the African variety of World Music without African dance rhythms. Thus, the late famous Ghanaian highlife musician King Bruce, when manager of Accra's *Elephant Walk* studio had a tape made with drumulator returned from the United States, requiring that the band return to the studio to replace the drum-machine track with a live drummer. A number of music journalists have commented on the unexportable nature of current Ghanaian popular music.

Secondly, the introduction of machines interferes with the flow of creative energy that takes place between musicians in a live context — whether in the studio or on stage. Musicians inspire one another and create new ideas during a performance. For instance, many jazz musicians prefer to be recorded in one take. They prefer to avoid studio overdubbing techniques whereby the whole band never plays as a unit but instead records a few musicians at a time over a number of days. Indeed, the very vocabulary of jazz musicians shows their antipathy towards the excessive use of drum machines and overdubbing. They prefer improvisation, and talk of the music having 'swing', 'play' 'looseness', 'feel', 'soul' and 'groove'.

The same need for 'feel' applies to symphonic orchestras where, despite written scores, the subtle interpretations of the composition are done on the spot by the conductor and virtuoso musicians. This is why Art Music recordings are always made by the whole orchestras in one take and not by a series of overdubs. Yet for today's young Ghanaian pop artists, overdubbing is the norm. This is why some bands now cannot reproduce on stage what they have recorded in a multi-track studio. For example, a synthesized trumpet may appear on a studio recording of a band that has no trumpeter. As a result the band has to mime to its own works on television or even on live stage.

This brings us to a third major problem arising from modern recording and production methods: nowadays, there is little or no direct contact between the performers and their audience. Many older Ghanaian musicians will tell you that some of their ideas have been drawn from the immediate response of their audiences during performances. For instance, formerly singers responded to comments from their audience, or a rhythmic dialogue would take place between the percussionists and dancers. These are age-old folk traditions here in Ghana and elsewhere in the world. A fourth negative consequence of machine music in Ghana is that the clear human voice has been compromised by electronic gadgets such as harmonizers, phasers and double-tracking, and by the fact that the sound level of the singers is often very low as compared with the instrumental background. The sound of the human voice is literally getting lost in the ghostly electronic mix.

Last but not least of these problems is the fact that drum machines and synthesizers are putting percussionists and horn players out of work. For now all the sounds that these musicians supply can be simulated by one musical technician.

All these problems which are now being faced in Ghana began to effect the West in the early 1980s with the fashion of the computer generated disco music of groups like Kraftwork, Munich Machines and Donna Summers, all playing at an exact 154 beats per minute. However, over the last few years in Europe and North America there has been some reaction against modernistic machine music. One such reaction is a Western back-to-roots movement in which European and American youth have turned partially away from modern sounds towards folk music, non-Western World Music and the recycling of old pop songs from the past. Paradoxically, part of this recycling of the past uses the most advanced techniques. One current trick is the electronic sampling of the sounds of old stars like James Brown and Jimmy Hendrix, and the grafting of their phrases, shouts and guitar-licks into current works. (This, creates enormous copyright problems regarding the length of a sample in order for it to be copyrightable).

A second response of Western artists to electronic inputs has been to 'unplug'. Pop stars such as Neil Young and Eric Clapton unplug their electric instruments and play acoustically. Further, when a drum machine is now used in America and Europe, complementary live percussion (such as hi-hats, timbales and congas) are usually added. An instance is the work of Michael Jackson. In the early 1980s his songs were backed percussively by drum machines alone. But his later recordings use a drum machine on one track and a live drummer on another, carefully blended together to produce a live feel.

A third recent response by Western musicians has been their attempt to humanize electronic music. Ironically, all these effects depend upon the increased sophistication of digital equipment, in particular the increase in 'quantization'. This is the division of a musical measure into incredibly tiny metronomic beats, pulses or kicks. For example Michael Stewart (1987) has devised a 'feel spectrum' for livening up digitally sequenced music. If the drummer plays a few milliseconds ahead of the digital pulse he calls it 'snappy'; if he plays behind, it is called 'groovy'. Likewise David Jaffe (1985) uses 'tempo perturbations' that stagger the attack of the played note in relation to the exact metronomic pulse or kick. Meanwhile Kalle Nemvalts (1988) creates degrees of 'swing' by allowing the duration of the played drumnote to fill differing percentages of the spaces between digital pulses. Travis Charbeneaue (1989) utilizes 'time-shifting adjustments' to strike the 64th note ahead of the electronic pulse or behind it. All these rhythmic displacement tricks are attempts to simulate human imprecision, inaccuracy, ambiguity, leeway, and generally to create a more authentically live feel in otherwise mechanically exact electronic rhythms. Another way musical technology is being 'humanized' in the West is through the use of MIDI devices (Musical Digital Interface) that operate between a musical instrument and a computer. These are played in real-time, not the pre-set quanticized time of drum machines. An example is the DRUM KAT, which consists of special electronic MIDI pads that are beaten with drumsticks, just like an ordinary drum. The drum strokes create an electronic signal that triggers off the computer's digitally generated or sampled sound. An extension of this idea is found with the Bodysynth. This device is used by the American musician-composer Laurie Anderson. Electronic sensors are stuck all over the artist's body and are triggered by the movement of the musician's or dancer's muscles. Thus the whole human body becomes a musical instrument.

So in spite of the West's general fascination with electronic sounds, recent moves have been developed by musicians and composers to reassert themselves in the three ways just described: via the Western back-to-roots trend, the performance of 'unplugged' pop stars, and the humanizing of music software programs.

After an initial flirtation with local hi-tech popular music during the 1980s, the electronic music scene is beginning to change in Ghana. In 1992 there were audience protests over the low-cost, locally produced, 'lip-synched,' music videos broadcast by Ghana Television (GTV) on the nation's then only television channel during Saturday evening primetime. In response, Ghana Television began a program of live dance band music called "For Your Dancing Feet" which is still running. In the early 1990s there was also a slight waning of the 'spinners' craze amongst the youth and the emergence cf a new generation of 'highlife' bands who play for live dances, including The Golden Nuggets, Western Diamonds, the current Marriots Band, Ankobra and Nakorex. Old-time style 'highlife' dances have also been organized by the ABC Brewery and the Ghana Television Club-House, specializing in the highlife classics of the 1950s and '60s. Cassette releases of old evergreen highlife favorites have recently been coming on the market as well, including those by The Black Beats, Tempos, African Brothers, Kakaiku, Alhaji Frempong and The Kumasi Trio.

The legal side of this interface of traditional music and modern technology appears with special clarity with regard to the oral tradition and the issue of copyrights.

The idea of copyright first appeared in 16th century Europe in connection with book publishing. In the 18th and 19th centuries copyrighting was extended to a wider technology and to the fine arts. Because of its origin the notion of copyright carries three basic Eurocentric assumptions:

1. A specific artwork or intellectual idea is created by a single or fixed set of particular individuals; its author is therefore easily identifiable.
2. Older artistic forms rooted in pre-industrial peasant society (i.e. folklore) are public property, because their authors are unidentifiable, hence anonymous.
3. In accord with English law (on which much of Ghanaian contract law is based) there can be no copyright unless a work has been written down, recorded or otherwise reduced to material form. This is a clear reflection of copyright's origin in book publishing.

Since the 19th century, when copyright really became effective in Europe, there has been a clear demarcation between anonymous folk music, on the one hand, and popular or classical works that are composed by identifiable contemporary individuals on the other. The term 'folk music' applies to pre-industrial art forms publicly owned and preserved in museums and archives — in contrast to individually and privately owned artistic and intellectual creative works. Thus in Europe the realms of the folk-music archivist and the copyright official do not overlap. However, in many non-industrial countries (including those in Africa) there is a living folk tradition simultaneously co-existing with privately owned, creative works. Outside Europe the realms of folklore and copyright do overlap. Indeed the very (European) concept of 'folklore' has to be re-assessed in the context of non-technocratic cultures. Moreover, in Ghana and many other African countries art and cultural works are often not written down nor materialized in any way; they constitute part of a persistent living oral tradition.

There are four specific problems in applying to Ghana and other African countries European assumptions about 'folklore' and 'copyright':

There is a widespread misconception that only literary or other materially recorded works (i.e. printed, scored, choreographed, taped artwork) can generate royalties. On this view, since African folklore is oral, it cannot have a definite, fixed authorship and therefore cannot be copyrighted. This view favors literate artists in affluent technocratic societies at the expense of nonliterate artists based in low-income, nonindustrialized countries. But often the author(s) of oral works can in fact be identified, as noted by Anyidoho and Tsikata (1988). They and Dekutsey (1988) give the examples of the 'unwritten copyright' of Somali poetry and the oral Ewe funeral poems of Akpalu and other traditional poet-cantors. Anyidoho (1983) also highlights the Ewe Haikotu drum clubs in which the composer of the words and tunes first prepares the performance with the other members of the group in closed session, before presenting it to the public. Similar to this practice is the Eguamala dance drumming of the Bendel State of Nigeria, where the known composer and group rehearse for two years in secrecy playing their work publically, as noted by Okwesa (1990). Subsequently, they can sell the whole work outright since initially it is the private property of the group that created it.

In a speech by Dr. Mohammed Ben Abdullah, Secretary of the National Commission on Culture at the 1991 Inauguration of the Ghana Folklore Board of Trustees, folklore was defined to be:

> [All the] literary, artistic and scientific works belonging to the cultural heritage of Ghana which were created, preserved and developed by ethnic communities of Ghana or by unidentified Ghanaian authors.

The distinction between folklore and contemporary artistic idioms is simple enough to make in the Western situation where the oral folklore tradition is dead or has to be artificially preserved. But it becomes exceedingly complex to apply in the case of a living tradition as exists in Ghana. This problem was documented in the 1989 report of WIPO (World Intellectual Protection Organization) on "The Protection of Expressions of Folklore." There it is mentioned that one of the major obstacles to creating an international agreement for the protection of folklore is the "lack of appropriate sources for the identification of folklore to be protected." The following list of nine possible permutations that may occur demonstrates how difficult it is to define folklore, and to separate it from the other contemporary composed performing arts of Ghana. Determining who owns what in this context is no easy task.

Varieties of folkloric or folkloric-inspired Ghanaian musical genres includes the following:

1. Traditional music, dance, drama and poetry that have been created either communally or so long ago that it is beyond the reach of copyright (75 years since the death of the composer(s)). This is 'folklore' in the sense defined above by Dr. Abdullah above.
2. Modern neo-traditional genres (such as Kpanlogo, Akpalu, Borborbor, among others) whereby individual or group composers can be identified and fall within the copyright period (i.e. the composer(s) may be still alive, or the 75 years since their death has not elapsed).
3. Popular dance-music that draws heavily on traditional tunes, forms and poetry: this category includes all contemporary dance bands, guitar bands, concert-party bands and cultural groups that employ combinations of traditional and modern instrumentalists. These groups play music based on traditional highlife, *adowa*, *agbadza* and other folkloric genres, using traditional melodies, poetry, proverbs, lullabies, children's songs, ceremonial songs, work songs, war songs and funeral songs.

4. Popular Ghanaian music of dance and guitar bands that incorporates folkloric or popular music elements from other African countries, with or without a Ghanaian folkloric content: examples include the local Ghanaian use of 'Congo Jazz', South African Kwela music and Senegambian griot music.
5. 'Serious' or 'Art' music that draws heavily on the traditional motifs mentioned in (3) above, but is composed, scored and orchestrated for piano or symphonic orchestras.
6. 'Serious' scored and orchestrated music that includes elements from the folklore of other African countries, with or without a Ghanaian component, such as Pan-African compositions.
7. Commercialized folkloric music used for cabarets and the tourist trade.
8. Government/para-statal/university traditionally oriented dance ensembles that are performed on stage and are professionally choreographed. This is the nearest Ghanaian equivalent to the preserved form of 'folklore' found in Europe and in the United States.
9. European folkloric elements that are incorporated into Ghanaian music. An example is local Ghanaian gospel music that sometimes uses the melodies of old European hymns and folksongs.

The European Division of Musical Components that Accrue Copyright Composer Royalties. In the West, composer royalties are divided so that 50 percent goes to pay for the lyrics and 50 percent for the music or melody. In African music, rhythm is so important that royalties should be broken down into three components, namely, lyrics (33 percent), melody (33 percent), and rhythm (33 percent). This issue of distribution of entitlements becomes even more complex when one takes into consideration the fact that African music is often polyrhythmic. That is, not just one but multiple rhythms and cross melodies are used simultaneously. This very complexity created a serious dilemma at the 1981 conference of the International Association for the Study of Popular Music (IASPA) held in Amsterdam. Two officials of an American copyright organization became very excited about a snippet of the tune "Somewhere Over the Rainbow" that they heard in one of Ebeneezer Obey's Nigerian Juju songs. They insisted that the American composer should be compensated by the Nigerian one. It was pointed out, however, that they had heard only one of several melodies that were going on simultaneously in the music. There was a Juju refrain, a palm-wine-music guitar riff, a Hawaiian style of guitar, a touch of Fela Kuti's Afrobeat, not to mention the melody of Obey's own voice. So talking about royalties for snatches of a cross melody in polyrhythmic music becomes very difficult indeed, especially for people not trained to hear multiple rhythms. A final point about multiple components is that African music is usually associated with specific dances. So in the African situation, royalty-accruing components could be even further subdivided into four categories, namely: the lyrics, the melody, the rhythm and the dance-step. African musical composition is far more intricate and subtle in this respect than the simple Western division of components into lyrics and melody.

The Impact of Copyright on Existing Ghanaian Performing Art Norms. A very important point brought up in the (1988) paper on copyright and oral literature by Anyidoho and Tsikata is their explication of the differences between the concepts of composer and performer in Africa and in the West. In Europe and the United States, these two roles are usually quite distinct, whereas in Africa most often the composer and the performer are the same individual. In African oral performing arts there exists what Anyidoho and Tsikata call the "centrality of performance." Adding to the confusion for a copyright administrator, in African performing arts the audiences often have a creative role, since they are expected to chant, clap and carry out dance-dialogues with the drummers and musicians. This is quite unlike European music (especially the classical variety) where the motionless audience sits quietly and claps only after the performance, or after a significant portion of it, and only then as an interruption, not throughout the whole or as an integrated part of the performance as in Africa.

Another point brought up by Anyidoho and Tsikata is the "great latitude for borrowing, adaptation and improvisation" that exists in Ghanaian and other African performances. This contrasts with the typical performance in Europe and the US where musical content is fixed by the score sheet and the conductor's baton. Again a problem is posed for copyright administration concerning the degree of originality in a reworked piece of African music, dance or drama. The legal implications of these different artistic norms in Africa and in the West surfaced in 1990 during a Ghanaian High Court case between pianist Ray Ellis and producer Kwadwo Donkor. The pianist claimed rights to some of the composer royalties for the already copyrighted highlife tunes he played instrumentally on the record, since he believed he was re-interpreting the songs he was playing. However, because he had been paid merely as a performing session-man by the producer, Ellis lost the case. This dispute highlights the gray areas between an `arrangement' and an `adaptation' of a song. An arrangement is only a readjustment of a musical work's distinct components, for instance the key or orchestration may be changed. According to both the WIPO report and Ghana's PNDC Copyright Law 110, an arrangement can accrue no royalties. An adaptation, on the other hand, is the creation of a fresh derivative of an original work, and so it can attract royalties. An adaptation is what Ellis thought he was creating.

Ghana's PNDC 110 Copyright Law of 1985 vests works of Ghanaian anonymous folklore in the state for perpetuity and prohibits their use without the permission of a government Secretary (i.e. a Minister of Parliament) who may charge a fee. This ministerial function was taken over by the Ghana Folklore Board of Trustees when it was inaugurated in 1991. For instance, in 1991 the Ghana Folklore Board received royalties from the American singer Paul Simon for his use of the folkloric melody "Yaa Amponsah" for the "Spirit Voices" song on his *Rhythms of the Saints* record album of the late 1980s. However, due to an ambiguity in the PNDC Copyright Law 110, there is no distinction as to whether it is a foreigner or a Ghanaian national who has to gain permission and pay a fee before using folklore. In 1996 the Folklore Board decided to extend its initially sensible and just policy of collecting royalties from foreigners for Ghanaian folklore to Ghanaian nationals themselves. This extension of the law to Ghanaians will have at least four negative consequences, listed below.

Governmental Censorship and Cultural Stunting. The idea of the Ghanaian government owning the copyright on the nation's folklore is a reasonable one in light of the potentials for 'First World' commercial exploitation, mutilation, distortion and trivialization of 'Third World' cultural traditions. Yet the extension of this idea to a policy of demanding a fee from Ghanaians for permission to use their own folklore poses serious risks. These risks were noted in the 1989 WIPO report itself. The report discusses the need for "a proper balance between protection against abuses of expressions of folklore. . . .[vs.] . . . freedom and encouragement . . . of their further development, dissemination and also adaptation."

This need for 'balance' was mentioned in Dr. Abdullah's speech of 1991. Anyidoho and Tsikata12 also point to the danger of "exaggerated claims of state ownership" that could "fossilize and stunt" the development of local oral traditions. Moreover, since there is so much interaction between Ghanaian folkloric and popular genres (unlike in Europe and the US), this stunting could also affect popular music, dance and drama as well. The result would lead not only to a cultural tragedy, but also to an economic disaster. With the current Western interest in folk-oriented 'World Music', Ghanaian popular performance with a strong folkloric content is a potentially renewable source of foreign exchange for the country. Moreover, the WIPO report itself states that the protection of 'Third World' folklore from 'First World' distortion and commercialization should apply only beyond the country in which it originates. To apply this ruling within Ghana to nationals will have the negative effect of setting up a government or para-statal 'censor' in the arts. Consider the example of local *Kpanlogo*. Although today this genre is considered to be a precious part of Ghana's cultural heritage, initially it was frowned upon by some members of the Arts Council at the time of the genre's inception in the 1960s. They thought the dance was indecent and, if they had been granted the power to do so, they would have banned it from the outset. A similar non-Ghanaian case is that of the popular music in the United States that evolved out of African-American and, indeed, African folk music. If at the turn of the century the American government had been entitled to a policy of preventing the distortion of its own folklore, Blues and Jazz would surely never have become that country's national music. For in their infancy these genres were called the 'Devil's Music' and were associated with lowlife 'Boogie Houses,' 'Jook Joints' and the red-light Storyville district of New Orleans.

In short, the imposition of copyright regulations to constrain Ghanaians attempting to use their own folklore will prevent the commercialization, adaptation and development of Ghana's own indigenous musical heritage. This will wholly discourage the overall promotion of that heritage — in contrast with the renaissance of musical traditions that has occurred in Western countries. For in European countries and in the Americas, prohibitive laws are not imposed on nationals using their own folklore, since folklore is considered to be part of the public domain. Ghana will therefore disadvantage itself vis-a-vis these nations by putting an actual disincentive on contemporary Ghanaian musicians who manifestly want to recycle and adapt ancestral works to their own modern era of music.

The Problem of the Same Folklore Existing in Two or More African Countries. The 1989 WIPO report notes the problem of similar folkloric genres existing in several countries. This is particularly pertinent to Africa where the national borders do not always correspond to ethnic ones. Anyidoho and Tsikata discuss the examples of the Dagarte people and the confusion that can arise from Ghana's 'nationalizing' a folklore that also exists outside its geographical borders. They remark that "Burkina Faso has as much right as does Ghana to claim Dagarte folklore as its national cultural heritage." Similar examples are the Agbadza dance music found both in Ghana and in Togo, and the Adowa dance music found both in Ghana and in Eastern Cote D'Ivoire. There are also traditional musical features and rhythms in Ghana (such as the bell pattern of Tigari) that one will find located all over Africa. The correct classifications arising from these folkloric overlaps will therefore involve copyright organizations from all over the continent.

Possible Negative Consequences for Ghana's Creative Cultural Development Resulting from Folkloric Fees on Ghanaian Nationals. It is worth spelling out how taxation extracted from Ghanaians for their use of folklore may damage the local contemporary performing arts. Firstly, fee charges for using local resources could lead to an ever increasing adoption of foreign music by Ghanaian artists already heavily under the influence of imported music. Secondly, in order to circumvent such taxes, Ghanaian musicians may resort to utilizing African musical styles found outside Ghana that resemble Ghanaian ones (e.g. the Agbadza, Adowa, Tigari and Dagarte folklore). To illustrate this potential problem, we can imagine the 18th century when there was a living folklore in Britain as there is now in present-day Ghana, with an area of artworks being created by known individuals. Suppose an alien agency had suddenly appeared in Britain at that time and persuaded the King and Parliament to 'nationalize' and tax their folkloric works. This would have been a calamity for subsequent British popular and classical music, particularly that of the 'Romantic' composers of the 19th century since much of their work was based on their own local folklore. As a result, British Romantic composers might have gone to other European countries where the tax law did not apply, and consequently they would have helped to develop those other national cultures instead of their own.

The State Versus the Locality. There is yet another foreseeable negative consequence of the Ghanaian state collecting royalties and granting permission for Ghanaians to use their own folklore commercially. It may lead to a future full of conflicts between the central government and ethnic regional leaderships over the ownership of folkloric works produced in a particular province. The state claiming univocal ownership of all Ghana's anonymous folkloric works could create tensions with groups that have communally created and established distinct genres of folklore. In the case of performance, such groups would include musical families, age-sets, *asafo* (warrior) companies, traditional religious cults, secret societies, musical clubs and guilds, and chiefs' courts. For instance, the *goje* or one-stringed fiddle music of the Dagomba people of northern Ghana is in the hands of specialized praise-singing guilds composed of men who hand down their skills and repertoires to their sons. Another case in point is the *adowa*, *kete* and other drum-dances, which belong to the Asante royal court in Kumasi.

So who owns this music? Is it the property of the Dagomba guilds and the Asantehene (the Asante King)? Or does it belong to the centralized state? A modern state, unless it is totalitarian, can never own a people's indigenous culture. The state is a custodian of that culture. In principle, a country's anonymous traditional culture is the inalienable property of those individuals, groupings and ethnic communities who comprise the sovereign nation. As far as a country's nationals are concerned, the nation's folklore should be a component of the public domain and not the property of any agency in the state's bureaucracy. From a practical standpoint, the possibility of legal disputes between the central state vs. ethnic, clan, religious and other provincial groupings over the property rights to traditional artistic works is too awful to contemplate. Such conflicts do not now and never have transpired in the Western industrially dominated nations; and they are quite as unnecessary in industrially austere nations such as Ghana.

6

Audio-Visual Technology, Photography and Design

Introduction

The purpose of this section is to provide the reader with details of the various audio-visual technologies available at the UCD Michael Smurfit School of Business, and to provide advice and guidance on the use of these technologies. The Virtual Learning Environment (VLE) at the Smurfit School is an essential element in the schools e-learning/e-teaching strategy. The VLE incorporates an online collaboration facility, wired/wireless networks and experiential learning. The Smurfit School has a number of state-of-the-art Technology Enhance Classrooms (TEC) and mobile audio-visual technologies which complements this unique environment. It is the role of the UCD Information and Learning Technology Group (ILTG) to ensure a strategy and appropriate support services are in place when providing these technologies to the user.

Video

Video is the technology of electronically capturing, recording, processing, storing, transmitting, and reconstructing a sequence of still images which represent scenes in motion. Video technology was first developed for television systems, but has been further developed in many formats to allow for consumer video recording. Video can also be viewed on through the Internet as video clips or streaming media clips on computer monitors. Video is different than film, which captures a moving image as a sequence of still pictures photographically.

Description

The term *video* (from the Latin for "I see") commonly refers to several storage formats for moving pictures: digital video formats, including DVD, QuickTime, and MPEG-4; and analog videotapes, including VHS and Betamax. Video can be recorded and transmitted in various physical media: in magnetic tape when recorded as PAL or NTSC electric signals by video cameras, or in MPEG-4 or DV digital media when recorded by digital cameras. Quality of video essentially depends on the capturing method and storage used. Digital television *(DTV)* is a relatively recent format with higher quality than earlier television formats and has become a standard for television video. *(See List of digital television deployments by country.)*

3D-video, digital video in three dimensions, premiered at the end of 20th century. Six or eight cameras with realtime depth measurement are typically used to capture *3D-video* streams. The format of *3D-video* is fixed in MPEG-4 Part 16 Animation Framework Extension (AFX).

In the UK, Australia, The Netherlands and New Zealand, the term *video* is often used informally to refer to both video recorders and video cassettes; the meaning is normally clear from the context.

Characteristics of Video Streams

Number of Frames Per Second

Frame rate, the number of still pictures per unit of time of video, ranges from six or eight frames per second (*fps*) for old mechanical cameras to 120 or more frames per second for new professional cameras. PAL (Europe, Asia, Australia, etc.) and SECAM (France, Russia, parts of Africa etc.) standards specify 25 fps, while NTSC (USA, Canada, Japan, etc.) specifies 29.97 fps. Film is shot at the slower frame rate of 24fps, which complicates slightly the process of transferring a cinematic motion picture to video. To achieve the illusion of a moving image, the minimum frame rate is about ten frames per second.

Interlacing

Video can be interlaced or progressive. Interlacing was invented as a way to achieve good visual quality within the limitations of a narrow bandwidth. The *horizontal scan lines* of each interlaced frame are numbered consecutively and partitioned into two *fields*: the *odd field* consisting of the odd-numbered lines and the *even field* consisting of the even-numbered lines. NTSC, PAL and SECAM are interlaced formats. Abbreviated video resolution specifications often include an *i* to indicate interlacing. For example, PAL video format is often specified as *576i50*, where *576* indicates the vertical line resolution, *i* indicates interlacing, and *50* indicates 50 fields (half-frames) per second.

In *progressive scan* systems, each refresh period updates all of the scan lines. The result is a higher perceived resolution and a lack of various artifacts that can make parts of a stationary picture appear to be moving or flashing. A procedure known as deinterlacing can be used for converting an interlaced stream, such as analog, DVD, or satellite, to be processed by progressive scan devices, such as TFT TV-sets, projectors, and plasma panels. Deinterlacing cannot, however, produce a video quality that is equivalent to true progressive scan source material.

Video Resolution

The size of a video image is measured in pixels for digital video or horizontal scan lines and vertical lines of resolution for analog video. In the digital domain (e.g. DVD) standard-definition television (SDTV) is specified as *720/704/640×480i60* for NTSC and *768/720×576i50* for PAL or SECAM resolution. However in the analog domain, standard definition equates to about 240x480 (NTSC) or 240x576 (PAL) pixels for VCR quality, to 400x480 (NTSC) or 400x576 (PAL) pixels for TV broadcasts (i.e. the number of horizontal scanlines [from top to bottom] remain constant, but the horizontal resolution [from left to right] varies).

Aspect ratio is preserved because of non-square "pixels". New high-definition televisions (HDTV) are capable of resolutions up to *1920×1080p60*, i.e. 1920 pixels per scan line by 1080 scan lines, progressive, at 60 frames per second. Video resolution for 3D-video is measured in voxels (*volume picture element*, representing a value in three dimensional space). For example 512×512×512 voxels resolution, now used for simple 3D-video, can be displayed even on some PDAs.

Aspect Ratio

Aspect ratio describes the dimensions of video screens and video picture elements. The screen aspect ratio of a traditional television screen is 4:3, or 1.33:1. High definition televisions use an aspect ratio of 16:9, or about 1.78:1. The aspect ratio of a full 35 mm film frame with soundtrack (also known as "Academy standard") is around 1.37:1. Pixels on computer monitors are usually square, but pixels used in digital video often have non-square aspect ratios, such as those used in the PAL and NTSC variants of the CCIR 601 digital video standard, and the corresponding anamorphic widescreen formats. Therefore, an NTSC DV image which is 720 pixels by 480 pixels is displayed with the aspect ratio of 4:3 (which is the traditional television standard) if the pixels are thin and displayed with the aspect ratio and 16:9 (which is the anamorphic widescreen format) if the pixels are fat.

Color Space and Bits Per Pixel

Color model name describes the video color representation. *YIQ* was used in NTSC television. It corresponds closely to the *YUV* scheme used in NTSC and PAL television and the *YDbDr* scheme used by SECAM television. The number of distinct colours that can be represented by a pixel depends on the number of *bits per pixel* (bpp). A common way to reduce the number of bits per pixel in digital video is by chroma subsampling (e.g. 4:4:4, 4:2:2, 4:2:0).

Video Quality

Video quality can be measured with formal metrics like PSNR or with subjective video quality using expert observation.

The subjective video quality of a video processing system may be evaluated as follows:

- Choose the video sequences (the *SRC*) to use for testing.
- Choose the settings of the system to evaluate (the *HRC*).
- Choose a test method for how to present video sequences to experts and to collect their ratings.
- Invite a sufficient number of experts, preferably not fewer than 15.
- Carry out testing.
- Calculate the average marks for each *HRC* based on the experts' ratings.

Many subjective video quality methods are described in the ITU-T recommendation BT.500. One of the standardized method is the *Double Stimulus Impairment Scale* (DSIS). In DSIS, each expert views an *unimpaired* reference video followed by an *impaired* version of the same video. The expert then rates the *impaired* video using a scale ranging from "impairments are imperceptible" to "impairments are very annoying".

Video Compression Method (Digital Only)

A wide variety of methods are used to compress video streams. Video data contains spatial and temporal redundancy, making uncompressed video streams extremely inefficient. Broadly speaking, spatial redundancy is reduced by registering differences between parts of a single frame; this task is known as *intraframe compression* and is closely related to image compression. Likewise, temporal redundancy can be reduced by registering differences between frames; this task is known as *interframe compression*, including motion compensation and other techniques. The most common modern standards are MPEG-2, used for DVD and satellite television, and MPEG-4, used for home video.

Bit Rate (Digital Only)

Bit rate is a measure of the rate of information content in a video stream. It is quantified using the bit per second (*bit/s*) unit or *Megabits per second* (*Mbit/s*). A higher bit rate allows better video quality. For example VideoCD, with a bit rate of about 1 Mbit/s, is lower quality than DVD, with a bit rate of about 5 Mbit/s. HDTV has a still higher quality, with a bit rate of about 20 Mbit/s.

Variable bit rate (VBR) is a strategy to maximize the visual video quality and minimize the bit rate. On fast motion scenes, a variable bit rate uses more bits than it does on slow motion scenes of similar duration yet achieves a consistent visual quality. For real-time and non-buffered video streaming when the available bandwidth is fixed, e.g. in videoconferencing delivered on channels of fixed bandwidth, a constant bit rate (CBR) must be used.

Stereoscopic

Stereoscopic video requires either two channels — a right channel for the right eye and a left channel for the left eye or two overlayed color coded layers. This left and right layer technique is occasionally used for network broadcast, or recent "anaglyph" releases of 3D movies on DVD. Simple Red/Cyan plastic glasses provide the means to view the images discretely to form a stereoscopic view of the content. New HD DVD and HD Blu-ray disks will greatly improve the 3D effect, in color coded stereo programs. The first commercially available HD players are expected to debut at the 2006 NAB Show in Las Vegas in April. See articles Stereoscopy and 3-D film.

Video Conferencing

Here at the UCD Michael Smurfit School of Business, there is Video Conferencing technology available to all academic and administrative functions. The system available within the school is a mobile IP (Internet Protocol) system. IP is the latest method of communication for Video Conferencing technologies. A Video Conference is a live connection between people in separate locations for the purpose of communication, usually involving audio and often text as well as video. At its simplest, videoconferencing provides transmission of static images and text between two locations. At its most sophisticated, it provides transmission of full-motion video images and high-quality audio between multiple locations.

Meeting Scenario

Facilitating attendance at meetings is one of the simplest yet most popular uses of videoconferencing. For meetings that regularly take place and require face-to-face communication, videoconferencing can substitute for the actual physical presence of remote participants.

- Reduces travel costs and time
- Makes meeting attendance more convenient.
- Makes meetings more likely to occur.
- Frequent and/or ad hoc meetings that might not have been scheduled due to travel costs and timing can be enabled via videoconferencing.
- Enhances the sense of teamwork among people at different locations
- Videoconferencing provides remote participants with much of the face-to-face familiarity that comes with physical presence.

Collaborative work can be enhanced further through the integration of videoconferencing with collaborative electronic tools (data transfer, shared whiteboards, shared applications.)

Classroom Scenario

A particularly exciting type of "meeting" that may be enhanced and expanded through the use of videoconferencing is classroom instruction. Certainly all of the factors listed above for furthering the success of videoconferencing within general meetings affect the classroom as well.

- Remote participant(s) may be additions to the instruction itself, such as expert speakers or co-instructors.
- Instructor accessibility in the physical classroom can easily overtake the presence and command of the remote instructor, encouraging side conversations and inattention to remote instruction.

Technical and Support Information

The Video Conferencing System used at the Smurfit School is a Polycom VSX 7000. For further details on the Polycom VSX 7000 see our list of reading materials below.

- HEAnet Video Streaming and Video Conferencing
- Polycom VSX 7000 Datasheet
- Polycom VC Collaboration Guide
- Polycom VSX 7000 User Guide

If you would like a demonstration or training on the Schools Video Conferencing technology, or would like to discuss with a member of the ILTG, how VC might help enhance your lectures/meetings, please complete the simple request form located here. You may also use this form to request the VC technology for any up coming events.

Video Conferencing equipment is for use on the Smurfit School campus only. ILTG require that a test VC session is conducted with the remote site at least three working days in advance of the actual event. To view our Audio Visual Technology Policies, please click here.

Mobile Equipment

There are a number of mobile projectors and notebook computers that can be set up for special events and occasions. If you require this equipment then it must be booked through the AV Booking section, the username and the password for this section is available only through the ILTG. This service is only available to staff members.

Students can also avail of this but only if they contact a staff member and have them book and take responsibility for the equipment.

How to Order Equipment

In order to book the equipment the online form must be filled out. Once this has been completed you will receive an email to confirm that the ILTG have received your request. Please note that receiving this email is not confirmation that the equipment is booked for you. An ILTG technician will contact you by phone in order to establish that the equipment is available.

Producing Video

RealNetworks introduced RealVideo with RealSystem 4, making streaming video available over the Internet. This chapter covers RealVideo production techniques, providing tips for capturing high-quality video, working with digitized video source files, and using RealProducer to encode your clips.

Understanding RealVideo

A video consists of two parts: the visual track and the soundtrack. In a RealVideo clip, the soundtrack is encoded with RealAudio codecs, and the visual track is encoded with a RealVideo codec. Both tracks are packaged in a RealVideo clip that, like a RealAudio clip, uses the file extension .rm. This section explains how RealVideo encodes a source video for streaming. This information will help you produce high-quality streaming clips.

RealVideo Bandwidth Characteristics

Because RealVideo uses RealAudio to encode a video's soundtrack, a chunk of the clip's bandwidth first goes toward the audio. The visual track is then squeezed into the bandwidth that's left. For 28.8 Kbps modems, for example, RealVideo clips stream at 20 Kbps, leaving 8.8 Kbps of modem bandwidth for overhead. How much bandwidth the visual track gets depends on how the audio is encoded. With a 5 Kbps RealAudio voice codec for the soundtrack, the visual track gets 15 Kbps. With an 11 Kbps music codec, though, the visual track gets just 9 Kbps. At low bandwidths, how you encode the soundtrack can affect how the visual track looks. RealAudio music codecs typically consume more bandwidth than do voice codecs. Music's greater frequency range requires more data than does speech, so a music soundtrack consumes more bandwidth than a spoken one. A video with an audio narration might therefore look better than one accompanied by music, as there would be more bandwidth available for the visual track. At higher streaming speeds, the soundtrack uses proportionally less of the clip's bandwidth, so differences in soundtrack encoding affect visual quality less. At speeds above 100 Kbps, you get high-quality sound that uses no more than a quarter of the clip's streaming bandwidth.

RealVideo Frame Rates

Like RealAudio, RealVideo is "lossy," meaning that it throws out nonessential video data when encoding a clip. One way that RealVideo squeezes down clip sizes is by reducing the video's frame rate. The higher the frame rate, the smoother the motion:

- The standard frame rate for full-motion video is 24 to 30 frames per second (fps). At this speed, the human eye perceives movement as continuous—a phenomenon known as *persistence of vision*.
- A common rate for streaming video that approximates full-motion video is 15 fps. To most people, a 15 fps video flows smoothly, though not quite as fluidly as one at a higher rate.
- Below 15 fps, a video looks jerky.
- Below 7 fps, a video looks very jerky.
- Below 3 fps, a video essentially becomes a slideshow.

Most source videos start out at 15 to 30 fps. During encoding, RealVideo adjusts this frame rate downward as necessary, keeping the rate up in high-action scenes, reducing it in slow ones. Thus, your encoded clip will not have just one frame rate, but a mix of frame rates that varies with its content. If you follow good production practices, your clips will typically stream over slow- to medium-speed connections at 7 to 15 fps. At higher speeds, you'll get 15 to 30 fps. Many factors, though, affect a RealVideo clip's frame rate:

- The video's window size greatly affects frame rate. If you use too large of a window for your target bandwidth, you will not get a high frame rate. For more information, see "RealVideo Window Sizes".
- RealVideo 8 provides video quality superior to that produced by older RealVideo codecs. Using an older codec may result in a lower frame rate.
- Visually complex videos that show many objects moving across the screen simultaneously are hard to encode and may result in too low a frame rate.
- RealProducer gives you an option for smoother motion. Choosing this option raises the clip's overall frame rate and reduces visual quality, whereas choosing the option for better image quality lowers the frame rate.
- In a video that has a mix of fast and slow scenes, variable bit-rate encoding (VBR) and two-pass encoding generally help the fast scenes achieve a higher frame rate. See "RealVideo Options" for more information.
- When encoding with RealProducer Plus, you can lower the bit rate of the RealAudio codecs used for a given clip. This gives more bandwidth to the visual track, helping to raise the frame rate.

- Scalable Video Technology (SVT) enables RealPlayer to lower the frame rate as necessary during playback to lighten a computer's CPU load. For more information, see "Scalable Video Technology".

RealVideo Clarity

In addition to changing its frame rate, RealVideo can reduce a clip's streaming size by throwing out pixel data. A video stores information about each pixel in the frame. RealVideo, on the other hand, stores data for pixel groups. When bandwidth is tight, RealVideo shoehorns pixels with slightly different RGB values into the same group. These pixels then look identical rather than nearly identical. This may result in a loss of detail if compression is too high. The following illustration compares a smooth video with one that has lost detail through too much compression. By using good production practices as described in this chapter, you can help keep the video's clarity intact during encoding. Also note the following points:

- The video's window size affects visual clarity. If you use too large of a window for your target bandwidth, visual clarity may suffer. For more information, see "RealVideo Window Sizes".
- When you encode with RealProducer, you can choose an option for better image quality. The video may be jerkier, though, because increasing the pixel data reduces the frame rate.
- A video with relatively stationary subjects ("talking heads") will have better visual quality than a video with rapid scene changes and a lot of movement.
- If you plan to launch a video in double- or full-screen mode as described in "Setting a Presentation's Starting Mode", boost video clarity as much as possible during production and encoding. RealPlayer enlarges the clip by duplicating its pixels, which magnifies any defects.

RealVideo Window Sizes

The four common RealVideo clip sizes that maintain the 4:3 aspect ratio used in television. For each clip size, the table indicates the general playback quality you'll get when streaming a RealVideo 8 clip to various target audiences. "Excellent" video quality means few visual artifacts and a frame rate that results in consistently smooth playback. If you plan to stream clips over modems, you can first encode your clip at 320 by 240 pixels to test its quality. If you want better quality, shrink the video window with your editing software or with RealProducer during encoding.

Different Window Sizes for Different Bandwidths

When you want to encode a single video for both low-speed and high-speed connections, you need to decide what video window size to use. Although with SureStream technology you can easily create a single RealVideo clip that streams at many bandwidths, using too large a window results in low frame rates for viewers with dial-up modems. Therefore, you may want to use a small video window to reach the widest audience. High-speed viewers, however, will not receive the benefit of their hefty bandwidth. You can resolve this dilemma by creating two or more versions of your video, each for a different window size. You can use your video editing software to do this, or use RealProducer to resize or crop the video during encoding. Then encode each video for a few different streaming speeds. You can make the clips available through separate links, or use a SMIL <switch> tag to let RealPlayer choose which version to play.

RealVideo Codecs

RealVideo 8 is the standard RealVideo codec, but you can also encode with one of two RealVideo G2 codecs. The codec you use encodes all of a clip's SureStream streams. You cannot encode half the streams with the RealVideo 8 codec, for example, and the other half with a RealVideo G2 codec.

RealVideo 8 Codec

The RealVideo 8 codec results in visual quality markedly superior to that produced by the RealVideo G2 codecs. It requires more processing power, though, so encoding a clip with it takes longer than encoding the clip with a RealVideo G2 codec. RealPlayer 8 and later can play RealVideo 8 clips. Earlier versions of RealPlayer are prompted to autoupdate to RealPlayer 8. RealNetworks recommends using this codec unless you need faster encoding performance during broadcasts, or you need to stream video to earlier versions of RealPlayer.

RealVideo G2 Codecs

The RealVideo G2 codecs are older codecs used by RealProducer G2 and RealProducer 7. These codecs encode video clips faster than the RealVideo 8 codec does, but their visual quality is poorer. For a given streaming speed, using an older RealVideo codec rather than RealVideo 8 results in either a reduced frame rate or diminished visual quality at the same frame rate. Use one of the following RealVideo G2 codecs for faster encoding during broadcasts or if you need to stream video to versions of RealPlayer that cannot upgrade to Release 8:

- RealVideo G2 with SVT

  The RealVideo G2 with SVT codec is compatible with RealPlayer G2 Update 1 (version 6.0.6) or later. RealPlayers with lower version numbers are prompted to autoupdate to the latest version of RealPlayer before viewing the clip.

- RealVideo G2

  The RealVideo G2 codec without SVT is compatible with RealPlayer G2 and later. It is not compatible with RealPlayer 5 or earlier.

RealVideo Standard Codec

In RealProducer, you cannot explicitly choose the RealVideo standard codec, which was the default codec before RealSystem G2 was released. RealProducer uses this codec solely for backward compatibility with RealPlayer 5.

Scalable Video Technology

The RealVideo 8 and RealVideo G2 with SVT codecs include Scalable Video Technology (SVT), which scales down frame rates when clips play on slower computers. RealVideo's variable frame rate means that one scene may be encoded at 7 fps, whereas another one is encoded at 15 fps. High frame rates take a lot of processing power to decompress. Although fast PCs handle high frame rates well, slower PCs may have trouble. With SVT, RealPlayer can lower the frame rate "on the fly" to keep a PC's CPU from sputtering. So although a given scene is encoded at 15 fps, it may play on some RealPlayers at 8 fps if those computers lack the power to decompress 15 fps video clips.

Steps for Streaming RealVideo

When producing a RealVideo clip, you should choose the best source material and best equipment possible. The goal throughout the video production process is to get optimum video quality for each streaming speed.

The following steps summarize how to create a RealVideo clip:

1. Capture the video content.

   To start video production, you capture the source video by shooting a scene with a video camera, for example, or gathering prerecorded content from a tape, satellite, laserdisc, or other source.

2. Digitize and edit the video file.

   You next digitize the video to convert it to a standard file format, such as AVI or QuickTime. With your preferred video editing software, you can then edit the video as necessary. If you are broadcasting live, however, you encode the streaming video directly from the source.

3. Encode the RealVideo clip.

   With your digitized file optimized or your live broadcast ready to go, you encode your source as a RealVideo clip. When you do this, you target a network bandwidth or a set of bandwidths.

4. Deliver the RealVideo clip.

   With your presentation ready to go, you make your RealVideo clip or broadcast available through your Web site. If you are combining video with another streaming clip, you write a SMIL file that assembles the pieces.

Recording Video

Read this section carefully if you intend to shoot a new video rather than use existing video content. Because video loses image quality if it's highly compressed, always start with the best video source available.

Source Media Quality

Whether you shoot a video yourself or digitize existing material, start with a high-quality video media. The following are common video formats, listed in order of descending quality:

1. Betacam SP, also known simply as Beta. This format is common among video production professionals.
2. DV, miniDV, DVCam, or DVCPro.
3. Super-VHS (S-VHS) or HI-8mm.
4. VHS, 8mm.

Video Staging

Consider the video's final frame size before you shoot the first frame. Streaming over 28.8 Kbps modems requires a small video window, so you need to frame important visual elements well. For recommended window sizes, see "RealVideo Frame Rates".

Scene Changes and Movement

The fewer things that change from frame to frame, the sharper the image will appear in a low-bandwidth video. You can do the following to cut down on unnecessary movement:

- Use a mounted camera rather than hand-held one. This greatly reduces the movement you inadvertently introduce into the scene when recording.
- Don't have a rapidly moving object fill the entire frame. But you don't want to pull the camera back too far either. You need to find a happy medium between close-ups and panoramic shots.

Of course, you don't want to eliminate all dynamic elements. When you do include rapid movement, allow enough time for objects to resolve. Because of low frame rates and high compression, objects coming to rest may appear blurry at first. If you have a dialog box popping up on a computer screen, for example, have the box remain stationary for a few seconds so that the image resolves.

Colors and Lighting

Bright lighting at a constant exposure keeps the foreground detail crisp. Use uniformly dark colors for backgrounds, and uniformly light colors (but not whites) for clothing. Complex textures such as paisley and stripes degrade the final image quality with unwanted visual effects.

Digitizing Video

If you are not broadcasting RealVideo streams live, you digitize the source video on your computer or video editing station. You can then edit the file with your preferred editing software before encoding it as a RealVideo clip. This section provides tips for digitizing video.

S-Video Output

Video playback devices commonly have at least two common output types—S-video and composite. Use S-video, as it produces better results.

Color Depth

Always use 24-bit color. Lower color resolution results in poor clips.

Digitized Video Formats

It is better to work with uncompressed formats. Otherwise, you compress the source once when you digitize it and again when you encode it as RealVideo. This double compression can decrease the image quality. Use a compressed source format only if your RealVideo encoding tool supports the file as input. You can use compressed AVI files as long as the computer used to encode RealVideo clips has the same Video for Windows driver used to compress the AVI file.

Video Capture Frame Rates

Capture the video content at 15 frames per second (fps) if your clip will stream at less than 100 Kbps. For higher-speed streaming, capture it at 30 fps. Because a RealVideo clip's frame rate varies, some scenes may be encoded at less than the capture rate depending on bandwidth constraints. SVT enables RealPlayer to lower the frame rate on computers that have low processing power, ensuring that high frame rates will not overburden slow computers.

Video Capture Screen Sizes

Unless you are short on disk space or your video capture card recommends a different window size, capture video in a window 320 pixels wide by 240 pixels high. You can capture full-motion video at the full-screen size of 640 by 480 pixels if:

- Your clips will stream at speeds higher than 100 Kbps.
- Your encoded clips will be larger than 320 by 240 pixels.
- You have a video workstation capable of digitizing full-motion, full-screen video. Standard PCs typically cannot handle this large a load.

Using your editing software or RealProducer, you can reduce the window size for your RealVideo clip if necessary. For recommended RealVideo window sizes, see "RealVideo Window Sizes".

Computer Speed and Disk Space

Because video capture places a large burden on a computer's CPU and hard drive, be sure to use a fast computer. To avoid dropping frames during video capture, use a hard drive specially made for audio and video work. On Windows computers, you can use any video capture card that supports Video for Windows.

Use the following formula to calculate the approximate size in megabytes of a digitized video file:

(pixel width) x (pixel height) x (color bit depth) x (fps) x (duration in seconds)
8,000,000

Suppose you want to capture a three-minute video at 15 frames per second, with 24-bit color, in a window that is 320 by 240 pixels. As you can see from the following equation, your digitized source file would be approximately 622 MB:

(320) x (240) x (24) x (15) x (180) / 8,000,000 = 622 Megabytes

If necessary, you can conserve disk space by decreasing the window size or lowering the frame rate, or both.

Video Source File Size Limit

The Macintosh and some Windows file systems limit a single file to 2 GB (2048 MB) in size. At a 320-by-240 window size and 15 fps, this translates to about 9.5 minutes of video. Certain video production programs support the OpenDML (AVI 2.0) standard, which allows the creation of files larger than 2 GB. RealProducer may be able to accept a video source file larger than 2 GB as input, depending on the production software used to create the file. If you plan to produce long videos or videos with a large window size, check whether or not your video production software is limited to a 2 GB output file size. If it is not limited to 2 GB, create a video file larger than 2 GB and test to determine if RealProducer can accept the file as input.

Encoding RealVideo with RealProducer

To produce RealVideo clips, you start with video input from a live source, a digitized file, or media such as a tape or CD. You then encode a RealVideo clip from this input using a RealVideo encoding tool. The most widely used tools for encoding RealVideo are RealProducer Basic (a free product) and RealProducer Plus, which are available from RealNetworks at:

http://www.realnetworks.com/products/producer/info.html

RealProducer on Macintosh accepts the input formats widely used on that platform, whereas RealProducer on Windows or UNIX supports the formats widely used on those platforms. Check the RealProducer manual for your operating system for a list of accepted formats, which may include:

- AVI (.avi), uncompressed (recommended) or compressed
- MPEG-1 (.mpg)
- QuickTime (.mov), uncompressed (recommended) or compressed

When you encode RealVideo clips, you choose a bandwidth target or set of targets, then set parameters such as audio type (voice or music) and an emphasis on either smooth motion or sharp images. RealProducer then decides which RealAudio codecs are best to use for the soundtrack. It uses SureStream technology to encode the RealVideo clip for all your bandwidth choices, ensuring that each stream requires only a few seconds of preroll.

RealVideo Streaming Speeds

For all practical purposes, RealVideo's streaming bit rate is infinitely scalable. You can encode RealVideo at any speed you want, from 20 Kbps to hundreds or thousands of kilobits per second. Plus you can encode precisely at any bandwidth you choose, such as 89 Kbps, 117 Kbps, 575 Kbps, 1.5 Mbps, and so on. With RealProducer Plus, you do this by adjusting RealVideo's target audience settings. If your RealVideo clip will play in parallel with another clip, you may need to lower RealVideo's bit rate for each target audience. This way, the clip does not consume all of a connection's bandwidth. For a 56 Kbps modem, for example, RealProducer standardly encodes the clip to stream at 34 Kbps. Using the RealVideo target audience settings, you can lower this value to 20 Kbps, for example, leaving 14 Kbps free for another clip.

Whenever you lower RealVideo speed, the new bit rate includes the rate of the RealAudio codec used for the soundtrack. If you use a 32 Kbps RealAudio codec and set a total RealVideo bit rate of 36 Kbps, you will not have much bandwidth left for the visuals (maybe a frame every few seconds). You'll need to select a lower-bandwidth RealAudio codec. There are no strict rules for the ratio of soundtrack bandwidth to total RealVideo bandwidth. The ratio depends entirely on whether you want to emphasize the audio track or the visuals. RealVideo normally allots no more than 25 percent of the total bandwidth to the soundtrack because the visual information contains much more data. At bandwidths of several hundred kilobits per second, you can use considerably less bandwidth for the soundtrack in relation to the visual track.

Video Compatibility with RealPlayer 5

RealProducer can include in SureStream clips a stream that RealPlayer 5 can play. This backward-compatible stream is set for your lowest target bandwidth. For example, if your clip targets 28.8 Kbps modems, 56 Kbps modems, and DSL speeds, the RealPlayer 5 stream is for 28.8 Kbps modems. It uses older RealAudio and RealVideo codecs, and RealServer streams it to RealPlayer 5 using the older PNA protocol rather than the newer RTSP.

RealVideo Filters

RealProducer's preferences include filtering options you can use when encoding RealVideo clips. These filters remove artifacts that appear in the encoded clips because of the methods used to create the source video.

Noise Filters

Noise distortion is similar to the "snow" that often shows up on TV screens as a result of signals received over an antenna. RealProducer has low and high noise filters you can use if your source video clip has a little noise or a lot of noise, respectively. The best way to eliminate noise, though, is to follow good production practices, as described in "Recording Video".

Resizing Filters

When you resize a RealVideo clip with RealProducer, you can use a resizing filter that performs either a fast resize or a high-quality resize. These resizing options affect the source video only when you make the clip smaller. They tell RealProducer to throw out video data by using either a quick method (fast resize) or a complex analysis (high-quality resize). A high-quality resize results in a superior image, but it also lengthens the encoding time.

Inverse-Telecine Filter

The Inverse-Telecine filter is for cinematic film that was transferred to NTSC video. It has no effect on PAL video. Film is usually photographed at 24 frames per second (fps), and the film-to-video conversion (called "telecine") duplicates some frames to achieve the NTSC standard of 30 fps. To strip out redundant frames, use the inverse-telecine filter when encoding NTSC video that was transferred from film and has a frame rate of 25 to 30 fps.

De-Interlace Filter

The de-interlace filter removes jaggedness from interlaced video. It is useful only for interlaced source video that is at least 240 lines high. Typical source video used for television is 480 lines high. If you digitize the video with a video capture card that captures at 240 lines or fewer, the card throws out either the odd or the even lines, de-interlacing the video itself.

RealVideo Options

The RealProducer preferences include several RealVideo encoding options that affect the quality of RealVideo clips by modifying RealProducer's encoding methods.

Variable Bit Rate Encoding

Variable bit rate (VBR) encoding is optional for RealVideo. It varies a clip's playback bit rate while keeping the *streaming* bit rate constant. This gives more bandwidth to scenes that are hard to compress and less to scenes that are easy to compress. In a video that streams at 225 Kbps, for example, one second may get 150 Kb of data while another gets 300 Kb. VBR encoding generally provides video quality superior to that achieved with constant bit rate (CBR) encoding, making the most difference in videos with a mix of high- and low-action scenes.

Two-Pass Encoding

With two-pass encoding, RealProducer runs through the source video once to gather information. It then makes a second pass to encode the RealVideo streams. Two-pass encoding helps the most with variable bit rate (VBR) encoding. With this type of encoding, RealProducer analyzes the entire source video first to determine how best to vary the playback bit rate. Without it, RealProducer analyzes small sections of the source video during encoding, creating a string of VBR sections within the clip.

Loss Protection

RealProducer's loss-protection feature adds error-correction data to RealVideo streams, helping them maintain quality in lossy environments. RealProducer adds as much error-correction data as it can without lessening the video quality. Although you'll get more benefit from this feature when streaming across the Internet rather than over an intranet, it is useful to turn loss protection on for all encoded content.

Support and Maintenance

ILTG audio-visual technology support technicians are available throughout the year to address any problems which may arise with the use of classroom audio-visual technology. Should you have a query in relation operating the audio-visual technology, you can contact our AV staff using the green button on the classroom telephones. This provides a direct link to our AV staff, we will try to ascertain what the exact problem is over the phone and provide advice on how to rectify the problem. If the problem is one which cannot be rectified over the phone our AV support technician will visit the classroom and will endeavour to rectify any problems.

Third Party Support

Our third party Audio-Visual supplier are onsite once a month to perform maintenance checks and proactive testing of all classroom audio-visual equipment. During these checks all projectors are cleaned, any new problems are also investigated. If our suppliers cannot resolved a problem onsite, they will take the equipment off site for repairs and a temporary solution will be put in place.

The Smurfit School's classroom audio-visual technology is also supported under a maintenance agreement. In the event that there is a problem with a piece of AV equipment, we will liaise with our supplier directly to ensure that the problem is resolved as soon as possible.

Photography

Photography is the process of making pictures by means of the action of capturing light on a film. Light patterns reflected or emitted from objects are recorded onto a sensitive medium or storage chip through a timed exposure. The process is done through mechanical, chemical or digital devices known as cameras.

The word comes from the Greek words öùò *phos* ("light"), and ãñáößò *graphis* ("stylus", "paintbrush") or ãñáöÞ *graphê*, together meaning "drawing with light" or "representation by means of lines" or "drawing." Traditionally the product of photography has been called a photograph. The term *photo* is an abbreviation; many people also call them *pictures*. In digital photography, the term *image* has begun to replace *photograph*. (The term *image* is traditional in geometric optics.)

Photographic Image-Forming Devices

The camera or camera obscura is the image-forming device and photographic film or a digital storage card is the recording medium, although other methods are available. For instance, the photocopy or xerography machine forms permanent images but uses the transfer of static electrical charges rather than photographic film, hence the term electrophotography. Rayographs published by Man Ray and others are images produced by the shadows of objects cast on the photographic paper, without the use of a camera. Objects can also be placed directly on the glass of a scanner to produce digital pictures. Photographers control the camera and lens to "expose" the light recording material (usually film or a charge-coupled device; a complementary metal-oxide-semiconductor may also be used) to the required amount of light. After processing, this produces an image. The controls usually include but are not limited to:

- **Focus of the lens**
- **Aperture of the lens** - adjustment of the iris, measured in f-stops, which controls the amount of light entering the lens. Aperture also has an effect on focus and Depth of field.
- **Shutter speed** - adjustment of the speed (often expressed either as fractions of seconds or as an angle, with mechanical shutters) of the shutter to control the amount of time during which the imaging medium is exposed to light per each exposure. Shutter speed may be used to control the amount of light striking the image plane, though doing so has implications for the amount of motion blur visible in the exposed image.
- **White balance** - on digital cameras, electronic compensation for the color

temperature associated with a given set of lighting conditions, ensuring that white light is registered as such on the imaging chip and therefore that the colors in the frame will appear natural. On mechanical, film-based cameras, this function is served by the operator's choice of film stock. In addition to using white balance to register natural coloration of the image, photographers may employ white balance to aesthetic end, for example white balancing to a blue object in order to obtain a warm color temperature.

- **Metering** - measurement of exposure at a midtone so that highlights and shadows are exposed according to the photographer's wishes. Many modern cameras feature this ability, though it is traditionally accomplished with the use of a separate light metering device.
- **ISO** - traditionally an indicator of the selected film speed on film cameras, ISO ratings are employed on modern digital cameras as an indication of the imaging chip's light sensitivity.
- **Auto-focus point** - on some cameras, the selection of a point in the imaging frame upon which the auto-focus system will attempt to focus. Many SLR cameras feature multiple auto-focus points in the viewfinder.

Many other elements of the imaging device itself may have a pronounced effect on the quality and/or aesthetic effect of a given photograph; among them are:

- Focal length and type of lens (telephoto, macro, wide angle, or zoom)
- Filters or scrims placed between the subject and the light recording material, either in front of or behind the lens
- Inherent sensitivity of the medium to light intensity and color/wavelengths.
- The nature of the light recording material, for example its resolution as measured in pixels or grains of silver halide.

Remembering Camera controls are inter-related, as the total amount of light reaching the film plane (the "exposure") changes proportionately with the duration of exposure, aperture of the lens, and focal length of the lens (which changes as the lens is focused, or zoomed). Changing any of these controls alters the exposure. Many consumer-grade cameras may be set to adjust most or all of these controls automatically, with little or no input from the operator. This automatic functionality may be useful to amateur photographers, who may not have mastered the ability to expose their photographs manually.

The duration of an exposure is referred to as shutter speed, often even in cameras that don't have a physical shutter, and is typically measured in fractions of a second. Aperture is expressed by an f-number or f-stop (derived from focal ratio), which is proportional to the ratio of the focal length to the diameter of the aperture. If the f-number is decreased by a factor of, the aperture diameter is increased by the same factor, and its area is increased by a factor of 2. The f-stops that might be found on a typical lens include 2.8, 4, 5.6, 8, 11, 16, 22, 32, where going up "one stop" doubles the amount of light reaching the film, and stopping down one stop halves the amount of light.

Exposures can be achieved through various combinations of shutter speed and aperture. For example, f/8 at 1/125th of a second and f/4 at 1/500th of a second yield the same amount of light. The chosen combination has an impact on the final result. In addition to the subject or camera movement that might vary depending on the shutter speed, the aperture (and focal length of the lens) determine the depth of field, which refers to the range of distances from the lens that will be in focus. For example, using a long lens and a large aperture (f/2.8, for example), a subject's eyes might be in sharp focus, but not the tip of the nose. With a smaller aperture (f/22), or a shorter lens, both the subject's eyes and nose can be in focus. With very small apertures, such as pinholes, a wide range of distance can be brought into focus.

Image capture is only part of the image forming process. Regardless of material, some process must be employed to render the latent image captured by the camera into the final photographic work. This process consists of two steps, development, and printing. During the printing process, modifications can be made to the print by several controls. Many of these controls are similar to controls during image capture, while some are exclusive to the printing process. Most controls have equivalent digital concepts, but some create different effects. For example, dodging and burning controls are different between digital and film processes. Other printing modifications include:

- Chemicals and Process used during film development
- Duration of exposure (equivalent to shutter speed)
- Printing Aperture (equivalent to aperture, but has no effect on depth of field)
- Contrast
- Dodging (Reduction in exposure of certain print areas, resulting in a lighter areas)
- Burning (Increase in exposure of certain areas, resulting in darker areas)
- Paper Quality (Glossy, Matte, Etc)

Uses of Photography

Photography has gained the interest of many scientists and artists from its inception. Scientists have used photography to record and study movements, such as Eadweard Muybridge's study of human and animal locomotion (1887). Artists are equally interested by these aspects but also try to explore avenues other than the photo-mechanical representation of reality, such as the pictorialist movement. Military, police and security forces use photography for surveillance, recognition and data storage. Photography is used to preserve memories of favorites and as a source of entertainment, any trobles u may have take to green_day_leslie@hotmail.com

History of Photography

Chemical Photography

For centuries images have been projected onto surfaces. As argued by artist David Hockney, some artists used the camera obscura and camera lucida to trace scenes as early as the 16th century. However, this theory is heavily disputed by today's contemporary realist artists who find the device almost impossible to use. Furthermore, these artists are able to produce work of extremely realistic and accurate quality using techniques of measurement and observation passed down in generations old traditions, and not any sort of tracing. These traditions were used by the old masters in their lineage and it is not plausible that the camera obscura would have been widely used, as other freehand techniques are more accurate and very easy to use with proper training. These early cameras did not fix an image, but only projected images from an opening in the wall of a darkened room onto a surface, turning the room into a large pinhole camera. The phrase *camera obscura* literally means darkened room. While this early prototype of today's modern camera may have had modest usage in its time, it was an important step in the evolution of the invention.

The first photograph was an image produced in the 1820s by the French inventor Nicéphore Niépce on a polished pewter plate covered with a petroleum derivative called bitumen of Judea. Produced with a camera, the image required an eight-hour exposure in bright sunshine. Niépce then began experimenting with silver compounds based on a Johann Heinrich Schultz discovery in 1724 that a silver and chalk mixture darkens when exposed to light.

In partnership, Niépce, in Chalon-sur-Saône, and Louis Daguerre, in Paris, refined the existing silver process. In 1833 Niépce died of a stroke, leaving his notes to Daguerre. While he had no scientific background, Daguerre made two pivotal contributions to the process. He discovered that exposing the silver first to iodine vapour, before exposure to light, and then to mercury fumes after the photograph was taken, could form a latent image. Bathing the plate in a salt bath then fixes the image. In 1839 Daguerre announced that he had invented a process using silver on a copper plate called the Daguerreotype. A similar process is still used today for Polaroids. The French government bought the patent and immediately made it public domain.

In 1832, French-Brazilian painter and inventor Hercules Florence had already created a very similar process, naming it *Photographie*, and William Fox Talbot had earlier discovered another means to fix a silver process image but had kept it secret.

After reading about Daguerre's invention Talbot refined his process, so that it might be fast enough to take photographs of people. By 1840, Talbot had invented the calotype process. He coated paper sheets with silver chloride to create an intermediate negative image. Unlike a daguerreotype a calotype negative could be used to reproduce positive prints, like most chemical films do today. Talbot patented this process, which greatly limited its adoption. He spent the rest of his life in lawsuits defending the patent until he gave up on photography. Later George Eastman refined Talbot's process, which is the basic technology used by chemical film cameras today. Hippolyte Bayard had also developed a method of photography but delayed announcing it, and so was not recognized as its inventor.

In 1851 Frederick Scott Archer invented the collodion process. Photographer and children's author, Lewis Carroll, used this process.

Slovene Janez Puhar invented the technical procedure for making photographs on glass in 1841. The invention was recognized on July 17 1852 in Paris by the Académie Nationale Agricole, Manufacturière et Commerciale.

Herbert Bowyer Berkeley experimented with his own version of collodian emulsions after Samman introduced the idea of adding dithionite to the pyrogallol developer. Berkeley discovered that with his own addition of sulphite, to absorb the sulphur dioxide given off by the chemical dithionite in the developer, that dithionite was not required in the developing process. In 1881 he published his discovery. Berkeley's formula contained pyrogallol, sulphite and citric acid. Ammonia was added just before use to make the formula alkaline The new formula was sold by the Platinotype Company in London as Sulpho-Pyrogallol Developer.

Popularization

The Daguerreotype proved popular in responding to the demand for portraiture emerging from the middle classes during the Industrial Revolution. This demand, that could not be met in volume and in cost by oil painting, added to the push for the development of photography. Daguerreotypes, while beautiful, were fragile and difficult to copy. A single photograph taken in a portrait studio could cost USD $1,000 in 2006 dollars. Photographers also encouraged chemists to refine the process of making many copies cheaply, which eventually led them back to Talbot's process.

Ultimately, the modern photographic process came about from a series of refinements and improvements in the first 20 years. In 1884 George Eastman, of Rochester, New York, developed dry gel on paper, or film, to replace the photographic plate so that a photographer no longer needed to carry boxes of plates and toxic chemicals around. In July of 1888 Eastman's Kodak camera went on the market with the slogan "You press the button, we do the rest". Now anyone could take a photograph and leave the complex parts of the process to others, and photography became available for the mass-market in 1901 with the introduction of Kodak Brownie.

Since then color film has become standard, as well as automatic focus and automatic exposure. Digital recording of images is becoming increasingly common, as digital cameras allow instant previews on LCD screens and the resolution of top of the range models has exceeded high quality 35 mm film while lower resolution models have become affordable. For the enthusiast photographer processing black and white film, little has changed since the introduction of the 35mm film Leica camera in 1925.

Economic History

In the nineteenth century, photography developed rapidly as a commercial service. End-user supplies of photographic equipment accounted for only about 20% of industry revenue.

With the development of digital technologies and of communications devices, such as camera phones, understanding the economics of image use is becoming increasingly important for understanding the evolution of the communications industry as a whole.

Photography Types

Color Photography

Color photography was explored throughout the 1800s. Initial experiments in color could not fix the photograph and prevent the color from fading. The first permanent color photo was taken in 1861 by the physicist James Clerk Maxwell.

One of the early methods of taking color photos was to use three cameras. Each camera would have a color filter in front of the lens. This technique provides the photographer with the three basic channels required to recreate a color image in a darkroom or processing plant. Russian photographer Sergei Mikhailovich Prokudin-Gorskii developed another technique, with three color plates taken in quick succession.

Practical application of the technique was held back by the very limited color response of early film; however, in the early 1900s, following the work of photo-chemists such as H.W. Vogel, emulsions with adequate sensitivity to green and red light at last became available.

The first color film, Autochrome, invented by the French Lumière brothers, reached the market in 1907. It was based on a 'screen-plate' filter made of dyed dots of potato starch, and was the only color film on the market until German Agfa introduced the similar Agfacolor in 1932. In 1935, American Kodak introduced the first modern ('integrated tri-pack') color film, Kodachrome, based on three colored emulsions. This was followed in 1936 by Agfa's Agfacolor Neue. Unlike the Kodachrome tri-pack process the colour couplers in Agfacolor Neue were integral with the emulsion layers, which greatly simplified the film processing. Most modern color films, except Kodachrome, are based on the Agfacolor Neue technology. Instant color film was introduced by Polaroid in 1963.

As an interesting side note, the inventors of Kodachrome, Leopold Mannes and Leopold Godowsky, Jr. were both accomplished musicians. Godowsky was the brother-in-law of George Gershwin and his father was Leopold Godowsky, one of the world's greatest pianists. Color photography may form images as a positive transparency, intended for use in a slide projector or as color negatives, intended for use in creating positive color enlargements on specially coated paper. The latter is now the most common form of film (non-digital) color photography owing to the introduction of automated photoprinting equipment.

Digital Photography

Traditional photography was a considerable burden for photographers working at remote locations (such as press correspondents) without access to processing facilities. With increased competition from television there was pressure to deliver their images to newspapers with greater speed. Photo-journalists at remote locations would carry a miniature photo lab with them and some means of transmitting their images down the telephone line. In 1981 Sony unveiled the first consumer camera to use a CCD for imaging, and which required no film — the Sony Mavica. While the Mavica did save images to disk, the images themselves were displayed on television, and therefore the camera could not be considered fully digital. In 1990, Kodak unveiled the DCS 100, the first commercially available digital camera. Its cost precluded any use other than photojournalism and professional applications, but commercial digital photography was born.

Digital imaging uses an electronic sensor such as a charge-coupled device to record the image as a set of electronic data rather than as chemical changes on film. Some other devices, such as cell phones, now include digital imaging features. Even though there are no chemical processes, a digital camera captures a frame of whatever it happens to be pointed at, which can be viewed later.

Although digital imaging is conceptually no different from ordinary chemical photography, it has certain distinctions. The primary difference lies in that photography inherently resists manipulation due to the fact that it is an analog process involving film, optics and photographic paper, while digital imaging is a highly manipulative medium since it is purely digital from the beginning. This difference allows for a degree of image post-processing which is comparatively difficult in photography, and thus the distinction has less to do with visual dissimilarities, and far more to do with their quite different communicative potentials and applications. Another basic difference is that at no point in the process is the image truly photographic, or etched by light, as in the chemical processes used to make negatives and prints. It is at first an interpretation by the camera of light intensities detected by a grid of sensors. It only becomes a viewable image only after being translated and reproduced on a display or printing device.

Digital imaging is replacing photography in the consumer and professional markets at a rapid pace. In 10 years, digital point and shoot cameras have become widespread consumer products. These digital cameras now outsell film cameras, and many include features not found in film cameras such as the ability to shoot video and record audio. Kodak announced in January 2004 that it would no longer produce reloadable 35 mm cameras after the end of that year. This was interpreted as a sign of the end of film photography. However, Kodak was at that time a minor player on the reloadable film cameras market. In January 2006 Nikon followed suit and announced that they will stop the production of all but two models of their film cameras, they will continue to produce the low-end Nikon FM10, and the high-end Nikon F6. On May 25, 2006 Canon announced they will stop developing new film SLR cameras.[2] The price of 35 mm and APS compact cameras have dropped, probably due to direct competition from digital and the resulting growth of the offer of second-hand film cameras.

Because photography is popularly synonymous with truth ("The camera doesn't lie"), digital imaging has raised many ethical concerns. Many photojournalists have declared they will not crop their pictures, or are forbidden from combining elements of multiple photos to make "illustrations," passing them as real photographs. Many courts will not accept digital images as evidence because of their inherently manipulative nature. Today's technology has made picture editing relatively easy for even the novice photographer. Even beginners can easily edit color, contrast, exposure and sharpness with the click of a mouse, whereas those same procedures would have taken an extensive amount of time in a traditional darkroom.

Photography Styles

Commercial Photography

The commercial photographic world can be broken down to:

- Advertising photography: photographs made to illustrate a service or product. These images are generally done with an advertising agency, design firm or with an in-house corporate design team.
- Fashion and glamour photography: This type of photography usually incorporates models. Fashion photography emphasizes the clothes or product, glamour emphasizes the model. Glamour photography is popular in advertising and in men's magazines. Models in glamour photography may be nude, but this is not always the case.
- Editorial photography: photographs made to illustrate a story or idea within the context of a magazine. These are usually assigned by the magazine.
- Photojournalism: this can be considered a subset of editorial photography. Photographs made in this context are accepted as a truthful documentation of a news story.

- Portrait and wedding photography: photographs made and sold directly to the end user of the images.
- Fine art photography: photographs made to fulfill a·vision, and reproduced to be sold directly to the customer.

The market for photographic services demonstrates the aphorism "one picture is worth a thousand words," which has an interesting basis in the history of photography. Magazines and newspapers, companies putting up Web sites, advertising agencies and other groups pay for photography.

Many people take photographs for self-fulfillment or for commercial purposes. Organizations with a budget and a need for photography have several options: they can assign a member of the organization, hire someone, run a public competition, or obtain rights to stock photographs.

Photography as an Art Form

During the twentieth century, both fine art photography and documentary photography became accepted by the English-speaking art world and the gallery system. In the United States, a handful of curators spent their lives advocating to put photography in such a system, with Alfred Stieglitz, Edward Steichen, John Szarkowski, and Hugh Edwards the most prominent among them. The aesthetics of photography is a matter that continues to be discussed regularly, especially in artistic circles. Many artists argued that photography was the mechanical reproduction of an image. If photography is authentically art, then photography in the context of art would need redefinition, such as determining what component of a photograph makes it beautiful to the viewer. The controversy began with the earliest images "written with light": Nicéphore Niépce, Louis Daguerre, and others among the very earliest photographers were met with acclaim, but some questioned if it met the definitions and purposes of art.

Visual Design

Color

Color is a good tool for communicating information in a user interface. For example, it can be used to:

- strengthen a desktop's look and feel by enhancing a theme
- accent a dynamic alert in a system management application
- emphasize an element in a long list to expedite scanning
- add aesthetically pleasing details to an icon

However, color should always be regarded as a useful addition to your design, not as a necessity. Never depend upon colors alone to display important information, and keep in mind that if colors cannot be perceived correctly (for example, the user has an 8-bit system, or is colorblind), your application should still be usable.

Palette

A 32-color palette has been developed for the GNOME desktop. The palette may be downloaded from http://developer.gnome.org/projects/gup/images/ximian-palette. To use it in The GIMP, save it to your ~/.gimp_1.2/palettes folder, and restart The GIMP. A single, consistently-used palette helps give a unified look and feel to the desktop while minimizing visual distractions. If you need a color that is darker or lighter than the colors in this basic palette (e.g., for antialiasing), choose a color that is closest to the hue you need, then darken or lighten as required.

Hue, Brightness, Contrast

Users with vision disorders, such as colorblindness or low vision, require alternatives to default settings. A good user interface anticipates these needs by providing customizable preferences and support for accessible themes. Even better is an application that is already configured with carefully-chosen color and contrast defaults.

An estimated 11% of the world population has some sort of colorblindness. Those affected typically have trouble distinguishing between certain hues such as red and green (deuteranopia or protanopia), or blue and yellow (tritanopia). Therefore it is necessary to allow the user to customize colors in any part of your application that conveys important information. This means that your application must effectively convey information using just the colors from any theme that the user chooses. A useful tool for reviewing information about colorblindness and checking legibility of images for colorblind users is Vischeck, an online tool that simulates the way an image or a website might appear to a user who has deuteranopia, protanopia, or tritanopia. Other users have more problems with contrast levels rather than hue on their screen. Some users require a high level of contrast between background and foreground colors, such as black on white, white on black, or some other high-contrast combination. Others can experience discomfort unless they use low-contrast settings, such as gray text on a lighter gray background.

You can meet these needs by ensuring your application supports the accessible GNOME themes (found in the gnome-themes module in cvs), which include high and low contrast themes, and large print themes. This means you must supply default and large sizes of high-, low- and regular-contrast icon sets with your application.

Guidelines

- Use the GNOME color palette. If you need a darker or lighter shade, start from one of the colors from the palette and darken or lighten as needed.

- Do not use color as the only means to distinguish items of information. All such information should be provided by at least one other method, such as shape, position or textual description.
- Ensure your application is not dependent on a particular theme. Test it with different themes, especially high and low contrast accessibility themes, which use fewer colors, to ensure your application respects the settings. For example, all text should appear in the foreground color against the background color specified in the chosen theme.
- Select colors carefully. When they need to be recognizably different, select the light colors from orange, yellow, green or blue-green, and darker colors from blue, violet, purple or red, as most people affected by colorblindness already see blue, violet, purple and red as darker than normal.

Window Layout

General

Placement of visual components in an application is important because relationships between elements are indicated by their positions. This is called "layout" in interface design. A clean layout is crucial to creating a smooth visual flow of information for the user. This section describes the proper component placement and spacing to use in GNOME applications. The major components discussed will be labels, icons, radio buttons and checkboxes, text fields, command buttons, and drop-down menus.

Dialogs

When a user is scanning a complex preferences dialog consisting of many labels and corresponding checkboxes, text fields, and combo boxes, it is easy to see how she can quickly become hindered by poor layout in the visual design.

As the labels are all similar in length, they should be left-aligned. Now the user has a firm left margin to anchor the eye and scan the list of items vertically more easily. If most of the labels in a group greatly differ in length, right-align them instead, so that the controls do not end up too far away from their corresponding labels.

Using frames with visible borders to separate groups within a window is deprecated. Use spacing and bold headers instead. This is more effective because there are fewer gratuitous lines to distract the user from the main content in the window. Try to keep components consonant with each other in terms of size and alignment. This is particularly important within a group of controls, so that the user's ability to quickly scan information is not sacrificed. Minimize as much as possible the need for the user's eye to jump around when scanning a layout.

Guidelines

- Leave a 12-pixel border between the edge of the window and the nearest controls.
- Leave a 12-pixel horizontal gap between a control and its label. (The gap may be bigger for other controls in the same group, due to differences in the lengths of the labels.)
- Labels must be concise and make sense when taken out of context. Otherwise, users relying on screenreaders or similar assistive technologies will not always be able to immediately understand the relationship between a control and those surrounding it.
- Assign access keys to all editable controls. Ensure that labels immediately precede their associated control in the tab order, so that the access key will focus to or activate the correct control when pressed.

Spacing and Alignment

Provide adequate space between controls and groups of controls. This white space will make it easier for the user to find the information they need.

Guidelines

- As a basic rule of thumb, leave space between user interface components in increments of 6 pixels, going up as the relationship between related elements becomes more distant. For example, between icon labels and associated graphics within an icon, 6 pixels are adequate. Between labels and associated components, leave 12 horizontal pixels. For vertical spacing between groups of components, 18 pixels is adequate. A general padding of 12 pixels is recommended between the contents of a dialog window and the window borders.
- Break long lists of choices into smaller groups. For lists of less than about eight items, use radio buttons or check boxes. For longer lists, use a list control or option menu.
- Try to keep elements of the same type left-aligned with each other. For instance, the group titles (General and Actions) are left-aligned and justified with each other.
- Indent group members 12 pixels to denote hierarchy and association.
- Minimize the number of alignment points in your window. An alignment point is an imaginary vertical or horizontal line through your window that touches the edge of one or more labels or controls in the window.
- Right-justification within groups or the overall window (as indicated by the line labelled "justification" in pleasing to the eye, but not crucial.

- Lay out components left-to-right, top-to-bottom. Generally, the first element the user is meant to encounter should be in the top-left, and the last in the bottom right. Keep in mind that when localized for non-western locales, interfaces may be reversed so that they read from right to left.
- Using "white" or blank spacing and indentation to delineate groups is cleaner and preferable to using graphical separators such as frames.
- Align controls in your layout EXACTLY. The eye is very sensitive to aligned and unaligned objects. If nothing lines up with anything else in a window, it will be very hard for the user to scan the contents and find the information he wants. Two things that almost line up, but not quite, are equally distracting.
- Be consistent. Use the same spacing, alignment, and component sizes in all dialogs appearing in your application. The OK and Cancel buttons, for example, should all appear exactly 12 vertical and horizontal pixels from the lower right corner of every dialog window.
- Ensure that light and dark areas as well as spacing are equally distributed around the window. Keep in mind that every control or group of controls in your window has a visual "weight," depending on its overall size, color, and how much white space it includes. Darker, larger areas are "heavier," while paler, smaller areas are "lighter."
- Do not design windows that are more than 50% longer in one dimension than in the other. People are more comfortable looking at windows and dialogs whose dimensions stay within the golden ratio (about 1.6 to 1), a ratio that artists and architects have used to create aesthetically-pleasing buildings and paintings for thousands of years.

Technical Details for Proper Layout

Set Border Width for the GtkDialog to 12. Place a GtkVBox containing as many rows as you wish to have categories inside the control area of the GtkDialog, and set the Spacing for the GtkVBox to 18. In turn, each category should be composed of a GtkVBox with two rows. Set the Spacing to 6.

- In the top row, place a label for the category header. Make the label bold using the Pango markup
  <span weight="bold">*Category Header*</span>

  Set the label property Use Markup to Yes, and X Align to 0.0 to left align the label.
- Place a 2-columned GtkHBox in the lower row of the top-level GtkVBox.
  - In the left column, place a label containing four space characters. This will serve to indent the category contents.

- In the right column, place a GtkVBox containing a row per control you wish to place in the category. Set the Spacing to 6.
  - For left-side labelled controls such as text boxes, option menus, and many others, place a 2 columned GtkHBox inside the row with a label in the left column and the corresponding control in the right. Set the Spacing on the GtkHBox to 6. Place all labels such as this (for the whole window) in the same GtkSizeGroup (there is currently no way to do this using only Glade, you will have to use code as well). This will align the controls to their right, even between categories, which is important for allowing quick visual scans.
  - For right-side labelled controls such as check boxes and radio buttons, simply place them directly in the row.

Text Labels

To a user with normal vision, textual output provides the majority of the information and feedback in most applications. To a visually-impaired user who may not be able to see or understand any additional graphical output, clear textual output is critical. You must therefore choose and position text carefully on the screen, and leave the choice of fonts and sizes to the user, to ensure that all users are able to use your application effectively.

Spacing and Alignment

Use spacing and alignment of text uniformly throughout your application. A basic rule of thumb is to put space between user interface components in increments of 6 pixels, going up as the relationship between related elements becomes more distant.

Guidelines

- If the label precedes the control it is labelling, end the label with a colon. For example, Email: to label a text field into which the user should type their email address. This helps identify it as a control's label rather than an independent item of text. Some assistive technology screen review utilities may also use the presence of a colon to identify text as a control label.
- When you use static text to label a control, ensure that the label immediately precedes that control in the Tab order. This will ensure that the access key (underlined character) you assign to the label will move focus to or activate the correct control when pressed.
- Left-align components and labels, unless all the labels in a group have very different lengths. If they do, right-align the labels instead, to ensure that no controls end up too far away from their corresponding labels.

- Choose label names carefully. Label objects with names that make sense when taken out of context. Users relying on screenreaders or similar assistive technologies will not always be able to immediately understand the relationship between a control and those surrounding it.
- Be consistent with label usage and semantics. For example, if you use the same label in different windows, it will help if it means the same thing in both windows. Equally, don't use labels that are spelled differently but sound the same, e.g., "Read" and "Red", as this could be confusing for users relying on screenreaders.
- Don't use the same label more than once in the same window. This makes life difficult for users relying on tools like magnifiers or screen readers, which cannot always convey surrounding context to the user.
- Do not hard-code font styles and sizes. The user should be able to adjust all sizes and typefaces.
- Do not use more than two or three different fonts and sizes in your application, and choose visually distinct rather than similar-looking fonts in one window. Too many font sizes and styles will make the interface look cluttered and unprofessional, and be harder to read. In general, always use fonts from the current theme, and specify relative rather than absolute sizes.
- Do not use graphical backdrops or "watermarks" behind text, other than those specified by the user's chosen theme. These interfere with the contrast between the text and its background. This can cause difficulty for users with visual impairments, who will therefore normally choose themes that always use plain backdrops.

Capitalization

Two styles of capitalization are used in GNOME user interface elements:

Header Capitalization

Capitalize all words in the element, with the following exceptions:

- Articles: *a*, *an*, *the*.
- Conjunctions: *and*, *but*, *for*, *not*, *so*, *yet* ...
- Prepositions of three or fewer letters: *at*, *for*, *by*, *in*, *to* ...

Sentence Capitalization

Capitalize the first letter of the first word, and any other words normally capitalized in sentences, such as application names.

Capitalization Style Guidelines for User Interface Elements

Element	*Style*
Check box labels	Sentence
Command button labels	Header
Column heading labels	Header
Desktop background object labels	Header
Dialog messages	Sentence
Drop-down combo box labels	Sentence
Drop-down list box labels	Sentence
Field labels	Sentence
Filenames	Sentence
Graphic equivalent text: for example, Alt text on web pages	Sentence
Group box or frame labels	Header
Items in drop-down combo boxes, drop-down list boxes, and list boxes	Sentence
List box labels	Sentence
Menu items	Header
Menu items in applications	Header
Menu titles in applications	Header
Radio button labels	Sentence
Slider labels	Sentence
Spin box labels	Sentence
Tabbed section titles	Header
Text box labels	Sentence
Titlebar labels	Header
Toolbar button labels	Header
Tooltips	Sentence
Webpage titles and navigational elements	Header

Fonts

Only use the fonts that the user has specified in their theme, and in sizes relative to the default size specified in their theme. This will ensure maximum legibility and accessibility for all users.

Do not mix more than two or three font sizes and styles (underlined, bold, italicized) in one window, as this will look unprofessional and distract the user from the information being conveyed.

Provide alternatives to WYSIWYG where applicable. Some users may need to print text in a small font but edit in a larger screen font, for example. Possible alternatives include displaying all text in the same font and size (both of which are chosen by the user); a "wrap-to-window" option that allows you to read all the text in a window without scrolling horizontally; a single column view that shows the window's contents in a single column even if they will be printed in multiple columns; and a text-only view, where graphics are shown as placeholders or text descriptions.

Visual Workplace-Visual Thinking: Introduction

Creating Enterprise Excellence Through the Technologies of the Visual Workplace

The technologies of the visual workplace represent a comprehensive strategy for installing vital information as close to the point of use as possible. Through this elegant and powerful chain of methods, we eradicate motion – caused by chronic information deficits in the workplace – even as we generate new levels of employee inventiveness and contribution, even as we align the enterprise.

As you will discover by the time you compete this book, workplace visuality creates a set of outcomes that work in parallel with lean outcomes.

Visual builds the details of work into the physical environment and thereby improves adherence, enabling people to work precisely with increasing self-regulation. Lean defines, extends, accelerates, and controls the flow of work that visual spells out, dramatically reducing lead-time and flow distance. Visual imbeds lean gains into the physical workplace and creates self-leadership and alignment on every level of the organization. Visual and lean work hand-in-hand, as do the wings of a bird. Neither is more important; they are of equal importance.

There is understandable confusion on this point because nearly every early training session on lean has a built-in module under the "5-S" rubric that teaches the importance of borders and home addresses, two elements of workplace visuality. This leads people to mistakenly assume that the lean approach incorporates visual. It does not.

In fact, as you move through the chapters of this book, you will see that applying 5S solely within the context of lean not only gives implementers a false belief that they are implementing workplace visuality, it also vastly reduces the impact that so-called "5S" can contribute to the company's journey to excellence. In nearly twenty-five years of research and implementation, I have never found an approach more powerful than workplace visuality in liberating, empowering, and aligning the workforce – not just value-add employees but all employees, including managers and executives. And this is only one aspect of its power. From its foundation (so-called "5S") to visual guarantees (viz., poka-yoke systems), the visual workplace is so much more. Because organizations have an incomplete understanding of the visual approach, they under-implement and therefore under-use the remarkable set of principles, concepts, methods, tools, practices that constitute the technologies of the visual workplace.

A New Understanding

This book invites you to consider a wholesale upgrade of your vision and understanding of the visual approach – one that would populate the operational landscape with hundreds, even thousands, of visual devices and visual mini-systems that would in their turn entirely redefine, even revolutionize, the way work gets done, waste is reduced, employees are involved, customers are served, and profit is made in your organization. Imbedded in this invitation is the promise of a new enterprise, one that reaches for and gains excellence as a way of doing business, as part of daily work. That excellence is founded upon the emergence of a new core competency in the corporation, one that I call *visual thinking*.

- Visual thinking is the ability of each employee to recognize motion and the information deficits that cause it – and then to eliminate both through solutions that are visual.

Visual thinking, which fits hand-in-glove with lean principles and outcomes, is the doorway to the tomorrow you have been seeking, whatever the industry, whatever the venue.

How to Use This Book

The first in a new series of books on visuality in the workplace, Visual Workplace-Visual Thinking focuses on what workplace visuality is, why it is important, and how its fundamental values and premises lead to visual outcomes that are effective, expansive, renewable, and, above all, sustainable. Ultimately, this is a book about visual thinking and how to create a workforce of visual thinkers. It is written for executives, managers, supervisors, team leaders, and union leadership in its entirety – in short, for anyone and everyone who must work through others to achieve their own objectives. The second and third books in this new series, *Work That Makes Sense* and *Visuality In Action*, focus on the visual contribution of operators and line employees – the value-add level of the enterprise. Other conceptual and how-to books will follow, addressing such key visual outcomes as visual displays, visual standards, visual metrics and visual problem-solving, visual controls and visual pull systems, and the leadership conversion that the journey to enterprise excellence requires.

My purpose in telling you this is not to take an opportunity to market our other wares but to help you stretch your thinking further about what the visual workplace is and why it is important. This book is most emphatically *not* an implementation manual, even though it provides many details on the previously misunderstood field of workplace visuality. While it explains what each visual workplace technology is, implementation requires much more detail. What is required is a known sequence of steps that yields early success (the easy part) and ensures long-term sustainability – that elusive holy grail of all improvement activity. The improvement workscape is already littered with too many failed implementations – failed because either the initiative caused more harm than good and/or because improvements did not last.

Primarily, then, this is a book about knowledge, not know-how. It has four sections. Section One focuses on basic concepts and principles, with Chapter I discussing enterprise excellence and the pure power of visual information sharing. Chapter II presents the eight building blocks of visual thinking and is as close to a methods primer as you will find in this volume.

The second section of the book focuses on the culture of work, beginning with the discussion in Chapter III of the role of executives in discovering and developing new facets of leadership – including initiating the empowerment conversion that results in a deeply engaged, spirited, inventive, and aligned workforce. Chapter IV discusses the evolution of individual employees into visual thinkers, capable of creating a genuinely visual work environment.

The three chapters in the book's third section detail the technologies of the visual workplace, what they are, why they are important, and who takes the lead in implementing them – visual order, visual standards, visual displays, visual metrics, visual problem-solving, visual controls, visual pull systems, and visual guarantees. The book concludes with a discussion of the visual and lean paradigms, how they support each other, and where the most common mistakes are made in bringing them into alignment – for aligned they must be if excellence in the enterprise is to be achieved and sustained.

Graphics and charts along with over a dozen photographic folios of actual examples anchor your understanding. Other photographs of visual solutions populate the text. I hope many of these will knock your socks off, much as they knocked off mine when I first saw them.

As you turn the last page, it is my sincere wish that you will have gained a much deeper and more complete understanding of why workplace visuality is crucial to your company's journey to excellence and your own. If all goes well, by book's end, you may also be well on your own way to becoming a visual thinker. I would be so very pleased if you were.

Visual Technologies and their Assessment in Undergraduate Teaching and Learning

Activities

There were two stages: planning and design by the two project participants, and implementation with the participation of the students. We used funds from the UWS

Teaching Innovation Fund for tutorial support to facilitate both stages. We also used Blackboard to support each module and others throughout the year.

During Teaching Block 1 we planned and designed the schedule and logistics of the practical teaching and learning. The project was aimed at developing assessment strategies, but it was necessary to develop simple and effective means to provide adequate training. After a lengthy process we successfully negotiated facilities with the university and found staff to provide training in scanning and editing over the period February to April: a postgraduate, and a freelance news cameraman. Researching the design was a challenge due to a shortage of existing guidelines. The booklet on 'portfolios' from the Generic Learning Centre had been helpful in devising the hard-copy portfolio used previously as a means of assessment, but there did not seem to be any resource which suggested ways of tackling using the CD-ROM as a learning device, or ways of assessing it. Criteria for assessing video work are limited to university courses such as Manchester's MA in Visual Anthropology, and guidelines provided for selecting ethnographic films at festivals. It was also necessary to revise existing module outlines and process paperwork with Quality Committees.

Both modules were taught in Teaching Block 2. The 50 minute 'scanning training' session was deemed equivalent to a 1,000 word piece of 'formative coursework' for the module, hence students did not feel that they were having to do more for this module than for others. The scanning training went extremely well with 100% attendance, and the tutor found time in 50 minutes to introduce the students to Power Point, which some were able to use in the CD-ROMs. The trainer kept weekly 'Surgery Hours' and offered 'Emergency Surgeries' in the week before work was due. Video editing training started in the fourth week after all the students had filmed a basic exercise and received detailed feedback. Working in the same groups, they filmed and logged 30 minutes max of material, and were taught in one hour to capture and cut short films of 5 minutes; in future it should be two hours. These exercises were debriefed in a seminar with the editing tutor present. For the final projects, student teams (of two, and in one case, three, initially) had access to three cameras over three weeks and tutorial help for two half days per team over two weeks. They were required to film 60 minutes of rushes, which they had to cut into films of not more than 10 minutes. The process was very compressed, with no time for feedback on rough cuts. All guidance was from the tutor, and the lecturer refrained in the name of fairness from seeing the work until it was finished.

For both parts of the project we researched and designed documentation for discussion with the students. Time was set aside for consulting the students taking the modules to discuss and determine assessment criteria. For the CD-ROMs, they were grouped in twos and threes, and asked to discuss what criteria they felt were most appropriate, having been provided with the 'bench-marking' criteria for Anthropology, and the Learning Outcomes for the module for level 2 and level 3. In

Visual Anthropology two one-hour seminars were dedicated to assessment and took the form of focus groups. Discussion documents were provided, as well as the discipline-specific documentation used for the CD-ROM group. For the Visual Anthropology students, the main points of concern were the balance of marks between the video and the reflexive report (which together formed 50% of the module assessment), and how anthropological relevance should be assessed. The group decided on a 50/50 balance of marks, and an assessment of anthropological relevance limited to the written report. The process of assessment involved reading the reports, seeing the films with the students as a group, then re-viewing the films and re-reading the reports. Both the second marker (who followed a similar procedure alone) and the external were asked to view all eight films.

In neither case did the students support formal peer-assessment, nor did the technical trainers contribute to formal assessment. We did however ask for informal technical feedback in both modules.

Outcomes

For both modules, standard feedback report forms for assessed work were amended on the basis of student recommendations. For the CD-ROMs for The History of Anthropological Theory, Content and Structure were deemed the two most important criteria of evaluation (35% each), then Technical Competence (20%) and Written Expression least (10%), at both level 3 and level 2. For Visual Anthropology a different form had to be constructed. In Visual Anthropology, students proved reluctant to trust to their image production, and opted for a 50-50 balance of marks between the video and the reflexive report. Ironically, everyone would have gained higher marks if the original proposal of 65% for the film and 35% for the report had been followed. Once the marks are finalized, students will be given a final chance to give feedback to finalize recommendations for future practice.

In The History of Anthropological Theory, 24 level 3 students and 15 level 2 students produced CD-ROMs, 39 in all. All demonstrated a basic technical competence in scanning, and some displayed very high levels of technical proficiency in design and presentation. Topics included original research into a distant relative from Victorian times who had published an ethnographic survey of a part of India, using family documents and other memorabilia, early explorers (Lady Mary Wortley Montagu, Isabella Bird, and Mary Kingsley), expeditions (Torres Straits, Jesup North Pacific, Lewis and Clark), and the early ethnographic filmmaker, Robert Flaherty (this by students also doing Visual Anthropology). A sample of work was marked by both project participants. Highest marks were gained by those students who devised labelled 'pathways' through the material, and evaluated its usefulness for other users (the Content and Structure criteria). It was clear that, apart from technical competence in scanning and, in some cases employing Power Point, students had acquired valuable skills in structuring the presentation of such materials in a logical and 'user-friendly' way.

In Visual Anthropology, 15 students worked in 7 teams (and eventually 8), to research and produced 'portraits' of persons or places in and around Swansea. The topics included a family sportswear business, a man who swims everyday in the Bristol Channel, a circus-skills training session, school visits to the University's Egypt Centre (a reflection of a joint honours Anthropology and Egyptology student doing the module), an art class, skateboarding, a woman working for SUSTANS, and anti-war demonstrations. All films were assessed in the class of 2.1 and upwards, but some of the reports did not show such a high level of attention, so some marks were pulled down.

In the case of Visual Anthropology there was an extra outcome. Six Swansea students, three of whom had done the module, participated in a field school organised out of the University of Glamorgan. The project convenor acted as Assistance Director of the School and Director of the visual project, which aims to produce a 25 minute video. She ran an initial training day, and the three Swansea students acted as tutors, with ongoing responsibility to oversee filming practice for the rest of the field school. A viewing of 10 hours of rushes at the end of the school showed what an excellent job they had done, so they were well able to transfer their skills. We are currently expecting the film to be edited in Swansea by two students who participated on the field school and another visual anthropology student; of the three, two did the visual anthropology module, and will train the third student who didn't.

Implications

I begin with the comments from our external examiner, Dr Garry Marvin:

'Two areas that are new to me this year deserve the highest praise - the production of CD ROMs for the History of Anthropological Theory and the video films for Visual Anthropology. In both of these courses the students have been encouraged to use their imagination and skills to produce truly original work rather than repeating and commenting on the work of other anthropologists. Obviously a huge amount of thought and effort has gone into the planning of these courses and, within the limited resources available, great effort has been made to provide the students with the necessary training to produce their CD ROMS and videos. I am afraid that I am someone whose eyes usually glaze over at the mention of 'transferable skills' but in these two courses there really are genuine and significant transferable skills. The ability to design a project on CD ROM with all the necessary research into web resources, the creative use of graphics and the hyperlinks etc and the skills of visual production in terms of design, filming and editing are skills that will certainly have a potential use outside the academic world. These two courses successfully bring new media into productive contact with academic anthropology and constitute a most valuable addition to the range of anthropology on offer at Swansea. Such courses inevitably require considerable resourcing and I hope that the University will consider the possibility of offering more funding to allow their further development.'

The students were challenged and although there were steep learning curves in both cases, there was general enthusiasm about the opportunities to use these new methods as part of an academic curriculum (some student comments may be found in the appendices). There were practical problems in 'embedding' these practices, as the Library and Information Services section of University of Wales Swansea cannot at present support specialist IT undergraduate training in scanning and editing software. In terms of sustainability, resources will be needed each time the modules are taught to fund this training. Access to the faculty IT room would also be crucial for scanning training. As far as video editing is concerned, the university's stand-alone 'Purple' system will be available and operates very reliably and to a high standard. For the future, to open up the video training to a wider number of students at different level, it would be necessary to find resources for editing software that could be used in a newly opened self-study computer laboratory. The cost of access however would be a loss of reliability.

To promote best practice in our institution, we intend to hold a School seminar about the C-SAP project in the hope of encouraging colleagues in using visual technologies and assessment in their own module topics. A version of this report will also go to the UWS Teaching Innovation Committee that matched C-SAP funds for this project. The University's Learning and Teaching Committee is also aware of this project and its potential, and will be presented with a copy of this report.

In the long term we need to consider how these two sets of skills fit into the wider skills training platform provided by universities, and how much priority they should be given. If more information-delivery can be done through Blackboard, space for a module could be made available. In the meantime, Blackboard usage by students and staff is patchy. Institutional support for basic staff training is good, but there is no institutional support whatsoever to assist with packaging and transferring course material to Blackboard. A final comment is that visual assessment cannot be essentialized any more than 'written assessment' can. Assessment criteria have to be associated with the overall learning outcomes and skill acquisition for the module, as well as reflecting disciplinary benchmarking criteria and standards.

Sound of Music: An Introduction

All musicians work with sound in one fashion or another, yet most have little understanding of its properties. Computer musicians, in particular, can benefit in myriad ways from an understanding of the mechanisms of sound, its objective measurements and the more subjective area of its perception. Not only is this understanding crucial to the proper use of common studio equipment and music software, but novel compositional strategies can be derived from exploiting much of the information contained in this chapter. One would expect a painter to know about the properties of paint—the same should hold true for the composer's understanding of acoustics and psychoacoustics.

The physics of sound (acoustics) is often confused with the way in which we perceive it (psychoacoustics). This chapter begins with a study of sound's physical characteristics and common measurements, followed by a discussion of human aural and musical perception.

Sound

We live at the bottom of a sea of air. As with the ocean, the farther down one goes, the greater the density of molecules and the greater the pressure it exerts on us. The average atmospheric pressure, as it is called, is measured in many different units, but the one most people are familiar with is barometric pressure (measured in *millibars*). Altitude, temperature and weather conditions affect barometric pressure (low barometric pressure, for example, is often associated with storm systems). If the micro-pressure level surrounding us remains steady or changes very slowly, we experience silence. Even so, individual air molecules themselves always exhibit at least a minimum rate of motion without causing perceptible pressure changes.

Sound is produced by a rapid variation in the average density or pressure of air molecules above and below the current atmospheric pressure. We perceive sound as these pressure fluctuations cause our eardrums to vibrate. When discussing sound, these usually minute changes in atmospheric pressure are referred to as sound pressure and the fluctuations in pressure as sound waves. Sound waves are produced by a vibrating body, be it an oboe reed, guitar string, loudspeaker cone or jet engine. The vibrating sound source causes a disturbance to the surrounding air molecules, causing them bounce off each other with a force proportional to the disturbance. The energy of their interaction creates ripples of more dense (higher pressure) to less dense (lower pressure) air molecules, with pressures above and below the normal atmospheric pressure. When the molecules are pushed closer together it is called compression; when they are pulled apart, it is called rarefaction. The back and forth oscillation of pressure produces a sound waves.

Sound Travel

The speed at which sound propagates (or travels from its source) is directly influenced by both the medium through which it travels and the factors affecting the medium, such as altitude, humidity and temperature for gases like air. Bad news for Star Wars fans—there is no sound in the vacuum of space because there are too few molecules to propagate a wave.

It is important to note that the speed of sound in air is determined by the conditions of the air itself (e.g. humidity, temperature, altitude). It is not dependent upon the sound's amplitude, frequency or wavelength. To calculate the approximate speed of sound in dry air at sea level, use the following formula:

$$V = 331.4 + 0.6T_c$$

V = velocity (m/s), T_c = temperature in Celsius

Using this formula, the speed of sound at 20° Celcius (68° Fahrenheit) is:

344 meters per second (m/s)
1128 feet per second (f/s)
770 miles per hour (mph)

Sound Waves

Sound waves are often characterized by four basic qualities, though many more are related:

*Frequency, Amplitude, Wave Shape and Phase**

Some sound waves are periodic, in that the change from equilibrium (average atmospheric pressure) to maximum compression to maximum rarefaction back to equilibrium is repetitive.

It is possible to measure frequency in seconds per cycle or periods, but it is far more common for sound measurements to use cycles per second or simply cps.

Periodic motion depends on two prime factors; 1) *elasticity*, in that medium being distorted return to its original state (equilibrium), and 2) a source of *energy* to initiate and sustain motion. In the case of sound waves, the atmospheric pressure will return to the ambient pressure without an energy source to disturb it, and any vibrating surface will constitute an energy or excitation source.

Simple harmonic motion, the motion described by mass/spring example and pictured above, is represented in sound as a sine wave, which traces the mathematical shape of it namesake. A sinusoidal wave (which also includes a cosine wave) is the *only* wave shape that produces a single frequency, as we will see in the waveform chapter. With any minute deviations in the sine shape, additional frequencies will be generated.

Frequency

The number of cycles per unit of time is called the frequency. For convenience, frequency is most often measured in cycles per second (cps) or the interchangeable hertz (Hz) (60 cps = 60 Hz), named after the 19th C. physicist. 1000 Hz is often referred to as 1 kHz (kilohertz) or simply '1k' in studio parlance.

Ampitude

Amplitude is the objective measurement of the degree of change (positive or negative) in atmospheric pressure (the compression and rarefaction of air molecules) caused by sound waves. Sounds with greater amplitude will produce greater changes in atmospheric pressure from high pressure to low pressure. Amplitude is almost always a comparative measurement, since at the lowest-amplitude end (silence), some air molecules are always in motion and at the highest end, the amount of compression and rarefaction though finite, is extreme. In electronic circuits, amplitude may be increased by expanding the degree of change in an oscillating electrical current. A woodwind player may increase the amplitude of their sound by providing greater force in the air column i.e. blowing harder.

Digital Video

The defining technology of multimedia is digital video. Or, more precisely, our ability to handle full motion video information within a digital environment. This ability is based entirely upon one technique—the technology of digital compression. But before considering briefly how the processes of compression work, it is worth framing the reason why video itself presents such a technological challenge to digital media systems. The simple reason is that once video goes digital it takes a huge amount of digital information to describe it. The problem is related not only to the complexity of rendering a high quality colour image but also to the demanding task of keeping up with the continuing rapid changes of image that characterise the way video delivers its impression of on-screen motion.

The exact amount of digital information needed to represent video depends largely on the quality of resolution with which the images are rendered. In a computer environment, screen displays are made of thousands of illuminated pixels, points on the screen which can be individually illuminated to form a viewable image. By refreshing the pixels with new instructions, images can be made to change and if they do so sufficiently quickly, one result can be animation, computer-generated motion.

There is a straightforward relationship between the resolution of a particular type of screen and the amount of data needed to support that resolution. For example, one of the standard monitor resolutions now widely used in computing is called VGA (video graphics array). A typical VGA screen consists of 640 pixels across and 480 pixels down. This means a screenful of information is provided by 307,200 illuminated dots, quality of resolution depends not only on this absolute number of but also on the number of colours and intensities which can be utilised at each pixel. The data needed to provide this colour/intensity control are provided in the form of a bit code. Codes based on a higher number of bits can deliver more colours and intensities than those using very few bits. In the case of VGA, the size of the code is typically four bits for each pixel. In other words, every two pixels accounts for one byte of information. At

VGA resolution, therefore, a static screenful of information needs 153,600 bytes (153.6 kilobytes).

Now let us look at television information and gain some sense of the amount of data needed to represent motion video. In the United States and Japan the system of encoding analogue television signals is called NTSC (National Television System Committee). It defines a television image in 520 horizontal lines of information, updated 60 times each second. In the UK and most of Europe, the PAL (phase alternation line) standard is used. Although similar in concept to NTSC, PAL uses 625 lines updated 50 times each second. Each update in fact provides half a frame of information. Since television pictures are built up by interlacing two half-frames, the factor of 50 updates per second means that the picture is updated at 25 complete frames each second. The horizontal resolution along one of the PAL lines is equivalent to about 700 dots, each a separately luminescing spot on the cathode ray screen. This means that a screenful of PAL television is represented by roughly half a million dots. Translating the colour quality required into digital terms means that each of these dots has to be addressed by the equivalent of 16 bits of information. Therefore 25 frames per second equates to around 20 megabytes of data every second. This is the rate of data transfer needed to produce television quality video in full motion on a full screen. Even a single, still image at this quality requires about 800 kilobytes of data.

It is worth noting — because it is a widely exploited feature of PC-based multimedia— that it does not have to be like this. We can drastically reduce the amounts of data involved by simply cutting the size of the video image. If full screen video needs around 20 megabytes a second, quarter screen video needs only 5. Reduce the image further and you similarly cut the data load. You can go further. We saw in the arithmetic above that a major ingredient in fuelling the data load is the fact that video data are refreshed at 25 frames per second (in Europe). If we sacrifice both frame rate and picture size, we can cut the data load still further. Indeed, the degree of sacrifice may not be great. After all, if 25 frames per second represents what is technically described as full motion, would the eye of the consumer really notice a drop to 20? In practice—depending on the video footage involved—digital producers can go as low as 15 frames per second and still retain much of the quality of full motion, even if the video gets a little jerky when the action hots up. If you want to take risks, you can also cut the data still further by reducing the amount of colour data in the images and making do with a grainy greyness instead of sharp, contrasty video quality. A trade off among frame rate, picture size and (possibly) colour resolution, therefore, can substantially reduce the technical demands of digital video. But the Holy Grail remains the effort to deliver full screen, full motion at good quality resolution.

Compromises aside, the huge amounts of information needed to convey images such as full screen colour stills or full screen, full motion video represent one of the greatest challenges for multimedia technology. The problem is both one of storage and processing power. It may be more of one than the other, depending on the approach of the multimedia system. For example, in the sector of the multimedia industry focusing on compact disc media, even the huge capacity of the disc looks modest compared to the demands of video. A compact disc—for all its hundreds of megabytes of storage space-could hold only about 30 seconds of uncompressed 'television quality' full screen video. And even if we wanted to store such a short segment, we could never get it off the disc fast enough to replicate full motion. The rate of data transfer needed would be well beyond the maximum capabilities of most compact disc systems. This is a problem of storage and transfer. As far as delivering the end product is concerned, somewhere in the chain a powerful computer is needed. In the 1980s, multimedia could never have been a viable industry simply because most of the computers of the day were not powerful enough for the job. And those that had the power were far too expensive to be used except in specialist, high value applications. But today multimedia can address a big audience because its principal delivery technology is widely and cheaply available. In simple terms, desktop computers of the late 1990s—and appliances based on the same underlying technology — are now powerful and cheap enough to deliver multimedia quite routinely to millions of people all over the world.

While multimedia in general needed to await the arrival of affordable computing power to deliver its fruits, digital video within multimedia relics foremost on techniques of compression which squeeze huge digital video files down to more manageable size and then allow the same files to be decompressed at the point of delivery.

The Beginnings of Optical Media

Before we examine the rise of the compact disc, we should spend a moment to reflect on its immediate antecedent, the video disc. Although it has much apparently in common with compact disc media, the original form of optical disc differed in one fundamental way. It was an analogue medium while compact disc took the same underlying technology into the digital age.

In the early 1980s, at the same time that the first home computer boom was at its height, the LaserVision video disc was exciting considerable interest as a publishing medium. It is not hard to see why. LaserVision (originally a proprietary name coined by Philips and, today, known generically as 'laser disc') emerged from the laboratories of Philips in the late 1970s. It is based on encoding multimedia information on the reflective surface of a silvered 12-inch disc. The encoding is done by a fine laser beam burning a series of microscopic pits into the disc surface. During playback, another laser beam passes over the surface of the spinning disc, acting as a stylus made of light. The way the light beam is reflected from the surface of the disc is affected by the presence of the pits, areas where the reflective surface has been burned away during the original encoding process. This modulation in the laser beam caused by the varying reflectivity is itself detected, decoded and reconstituted as the original multimedia information. Using this process, full morion, full frame video can be delivered together with the full range of other media types-still images, high quality sound and animations.

There are none of the problems of digital image data because the video disc is not digital. The laser beam, reading the pit code on the disc, is affected by the varying length of the pits. This creates a continuously changing value, characteristic of analogue information. Although not a digital medium, the video disc is nonetheless the starting point for modern interactive multimedia development. There are two main reasons. First, a standard disc offers up to 55,000 frames of information, each with its own unique electronic address or frame number. This makes it possible to access any individual frame by calling up that address and displaying its contents. Second, because the disc offers radial access to its contents, an individual frame or sequence of frames can be located and retrieved very quickly. The combination of these two factors means that by placing access to the disc under computer control, it is possible to create an interactive multimedia experience. Contrast this with efforts to use a linear medium such as videotape interactively—the only other interactive alternative in the late 1970s and early 1980s. Even with careful design, the time taken to wind a tape back and forth to locate required information makes it laborious and frustrating, even in the simplest applications.

The computing muscle used for rapidly locating and retrieving required information from the disc is supplied either by a separate microcomputer linked to a laser disc player or a microprocessor built into the player itself. Software suitably designed for the particular application is employed to control the user's interaction with the multimedia data on the disc. This means that the choices a user makes determine the particular pathway that the user takes through the multimedia information, with the computer drawing as required on the text, sound, still images and moving video stored on the disc. Used this way, the video disc is no more than a peripheral to the computer, much as any external disk drive might be. It is simply a physical source of stored, displayable information, accessed by a computer as a part of an interactive product designed for a given purpose.

The manufacturers of video disc players in the late 1970s and early 1980s had high hopes for commercial success across consumer, professional and business markets. The reality has fallen far short of these early expectations. Although we cannot properly analyse the fortunes of the interactive video industry here, we can at least summarise. The only substantial markets for interactive products have proved to be in dedicated applications. In these, video discs have been commissioned to address a single, bespoke purpose rather than to provide a product speculatively for a wide range of possible customers. Generally, these bespoke applications have been in the fields of industrial and professional training and in experimental retail promotion such as point-of-sale and point-of-information systems which—on the whole—have gone nowhere.

It is too soon to say, however, that the video disc should be consigned to the scrap heap of technological history, particularly since the above comments relate only to applications offering significant degree of interactivity. In 1992, the European Laser Disc Association (ELDA) published sales statistics showing a remarkable resurgence in Europe of consumer market interest in largely linear playback of feature films and music vide:

This came as no surprise to Japanese and US video disc companies Figures for their markets show substantial growth in consumer sales during the early 1990s. In Japan, for example, manufacturing figures for player rose from 500,000 in 1987 to nearly 1.3 million in 1991. Of the 1991 figure, about 550,000 were exported, mainly to the United States. The Japanese consumer market in 1992 had the choice of about 10,000 generic titles, most published by leading hardware manufacturer Pioneer. In the United States, the installed base of players has grown from 120,000 in 1988 to just under 300,000 in 1992. More recent statistics show a continuing substantial use of video discs in the US and Japanese markets. By the end of 1994, the total US consumer market stood at 1.5 million players with annual hardware sales holding steady at around 280,000. There were over 8,500 tides available. In Japan, the installed base of players had reached 4.7 million by the end of 1994 with annual sales running at over 400,000. The total number of consumer titles stood at nearly 18,500, mainly feature films, popular music and karaoke.

In Europe—in a move that speaks volumes—ELDA recently transformed itself into the European Platform for Optical Discs (EPOD) and now acts as a trade clearing house on marketing-related matters relating not only to video disc markets but the full range of CD media. Despite its change of name and orientation, the organisation continues to report surprisingly strong installed base figures for linear playback hardware. The figures for 1993-4 look like this (all figures are thousands):

	Benelux	*France*	*Germany*	*Spain*	*UK*	*Italy*	*Rest of Europ*	*Total*
End 1993	16	200	42	72	16	28	23	381
End 1994	18.5	230	48	126	22.5	29	29	484.5

These are not huge figures for a long-established technology, however, especially when compared, say, to Inteco Corporation's estimate for PC CD-ROM drives in European homes. At the end of 1994, Inteco reckoned that 2.7 million European homes had such drives, up from 360,000 the year before. But while video disc hardware markets are not growing fast, they are still growing. As the hardware base edges upward, sales of software are also rising. EPOD reports the following releases of new titles in Europe in 1994:

	Film	*Classical music*	*Pop/jazz*	*Total*
France	629	563	221	1,443
Germany	396	568	221	1,205
UK	204	548	191	963
Spain	169	568	196	948

Sales overall were up over 12 per cent in unit terms over 1993 with 2.3 million discs selling in 1994 compared to just over 2.0 million the previous year. However, these healthy-seeming numbers are heavily skewed by the efforts of a single Spanish publisher called Planeta Spain which has had an extremely successful time selling a package of hardware and software door-to-door. On its own, Planeta Spain contributed about half the total of European unit sales of discs during 1993 and 1994.

Currently, in Europe as in Japan and the United States, title catalogues are dominated by linear entertainment product. In other words, the video disc's survival seems to be based on its qualities as a high performance playback medium offering the best in sound and video combined. The competitive issue in the consumer market for digital media such as the new interactive CD multimedia platforms—and in particular, the forthcoming high density CD formats—is therefore not content and functionality but the fact that another demand is potentially being made on the all-too-limited consumer purse.

Old and non-digital as it is, video disc technology is — at the time of writing—still the only widely available platform available that can deliver high quality, full motion, full frame video complete with a range of trick frame features such as forward and backward variable speed motion and perfect freeze frames. As well as offering excellent interactive video potential in itself, it continues to provide a useful stored source of video imagery for use in real-time digital video systems using digitising interface adapters. While the future may well belong to thoroughbred digital systems, right now it is a question of satisfying today's needs with today's technology. Superior as the unified digital environments for multimedia may be, right now they simply cannot deliver high quality video in a form you can easily buy. New high density formats will be arriving in the market during 1997 but will initially be expensive. In addition, a potential format war is likely to confuse consumers until—like VHS video and Betamax—the market-place works out what it wants. The promise of high quality, feature length video in digital form is certainly there but, for the moment, if we want such video to use today in linear and interactive applications, we still have to compromise on the digital ideal. Of course, you will have to want interactive video quite badly because interactive video discs and their players are costly. So, as far as interactive applications are concerned, video disc still looks like an answer in search of a question that can afford it.

It is of course only a question of time. Video discs have a brief window of opportunity remaining before the digital video discs and interactive high density compact disc media cut the ground from beneath them. The analogue video disc is not yet quite dead but it is certainly dying. The future, therefore, is digital and that means the dominance-in various flavours—of compact disc technology.

Multimedia Entertainment in the Home

Games was, in principle, a simple category to exploit because it belonged to a pre-existing genre. CD-I's problem in this sector was simply that the technology had not been optimised for game play. Other hardware makers with a tight specialism in games-such as Sega and Sony-both espoused CD-ROM 'black box' technology by creating new multimedia machines designed to squeeze the maximum games-playing potential from the systems. The result has been specialist CD-ROM players such as Sega's Saturn and Sony's Playstation which combine immense computing power with CD technology at incredibly low prices. As a result, the technology hits the high volume mainstream of the video games market while CD-I struggles in the shallows as 'a machine on which games can be played' rather than competing as a dedicated games console that can really deliver the business.

In the area of movies, CD-I is on firm ground and indeed Philips have been instrumental in creating a new sub-category of the CD-ROM standard known as VideoCD which plays-among other platforms-on CD-I. VideoCD is merely a flavour of CD-ROM that sacrifices interactivity for an ability to replay linear, full screen, full motion movies. In other words, because it has limited interactive features, comparable to the kind offered by CD-audio-the ability to shuffle and programme the playback of 'tracks'-it does not need to dip down into the operating system of its host machine. This means that so long as the host has the appropriate means of handling the video data built into its electronics, it can play VideoCD titles. VideoCD is, therefore, the first true cross-platform, multimedia CD format.

There are two levels at which taking this direction presented special problems and special advantages for Philips. The problems were both technological and commercial. At a technological level, creating a CD-ROM video standard meant being able to compress-in a universally standard way-the huge amount of digital information needed to represent a complete video so that it could be stored on a disc. Second, it meant making it possible for CD-I players to decompress this information so that the reconstructed video could be played back on a TV screen in real time. This was a big task. As we saw, a single frame of full screen TV quality video needs almost a whole megabyte of digital information to represent it fully. And to deceive the eye into thinking it is watching 'full motion', that frame has to be refreshed 25 times a second in Europe or 30 times a second in the Unites Sates (because, although eyes are much the same, television standards are not). In other words, on a European basis, about 20 megabytes of data every second need to be processed, transferred and displayed by the multimedia player in order for the screen to produce a full screen, full motion video experience.

If the multimedia is being delivered from a CD-ROM, the problem is complicated still further. Aside from the raw storage issue — and 650 megabytes of CD-ROM is soon consumed by accompressed video information-there is an additional limitation in the underlying technology. CD-ROM is derived from its CD-audio forebear. CD-audio was optimised to give maximum linear play time rather than to allow interactivity and fast data transfer. This process of optimising the technology included a standard speed at which the disc was spun in the player. Because data on a CD can be read by the laser stylus only when the disc physically passes beneath the stylus, the speed at which the disc spins defines the rate at which the stylus can retrieve information from its surface. It turns out that for standard CD systems this rate of transfer is around 150 kilobytes per second. So, even if we stored 33 seconds of accompressed video on a CD-which is about the most we could achieve-we could not retrieve it anything like fast enough to deliver full motion because we would need to take data from the disc at many times is maximum rate. One solution, of course, is to spin the disc faster and-as the CD-ROM market has matured-double and quadruple speed CD-ROM drives have emerged. But at the time this issue was first being resolved the 'speed of light' for drives was firmly 150 kilobytes per second and the implications of this ultimate limitation had to be addressed.

CD Video

We have already discussed the process of compressing and decompressing digital video. But to save us making awkward cross-references to that earlier material we will reprise some of it in the particular context of CD media to see how such compression-decompression schemes are bringing video to the experience of multimedia CD-ROM.

The business of compressing data sufficiently to achieve at the least the storage part of the equation was well established and-by the early 1990s-already enshrined in an international technical standard called MPEG (Motion Picture Experts Group-the name of the original team that figured the standard out). Its first phase standard is actually called MPEG-1. Uprated and more extreme compression schemes based on the same underlying mathematics are also now established. Most importantly of these, MPEG-2 is now about ready to begin delivering the first high density CD-ROM media and to transform digital data and television broadcasting.

This, however, addresses one part of the problem. Compressed digital signals or data can be fitted into less bandwidth-in the case of transmitted media-or squeezed onto less CD-ROM real estate in the case of offline, packaged media. But once compressed, the user still has to decompress it in order to view the original, reconstructed information. In other words, finding an effective way of compressing the data is only half the battle.

If the means of compression, for example, requires users to have a Cray supercomputer to decompress the data, the scheme is plainly commercial nonsense. If it is to be useful, digital compression technology must also allow easy and cheap decompression by end users — otherwise it is like teaching a dog to dance on one leg: interesting, clever, but ultimately totally pointless.

As we implied earlier, MPEG compression is the real heavyweight contender among compression schemes, delivering excellent quality at an affordable encoding price. The level of performance it delivers, however, permits only 72 minutes of video per CD-ROM-so feature films have to be delivered in two or three disc sets-and the quality of playback is generally no better than VHS tape quality. However, it is an immediately available, 'good enough' solution. Its real drawback is less its overall performance than the grunt it requires of host computers in order to decompress the information it delivers. In practical terms, this means that to handle MPEG video, most of the desktop computers in use today need a power boost in the shape of a dedicated MPEG chip, designed to handle the decompression for the PC. The big advantage for the proprietary CD-ROM multimedia players-the so-called 'black boxes'-is that the chips needed to decompress MPEG video and other data can be included in the 'black box' itself-the razor can be sold with the razor blade. The hardware, after all, is dedicated to a particular purpose and it can generally be assumed that customers will want what is offered or else they would not buy it in the first place. In the case of CD-I, for example, VideoCD -which is designed around MPEG-1 compression-is an integral part of Philips' offering so building in an MPEG chipset and including it in the pricing of CD-I players makes obvious sense in terms of Philips' market proposition.

The situation, however, is completely different in the generic world of PC CD-ROM. Here different PC manufacturers provide a myriad of variations upon a hardware theme, each trying to make their computers distinctive at a competitive price for an increasingly discerning audience. Most fundamentally, of course, PCs from any manufacturer are, almost by definition, general purpose devices. In other words, in functional terms, they lie at the opposite end of the spectrum from dedicated devices such as CD-I players and games consoles. PCs offer a range of possible functions driven by the wide range of applications software that can be run on them. It may well be that increasing numbers of PCs have more or less standardised multimedia capabilities built into them but we are a long way, for example, from being able to assume that PC users will routinely want to play VideoCD or, more generally, to access full screen, full motion video as a feature of interactive CD-ROM titles. This means something very simple in commercial terms. If people do not want it routinely, they should not routinely be made to pay for it as a part of the price of their hardware. It makes better sense to give purchasers the option of buying the PC without MPEG video chips inside and acquiring those chips as an upgrade if it turns out to be something they do want in future. Out of this simple idea has grown a massive spin-off business from the PC industry, solely concerned with creating and marketing upgrade kits, to deliver not only MPEG decompression but also a wide range of bolt-on functionalities for PCs.

For a combination of reasons, MPEG cards for PCs have not yet sold strongly although they are now widely available from a range of suppliers both in the United States and Europe. We are, of course, moving towards the time when MPEG will be cheap enough and compact enough to be included within PCs at very little additional cost. In much the same way as PCs are routinely being sold with built-in CD-ROM drives, therefore, we will soon find them coming equipped with MPEG video chips whether we are interested in video or not. Meantime, however, multimedia CD-ROM publishers have to address as wide a market as possible and cannot rely on customers having the necessary MPEG chips in their machines or being willing to make a special purchase and go through all the anguish of installing such chips, merely to view their latest CD-ROM title. In other words, publishers have to find a generic means of delivering video if they wish to include it at all. The most widely used solution is to dispense with MPEG schemes-which continue (largely and currently) to demand the decompression power of additional chipsets-and decompress the stream of digital video data using instead a much weaker system based not on special hardware but on a proprietary computer program designed specially for the purpose.

Meanwhile, VideoCD is now one of the main drivers of market demand for CD-I and deals by Philips acquiring VideoCD rights from major Hollywood studios have ensured a steady flow of high profile titles. Elsewhere independent publishers-particularly in Europe and Japan-have other turned their own video assets into VideoCD titles or acquired rights to enable them to issue VideoCDs based on other people's assets. The great attraction has been the low cost of encoding the video and, therefore, the commercial ease of transferring content from tape to disc, and the lure of a cross-platform format. The fact that the cross-platform nature of VideoCD has so far been a more theoretical than practical benefit has done little to stem the enthusiasm of the proponents of VideoCD and hundreds of titles are now available with many more in preparation.

The Digital Video Disc

The enthusiasm for VideoCD, based as it is upon the original MPEG-1 standard, has been noticeably muted in the United States. While Europe and Japan embraced the standard as a 'here and now, good enough' solution, US hardware and software companies stood back, questioning whether a system based on MPEG-1 really offered the added values needed to create a CD-based video standard that could compete with the utility and installed base of conventional videotape. While VideoCD was plainly a 'here and now' technology-at least, so far as CD-I was concerned -was it 'good enough' to make a substantial market breakthrough? For US companies, therefore, the issue was whether MPEG-1 was really the right horse to back. Perhaps being geographically close to the home of the movie industry affected their thinking because it was certainly true that Hollywood regarded MPEG-1 as far from being the Nirvana of a replacement for videotape. As far as the studios were concerned, VideoCD rights were a useful source of additional income-particularly at the prices Philips has been prepared to pay-so long as the deals were for movies which had already been fully exploited in conventional video formats. In other words, with a few exceptions, the majors were prepared to play along with VideoCD so long as it carried no threat to its mainstream revenue sources-box office, video and TV.

But was there any alternative to VideoCD on the horizon? Was there even the prospect of another horse to back? Certainly, when Philips launched VideoCD in 1994, it resolutely faced down suggestions from the industry that MPEG-1 systems were merely using an interim technology. It backed VideoCD to the hilt because VideoCD was the short-term saviour of CD-I and needed to be promoted strongly as a consumer product for the long term. In reality, however, Philips, together with its CD-I partners, Sony, was already developing the real video format for the long term and, as expected, it was based on a combination of MPEG-2 decompression combined with a revised form of CD-ROM technology offering vastly greater storage capacity than the existing generation of CD-ROM systems.

Late in 1994, Philips and Sony found their hand forced by an unexpected move by an alliance of hardware and software companies led by Toshiba. Toshiba announced it was going to establish its own variety of high density CD-ROM standard, apparently ahead of the system being worked on by Philips and Sony. Toshiba's concept appeared to be similar to the Philips/ Sony format. It also used a double layer of recording media on the disc with a clever technology with a variable focus laser enabling the laser stylus to read both layers independently. However, it differed in suggesting that the discs should be double sided. Nobuyuki Idei, Sony Corporation's managing director, immediately issued a statement reaffirming Sony's commitment to the single-sided, double-layer, high density specification and saying that 'after careful evaluation and consideration with Philips, Sony has no plans to support the specifications proposed by an alliance of seven companies'. The gang of seven that Idei referred to was led and masterminded by Toshiba but included some powerful allies such as one-time CD-I ally Matsushita, media giant Time Warner, Hitachi, Pioneer, MCA and Thomson.

Idei's statement was effectively a declaration of a format war despite the fact that there were strong similarities between the two. Both were based on MPEG-2 encoding and relied on variable rues of transferring data from the disc to the player in order to optimise the length and quality of playback. Both were also based on offering double play options. In other words, the standard playback for both formats is about 140 minutes -sufficient for most feature movies-but a 'double up' option is available to create 280 minutes of playback. One of the major differences between the two systems was how they each offered this. In the case of Sony and Philips approach, a second information layer was to be bonded to and located above the initial, standard layer. Toshiba's strategy is also to use two information layers but to bond them back-to-back to create a double-sided system.

Sony's rejection was ostensibly based on its view of the comparative quality and manufacturing costs of the two formats. Sony (and by implication, Philips) claimed that its single-sided approach combined high quality playback (comparable with video disc) with ease and, therefore, economy of manufacture. It pointed out that the new format will need only minor modification to existing CD manufacturing equipment and that players will require only a single laser pickup to read both conventional and high density CD media. This last point was crucial because it explicitly indicated that the Sony/Philips standard would mean that players can be made backwardly compatible with existing CD-ROM and VideoCD titles. Sony had certainly hitched their argument to the key issue. Despite Toshiba's strong backing, its double-sided approach suggested that mastering and pressing plants would have to re-tool with special lathes and replicators to handle the new discs. Players too were unlikely to be cheap. The actual price depended on the engineering approach but unless users were going to flip double-sided discs over themselves, players would need two optical pickups. Leaving aside the complexity of just making this work, MPEG-2 players with double optics were unlikely to be a consumer priced item in the foreseeable future despite Toshiba's bold claims about $500 price points by 1996.

What did all this mean for VideoCD-the existing linear video standard-and for the real future of high density linear and interactive CD-ROM developments? It is important to appreciate two important sub-texts to the public posturing by both camps.

The first derives directly from Hollywood. The major studios-hugely influential as the source of a rich flow of high value content-were taking a big interest in the future of digital video. As we noted, earlier, apart from some careful deal-making over VideoCD rights, Hollywood was still waiting for a replacement for its cash cow, videotape, that would offer some distinctive added values. As far as it was concerned, VideoCD, with all the limitations of MPEG, was not it. Hollywood did not like the quality and it liked even less the maximum 72 minutes playing time which meant movies had to be delivered on multidisc sets. In fact, Hollywood had a very clear shopping list of features it was looking for in any new system. Discs must have enough play time to carry a complete feature film. This meant enough capacity to store at least 140 minutes of video, preferably much more. The playback quality had to be far superior to VHS. Ideally it should be comparable to the broadcast quality and stereo sound offered by analogue videodiscs and should also allow multiple soundtracks for dubbing purposes. The hardware and software would need to be parent friendly so a lock to provide unauthorised playback by children was essential. And, finally, the system must embody a foolproof anti-piracy device.

This was Hollywood's ideal shopping list-or, at least, the main items from it-and whether or not it could possibly get all that it wanted was less important than the power and strength of its lobby. By taking a public and prescriptive stand, the movie industry was effectively shaping the future of high density CD-ROM formats as a medium to play back movies. Not surprisingly, therefore, the format soon stopped being called high or super density and took on the generic title DVD, standing for digital video disc. This implied that interactivity was consigned firmly to the back seat. The use of high density for video-rich interactive applications in education, information and entertainment was purely secondary to creating a medium for playing back linear movies.

The second sub-text concerned control of patents. Seen from outside the scrum, the obdurate positions of Toshiba and its allies on the one hand, and Philips and Sony on the other, looked like an exercise of crass obstinacy. After all, a format war would benefit no one and the difference between the two technological solutions was really not great. Despite the high-minded talk about which system was 'superior' the real issue behind the spat was hardly discussed. The war was not a phoney one despite the fineness of the differences between the two sides. And neither was it a war-as it appeared to be — about formats. The real struggle was for the control of patents. Philips and Sony together were the creators of contact disc technology. As its creators, they also became proprietors of a number of key underlying patents which-translated into manufacturing licences- generate for both corporations huge sums in royalties from hardware manufacturers and disc replicators. For every CD audio or CD-ROM device made and for every disc pressed, Philips and Sony receive a payback. The development of ever more pervasive CD-based standards, therefore, was much more than a way of growing the opportunities for Philips and Sony to sell more of its own products. It was a way of selling more of everybody else's products too and so sustain and build their royalty cash flows. The battle by Toshiba to establish a new high density standard, therefore, was more than a threat to take a lead in the manufacture of its own VideoCD products. It was a threat to Philips' and Sony's continuing control of underlying patents and to the revenues that such parents guarantee.

In the middle of a long hot August 1995, in Europe, Philips finally came up with a compromise aimed at defusing the conflict and avoiding a costly and pointless battle in the market-place. At the rime of writing, it is still too early to determine who has won and lost in this battle for control of the next major stage in CD-ROM evolution but it appears there has been give and take on both sides. The differences between the Toshiba-led Super Density Alliance and the Philips-Sony initiative had been getting more subtle as the months had passed but the final resolution appears to lean more towards Toshiba than Philips. A double-layer disc technology is going to be used-as first proposed by Toshiba-but both layers will be read from one side, as suggested by Philips and Sony. The outcome is a two-pronged standard offering backward compatibility with existing conventional density formats. There will be a single-sided, single-layer disc format providing a storage capacity of 4.7 gigabytes (a gigabyte is a thousand megabytes and the high density figure compares with 0.6 gigabytes currently offered by standard CD-ROMs). Using MPEG-2 compression, this will make it possible to accommodate all but the very longest feature movies on a single disc at a quality comparable to today's videodiscs. There will also be an ultra high density format using double-layering to give 8.5 gigabytes of storage. This is likely to be used for major, video-rich interactive applications. The first titles conforming to the new standards will be released with the first tranche of DVD players late in 196 or early in 1997. There are as yet no public plans for interactive tides using the high density formats and few expect them to emerge until late 1997 at the earliest.

Even if the technological issues appear to have been resolved, however, a continuing source of concern for Philips and Sony is whether it can continue to claim ownership of underlying CD standards. In other words, even if the format war is over, the patent war may only just be beginning.

Developments in Distribution Channels

To gain an impression of how much further retail support still has to go before a really effective infrastructure is available, we only have to look at the estimated penetration of multimedia in the key retail sectors. Late in 1994, Richard Bowers, the Executive Director of the US Optical Publishers Association, published results of a study carried out in the previous summer. He found that the real focus of retail distribution remained in the specialist software Stores. Out of 5,300 such stores in the United States about 4,500 were stocking multimedia CD-ROM titles. This is a penetration of 85 per cent. Elsewhere the picture, though fast evolving, was more patchy. Out of 16,500 computer and consumer electronic stores, for example, 2,000 (12.2 per cent) were stocking CD-ROM titles. Bookstores were beginning to emerge as a new and important sector. Out of 11,000 nationwide, around 500 (4.5 per cent) had made a commitment to CD-ROM but many others were planning to enter the market before Christmas. Bowers believed that bookstores would be the biggest single growth sector of 1995. Video stores were also expected to rapidly expand their involvement in multimedia, with Blockbuster leading the way with its formidable 4,000 store network. In the area of department stores, the plans of the major chains are crucial. In 1994, Bowers found, fewer than 500 such stores out of over 10,000 were stocking CD-ROMs. The turnaround in this sector-when it occurs-will have a huge impact because of the high volumes that such chains can achieve deploying their very high profile shelf space.

Even the anticipated growth in book and video retailers and department store chains stocking titles-a process which is taking much longer to develop than Bowers had thought in 1994-is unlikely to bring much immediate relief to the immense congestion in US distribution channels. Indeed, whatever relief does emerge may come too late for many developers depending on cash flow from sales of titles they have joint ventured with larger content companies. Flush with recent injections of venture capital from bankers and financiers with a simplistic and rosy-eyed view of the growth of the consumer market, these small outfits have been at the forefront of the surge in new titles. They are now becoming the first to feel the backlash of the distribution crisis. The fully featured, big budget titles they have created need to find high volume outlets to recoup their investments on any reasonable timescale and, despite the significance of direct selling and bundling, serious volume can best be achieved through high street exposure.

The problems in getting shelf space most obviously hit small players with small lists or even just a single tide to their name. But the majors are also feeling the pressure. Microsoft, for example, with all its power in the market-place and a large number of titles available in its Home brand series, is finding that it can gain consistent retail distribution only for a handful of its perennial bestsellers. Elsewhere, affiliate label programmes are also under pressure with organisations like Comptons New Media, Time Warner Interactive and Mindscape all having real difficulty in getting the full range of the titles in their care into the market. A serious commercial squeeze is being made even more dangerous by a rampant drive to cut street prices-at least, in the US market. In 1995, Microsoft, for example, slashed US prices of all its titles by an average of around 30 per cent. Publishers of mainstream encyclopedias such as Grolier, Comptons and Microsoft have seen their prices slip from around $200 in 1994 to under $50 by late 1995. Elsewhere, specialist publishers such as Softkey have established new ground with budget and infotainment titles, priced at under $20. The intent behind the downward spiral in pricing is clear. The hunt is on for shelf space and with it the ultra-high volumes of sale that will compensate for the crumbling price points. But results so far suggest that drastic price cutting is demolishing fragile margins rather than delivering the broadly based competitive advantage being sought. Falling prices may look good for consumers but, through their savage impact on margins, are threatening to destroy the underlying publishing industry. Price cutting alone, of course, is not the key issue. The real problem is price cutting products that have to fight their way through a pressurised value chain where distributors, sub-distributors and retailers all expect to take deep discounts out of the revenue stream. The price wars being fought in the United States have not yet fully impacted on the less well developed European market. But they will. Imported products from the States are already falling in price and while exporters will try to price to the higher levels acceptable to Europeans, the downward slide is inevitable. Where the imported products go, indigenous products must surely follow.

CD-ROM's End Game

Increasingly, the multimedia CD-ROM industry is suffering serious commercial pain and some battered developers and publishers are beginning to question the unquestionable. Despite all the hype and hope of recent years, does consumer CD-ROM publishing have a long-term future? It has been an unquestioned article of faith in the CD media industry that the consumer market needs only an installed base of technology before it lifts off in spectacular fashion to create a rich, diverse and profitable title publishing market. But this idea emerged in those halcyon days when surfing was a watersport, nets were used for fishing and getting wired was a problem your electrician sorted out. Today's electronic media market is dramatically different. Instead of a landscape dominated by familiar, offline packaged media like CD-ROM, we now have complex play-offs between offline and online media and a burgeoning market for selling new forms of content and services over global networks. Even offline's much lauded ability to handle high quality interactive multimedia is looking increasingly unconvincing as a unique proposition as even narrowband networks — the kind that rely on nothing more space age than a telephone line — become capable of delivering 'good enough' multimedia to an expanding population of wired consumers.

Meantime, out on the battlefields, blood is being shed in pursuit of the original dream. The developers, publishers and distributors of multimedia are struggling up and down the value chain to bring an ever larger volume of CD-ROM tides to a growing number of users with CD-ROM drives attached to or built into their PCs. But as we have already noted, possession of the hardware, however, does not necessarily imply its use. This is a key idea which should be engraved on the hearts of everyone trying to commercialise this market. Most vividly, in Europe-where hardware bases are rising exponentially-title sales remain patchy and generally unexciting. In the United States-where hardware figures are equally spectacular -sales volumes are coming but only in a sharply polarised fashion. About 10 per cent of the titles are generating 80 per cent of the revenues and the vast majority are unprofitable for everyone except the retailers. Which 10 per cent is making the running? Inevitably, that small proportion of the available titles able to gain some scarce and expensive shelf space at retail. In other words, gridlock in US distribution channels is making those consumers that want CD-ROM see only the tip of a publishing iceberg. Multimedia CD-ROM is increasingly expressing itself as a hit-driven business with little range in its offerings. While this obviously appeals to some consumers-after all, someone is buying nearly $2 billion worth of discs-it certainly lacks the depth of appeal needed to stir a deeply rooted, long-term publishing market.

Failures and difficulties of some leading developers-Amazing Media and Mammoth Microproductions in the United States and Attica and MDI in the UK-are early signs of growing commercial pressure in the value chain. It is most visible among the originators of multimedia titles because this community consists mainly of small, financially fragile organisations. But, be sure, the pain is already spreading up the chain and we will see once-committed, enthusiastic publishers soon retrenching and looking elsewhere for more stable and profitable sources of electronic publishing revenues.

This does not mean that the consumer CD-ROM market is on the brink of failure. Far from it. But it tells us that the market will not be the one we have long expected. Instead, it will resolve itself into a fast and furious hit-driven environment majoring on games and mainstream entertainment-including, within two to three years, a strong market for largely linear digital video disc (DVD) offerings, including a wide range of the world's most popular feature films and music videos. Reference and information will play a part but success will be limited to a few major tides which will dominate the market. For those still wanting to play in this business, therefore, the only available strategy is to cultivate niches and colonise them as quickly as possible before competitors move in and take the same, limited turf. A key area in which niches abound is education and focused, special interest publishing. So the message for the consumer market is not that it is doomed but that our original vision of it was naive and misplaced. To make money and prosper in the hard reality of the market-place we need either to make some big throws of the dice or take a more cunning view of the opportunities and become a shrewd, niche player.

Meantime, of course, a new form of publishing is emerging which increasingly merges offline and online media. We will examine online media in detail in following chapters but-even if it means readers looking ahead to clarify some of the terminology and concepts-it is worth mentioning right away the prospect of a powerful merger between offline and online publishing. As an infrastructure of network services unfolds, the possibility of embedding links to online sites within CD-ROM products looks increasingly plausible. The move to hybridise CD-ROMs in this way is already gathering pace rapidly in both the United States-where it is already an established publishing model-and, more slowly, in Europe, where a lack of consumer online services has so far held back commercial development.

The process of hybridising CD-ROMs offers major benefits for both publishers and customers. For customers, online links can enrich a CD-ROM title by providing access to additional information or even whole new tranches of product. A game-such as the bestselling *Myst*-can be sold as a fixed offline product and then updated over a network by downloading new chapters of the game to be stored on the user's hard disk and played using the software on-board the CD-ROM. Updates can also take the form of access to highly volatile information. Microsoft's 'Complete Baseball' -probably the first consumer hybrid-was aimed to provide a multimedia experience of baseball on the CD-ROM and access to latest sports results and news via a daily online link. Microsoft's latest audio counterpart of the bestselling *Cinemania,* a title called *Music Central,* allows you to go online and order the music titles you sample in the CD-ROM. New dimensions are also being added to information and reference products. Grolier Interactive's 1996 edition of its evergreen *Multimedia Encyclopedia* now contains hundreds of links to sites on the CompuServe network where its users can gain additional, related information or participate in forum discussions with other users with similar interests, exploring the same product.

The idea of communications of this kind is a powerful one-particularly since using a CD-ROM has traditionally been an inherently isolated (and, possibly, isolating) experience. Clearly, communication between publisher and customer via the hybrid links is a crucial means of building a relationship with the customer which can later be commercialised with new product and service offerings. But the same process of communication can just as easily take place amongst the users of the hybrid links themselves. In other words, hybrid CD-ROMs make it possible for publishers to build and manage communities of interest centred on their offline products but flourishing in the online environments. Such communities not only sustain but also spread interest in the offline product, strengthening sales potential, extending shelf life and enhancing the prospect of sequel or related new products. Despite the rhetoric of some commentators, hybridising CD-ROMs is not a sign of the predicted decline of CD-ROM media in favour of online products and services, a kind of halfway house en route to an entirely wired future. Much more important than that-it is a good, common-sense publishing model that works if applied with careful regard to its inherent technical and creative challenges and can be deployed to maximise profit and commercial advantage in a tough market-place which will do nothing but get tougher.

But the CD-ROM market is a coat of many colours and while the consumer market-in spite of all its difficulties-hogs the industry headline, the less glamorous but also less tormented professional, corporate and academic market sectors continue to grow and to offer serious publishing opportunities. An obvious reason why these sectors are more readily commercialised is that they do not lean so heavily on such an inefficient distribution infrastructure as retail. Instead, they rely largely on well-established direct marketing and direct selling models which publishers can more or less transfer from their traditional business experience. From a content development point of view, the markets are grounded, refreshingly, in defined and definable customer needs which can be turned by the publisher into the distinct added value features which ultimately sell the products. If such products fail to sell, it is more than bad luck or the injustice of an immature distribution system. It is bad publishing.

However, even in these well-established sectors, the outlook is troubled. Although the causes may be different, the low volume, high price market may be in as much long-term trouble as the high volume, low price one. Corporate, professional and academic information users are increasingly drifting towards the use of the new generation of low cost networks where range of choice, keen pricing and new product features are making online information sources more attractive than ever before. Long before an online consumer market is generating significant global revenues, professional, business-to-business and intra-business markets will have migrated online-not into the vastly expensive and unfriendly clutches of the online database industry of yesterday but to a welcoming, cost effective and increasingly Internet-based environment. Good news for users but bad for those publishers wedded to a future of CD-ROM publishing.

All of which demonstrates how important it has become not to define our businesses in terms of how we deliver our products but for what purpose we make them.

We now need to return to the simplification we introduced at the start or chapter 3. We pretended that the world of digital media was neatly divided into packaged media products-essentially bits embodied in atoms-and transmitted media products which are purely bits from the moment they are created to the moment they are delivered to their users. We have seen in the past few pages that this kind of simple division is a artificial way of structuring digital media sectors and the reality is that packaged and transmitted media are beginning to merge rich, hybrid publishing and distribution opportunities and a fundamentally new kind of experience for the users. However, we can as a matter of convenience and practical reality, maintain the fiction because while hybridisation is becoming increasingly important, most digital media developments still fall into one camp or the other. Our initial simplification, however, may soon get simpler. As we turn to consider transmitted media and the rise of the networks, we may well be studying the ultimate nemesis of CD-ROM media with hybrids merely a step on the road towards extinction. While we need to make the argument more fully, there is a strong case for believing that-except in niche applications such as digital video discs-the future of digital media is exclusively a wired one.

The notion of 'getting wired' is gaining common currency. One of the world's most successful new media magazines-admittedly one heavy with attitude and posturing-is actually called *Wired.* The metaphor suggests somehow gaining a physical cabled or wired connection to something -presumably a flow of information, entertainment and education. Leaving aside the issue of whether such physical connections are really needed, the underlying idea is important because it embodies an implicit reference to a term that has become one of the most widely used cliches of the media — 'the information superhighway'. The popular working understanding of the term is that it describes a vast, directed flux of digital information and communication carried amongst and to users in homes, universities, institutions and offices throughout the world, consisting of the richest imaginable synthesis of text, sound, images-including do. Accordingly everyone stampeded towards what looked at the outset like a golden opportunity, a licence to print money.

The reality has been quite different and while commentators like Negro-ponte may argue that the hype does not even begin to express the true magnitude of the impact of the Web, there is a serious issue of timescale to address. The pace of recent developments has been so rapid that it is tempting to think that the Web in particular and the Internet in general will soon become a mature environment for doing business. But the truth is that we are still in the first day of school. We not only have to master and improve the technologies underpinning the Internet to make it into a friendly, secure and pervasive environment but also need to build effective, new business models to create stable businesses that will prosper and flourish long term.

In previous chapter we looked at the rise of proprietary consumer networks-a phenomenon driven by the rapid computerisation of US and European homes and the emergence of the Internet as a mainstream online environment. In this chapter, we will focus on the single most important subset of the Internet for commercial activity-the World Wide Web. We will examine in particular the main basis for commercialising the Web and the key means of generating revenue from Web sites. Through examining its commercialisation, we will also be able to make sense of its devastating impact on the traditional business model of proprietary networks.

Selling Advertising

Perhaps as obvious as the idea of selling content is the prospect of selling advertising. Currently the most widely emphasised approach to revenue generation, the sale of advertising on a Web site is based fundamentally on that site's guaranteed ability to deliver eyeballs to the merchants taking the advertising space. In other words, a site's ability to attract advertisers and maintain a highly priced rate card is directly proportional to the size and focus of the constituency of users. Both factors-size and focus-are crucial. A large but demographically unfocused constituency may be desirable but a smaller but more focused one might be more so. In other words, size is not everything. If a site becomes the definitive stopping-off place for the world's fly fishermen, for example, the raw size of the constituency is less important than the fact that potential advertisers have a clear idea of main interests of the individuals making it up. Plainly such a site represents a golden opportunity for certain kinds of advertisers while others can avoid wasting their money.

Clearly, this argument holds good for both Web sites and proprietary online services. Most proprietary majors, however, have large unfocused constituencies with the important proviso that large means very large indeed. At the time of writing, for example, CompuServe has about 3.5 million subscribers worldwide while AOL counts over 4 million. These are big constituencies even if they represent a very mixed bag of individuals. On sheer size alone, they are potentially attractive to advertisers. However, proprietaries by their nature offer a wide variety of offerings to their subscribers and advertisers can therefore get the opportunity to lodge in areas of the service which attract demographically focused sub-sets of the overall constituency and so meet their need to spend their money addressing not just eyeballs but the right eyeballs.

Estimates vary wildly about how much advertising is currently taking place online. The US analysts Forrester Research believe that only about $10 million was spent in 1995 but that the scale of advertising will rapidly escalate over the next few years reaching a total spend of $2.2 billion by the year 2000. The reality of 1995 was probably closer to a spend of $60 million but whatever the exact figure, most analysts agree that the number is small. The steep escalation in revenue is based on three major factors coming into play over the years leading to the millennium. First, the emergence of effective ways to audit the effect of advertising on the Web. Software solutions are already emerging to address this issue. Second, a growing confidence and understanding by advertisers of how to utilise the interactive medium and leverage, in particular, its potential one-to-oneness. And third, the rise of standardised and trusted mechanisms to allow secure payments to be made over Internet connections.

Whatever the future may hold, it seems clear that substantial advertising revenues are being generated by only a relatively few high profile sites. In the course of 1995, for example, the HotWired site announced it was cash positive on the basis of its steadily growing income from advertising. Other sites such as Web directories and search engines-Yahoo, Lycos and others home pages, such as Netscape's, and highly popular content offerings, such as Sportszone, are all generating serious income. Elsewhere, advertising and advertising rate cards are more patchy. One thing is clear, however. All site owners with a consumer emphasis are chasing advertising as the key revenue source for their Web operations.

As we noted above, advertisers are undoubtedly at a disadvantage right now and the position will change only slowly. The key gap in the Web offering, as far as they are concerned, is auditing mechanisms for Web sites. Not only are advertisers seeking the right constituencies to address, they want to know which individuals in those constituencies have accessed their adverts and with what effect. In other words, advertisers seek some plausible way of measuring Web activity to tell them whether they are spending their (or their client's) advertising dollars effectively. Proprietary networks can deliver this because users accessing their services are individually identifiable and their actions online can be tracked step by step of the way. By contrast, the position for Web sites is more difficult. The technology of the Web makes it hard for site proprietors or advertisers to identify visitors unless they are required to register themselves beforehand. This is accordingly a widely used technique. Registration processes and passwords, even when no charge is being made for site access, however, are time consuming and tedious and are hardly an encouragement to new users or old ones who have (inevitably) forgotten their password. Even if sites can identify visitors, tracking what they do while connected to the site is a complex process and software-such as I/Pro or NetCount-is only now emerging capable of delivering useful data beyond the usual counting of so-called 'hits' which is no more than adding up the number of hypertext links on pages accessed by users while visiting a site. Other software designed to analyse increasingly more sophisticated usage data is also becoming available and packages such as Inverse's Market Focus and Open Market's WebReporter are becoming popular to save the laborious efforts of manual analysis.

There is still much progress to be made in this area of site exploitation and imminent developments will make a vast difference to the viability of sites, particularly because of the appeal that fully analysed tracking data have for advertisers. However, while server side usage and auditing software has a crucial role to play, client software is also going to contribute enormously to the personalising of site responses to incoming browsers. Netscape's browser for example now embodies a software system known as 'persistent client state HTTP cookies'. The cookies exist in the browser in order to allow site owners to tie together the various requests that a browser makes during a visit to the site. So, instead of seeing client activity as a flow of seemingly unrelated hits, site owners can see a client visit as a contiguous session and thereby analyse usage data far more powerfully. Cookies in Netscape browsers are identifiers which maintain and store information about a visitor's use of the site during the course of a single visit. The same cookies can contain information about the kind of browser, where it has been before it visited the site and, potentially, demographic data about the browser's user. In other words, if the cookie concept is more fully developed, it could effectively add to browsers a personalised identity card enabling sites to respond in a much more targeted way to visitors than they can at present.

An example of how this principle is already being used comes from the San Francisco based online specialist, C/Net. Using its own bespoke software, C/Net offers the opportunity to advertisers to tune their propositions differently for different site visitors. By using a mix of analysis of the incoming browser header information-which indicates the domain name and software identity of incoming browsers-and of registration data stored at the server based on personal information volunteered by visitors, C/Net can automatically provide basic demographic data to advertisers who can then deliver messages with emphases appropriate to the individuals accessing their advertising. For example, a computer supplier can ensure that the advert a Mac user sees does not try to sell PC products. Another advertiser might emphasise a corporate role in school resources for incoming browsers with 'edu' domain names and vary the offering to stress strengths in working with public sector organisations if the domain is 'gov.' Registration data could help a car manufacturer target older visitors with messages stressing safety and reliability while younger visitors receive a variant which focuses on a car's performance and design qualities. This approach to individualising site response is still in its infancy but is a crucially important future direction. Leveraging its potential, intense one-to-oneness lies at the heart of the successful commercialisation of the Web and the future of the entire online industry hangs upon it.

While the path of future direction is clear, the present reality is that for Web sites, counting hits is the best that can be offered. Understandably, therefore, advertisers are currently cautious or undecided about the of their move online. The potential benefits seem clear-access to global audiences or demographically defined cuts thereof and the possibility forging powerful, one-to-one relationships with individuals- –but the being asked plays badly against the current lack of measurable feedback. Advertisers simply do not have the reassurance they need yet that dollar they spend online is best spent online. But advertisers face an more challenging issue which many are only slowly beginning to appreciate. The nature of advertising online is fundamentally different from processes of advertising in the traditional media world. The techniques work on television or in print do not necessarily transfer to online environments and advertisers—together with all the content players of the media industry—have to be prepared to re-engineer their skills and commercial understandings in order to make their businesses work. Most importantly, interactive advertising is a one-to-one experience so far as the is concerned. Accessing an advert is a deliberate act by an individual and if the person has been persuaded to access it, the advert needs to deliver some real benefit. Punchy appeals for attention, or loud single-idea strap lines to sell a brand message, do not work online.

To be effective, advertising has to adapt to the new medium and that means close targeting of the audience, the use of communications to create two-way relationships with the audience and an increasing and deliberate blurring of the distinction between advertising and content. Such a blurring causes immediate concerns among regulators who are rightly dedicated to ensuring people know what is an advert and what is objective content without an advertising axe to grind. But it is possible to see the process as a benign means of supporting central content offerings with advertising content—information that is contextualised with the content to which it is related and which adds value to it. Additionally, the advertising must be genuinely interactive. It is not good enough to re-purpose advertising from the real world. Online must have what online needs and what online needs is the same for content sites as it is for advertising. So, whether a content site hosts an advertiser's offering or points from a button on the site to the advertiser's own site, it is vital that the content owner does more than sell space and walk away from the transaction. It is essential for site owners to develop a close, creative understanding with its advertisers so that the two communities can work together to create advertising that supports content and content that supports advertising. A meeting of minds is needed and every effort should be expended to achieve it. Interactive advertising in general and online advertising in particular will never work without it.

Content in the Digital World

We have used the rather crude and ruffianly term 'content' throughout this book, so reducing the subtleties and richness of our literary, artistic and musical heritage to something that sounds uncomfortably like a commodity. It is well to emphasise, therefore, that content is a jargon term like any other but in this case intended to carry with it all the infinite shades of possibility that lie in the media resources which fuel education, information and entertainment in our daily lives. Even in the digital age, content is not-nor ever will be-a commodity. Value, however, will be added to the experience of content in myriad ways and, if anything, our already rich media heritage should become richer still thanks to the scope and power of digital technologies.

There is a catchy, much used phrase which gives us a starting point. It tells us that 'content is king'. In other words, however many new platforms and channels of delivery emerge and whatever the technological complexities underpinning them, the information highways and byways will be silent and empty without content to suffuse them and bring them to life. More than most gross over-simplifications, this one is dangerous. And it is dangerous because it contains an important grain of truth. It is evident and demonstrable that information delivery is meaningless without information to be delivered; that vehicles for education and entertainment will go nowhere without the content that educates and entertains. It is rather like admitting that 'I think, therefore I am' is really just another way of saying 'I think, therefore something must exist which does the thinking'. So in a very rudimentary sense content is surely king, because without it the media industry, and the increasingly digital infrastructure surrounding it, would simply have no substance. But clearly, the 'content is king' sentiment goes much further than games of logic. It contains a note of smug triumphalism.

REFERENCES

A. Spoerri, Visual Tools for Information Retrieval, in *Proc. IEEE Symp. on Visual Languages*, IEEE CS Press, Los Alamitos, Calif., 1993, pp. 160-168.

A. Veerasamy and S. Navathe. Querying, navigating and visualizing a digital library catalog. In *Proceedings of the Second International Conference on the Theory and Practice of Digital Libraries*, 1995. 16

A. Veerasamy, S. Navathe, and S. Hudson. Visual interface for textual information retrieval systems. In *Proceedings of the Third Conference on Visual Database Systems*. IFIP 2.6, 1995.

Ahlberg, C., Williamson, C., and Shneiderman, B., Dynamic queries for information exploration: An implementation and evaluation, *Proc. ACM CHI92: Human Factors in Computing Systems*, (1992), 619- 626.

Andreas Dieberger. Providing spatial navigation for the world wide web. *Proceedings of COSIT 95 (Conference on Spatial Information Theory)*, pp. 93-106, 1995.

Andrews, K. Visualizing Cyberspace: Information Visualization in the Harmony Internet Browser, *InfoVis'95*, IEEE Press, Atlanta, 1995, pp. 97-104.

Anselm Spoerri. (1993) InfoCrystal: A visual tool for information retrieval & management. In *Proceedings of Information Knowledge and Management '93* , Washington, D.C., Nov 1993.

Asahi, T., Turo, D., and Shneiderman, B., Using treemaps to visualize the analytic hierarchy process, *Information Systems Research* **6**, 4 (December 1995), 357-375.

B. Bederson. Pad++: Advances in Multiscale Interfaces, in *CHI 94*, Conf. Companion, ACM Press, New York, 1994, p. 315.

Bartram, L., Ovans, R., Dill, J. and Havens, W. (1994) Intelligent graphical user interfaces for time-critical systems. In *Proceedings of Graphics Interface*, Banff, May.

Beard, D. V. and Walker, J. Q. (1990) Navigational techniques to improve the display of large two-dimensional spaces. *Behaviour and Information Technology*, **9**(6), pp. 451-466.

Bederson, B.B. Pad++: A Zooming Graphical Interface for Exploring Alternative Interface Physics, *Proc. UIST'94*, ACM Press, Marina del Rey, CA, 1994, pp. 17-26.

Bederson, Benjamin and Hollan, James. Pad++: A Zooming Graphical Interface for Exploring Alternate Interface Physics. *Proc. of UIST 1994*, ACM, New York.

Ben Shneiderman, Tree Visualization with Tree-Maps: 2-d Space-Filling Approach, *ACM Transactions on Graphics*, Vol. 11, No. 1, Jan 1992, 92-99.

Berge, C. (1973) *Graphs and Hypergraphs*, North-Holland, Amsterdam.

Bier, E. Snap-dragging in three dimensions. In *Proceedings of the 1990 Symposium on Interactive 3D Graphics*, pp. 193-204.

Bishop G., Fuchs, H., et al. Research directions in virtual environments: report of an NSF invitational workshop, March 23-24, 1992. In *Computer Graphics*, 26(3), pp. 153-177.

Bolt, R. A. 1984. *The Human Interface*. Lifetime Learning Publications, Belmont, Calif.

Boyle J., Eick S., Hemmje M., Keim D. A., Lee J. P., Sumner E.: Database Issues for Data Visualization: Interaction, User Interfaces, and Presentation , in: *Database Issues in Data Visualization*, Springer, 1994, pp. 210-229.

Brian Johnson, TreeViz: Treemap Visualization of Hierarchically Structured Information, *Proc. ACM CHI'92*, 369-370.

Brown, E. and Chignell, M. H. Learning by Linking: Pedagogical Environments for Hypermedia Authoring. (1993) *Journal of Computing in Higher Education*, 1993, 5(1), 27-50.

C. Ahlberg and E. Wistrand, IVEE: An Information Visualization and Exploration Environment, *Proc. Info. Vis. Symp. 95*, N. Gershon and S.G. Eick, eds., IEEE Computer Society Press, Los Alamitos, Calif., 1995, pp. 66-73. Also available on the World Wide Web at URL http://citeseer.ist.psu.edu/7914.html.

C. Ahlberg, E. Wistrand (1994), IVEE: An Environment for Automatic Creation of Dynamic Queries Applications, in *Proceedings CHI'95: Human Factors in Computing Systems*.

C. Gunn. Visualizing hyperbolic space. In *Computer Graphics and Mathematics*, pages 299—311. Springer-Verlag, October 1991.

C. Lynch and H. Garcia-Molina, *Interoperability, Scaling, and the Digital Libraries A Report on the May 18-19, 1995 IITA Digital Libraries Workshop* Reston, VA, August 22, 1995. http://www-diglib.stanford.edu/diglib/pub/reports/iita-dlw/main.html

C. M. Bowman, P. B. Danzig, D. R. Hardy, U. Manber, and M. F. Schwartz. *Harvest: A scalable, customizable discovery and access system*. Technical Report CU-CS-732-94, University of Colorado, August 1994. Available from ftp://ftp.cs.colorado.edu/ pub/ techreports/schwartz/Harvest.Jour.ps.Z.

C. Varela et al., DB: Browsing Object-Oriented Databases over the Web, *Proc. 4th Int'l Conf. on the World Wide Web*, 1996, available on the Web at URL http://www.w3.org/Conferences/ WWW4/Papers2/282/.

Card, S. K. and Henderson, D. A., Jr. 1987. A multiple, virtual-workspace interface to support user task switching. In *CHI+GI 1987*. ACM, New York.

Card, S., User perceptual mechanisms in the search of computer command menus, *Proceedings ACM CHI'82 Conference*, 190-196

Card, S.K., Pirolli, P., and Mackinlay, J.D. The Cost-of-Knowledge Characteristic Function: Display Evaluation for Direct-Walk Dynamic Information Visualizations, *CHI'94*, ACM Press, Boston, 1994, pp. 238-244.

Carriere, J. and Kazman, R. Interacting with Huge Hierarchies: Beyond Cone Trees, *InfoVis'95*, IEEE Press, Atlanta, 1995, pp. 74-81.

Catherine Plaisant, Brett Milash, Anne Rose, Widoff, Ben Shneiderman. LifeLines: Visualizing personal histories. *CHI 96 Conference Proceedings*, pp. 221-227, 1996.

Catherine Plaisant, Vinit Jain, video: *Dynamaps: Dynamic Queries on a Health Statistics Atlas*, CHI '94 Companion p. 439.

Chalmers, M. and Chitson, P. Bead: Explorations in Information Visualization, *SIGIT'92*, 1992, pp. 330-337.

Chang, Bay-Wei, and David Ungar. Animation: From Cartoons to the User Interface. *Proceedings of UIST. 1993*. Atlanta, Georgia:

Charoenkitkarn, N., Chignell, M. H., & Golovchinsky, G. (1995). Interactive Exploration as a Formal Text Retrieval Method: How Well can Interactivity Compensate for Unsophisticated Retrieval Algorithms? In *Proceedings of Third Text Retrieval Conference (TREC-3)* Gaithersburg, Maryland: National Institute of Standards and Technology (NIST). Paper and figures (postscript).

Charoenkitkarn, N., Chignell, M. H., & Golovchinsky, G. (1996). Is Recall Relevant? An Analysis of How User Interface Conditions affect Strategies and Performance in Large Scale Text Retrieval. In *Proceedings of Fourth Text Retrieval Conference (TREC-4)* Gaithersburg, Maryland: National Institute of Standards and Technology (NIST).

Charoenkitkarn, N., Tam, J., Chignell, M. H., & Golovchinsky, G. (1993). Browsing through querying: Designing for electronic books. In *Proceedings of Hypertext '93*, Seattle, WA: ACM Press. pp. 206-216.

Chignell, M. H., Golovchinsky, G., Poblete, F., & Zuberec, S. (1993). Information visualization and interactive querying for online documentation and electronic books. In *Proceedings of CASCON '93*, pp. 1011-1020. Toronto, Canada.

Chignell, M. H., Poblete, F., and Zuberec, S. (1993) An Exploration in the Design Space of Three Dimensional Hierarchies. In *Proceedings of the Human Factors Society '93*, pp xxx-yyy. 1993.

Christoph Schlieder. Reasoning about ordering. *Proceedings of COSIT 95 (Conference on Spatial Information Theory)*, pp. 341-349, 1995.

Christos Faloutsos and Dougtas Oard, A Survey of Information Retrieval and Filtering Method, http://www.glue.umd.edu/enee/medlab/filter/papers/survey.ps

Clifford Beshers and Steven Feiner. AutoVisual: Rule-based design of interactive multivariate visualizations. *IEEE CGA*, pp. 41-49, July 1993.

Conner, D.B., Snibbe, S.S., Herndon, K.P., Robbins, D.C., Zeleznik, R.C. and van Dam, A. Three-dimensional widgets. In *Proceedings of the 1992 Symposium on Interactive Three-Dimensional Graphics*, pp. 183-188.

Cooper, Muriel, et.al. Information Landscapes. MIT Technical Note. April, 1994.

Dan M. Russell, Mark J. Stefik, Peter Pirolli, Stuart K. Card. The Cost Structure of Sensemaking, *Proceedings of ACM InterCHI '93*. April 1993, pp. 269-276.

David Goldberg, David Nichols, Brain M. Oki, and Douglas Terry, Using collaborative filtering to weave an information tapestry, *Communications of the ACM*, vol. 35, no. 12, pp. 61-70, December 1992.

Dennis R. Proffitt, and Mary K. Kaiser, Perceiving Environmental Properties from Motion Information: Minimal Conditions, in Stephen R. Ellis (ed.), *Pictorial Communication in Virtual and Real Environments*, Bristol, PA: Francis & Taylor, Inc., 1991, pp. 47-60,

Dieberger, A. Browsing the WWW by interacting with a textual virtual environment - A framework for experimenting with navigational metaphors, accepted for *Hypertext'96*, Washington DC, 1996, p. forthcoming.

Dieberger, A. On Magic Features in (Spatial) Metaphors, *SigLink Newsletter*, 4, 3, (1995), pp. 8-10.

Doan, K., Plaisant, C., and Shneiderman, B., Query previews for networked information services, *Proc. Advanced Digital Libraries Conference* (May 1996).

Doug Schaffer, Zhengping Zuo, Lyn Bartram, John Dill, Shelli Dubs, Saul Greenberg, Mark Roseman. Comparing fisheye and full-zoom techniques for navigation of hierarchically clustered networks. In *Proceedings of Graphics Interface '93*, Toronto, Canada, May, Distributed by Morgan-Kauffman.

E. R. Gansner, S. C. North, and K. P. Vo. DAG - a program that draws directed graphs. *Software Practice and Experience*, 18(11), No v. 1988.

E. Rennison, Galaxy of News: An Approach to Visualizing and Understanding Expansive News Landscapes, in *UIST 94, ACM Symp. on User Interface Software and Technology*, ACM Press, New York, 1994, pp. 3-12.

E.G. Noik. A space of presentation emphasis techniques for visualizing graphs. In *GI '94: Graphics Interface 1994*, pages 225- 234, Banff, AL, Canada, May 1994.

E.G. Noik. Layout-independent fisheye views of nested graphs. In *VL '93: IEEE Symposium on Visual Languages*, pages 336-341, Bergen, Norway, August 1993.

Edward Tufte. (1983) *The Visual Display of Quantitative Information* . Graphics Press, Chelshire, CT, 1983.

Ellis S. [Ed.]. *Pictorial Communication in Virtual and Real Environments*, 2nd Ed. London, England: Taylor and Francis, 1993.

Eric A. Bier, Maureen C. Stone, Ken Pier, William Buxton, and Tony D. DeRose. Toolglass and Magic Lenses: The See-Through Interface. Proceedings of Siggraph '93 (Anaheim, CA, August), *Computer Graphics* Annual Conference Series, ACM, 1993, pp. 73-80.

Eric A. Bier, Maureen C. Stone, Thomas Baudel, William Buxton, and Ken Fishkin. A Taxonomy of See-Through Tools. *Proceedings of CHI '94,* (Boston, MA, April 24-28) ACM, New York, (1994), pp. 358-364.

Fairchild, K. M., Poltrock, S. E. and Furnas, G. W. (1988) SemNet: Three-dimensional graphic representations of large knowledge bases. In *Cognitive Science and its Application for Human-Computer Interface*, pp. 201-233, R. Guindon ed. Elsevier.

Fairchild, K.M. Information Management Using Virtual Reality-Based Visualizations, in Wexelblat, A. (Ed.) *Virtual Reality - Applications and Explorations*. Academic Press, 1993, p. Chapter 3.

Fairchild, K.M., et. al. Dynamic FishEye Information Visualizations, in Earnshaw, R.A., Gigante, M.A., and Jones, H. (Eds.). *Virtual Reality Systems*. Academic Press, 1993

Faloutsos C., Barber R., Flickner M., Hafner J., et al.: Efficient and Effective Querying by Image Content, *Journal of Intelligent Information Systems*, 1994, Vol. 3, pp. 231-262.

Faloutsos C., Lin K.: Fastmap: A fast Algorithm for Indexing, Data-Mining and Visualization of Traditional and Multimedia Datasets, *Proc. ACM SIGMOD Int. Conf. on Management of Data*, San Jose, CA, 1995, pp. 163- 174.

Feiner, S. (1988) Seeing the Forest for the Trees: Hierarchical Display of Hypertext Structure. In *Proceedings of the Conference on Office Information Systems 1988*, pp. 205-212, Palo Alto, March 23-25.

Feiner, S. and McKeown, K. Automating the Generation of Coordinated Multimedia Explanations, *Intelligent Multimedia Interfaces*, Maybury, M. Ed, AAAI Press/MIT Press, 1993. Cambridge, MA.

Feiner, S., Nagy, S. and van Dam, A. (1982) An experimental system for creating and presenting interactive graphical documents. In *ACM Transactions on Graphics*, **1**(1), pp. 59-77.

Fisher, S. S., McGreevy, M., Humphries, J., and Robinett, W. 1986. Virtual environment display system. In *Proceedings of ACM 1986 Workshop on Interactive 3D Graphics*. ACM, New York.

Florin, F. Information Landscapes, in Ambron, S. and Hooper, K. (Eds.). *Learning with Interactive Multimedia*. Microsoft Press, 1990, pp. 27- 49.

Frank M. Shipman III, Catherine C. Marshall, and Thomas P. Moran. Finding and using implicit structure in human-organized spatial layouts of information. *CHI 95 Conference Proceedings*, pp. 346-353, 1995.

Furnas, G. and Zacks, J. Multitrees: Enriching and Reusing Hierarchical Structure. *Proceedings of Human Factors and Computer Systems CHI*, 1994. Boston, Massachusetts.

Furnas, G. W. (1986) Generalized fisheye views. In *Proceedings of ACM CHI'86 Conference on Human Factors in Computing Systems*, pp. 16-23, Boston, Massachusetts, April 13-17, ACM Press.

G. Battista, P. Eades, R. Tamassia, and I. Tollis. *Algorithms for Drawing Graphs: an Annotated Bibliography*. Technical report, Brown University, June 1993.

G. Cybenko, Y. Wu, A. Khrabrov, and R. Gray, Information agents as organizers, in *CIKM Workshop on Intelligent Information Agents*, December 1994.

G. Fischer, The Importance of Models in Making Complex Systems Comprehensible, in M.J. Tauber and D. Ackermann (eds.), *Mental Models and Human-Computer Interaction 2*, Amsterdam: Elsevier, 1991, pp. 3-36.

G. G. Robertson, S. K. Card, and J. D. Mackinlay. The cognitive coprocessor architecture for interactive user interfaces. In *Proceedings of the ACM SIGGRAPH Symposium on User Interface Software and Technology*, pages 10—18. ACM Press, Nov 1989.

G. W. Furnas, T. K. Landauer, L. M. Gomez, and S. T. Dumais, The vocabulary problem in human-system communication, *Communications of the ACM*, vol. 30, pp. 964-971, November 1987.

Gaver, W.W. Oh What a Tangled Web We Weave: Metaphor and Mapping in Graphical Interfaces, *CHI'95 - Conference Companion*, ACM Press, Denver, CO, 1995, pp. 270-271.

George G. Robertson and J. D. Mackinlay. The document lens. In *Proceedings of the ACM Symposium on User Interface Software and Technology*. ACM Press, Nov 1993.

George G. Robertson, Stuart K. Card, and Jock D. Mackinlay. Information Visualization Using 3D Interactive Animation. *Communications of the ACM*, **36**(4), April 1993. pp. 57-71.

Gerhard Fischer and Curt Stevens. Information access in complex, poorly structured information spaces. *CHI 91 Conference Proceedings*, pp. 63-70, 1991.

Golledge, R.G. Path Selection and Route Preference in Human Navigation: A Progress Report, in Frank, A.U. and Kuhn, W. (Eds.). *Spatial Information Theory - Proceedings of COSIT'95*. LNCS 988, Springer, Semmering, Austria, 1995, pp. 207-222.

Golovchinsky, G. & Chignell, M. H. (1992). Making queries look like links: An interaction style for information exploration. *Computer Systems Technical Group Newsletter*, August 1992, 20-22.

Golovchinsky, G. and Chignell, M. H. (1996) Merging Hypertext and Information Retrieval in the Interface. Poster to appear at *SIGIR '96*, Zurich, Switzerland.

Golovchinsky, G. and Chignell, M. H. (1996) The Newspaper as an Information Exploration Metaphor. Dept. of Mechanical and Industrial Engineering Working Paper #96-05, April 1996. Submitted to *Journal of Information Processing & Management*.

Golovchinsky, G., & Chignell, M. H. (1993). Queries-R-Links: Graphical markup for text navigation. In *Proceedings of INTERCHI '93*, pp. 454-460. Amsterdam, The Netherlands: ACM Press.

Golovchinsky, G., Kamps, T., and Reichenberger, K. (1995) Subverting Structure: Data-driven Dynamic Diagram generation. *Proceedings of IEEE Visualization '95*, Atlanta, Georgia, Oct 29-Nov 3. pp. 217-223.

Grace Colby and Laura Scholl. Transparency and Blur as Selective Curs for Complex Visual Information. *Proceedings of SPIE '91* (San Jose, Feb). SPIE, 1991, pp. 114-125.

Grissom, S. and Perlman, G. *Step(3D): A portable discount usability evaluation plan for 3D interaction.* Department of Computer Science and Information Science, Ohio State University. OSU-CISRC-2/93-TR7, 1993.

Guy A. Story, Lawrence O'Gorman, David Fox, Louise Levy Schaper, H. V. Jagadish, The RightPages Image-Based Electronic Library for Alerting and Browsing, *IEEE Computer*, September 1992.

H. Wallach, and D.N. O'Connell, The Kinetic Depth Effect, *Journal of Experimental Psychology*, (45), 1953, pp. 205-217.

Harel, D. (1988) On visual formalisms. *Comm ACM*, **31**(5), pp. 514-530.

Hikmet Senay and Eve Ignatius. (1990) *Rules and principles of scientific data visualization.* Technical Report GWU-IIST-90-13, Institute for Information Science and Technology, The George Washington University, 1990.

Houde, S. and Solomon, G. Working Towards Rich & Flexible File Representations, *InterCHI'93*, ACM Press, Amsterdam, 1993, pp. 9-10.

Houde, S. Iterative design of an interface for easy 3D direct manipulation. In *Proceedings of CHI'92*, pp. 135-142.

Ivan E. Sutherland. Sketchpad: A man-machine graphical communications systems, Proceedings of the Spring Joint Computer Conference, 1963, 329-346, Baltimore, MD: Spartan Books.

J. Brown et al., *Visualization: Using Computer Graphics to Explore Data and Present Information*, John Wiley & Sons, New York, 1995.

J. C. Gower and P. G. N. Digby, Expressing complex relationships in two dimensions, in *Interpreting Multivariate Data* (V. Barnett, ed.), pp. 83-118, John Wiley & Son, INC., 1981.

J. Hagman (1994). The Cluster Analyzer & Visualizer - a Prototype for Data Exploration, Technical Report SSKKII-94.05, in *Proceedings of the Third International Conference in Central Europe on Computer Graphics and Visualisation 95*, Vol. 1, ed. Vaclav Skala, Univ. of West Bohemia, Pilsen, Czech Republic, 1995.

J. Hagman, 1994. *Information Visualization and Exploration - Potential and Requirements*, Technical Report SSKKII-94.03.

J. Lamping, R. Rao, and P. Pirolli, A Focus + Context Technique Based on Hyperbolic Geometry for Visualizing Large Hierarchies, in *CHI 95, Proc. ACM Conf. on Human Factors in Computing Systems*, ACM Press, New York, 1995, pp. 401-408.

J. Mackinlay. Automating the Design of Graphical Presentation of Relational Information. *ACM Transactions on Graphics*, 5(2):110-141, April 1986.

J. Nielsen. *Multimedia and Hypertext, The Internet and Beyond*. AP Professional, first edition, 1995.

J. Nielsen. The Art of Navigating Through Hypertext. *Communications of the ACM*, 33(3):296-310, March 1990.

J.A. Wise et al., Visualizing the Nonvisual: Spatial Analysis and Interaction with Information from Text Documents, *Proc. Info. Vis. Symp. 95*, N. Gershon and S.G. Eick, eds., IEEE Computer Society Press, Los Alamitos, Calif., 1995, pp. 51-58.

J.D.A. Henderson and S.K. Card, Rooms: The Use of Multiple Virtual Workspaces to Reduce Space Contention in Window-based Graphical User Interfaces, *ACM Trans. on Graphics*, Vol. 5, No. 3, July 1986, pp. 211-241.

J.E. Pitkow and Bharat K.A. WebViz: A Tool for World Wide Web Access Log Analysis. In *Proceedings of the First International World-Wide Web Conference*, Geneva Switzerland, May 1994.

Jacques Bertin. (1983) *Semiology of Graphics* . The University of Wisconsin Press, Madison, WI, 1983. Translated by William J. Berg.

Jade Goldstein and Steven F. Roth. Using Aggregation and Dynamic Queries for Exploring Large Data Sets. *Proceedings of CHI '94,* (Boston, MA, April 24-28) ACM, New York, (1994), pp. 23-29.

Jain, Vinit and Shneiderman, Ben. Data Structures for Dynamic Queries: An Analytical and Experimental Evaluation. *Proc. Conference on Advanced Visual Interfaces 94*, ACM, New York 1994, pp 1-11.

James E. Pitkow and Krishna A. Bharat. WebViz: A tool for world-wide web access log analysis. *Proceedings of the First International WWW Conference*, pp. ?, 1994?.

James R. Osborn and Alice M. Agogino. An interface for interactive spatial reasoning and visualization. *CHI 92 Conference Proceedings*, pp. 75-82, 1992.

Jerding, D.F. and Stasko, J.T. The Information Mural: A Technique for Displaying and Navigating Large Information Spaces, *InfoVis'95*, IEEE Press, Atlanta, 1995, pp. 43-50.

Jerry Lohse. A cognitive model for the perception and understanding of graphs. *CHI 91 Conference Proceedings*, pp. 137-144, 1991.

Jock D. Mackinlay, Stuart K. Card, George G. Robertson, Rapid Controlled Movement Through a Virtual 3D Workspace, *SIGGRAPH '90*, p. 171.

Jock Mackinlay. (1986) *Automatic Design of Graphical Presentations* . PhD thesis, Stanford University, 1986. Technical Report Stan-CS-86-1038.

John Lamping and Ramana Rao. Laying out an dvisualizing large trees using a hyperbolic space. *Proceedings of UIST 94*, pp. 13-14, 1994.

Johnson, B. and Shneiderman, B. (1991) Tree-maps: A space-filling approach to the visualization of hierarchical information structures. In *Proceedings of IEEE Visualization '91,* San Diego, CA, Oct 22-25, pp. 284-291.

Jones, W. and Dumais, S. The Spatial Metaphor for User Interfaces: Experimental Tests of Reference by Location versus Name, *ACM Transactions on Office Information Systems*, 4, 1, (1986), pp. 42-63.

Jun Rekimoto and Mark Green. The navigation grid: An effective technique for virtual space navigation. In *Proceedings of the Fifth Annual Western Computer Graphics Symposium*, 1993.

K.A. Olsen et al., Visualization of a Document Collection: The VIBE System, *Info. Processing and Management*, Vol. 29, No. 1, 1993, pp. 69-81.

Kahn, P. Visual Cues for Local and Global Coherence in the WWW, Communications of the ACM, 38, 8, (1995), pp. 67-69.

Kaltenbach, M., Robillard, F. and Frasson, C. (1991) Screen Management in Hypertext Systems with Rubber Sheet Layouts. In *Proceedings of Hypertext '91,* pp. 91-105, San Antonio, Dec 15-18.

Kandogan, E. and Shneiderman, B., Elastic windows: Improved spatial layout and rapid multiple window operations, *Proc. Advanced Visual Interfaces Conference 96*, ACM Press, New York, NY (May 1996).

Kaplan, N. and Moulthrop, S. Where No Mind Has Gone Before: Ontological Design for Virtual Spaces, *ECHT'94*, ACM Press, Edinburgh, 1994, pp. 206-216.

Keim D. A. Enhancing the Visual Clustering of Query-dependent Data Visualization Techniques using Screen-Filling Curves , *Proc. Int. Workshop on Database Issues in Data Visualization*, Atlanta, GA, 1995, to appear in: Springer Lecture Notes, 1996.

Keim D. A. Pixel-oriented Visualization Techniques for Exploring Very Large Databases, *Journal of Computational and Graphical Statistics*, March 1996.

Keim D. A. *Visual Support for Query Specification and Data Mining*, Dissertation, July 1994, Shaker Publishing Company, 1995, ISBN 3-8265-0594-8.

Keim D. A., Bergeron D., Pickett R. Test Data Sets for Evaluating Data Visualization Techniques, in: *Perceptual Issues in Visualization*, Springer 1994.

Keim D. A., Kriegel H.-P. Visually Supporting Data Mining of Large Existing Databases, *Proc. Int. Workshop on Database Issues in Data Visualization* , San Jose, CA, 1993.

Keim D. A., Kriegel H.-P., Ankerst M. Recursive Pattern: A Technique for Visualizing Very Large Amounts of Data , *Visualization '95*, Atlanta, GA, 1995.

Keim D. A., Kriegel H.-P., Seidl T. Supporting Data Mining of Large Databases by Visual Feedback Queries, *Proc. 10th Int. Conf. on Data Engineering*, Houston, TX, 1994.

Keim D. A., Kriegel H.-P., Seidl T. Visual Feedback in Querying Large Databases, *Visualization '93*, San Jose, CA, 1993, pp. 158-165.

Keim D. A., Lee J. P., Thuraisinghaman B., Wittenbrink C.: Database Issues for Data Visualization: Supporting Interactive Database Exploration, *Proc. Workshop on Database Issues for Data Visualization*, Atlanta, GA, 1995, to appear in: Springer Lecture Notes, 1996.

Keim D. A., Lum V.: Visual Query Specification in a Multimedia Database System, *Proc. Visualization '92*, Boston, MA, 1992, pp. 194-201.

Ken Fishkin, Maureen C. Stone. Enhanced dynamic queries via movable filters. *CHI 95 Conference Proceedings*, pp. 415-420, 1995.

Ken Perlin and David Fox. Pad: An Alternative Approach to the Computer Interface, *Proceedings of 1993 ACM SIGGRAPH Conference*, 57-64.

Kenneth P. Herndon and Tom Meyer. 3D widgets for exploratory scientific visualization. *Proceedings of UIST 94*, pp. 69-70, 1994.

Kenneth P. Herndon, Andries van Dam, and Michael Gleicher, Workshop on the Challenges of 3D Interaction, *CHI94*.

Kenneth P. Herndon, Robert C. Zelenik, Daniel C. Robbins, D. Brookshire Conner, Scott S. Snibbe, and Andries van Dam, Interactive Shadows, *Proceedings of UIST '92*, ACM SIGGRAPH, November 1992, pp. 1-6.

Kenrick J. Mock and V. Rao Vemuri, *Adaptive User Models for Intelligent Information Filtering*, http://www.glue.umd.edu/enee/medlab/filter/gwic.ps

Keywords: Hypermedia, Overview Diagrams, Information Visualization, Hierarchization

Keywords: Information Visualization, Overview Diagrams, BindFiltering, Hierarchizationing, Clustering,

Kidd, A. (1994) The Marks are on the Knowledge Worker. *Proceedings of Human Factors in Computing Systems CHI'94*, pp 186-191.

Koike, H. 1992. An application of three-dimensional visualization to object-oriented programming. In *Advanced Visual Interfaces (Proceedings of the International Workshop AVI'92)*, T. Catarci, M. F. Costabile, and S. Levialdi, Eds. World Scientific, Singapore, 180-192.

Koike, H. 1993a. The role of another spatial dimension in software visualization. *ACM Trans. Inf. Syst.* 11, 3 (July), 266-286.

Koike, H. 1993b. Implementation of a lisp printer using fractal views. In *Proceedings of 10th Conference of Japan Society for Software Science and Technology*, 101-104. In Japanese.

Koike, H. and Yoshihara, H. 1993. Fractal approaches for visualizing huge hierarchies. In *Proceedings of 1993 IEEE / CS Symposium on Visual Languages (VL'93)*. IEEE Computer Society Press, Los Alamitos, Calif., 55-60.

Kyoichi Arai, Teruo Yokoyama, Yutaka Matushita. A window system with leafing through mode: BookWindow. *CHI 92 Conference Proceedings*, pp. 291-292, 1992.

Lakoff, G. *Woman, Fire, and Dangerous Things: What Categories Reveal about the Mind*. University of Chicago Press, 1987. Chicago, Illinous.

Lakoff, G., and M. Turner. *Metaphors We Live By*. University of Chicago Press, 1980. Chicago, Illinous.

Larsson, James A. A Visual Approach to Browsing in a Database Environment. *IEEE Computer* 19, 6 (June 1986), pp. 62-71.

Leonard R. Wanger, James A. Ferwerda, and Donald P. Greenberg, Perceiving Spatial Relationships in Computer-Generated Images, *IEEE Computer Graphics & Applications*, May 1992, pp. 44-58.

Leonard R. Wanger, The Effect of Shadow Quality on the Perception of Spatial Relationships in Computer Generated Imagery, *Computer Graphics (Proceedings of the 1992 Symposium on Interactive 3D Graphics)*, 25(2), ACM SIGGRAPH, March 1992, pp. 39-42.

Lieberman, H. Powers of Ten Thousand: Navigating in Large Information Spaces (TechNote), *Proc. UIST'94*, ACM Press, Marina del Rey, CA, 1994, pp. 15-16.

Lin K., Jagadish H. V., Faloutsos C.: The TV-tree: An Index Structure for High-Dimensional Data, *VLDB Journal*, Vol. 3, 1995, pp. 517-542.

Lin, X. A Self-Organizing Semantic Map for Information Retrieval, *SIGIR'91*, 1991, pp. 262-269.

Lokuge, I. and Ishizaki, S. GeoSpace: An Interactive Visualization System for Exploring Complex Information Spaces, *CHI'95*, ACM Press, Denver, CO, 1995, pp. 409-414.

Lokuge, I., Gilbert, S.A., and Richards, W. *Mental Models for Touring Information Spaces*, 1995.

Luc Beaudoin, Marc-Antoine Parent, Louis C. Vroomen. Cheops: A compact explorer for complex hierarchies. *journal?*, pp. 87-92.

Lyn Bartram, Albert Ho, John Dill and Frank Henigman. The Continuous Zoom: A constrained fisheye technique for viewing and navigating large information spaces. *Proceedings of UIST 95*, pp. 207-215, 1995.

M. A. Hearst and J.O. Pedersen Re-examining the Cluster Hypothesi Scatter/Gather on Retrieval Results," *Proceedings of the 19th Annual International ACM / SIGIR Conference*, Zurich, 1996.

M. A. Hearst, TileBars: Visualization of Term Distribution Information in Full Text Information Access, *Proceedings of the ACM SIGCHI Conference on Human Factors in Computing Systems*, Denver, CO, ACM, May 1995, pp. 55-66. http://www.sims.berkeley.edu/~hearst/images/tb-refs.html

M. Benedikt, Cyberspace: Some Proposals, in *Cyberspace: First Steps*, M. Benedikt, ed., MIT Press, Cambridge, Mass., 1991, pp. 119-224.

M. L. Mauldin and J. R. R. Leavitt. Web-agent related research at the center for machine translation. In *Proceedings of the ACM SIGNIDR Meeting*, August 1994.

M. Sheelagh T. Carpendale, David J. Cowperthwaite, F. David Fracchia. 3-Dimensional pliable surfaces: For the effective presentation of visual information. *Proceedings of UIST 95*, pp. 217-226, 1995.

M.P. Consens and A.O. Mendelzon. GraphLog: A Visual Formalism for Real Life Recursion. In *Proceedings of 9th ACM SIGA CT-SIGMOD Symposium on Principles of Database Systems*, pages 404-416, 1990.

M.P. Consens and A.O. Mendelzon. The Hy + /GraphLog Visual Query System. In *Proceedings of the ACM-SIGMOD 1990 Annual Conference on Management of Data*, page 388, 1990. Video presentation summary.

M.P. Consens, A.O. Mendelzon, and D. Vista. Deductive Database Support for Data Visualization.

In *Proceedings of the 4th International Conference on Extending Database Technology*, pages 45-58, 1994.

M.P. Consens, F.Ch. Eigler, M.Z. Hasan, A.O. Mendelzon, M.G. Noik, A.G. Ryman, and D. Vista. Architecture and Applications of the Hy + Visualization System. *IBM Systems Journal*, 33(3):458-476, 1994.

M.P. Consens. *Creating and Filtering Structural Data Visualizations using Hygraph Patterns*. PhD thesis, Department of Computer Science, University of Toronto, February 1994.

MacEachren, A.M. *How Maps Work*, The Guilford Press, New York, 1995.

Mackinlay, J. D., Robertson, G. G. and Card, S. K. (1991) The perspective wall: detail and context smoothly integrated. In *Proceedings of ACM CHI'91 Conference on Human Factors in Computing Systems*, pp. 173-179, New Orleans, Louisiana, April 28-May 2, ACM Press.

Mackinlay, J.D., Rao, R., and Card, S.K. An Organic User Interface For Searching Citation Links, *CHI'95*, Denver, CO, 1995, pp. 67-73.

Mackinlay, J.D., Robertson, G.G., and DeLine, R. Developing Calendar Visualizers for the Information Visualizer, Proc. *UIST'94*, ACM Press, Marina del Rey, CA, 1994, pp. 109-118.

Maltz, D. and Ehrlich, K. Pointing The Way: Active Collaborative Filtering, *CHI'95*, ACM Press, Denver, CO, 1995, pp. 202-209.

Manojit Sarkar and Marc H. Brown (1992) Graphical fisheye views of graphs. In *Proceedings of ACM CHI'92 Conference on Human Factors in Computing Systems*, pp. 83-91, Monterey, California, May 3-7, ACM Press.

Manojit Sarkar and Marc H. Brown. Graphical fisheye views. *Communications of the ACM*, 37(12):73—84, December 1994.

Marchionini, G. *Information Seeking in Electronic Environments*. Cambridge University Press, 1995.

Marcia J. Bates. The design of browsing and berrypicking techniques for the online search interface. *Online Review*, 13(5):407, 1989.

Marshall, C.C. and Shipman, F.M. Searching for the Missing Link: Discovering Implicit Structure in Spatial Hypertext, *Hypertext'93*, ACM Press, Seattle, 1993, pp. 217-230.

Marshall, C.C. and Shipman, F.M. Spatial Hypertext: Designing for Change, *Communications of the ACM*, 38, 8, (1995), pp. 88-97.

Marshall, C.C., Shipman, F.M., and Coombs, J.H. VIKI: Spatial Hypertext Supporting Emergent Structure, *ECHT'94*, Edinburgh, 1994, pp. 13-23.

Marti A. Hearst. (1994a) *Context and Structure in Automated Full-Text Information Access* . PhD thesis, University of California at Berkeley, 1994. (Computer Science Division Technical Report UCB/CSD-94/836).

Marti A. Hearst. (1994b) Multi-paragraph segmentation of expository text. In *Proceedings of the 32nd Meeting of the Association for Computational Linguistics* , June 1994.

Marti A. Hearst. (1995) *An investigation of term distribution effects in Full-Text Retrieval*. Technical Report Report Number ISTL-QCA-1994-12-06, Xerox PARC, 1995. Submitted for publication.

Matthew Chalmers, Paul Chitson, Bead: Explorations in Information Visualization, *ACM SIGIR '92*, p. 330.

Matthew Chalmers. A linear iteration time layout algorithm for visualising high-dimensional data. *journal?*, pp. 127-132, .

Matthew Chalmers. Using a landscape metaphor to represent a corpus of documents. *Proceedings of COSIT 93 (Conference on Spatial Information Theory)*, pp. 377-390, 1993.

Matthias Hemmje, Clemens Kunkel, and Alexander Willet. Lyberworld - a visualization user interface supporting full text retrieval. In *Proceedings of the 17th Annual International Conference on Research and Development in Information Retrieval*, pages 249-259, 1994.

Maureen C. Stone, Ken Fishkin, and Eric A. Bier. The Movable Filter as a User Interface Tool. *Proceedings of CHI '94,* (Boston, MA, April 24-28) ACM, New York, (1994), pp. 306-312.

Max J. Egenhofer. Manipulating the Graphical Representation of Query Results in Geographic Information Systems. *Proceedings of the 1990 IEEE Workshop on Visual Languages*. IEEE Computer Society Press, Los Alamitos CA, 1990, pp. 119-124.

Michael F. Schwartz, Alan Emtage, Brewster Kahle, and B. Clifford Neuman. A comparison of Internet resource discovery approaches. *Journal of Computing Systems*, 5(4), Fall 1992.

Montello, D.R. Scale and Multiple Psychologies of Space, *COSIT'93*, Springer, Elba, 1993, pp. 312-321.

Mukherjea, S & Foley, J., D. (1995) Visualizing the World-Wide Web with the Navigational View Builder. *Computer Networks and ISDN Systems*, 27, 1075-1087

Mukherjea, S. and Foley, J.D. Showing the Context of Nodes in the World-Wide Web, *CHI'95 - Conference Companion*, ACM Press, Denver, CO, 1995, pp. 326-327.

Mukherjea, S., Foley, J.D., and Hudson, S. Visualizing Complex Hypermedia Networks through Multiple Hierarchical Views, *CHI'95*, ACM Press, Denver, CO, 1995, pp. 331-337.

N. Gershon and S.G. Eick, Visualization's New Tack: Making Sense of Information, *IEEE Spectrum*, Nov. 1995, pp. 38-56.

N. Gershon et al., Visualizing Internet Resources, in *Proc. Info. Vis. Symp. 95*, N. Gershon and S.G. Eick, eds., IEEE CS Press, Los Alamitos, Calif., 1995, pp. 122-128.

Nielsen, J. A Home-Page Overhaul Using Other Web Sites, *IEEE Software*, 12, 3, (1995), accessible at http://info.computer.org/pubs/software/face/05/face.htm.

Nievergelt, J. and Weydert, J. Sites, Modes, and Trails: Telling the User of an Interactive System where he is, what he can do, and how to get to places., in: Gurdj et al.: *Methodology of Interaction*. North-Holland, 1980, pp. 327-338.

Noik, E. G. (1993) Exploring large hyperdocuments: Fisheye views of nested networks. In

Proceedings of the ACM Conference on Hypertext and Hypermedia, Seattle, WA, November 14-18, ACM Press, pp. 192-195.

North, C., Shneiderman, B., and Plaisant, C., User controlled overviews of an image library: A case study of the Visible Human, *Proc. 1st ACM International Conference on Digital Libraries* (March 1996), 74-82.

O'Day, V. and Jeffries, R. Orienteering in an Information Landscape: How Information Seekers Get From Here to There, *InterCHI'93*, ACM Press, Amsterdam, 1993, pp. 438-445.

Olsen, K. and Korfhage, R.R. Desktop Visualization, *IEEE Symposium on Visual Languages '94*, IEEE Computer Society Press, 1994, pp. 239-244.

Olsen, K., et. al. Ideation Through Visualization: The VIBE System, *Multimedia Review*, 3, 3, (1992), pp. 48-59.

Osada, M., Liao, H., Shneiderman, B., AlphaSlider: searching textual lists with sliders, *Proceedings of the Ninth Annual Japanese Conference on Human Interface*, October 1993.

P. Pirolli and S. K. Card, Information Foraging in Information Access Environments, *Proceedings of the ACM SIGCHI Conference on Human Factors in Computing Systems*, Denver, CO, ACM, May 1995. http://www.sigchi.org/chi95/Electronic/documnts/papers/ppp bdy.htm

Parunak, H.V. Hypercubes Grow on Trees (and other Observations from the Land of Hypersets), *Hypertext'93*, ACM Press, Seattle, 1993, pp. 73-81.

Parunak, H.v. Hypermedia Topologies and User Navigation, *Proc. of Hypertext'89*, Pittsburgh, 1989, pp. 43-50.

Peter F. Sharp, and Russell Philips, Physiological Optics, in William R. Hendee and Peter N.T. Wells (eds.), *The Perception of Visual Information*, New York: Springer-Verlag, 1993, pp. 1-29.

Peter Pirolli, James Pitkow, Ramana Rao. Silk from a sow's ear: Extracting usable structures from the Web. *CHI 96 Conference Proceedings*, pp. 118-125, 1996.

Peter Pirolli, Patricia Schank, Marti Hearst, Christine Diehl. Scatter/gather browsing communicates the topic structure of a very large text collection. *CHI 96 Conference Proceedings*, pp. 213-220, 1996.

Peter W. Foltz and Susan T. Dumais, Personalized information delivery: An analysis of information filtering methods, *Communications of the ACM*, vol. 35, no. 12, pp. 51-60, December 1992.

Plaisant, C., Carr, D., and Shneiderman, B., Image-browser taxonomy and guidelines for designers, *IEEE Software* **12**, 2 (March 1995), 21-32.

Plaisant, C., Rose, A., Milash, B., Widoff, S., and Shneiderman, B., LifeLines: Visualizing personal histories, *Proc. of ACM CHI96 Conference (April 1996)*, 221-227, 518.

Poblete, F., Chignell, M.H., and Chaffey, A.V. *No Free Ride: When Information Visualization Doesn't Promote Learning of Information Structure*, University of Toronto, Dept. of Industrial Engineering report, Technical Report #96-01, 1996.

Poblete, F.P. *The Use of Information Visualization to Enhance Awareness of Hierarchical Structure*, Masters Thesis, University of Toronto / Dept. of Industrial Engineering, 1995.

R. Botafogo, E. Rivlin, and B. Shneiderman. Structural Analysis of Hypertexts: Identifying Hierarchies and Useful Metrics. *ACM Transactions on Office Information Systems*, 10(2):142-180, 1992.

R. Rao and S. K. Card. An Organic User Interface For Searching Citation Links, *Proceedings of the ACM SIGCHI Conference on Human Factors in Computing Systems*, Denver, CO, May 1995. http://www.sigchi.org/chi95/Electronic/documnts/papers/jdm_bdy.htm

R. Rao, J. O. Pedersen, M. A. Hearst, et al., Rich Interaction in the Digital Library, *Communications of the ACM*, 38 (4), 29-39, April 1995.

R. Rao, S. K. Card, W. Johnson, L. Klotz, and R. Trigg, Protofoil: Storing and Finding the Information Worker's Paper Documents in an Electronic File Cabinet, *Proceedings of the ACM SIGCHI Conference on Human Factors in Computing Systems*, April 1994.

R. Spence and M. Apperley, Data Base Navigation: An Office Environment for the Professional, *Behavior and Info. Technology*, Vol. 1, No. 1, 1982, pp. 43-54.

Ramana Rao, Stuart K. Card, Herbert D. Jellinek, Jock D. Mackinlay, George G. Robertson, The Information Grid: A Framework for Information Retreival and Retrieval-Centered Applications, *UIST '92*, p. 23.

Rao, R. and Card, S. K. (1994) The Table Lens: Merging graphical and symbolic representations in an interactive focus+context visualization for tabular information. In *Proceedings of the ACM CHI'94 Conference on Human Factors in Computing Systems*, pp. 318-322, Boston, April 24-28, ACM Press.

Reichenberger, K., Kamps, T., and Golovchinsky, G. (1995) Towards a Generative Theory of Diagram Design. *Proceedings of the Information Visualization Symposium '95*, Atlanta, Georgia, Oct 29-30, 1995. pp. 11-18.

Remde, J. R., Gomez, L. M. and Landauer, T. K. (1987) SuperBook: An Automatic Tool for Information Exploration - Hypertext? In *Proceedings of the ACM Hypertext'87 Conference*, Chapel Hill, NC., Nov 13-15, pp. 175-188.

Rennison, E. and Strausfeld, L. The Millennium Project: Constructing a Dynamic 3+D Virtual Environment for Exploring Geographically, Temporally, and Categorically Organized Historical Information, in Frank, A.U. and Kuhn, W. (Eds.). *Spatial Information Theory - Proceedings of COSIT'95*. LNCS 988, Springer, Semmering, Austria, 1995, pp. 69-91.

Rennison, Earl. Personalized Galaxy of News: Using a Learning Algorithm to Customize News Information Visualization, Navigation and Access. Submitted to *CHI 95*.

Rennison, Earl. *Using Genetic Algorithms to Explore Large Distributed Information Bases*. MIT Technical Note, April, 1994.

Richard A. Bolt, *Spatial Data Management*, Massachusetts Institute of Technology, 1979.

Richard Chimera. (1992) Value bars: An information visualization and navigation tool for multi-attribute listings. In *Proceedings of the ACM SIGCHI Conference on Human Factors in Computing Systems* , pages 293-294, May 1992.

Richard Chimera. Value Bars: An information visualization and navigation tool for multi-attribute listings. *CHI 92 Conference Proceedings*, pp. 293-294, 1992.

Richard Mander, Gitta Salomon, Yin Yin Wong, A 'Pile' Metaphor for Supporting Casual Organization of Information, *CHI '92*, p. 627.

Rieber, L.P. (1995) A Historical Review of Visualization in Human Cognition. *ETR&D*, 43, 1, pp 45-56.

Rifas, L. *The Dataforest: Tree Forms as Information Display Graphics*, PhD Thesis, University of Washington, 1994 (see the ECHT94 Position Paper).

Robert R. Korfhage, Query enhancement by user profiles, in *Proceedings of the Third Joint BCS and ACM Symposium*, 1984, pp. 111-122.

Robertson, G. G., Mackinlay, J. D. and Card, S. K. (1991) Cone trees: animated 3d visualizations of hierarchical information. In *Proceedings of ACM SIGCHI'91 Conference on Human Factors in Computing Systems*, pp. 189-194, New Orleans, Louisiana, April 28-May 2, ACM Press.

Rohrer, T. Feeling Stuck in a GUI Web: Metaphors, image-schemas, and designing the human computer interface - or - Metaphors we compute by: bringing magic into interface design, 1995.

Ronald Baecker, Ian Small, Richard Mander, Bringing Icons to Life, *CHI '91*, p. 1.

S. Feiner and C. Beshers, Worlds Within Worlds: Metaphors for Exploring *n*-dimensional Virtual Worlds, in *UIST 90, ACM Symp. on User Interface Software*, ACM Press, New York, 1990, pp. 76-83.

S. K. Card and P. Pirolli. The Cost-of-Knowledge Characteristic Function: Display Evaluation for Direct-Walk Dynamic Information Visualizations, *Proceedings of the ACM SIGCHI Conference on Human Factors in Computing Systems*, April 1994.

S. Mukherjea and J. Foley. Navigational View Builder: A Tool for Building Navigational Views of Information Spaces. In *ACM SIGCHI '94 Conference Companion*, pages 289-290, Boston, Ma, April 1994.

S. Mukherjea, J. Foley, and S. Hudson. Interactive Clustering for Navigating in Hypermedia Systems. In *Proceedings of the ACM European Conference of Hypermedia Technology*, pages 136-144, Edinburgh, Scotland, September 1994.

S.G. Eick, J.L. Steffen, and E.E. Sumner, SeeSoft—A Tool for Visualizing Software, *IEEE Trans. on Software Engineering*, Vol. 18, No. 11, Nov. 1992, pp. 957-968.

S.-H. Li and P. B. Danzig, *Two-dimensional visualization for Internet resource discovery*, Technical Report USC-CS-95-609, University of Southern California, 1995. 12

S.K. Card, G.G. Robertson, and W. York, The WebBook and the Web Forager: An Information Workspace for the World Wide Web, to appear in *CHI 96, ACM Conf. on Human Factors in Software*, ACM Press, New York, 1996.

S.K. Card, Human Factors and the Intelligent Interface, in G. Kohl and S.S. Nassau (eds.), *Combining Human Factors and AI: A New Frontier in Human Factors*, Proc. Symposium sponsored by the Metropolitan Chapter of the Human Factors Society, New York, 1984.

Samet, Hanan. *The Design and Analysis of Spatial Data Structures*. Addison Wesley, Reading, MA, 1990.

Sarkar, M., Snibbe, S., Tversky, O. and Reiss, S. (1993) Stretching the Rubber Sheet: A Metaphor for Visualizing Large Layouts on Small Screens. In *Proceedings of UIST '93*, pp. 81-91, Atlanta, Nov 3-5.

Schaffer, D. and Greenberg, S. (1993) Sifting through hierarchical information. In *Proceedings of posters and short papers ACM INTERCHI '93 Conference on Human Factors in Computing Systems*, Amsterdam, Holland.

Schaffer, D., et. al. Comparing Fisheye and full-zoom techniques for navigating large information spaces, *ACM Transactions on Information Systems*, to appear, (1996).

Seligmann, D. and Feiner, S. Automated Generation of Intent-Based 3D Illustrations. *Proceedings of the ACM SIGGRAPH 91*. Las Vegas, NV, 1991.

Shneiderman, B. (1991) Tree-maps. Excerpts from the *IEEE 1991 Visualization* Video.

Shum, S. Real and Virtual Spaces: Mapping from spatial cognition to Hypertext, *Hypermedia*, 2, 2, (1990), pp. 133-158.

Small, David, Suguru Ishizaki, and Muriel Cooper. Typographic Space. *Proceedings of CHI. 1994*. Boston, Massachusetts: ACM.

Snibbe, S.S., Herndon, K.P., Robbins, D.C., Conner, D.B. and van Dam, A. Using deformations to explore 3D widget design. In *Proceedings of SIGGRAPH'92*, pp. 351-352.

Staples, L. Representation in Virtual Space: Visual Convention in the Graphical User Interface, *InterCHI'93*, ACM Press, Amsterdam, 1993, pp. 348-354.

Stefanakis, E. and Kavouras, M. On the Determination of the Optimum Path in Space, in Frank, A.U. and Kuhn, W. (Eds.). *Spatial Information Theory - Proceedings of COSIT'95*. LNCS 988, Springer, Semmering, Austria, 1995, pp. 241-257.

Stephen C. Hirtle. Representational structures for cognitive space: Trees, ordered trees and semi-lattices. *Proceedings of COSIT 95 (Conference on Spatial Information Theory)*, pp. 327-340, 1995.

Stephen G. Eick and Graham J. Wills. Navigating large networks with hierarchies. *journal?*, pp. 204-210, .

Stephen G. Eick. Data Visualization Sliders. *Proceedings of UIST 94*, pp. 119-120, 1994.

Stephen Wehrend and Clayton Lewis. A problem-oriented classification of Visualization techniques. *journal?*, pp. 139-143, .

Steven Feiner and Clifford Beshers. Visualizing n-dimensional virtual worlds with n-vision. *Computer Graphics (1990 Symposium on Interactive 3D Graphics)*, pp. 37-38, Vol. 24, March 1990.

Steven H. Tang and Mark A. Linton. Pacers: Time-elastic objects. In *Proceedings of the ACM Symposium on User Interface Software and Technology*. ACM Press, Nov 1993.

Stuart K. Card, George G. Robertson, and Jock D. Mackinlay. The Information Visualizer, an Information Workspace, *Proceedings of ACM Human Factors in Computing Systems Conference (CHI '91)*, 181-188.

Suguru Ishizaki. Multiagent model of dynamic design: Visualization as an emergent behavior of active design agents. *CHI 96 Conference Proceedings*, pp. 347-354, 1996.

T. Kohonen, The self organizing map, *Proceedings of the IEEE Transactions on Computers*, vol. 78, no. 9, pp. 1464-1480, 1990.

T.A. van Dijk, and W. Kintsch, *Strategies of Discourse Comprehension*, New York: Academic Press, 1983.

Tam, J. C. and Chignell, M. H. (1992) Neighbourhoods and Links: Examining the Assumptions of Hypermedia. *Proceedings of 25th Annual Conference of the Human Factors Association of Canada*, Hamilton, Ontario, 1992, pp. 85-90.

The Webhound WWW Document Filtering System, MIT.

Thomas Erickson and Gitta Salomon. Designing a Desktop Information System: Observations and Issues, *CHI '91*.

Thüring, M., Haake, J.M., and Hannemann, J. What's Eliza doing in the Chinese Room? Incoherent hyperdocuments - and how to avoid them, *Hypertext'91*, San Antonio, 1991, pp. 161-177.

Tomihisa Kamada. *Visualizing Abstract Objects and Relations*. World Scientific, 1989.

Tufte, E.R. *Envisioning Information*, Graphics Press, Cheshire, 1990.

Tversky, B. Cognitive Maps, Cognititve Collages, and Spatial Mental Models, *COSIT'93*, Springer, Elba, 1993, pp. 14-24.

Tyson R. Henry, Scott E. Hudson , Interactive Graph Layout, *UIST '91*, p. 55.

U. Cavallaro et al., HIFI: Hypertext Interface for Information Systems, *IEEE Software*, Vol. 10, No. 6, Nov. 1993, pp. 48-51.

Veerasamy, A., Hudson, S., and Navathe, S. Querying, navigating and Visualizing an Online Library Catalog, GVU Tech report, 1996, accessible at ftp://ftp.cc.gatech.edu/pub/people/veerasam/sir.ps.

W. Johnson, S. K. Card, H.D. Jellinek, L. Klotz, R. Rao, Bridging the Paper and Electronic Worlds: The Paper User Interface, *Proceedings of INTERCHI*, ACM, April 1993. pp. 507-512.

Waern, Yvonne (ed.), *Cognitive Aspects of Computer Supported Tasks*, Tiptree, Essex: Anchor Press Ltd., 1989.

William C. Donelson. Spatial Management of Information, *Proceedings of 1978 ACM SIGGRAPH Conference*, 203-209.

Williamson, C., and Shneiderman, B., 1992. The Dynamic HomeFinder: Evaluating dynamic queries in a real-estate information exploration system, *Proc. ACM SIGIR92 Conference*, Copenhagen, Denmark, (June 1992), 338-346. Reprinted in Shneiderman, B. (Editor),

Sparks of Innovation in Human-Computer Interaction, Ablex Publishers, Norwood, NJ, (1993), 295-307.

Williamson, C., Shneiderman, B. *The Dynamic HomeFinder: Evaluating Dyunamic Queries in a RealEstate Information Exploration System*, University of Maryland CS-TR-2819, College Park, MD, 1992.

Wood, A., Drew, N., Beale, R. & Hendeley, B. HyperSpace: Web Browsing with Visualization. (1995) In *Proceedings of the Third International World Wide Web Conference*, pp. 22-26.

Wurman, R. S. *Information Anxiety: What to do when information doesn't tell you what you need to know*. Bantam Book, 1989. New York.

X. Lin, P. Liebscher, and G. Marchionini, Graphic Representation of Electronic Search Patterns, *J. Am. Society for Info. Science*, Vol. 42, No. 7, 1991, pp. 469-478.

X. Lin, Visualization for the document space, in *Proceedings of Visualization '92*, (Boston, MA), pp. 274-281, October 1992.

Y.K. Leung and M.D.Apperley. A review and taxonomy of distortion-oriented presentation techniques. *ACM Transactions on Computer-Human Interaction*, 1(2):126—160, June 1994.

Zeleznik, R.C., et al. An object-oriented framework for the integration of interactive animation techniques. In *Proceedings of SIGGRAPH'91*, pp. 105-112.

Zhengping Zuo, John Dill, and Lyn Bartram. Variable Zoom: A fisheye view of hierarchical networks. In *Proceedings of the Fifth Annual Western Computer Graphics Symposium*, 1993. 132

Zizi, M. and Beaudouin-Lafon, M. Accessing Hyperdocuments through Interactive Dynamic Maps, *ECHT'94*, ACM Press, Edinburgh, 1994, pp. 126-135.

7

Elements of Advanced Communication System

Hybrid DS/FH Spread Spectrum Communication System

Introduction

The system specification stage can be characterized as a translation of user demands into a technical specification. In this chapter we will concentrate on the trade-offs that exist during the system design stage. As an illustration, the design of a non cellular communication system referred to as *wissce* will be explained. This acronym "*wissce*" stands for Wireless Indoor Spread Spectrum Communication Equipment. This system will function as example of the design process throughout the remainder of this thesis.

This chapter is primarily focussed on system-level aspects. We however will keep in mind the implementation issues addressed in the previous chapter. In the next section the trade-offs that exist between the system parameters will be discussed, addresses the way the various clocks in *wissce* can be derived from a single time-base. The actual choice of parameters is made in At the end a conclusion shortly summarizes the results of the system specification stage and provides an summary of *wissce*'s system specification.

Clock Control

The term "clock-control" did not appear as a technical property. However, this does not mean that it is not a system issue, it just shows that a direct relation with the user demands is not obvious. The clock-control issue is related to the frequency plan in the transmitter front-end, the data-detection method and the requirements of the digital signal processing taking place in the transceiver back-end.

The usage of different clocks, a schematic view of a possible transceiver architecture. Both the transmitter (upper) and the receiver (lower) chain) are shown.

The translation from a baseband signal to the *rf*-transmit frequency is done in a number of steps (super heterodyne). In the transmission chain a frequency-hopping synthesizer (direct digital synthesizer: *dds*) takes care of data modulation (*mfsk*, via a frequency setting words: *fsw*), *fh*-spreading (also via the *fsw*) and *ds*-spreading (using a *ds*-code sequence). To generate the *ds*-code sequence, a code-clock (CK_{code}) is required. The output signal of the *dds*is both *ds*-spread and *fh*-spread and will be converted in two stages ($f_{LO}1$ and $f_{LO}2a$) to the *rf*-transmit frequency.

In the receiver chain the *rf*-signal is converted to baseband in two steps. First using local oscillator signal $f_{LO}1$ to go to an intermediate frequency and secondly using a second local oscillator signal to convert the signal to baseband. This second local oscillator is not fixed, it "hops" according to a pattern directed by frequency setting words (*fsw*). After the second conversion stage the signal is sampled using a sampling clock ($CK_{sampler}$) to enable the remaining of the processing (including *ds*-despreading) in the digital domain.

From the above discussion it appears that spreading is performed in the "analog" domain while despreading is done after sampling. The reason for this is that spreading is easily combined with the generation of the transmit signal (in the *dds*) while in the receiving chain more despreading paths are required (see section 7.3.3) so a digital *ds*-despreading operation is profitable.

Section 7.4 will more specifically address the front-end. A conclusion at this stage is that several clock-signals are required:

1. Front-end clocks, to enable the translation of baseband signals to and from high frequency *rf*-signals ($f_{LO}2a$ and $f_{LO}2b$)
2. An input clock to the frequency-synthesizer that performs the frequency-hopping spreading (CK_{DDS})
3. Several clocks used by the digital baseband processing: the sample-clocks ($CK_{sampler}$) and a number of processor clocks ($CK_{processor}$).

Front-end Clocks

Front-end clocks are required as local oscillator signals to translate baseband signals to high frequency *rf*-signals and vice versa. As there is a user demand to meet legal requirements, the *rf*-frequency is in the 2.4 GHz ISM-band. The exact local oscillator frequencies depend on the frequency plan of the front-end.

A related issue is the fact that when generating frequencies in the 2.4 GHz band, considerable frequency errors will appear due to the limited accuracy of a crystal oscillator. If applying a coherent data demodulation scheme, the frequency error must be controlled (by a carrier tracking loop). To avoid this effort, we chose a possibly non coherent data detection method (section 5.2.2) where the maximum acceptable frequency error follows from the modulation method.

There are two ways to compensate for the inaccuracy of standard crystal oscillators at an *rf*-frequency of 2.4 GHz: either by using a carrier-tracking loop or by applying a more accurate crystal oscillator. The inaccuracies in the output-frequency are mainly caused by temperature dependencies. A "more accurate" crystal oscillator can therefore be based on the principle of an *mcxo* (microprocessor controlled crystal oscillator) [BMH89] where using the property of a crystal that it can resonate at different frequencies simultaneously. A dual-mode oscillator provides both the fundamental frequency ($f_{fundamental}$) and the third overtone (f3-overtone). By frequency subtraction of the third overtone and three times the fundamental, a beat frequency is obtained:

$$f_{beat} = f_{3\text{-overtone}} - 3.\ f_{fundamental} \tag{1}$$

This beat frequency provides a measure for the temperature of the crystal. This measure can be used to control the output frequency, *mcxo*'s are commercially available and reported accuracies are better than 3.10^{-8} [O-T94).

Our approach towards an inexpensive implementation of this principle is to extract the beat frequency in the usual way and then use this frequency to control a fractional-N frequency synthesizer to get an accurate reference frequency [Reg].

To summarize: The main problem towards the generation of the clock-signals in the front-end is the accuracy. To solve the problem we propose to apply a crystal oscillator based on the principle of an *mcxo*.

fh-*Synthesizer Clock*

The *fh*-synthesizer clock is required as a reference clock to the frequency synthesizer that provides the "hopping" carrier. To enable rapid hopping from the one frequency to an other, a direct frequency synthesis technique should be applied. A direct digital synthesizer (*dds*) is an almost perfect compromise between all requirements and is therefore selected.

Every clock cycle a digital *frequency setting word* (*fsw*) is added to an accumulator. The contents of the accumulator represents the phase of the output signal. This phase representation is converted into a waveform and then into an analog output signal. By changing the *fsw*, it is possible to change the output frequency. In this way a "hopping" frequency synthesizer can be realized.

The "sampling"-frequency of the digital to analog converter should exceed twice the desired output frequency of the *dds*. As this "sampling"-frequency is equal to the clock frequency, the latter is an important parameter. To fix a value for this clock, the desired output frequencies should be known. The exact frequencies however are not fixed yet (dependent on, data speed, etc.), but the occupied bandwidth is about 10 MHz. This means:

1. As the *dds*has to "hop" throughout the whole frequency band of 10 MHz, the frequency-band to be covered is 10 MHz as well.
2. The clock-frequency should be as low as possible to save power and allow for an inexpensive implementation.
3. The center-frequency should be as high as possible to reduce mirror-frequencies in the front-end.
4. The combination of center-frequency and clock-frequency should be chosen in such a way that harmonics do not fold back in the desired frequency band.

If a center frequency of about 25 MHz is used, the clock frequency should then be approximately 80 MHz. The exact values should be chosen in such a way that they "fit" other constraints.

Baseband Processing Clocks

There are mainly 3 categories of low-frequency clocks: sample clocks, processor clocks and the transmitter code-clock.

Sample-Clock Signals

used in the analog to digital conversion of the input signals. Those clock signals were addressed in the section 5.2.7 on analog to digital interfacing.

Processor Clock Signals

As motivated in the previous chapter, the digital back-end will be implemented as an embedded system. The processor architecture which is the core of the embedded system as well as some of the application specific functional units need various clock-signals:

1. All processor clocks should be synchronous to avoid timing problems.
2. To enable an implementation on Sea-of-Gates, the main processor clock should not exceed 50 MHz.
3. The processor-clock should be high enough to enable the completion of a whole "software"-loop within a single symbol-period.
4. To control interfering signals, the exact processor clock frequency should be chosen in such a way that a fixed relationship with other clocks exist.

It is likely that the main processor clock will be in the range 30-50 MHz.

Code-Clocks

Two code-clocks exist in a transceiver: the receiver code-clock and the transmitter code-clock. In the receiving chain despreading is performed digitally (see section 5.2.7), the receiver code-clock will therefore be derived from the processor clock.

In the transmitter chain however, *ds*-spreading is performed in the transmitter-*dds*using a *ds*-code sequence that is generated within the processor framework. To enable the generation of the *ds*-code signal at the appropriate frequency a code-clock signal is required. The frequency of this clock is equal to the chip-rate:

$$r_c = N_{DS}.\mathrm{r}_{symb}. \tag{2}$$

As can be seen from this equation, the exact frequency of this clock signal depends on system parameters addressed before.

To summarize: in the clock control section we concluded that several clock signals occur in a transceiver. To avoid synchronization problems all clocks should be derived from the same reference clock which is accurate which implies a fixed relationships between all clocks.

The exact frequencies of a number of clock-signals are also dependent on several design issues discussed before. Those frequencies as well as a possible clock scheme will be discussed below.

System Specification

In chapter 3 the application domain of the target communication system was already briefly described. The goal of this section is to clarify the communication concept and evaluate the user demands. In this way a basis for the system specification can be found.

The concept of non-cellular communication systems requires no installation effort. A complete system only consists of a set of transceivers and is therefore mobile itself. A group of people might for instance go somewhere and still be able to communicate with each other as long as their relative distance is within specification.

So a non-cellular solution provides an enormous flexibility while it is also keeps prices acceptable in the sense that no additional investment in infrastructure is required, on the condition that the price of a single transceiver is comparable to the price of a mobile in a similar cellular system.

To enable communication, connections have to be made which requires a protocol. Such a protocol should fit the flexible nature of the proposed application domain and therefore has to be simple. A simple and effective protocol which will be used in the following, works as follows: an initiator starts transmission by making a call to an arbitrary other device (addressee). To this end the initiator transmits using the address (*cdma*-code) of the intended addressee. Once the addressee acquired synchronization, it gives an acknowledgement back to the initiator. If the initiator can synchronize to this message within a certain amount of time, the transmission of the intended data-message can start. The consequence of this approach is that during the synchronization stage both transceivers are transmitting simultaneously. During "normal" data communication this duplex connection is also required to remain synchronized. As a result the transmission system must provide full-duplex communication links.

Now that the non-cellular concept is explained, the user demands can be evaluated to fix technical parameters.

1. *Universal usage*

   Paramount to the user is undisturbed, low risk usage. For a large number of countries this means that a communication system has to obey legal requirements. The dutch situation requires spread spectrum communication systems to operate in the 2.4 GHz ISM-band. In most other western countries this frequency-band is available as well. The usage of this frequency band imposes a number of restrictions. The most stringent restriction is the bandwidth limitation. In the following we will refer to this user-demand as "meeting legal requirements".

2. *Reliable*

   Users wish error-free transmission. As complete error free transmission is not possible, the error probability should be minimized. In data communication it would be possible to "retransmit" erroneous messages on the cost of a lower transmission capacity. For voice applications however, this is not possible.

3. *In-door*

   The system is targeted for short distances so an important application will be as indoor communication equipment. Consequently operation in the (hostile) in-door environment should be possible.

4. *High transmission capacity*

   Pure data communication applications nowadays demand high transmission speeds. The transmission speed is however limited by the available bandwidth and the number of users that have to be allowed in the system.

5. *High active user capacity*

   A difference can be made between "active user capacity" and "total user capacity". The first capacity is determined by the amount of interference that can be allowed in the system. The total user capacity however, is determined by the number of available addresses (*cdma*-codes). At this point the focus is on the "active user capacity".

6. *Large area coverage*

   An important consideration is the maximum allowed distance between users. The system is meant for short-distances. For flexible usage however, this "short-distance" should be not too short. On the other hand the larger the distance, the higher the energy usage will be and the more interference will be generated for the other (near) users. The latter results in a worse mean receiving quality.

   The further users are apart, the worse the receiving quality will be. So the radio link will fail "softly".

7. *Low purchasing costs*

   The complete communication systems consists of only transceivers and is meant for the mass-market. In comparison with cellular systems, a non-cellular approach provides flexibility. It is however important that the price of a transceiver is comparable to that of mobiles in a similar cellular system. The purchasing costs therefore should be low.

8. Low operation costs

   Power consumption should be low to decrease operation costs. A service provider is not involved as the system does not depend on an infrastructure.

9. *Flexibility*

   The system should be flexible in the sense that many different applications can be allowed.

10. *Mobility*

    A complete communication system consists of only transceivers and is therefore mobile itself. For the situation in which a transceiver is used in a mobile situation (e.g. as hand-held), power consumption should be low as well.

11. *Short access time*

    The time to build a transmission link should be short.

The relation between important user-demands and technical specifications is given. At the top technical properties are given. In the first column the relative importance of a demand for the user is shown. A single "+" means "rather important" while "+++" expresses a meaning of "mandatory". For instance: "meeting legal constraints" is mandatory while "large area coverage" is only desirable. The next 7 columns to the right show the relation between user demands and technical properties like bandwidth, processing gain etc. A "+" on one hand expresses a positive relationship: the larger value of the property (for instance "larger bandwidth"), the higher the customer satisfaction. On the other hand a "-" shows a negative relationship, to satisfy the user the property should have a low value. The right 2 columns show properties for which grading does not make sense. A "+" expresses in these columns that a user-demand is in favor of the property while a "-" shows the opposite.

We observe that different user demands lead to contradictory technical solutions. For instance a "high user capacity" is in favor of a low symbol rate while "high transmission capacity" wants the opposite. This is the reason for taking the relative importance of all user demands into account.

The available *bandwidth* is an important system parameter and therefore the first property to be described in more detail (section 5.2.1). After fixing the available frequency-bands, it is logical to treat the *symbol-rate* and the *number of bits per symbol* to find a relation between *cdma* spreading-factor, bit-rate and available bandwidth (section 5.2.2). The *cdma*-spreading technique and *processing gain* is addressed in section 5.2.3 while the modulation-format itself is coped with in section 5.2.4.

The term *front-end complexity* can be interpreted as the number and quality of the components used in the front-end. As this property and the *output power* are strongly related, they are both dealt with in section 5.2.5. The required reliability ("reliable operation") is addressed in section 5.2.6, then finally section 5.2.7 addresses the interface between the analog and time-discrete domain.

Obtaining the system parameters is a highly iterative stage, all parameters influence each other. As a result it is difficult to discuss the system design process step by step. The following sections shows an attempt. However, cross-references throughout the sections can not be avoided.

Frequency Bands

In the Netherlands the available frequency band for spread spectrum communications is the so-called "2.4 GHz ISM-band" with a total of 30 MHz (2445-2475 MHz).

We saw that full-duplex communication links are required (page http://cas.et.tudelft.nl/~glas/thesis/node20.html - pgduplex http://cas.et.tudelft.nl/~glas/thesis/node20.html - pgduplex). If using a single frequency band for both receiving and transmitting, a transmitter will function as a near-interferer to its own receiver and correct data transmission is hardly possible. For this reason the available 30 MHz frequency band has to be divided into a transmission and a reception band. An additional problem is that both bands cannot be located directly next to each other: a guard-band is required to allow for filtering in the front-end.

At this stage a trade-off between occupied bandwidth for a single channel (BW_{total}) and requirements towards the front-end can be observed. The higher the occupied bandwidth, the higher the possible data speed and processing gain but the steeper (and more expensive) filters are required in the front-end. As a compromise we propose a guard-band of 10 MHz. This fixes BW_{total} to maximally 10 MHz as well.

An important issue is that as a transceiver can be both an initiator and an addressee, it should be possible to swap transmission and reception band. This imposes extra requirements on the front-end.

Transmission Capacity

It is clear that the user desires a high transmission capacity (overall data speed). However, it can also be seen that this user demand leads shows conflicts with the demands "low purchasing costs", "short access time", "meeting legal requirements" and others. As a result a compromise should be found.

The data speed can be increased independently of the occupied bandwidth by increasing the number of modulation levels (= number of bits per symbol). However, increasing this number of bits per symbol increases both the implementation cost and the bit error probability.

Summarizing: increasing the data speed leads to either a larger bandwidth occupancy or higher hardware costs and a worse bit error rate.

The trade-off between data speed and the number of modulation levels. This plot makes clear that it is advantageous to have a rather small number of modulation levels: the data speed increases with the " ^{2}log" of the number of levels while the data detection complexity increases linearly.

CDMA Technique

It was already shown that *cdma* (Spread Spectrum) techniques have very promising properties for using them in a communication system that has to provide ad-hoc communication links. However, each technique has its own disadvantages: direct-sequence suffers from the near-far effect, while it is hard to obtain a high processing gain with frequency-hopping.

In cellular systems the near-far effect can be reduced by applying power-control. Power-control is an algorithm in which the transmitted power of the mobiles is controlled in such a way that the received power of all mobiles at the base-station is equal. If such a power control algorithm functions as desired, near-far effects are not an issue in such systems. In non-cellular systems however, there is no base-station, consequently, power-control is hardly possible. To retain the advantages of both *ds*and *fh*while cancelling their shortcomings, a technique is selected that combines the large processing gain of *ds*with a reduction of the near-far effect due to *fh*http://cas.et.tudelft.nl/~glas/thesis/footnode.html - 1229http://cas.et.tudelft.nl/~glas/thesis/footnode.html - 1229.

This combined technique will be referred to as the hybrid *ds-fh*spread spectrum communication technique.

In this technique, a user-address consists of a frequency-hopping pattern of length N_{FH} and N_{FH} (possibly different) *pn-codes* of length N_{DS}. The start of a new set of *pn-codes* and an *fh*-sequence are linked. This is important when regarding the code-synchronization problem (chapter 7, page http://cas.et.tudelft.nl/~glas/thesis/node33.html - seccodesync http://cas.et.tudelft.nl/~glas/thesis/node33.html - seccodesync). An example user-address existing of an *fh*-sequence of length 7 and 7 *pn-codes*. Every data-symbol is combined with a *pn-code* causing the direct-sequence spreading. Subsequent data-symbols are transmitted in different *fh*-channels according to a certain sequence to perform *fh*-spreading. As a result we use neither fast nor slow frequency-hopping. A frequency-synthesizer only has to "hop" at a speed equal to the symbol-rate.

For constant and a small $BW_{\text{total}}\ r$ and a small δ_{mod}, the trade-off curves, can be obtained for three values of $BW_{\text{total}}\ r_{\text{symb}}$. Concerning this trade-off the following remarks can be made:

- It is likely that the *ds*-code will be made using shift-registers (so-called "shift register sequences" [Gol67]). The code-length is then 2^n-1 with n being an integer. For this reason, only the marked points are possible trade-off points.
- Increasing is advantageous (page http://cas.et.tudelft.nl/~glas/thesis/node7.html - page pghttp://cas.et.tudelft.nl/~glas/thesis/node7.html - pagepg) and can be realized at low implementation costs.
- Increasing results in the requirement for a more expensive *fh*-frequency-synthesizer and is for this reason undesired. A minimum number of *fh*-channels is however required to limit the influence of the near-far effect (near-interference).

To find a minimum value for the user demands "reliable operation" and "large user capacity" are translated into a technical compromise that maximally 2 near users may be present. As the frequency-hopping sequences are chosen in such a way that they have at most 2 partial hits with another sequence (see section 6.4.2), this compromise converts into the worst case possibility of having at most 4 partial hits per *fh*-sequence. Furthermore we need at least two frequency-hopping channels without near-interference to enable proper synchronization. As a result the minimum value of is 6, a vertical line representing.

After evaluating other trade-offs as well, section 5.4 will address the actual choice of the values of and N_{DS} and N_{FH}.

Modulation Format

An issue not yet addressed is the choice of modulation format. Requirements towards this digital modulation format are low implementation costs, the possibility of applying multi-level modulation (having multiple bits per symbol) and a low susceptibility to effects caused by the indoor radio-path.

Three likely candidates for the modulation format exist: amplitude modulation, phase modulation and frequency modulation. Detection of amplitude modulated symbols is problematic in combination with multi-level modulation while frequency-hopping in combination with phase shift keying is susceptible to multi-path effects and requires phase-continuous frequency hopping or a return-to-zero code. This leaves frequency shift keying (*fsk*) as the better alternative.

A well known disadvantage of *fsk*is that it requires a larger bandwidth (higher value of $_{mod}$) however this value will still be small in comparison with the already occupied spread spectrum bandwidth. Increasing the number of modulation levels is possible by using more than two frequencies. The resulting modulation technique is referred to as multiple frequency shift keying (*mfsk*). An additional property of frequency modulation is the possibility of non-coherent data detection. This saves hardware costs as a carrier tracking loop is not required if frequency errors are small.

Front-End Related Issues

The front-end of a transceiver is responsible for conversion and amplification of the transmitted signal from baseband to an *rf*-frequency and transmitting it. In addition the front-end should amplify the desired received signal and convert it to a baseband signal.

The maximum distance between transmitter and receiver depends on the transmitted power of a transmitter, the sensitivity of the receiver, the amount of interference that is added to the signal before data-detection takes place and the required bit error probability (*ber*).

The system is targeted for in-door communication so the distance will probably be much less than 1 km. Multi-path effects however, can dramatically reduce the received signal-to-noise ratio (see chapter 6, page http://cas.et.tudelft.nl/~glas/thesis/node27.html - secfading http://cas.et.tudelft.nl/~glas/thesis/node27.html - secfading). We will therefore require a free-space coverage of 1 km which corresponds to a loss of 100 dB.

How this translates to a required output-power, depends on the "quality" of the front-end (amount of interference added), the number of interfering users, the required *ber*and the relation between input signal to noise ratio (*snr*) to the baseband processing and *ber* (see chapter 6). Preliminary investigations showed that the required maximum output power will be below 1 mW.

Bit Error Probability

Reliable operation implies a low bit error probability (*ber*). This performance measure is dependent both on the received *snr*-level and the sensitivity of the receiver.

However, using the *ber*as a performance measure immediately introduces another problem. In an indoor environment fading heavily influences the *ber*-performance, while the multi-path situation (which introduces fading) can hardly be caught in a "typical" description. The multi-path properties are very irregular.

Yet a *ber*-performance measure is important as it gives the best indication of the "reliability" of a system. A *ber*-requirement of 10^{-6} in an unfaded channel (only Gaussian noise present) without error correction in combination with the existing multi-path effects and the application of error correcting coding is expected to result in a satisfactory performance.

In section 6.2 the multi-path effects on the relation between the *snr*and the *ber*will be analyzed.

Analog to Digital Interfacing

Analog to digital conversion consists of two parts: sampling and quantizing. In this section which deals with the system definition we will only consider the conversion from the analog to the time-discrete domain (sampling) as it has a large influence on the system architecture.

The more important issue in sampling is where in the architecture it takes place. Sampling directly at the antenna leads to a so called "software radio" [Mit95, Bai95, KS95]. This implies large demands on the sensitivity of the analog to digital conversion and the speed of the digital processing to follow. By moving the sampling operation from the antenna in the direction of the baseband processing, the analog part of radio gets more complex (and expensive) while the digital processing becomes simpler. As a compromise, sampling will be performed after *fh*-despreading and filtering.

A critical choice is the input center frequency:

1. zero-frequency is attractive as it enables a low sampling frequency. However due to non-linear effects, conversion to baseband also introduces a DC-component. This component is in general hard to deal with as this component is located in the middle of the desired signal and can saturate the sampler. Another drawback is that an extra conversion stage is required.
2. An intermediate frequency, in this situation the DC-component can be filtered out. A disadvantage however is the fact that the sampling frequency should be at last twice the highest signal frequency. So this alternative

increases the minimal sample frequency and consequently the speed of the digital processing.

3. Use an intermediate frequency but apply sampling and a frequency translation at the same time. In this way it is possible to convert the signal to DC and enabling a low sampling-frequency while the usual disadvantages of signals at DC are cancelled.

In the latter approach a low sampling frequency and the absence of any DC-component are combined and is therefore the more attractive one. A number of issues concerning the sampling frequency have to be dealt with:

- To minimize the required sampling-frequency, the input center-frequency should be "folded" back to DC. For this reason the sampling frequency has to be an integer times this center-frequency.
- If the desired frequency-band is converted to around DC, quadrature sampling is required to distinguish positive and negative frequency components. Consequently, the digital baseband signal (signal after analog to digital conversion) contains an in-phase and quadrature component.
- The sampling frequency should exceed twice the bandwidth of the baseband signal (Nyquist requirement).
- The sampling frequency should be asynchronous to the chip-rate (r_c) to enable proper code-tracking [FdD86].
- Bit error rate simulations showed that a sample frequency of about four times the chip-rate enables proper operation (the intended quantizing method also plays a role, see section 7.2.1.2 for more information on this aspect).

As the center of the intermediate frequency-band is converted to DC, quadrature sampling is required to enable a distinction between positive and negative frequency components. The quadrature sampling clock will be /2 rad. of the input center-frequency out of phase with the in-phase sampling clock. This introduces a quadrature error as a time corresponding to /2 rad. at the input-center frequency does not correspond to the same phase difference over the whole frequency band. This is a reason for choosing the input-center frequency high compared to the frequency band used by modulation ( ).

REFERENCES

Acredolo, L., & Goodwyn, S. (1996). *Baby signs.* Chicago, IL: Contemporary Books.

Alm, N. (1993). The development of augmentative and alternative communication systems to assist with social communication. *Technology and Disability,* 2(3), 1-18.

American Speech-Language-Hearing Association (2004). *Augmentative and alternative communication: Technical report.*

Baumgart, D., Johnson, J., & Helmstetter, E. (1990). *Augmentative and alternative communication systems for persons with moderate and severe disabilities.* Baltimore, MD: Paul H. Brookes Publishing Company.

Beukelman, D. (Ed.). (1992). [Topical issue]. *Seminars in Speech and Language*, 13(2).

Beukelman, D., & Miranda, P. (1998). *Augmentative and alternative communication: Management of severe communication disorders in children and adults (2nd ed.).* Baltimore, MD: Paul H. Brookes Publishing Company.

Beukelman, D., McGinnis, J., & Morrow, D. (1991). Vocabulary selection in augmentative and alternative communication. AAC: Augmentative and Alternative Communication, 7(3), 171-185.

Biklen, D. & Cardinal, D. (1997). *Contested words, contested science: Unraveling the facilitated communication controversy.* New York, NY: Teachers College Press.

Blischak, D. M. (1994). Phonological awareness: Implications for individuals with little or no functional speech. *AAC: Augmentative and Alternative Communication,* 10(4), 245-254.

Bondy, A. & Frost, L. (2002). *A picture's worth: PECS and other visual communication strategies in autism.* Bethesda, MD: Woodbine House.

Bornstein, H., & Saulnier, K. L. (1984). *The signed English starter.* Washington, DC: Gallaudet Press.

Bornstein, H., & Saulnier, K. L. (1987). *The signed English schoolbook.* Washington, DC: Kendall Green Publications.

Bornstein, H., Saulnier, K. L., & Hamilton, L. B. (Eds.). (1983). *Comprehensive signed English dictionary.* Washington, DC: Gallaudet Press.

Calculator, S. (1999). AAC outcomes for children and youths with severe disabilities: When seeing is believing. *AAC: Augmentative and Alternative Communication,* 15(1), 4-12.

Calculator, S. (1999). Look who's pointing now: Cautions related to clinical use of facilitated communication. *Language, Speech, and Hearing Services in Schools.* 30(4), 408-414.

Calculator, S. (2002). Use of enhanced natural gestures to foster interactions between children with Angleman Syndrome and their parents. *American Journal of Speech-Language Pathology.* 11, 340-355.

Calculator, S., & Jorgensen, C. (1991). Integrating AAC instruction into regular education settings: Expounding on best practices. *AAC: Augmentative and Alternative Communication,* 7(3), 204-214.

Capone, N. C. & McGregor, K. K. (2004). Gestural development: A review for clinical and research practices. *Journal of Speech, Language, and Hearing Research.* 47, 173-186.

Collier, B. (2000). *See what we say: Situational vocabulary for adults who use augmentative and alternative communication.* Baltimore, MD: Paul H. Brookes Publishing Company.

Cress, C.(2004). Augmentative and alternative communication and language: Understanding and responding to parents' perspectives. *Topics in Language Disorders.* 24(1), 51-61.

Cumley, G. D. & Swanson, S. (1999). Augmentative and alternative communication options for children with developmental apraxia of speech: Three case studies. *AAC: Augmentative and Alternative Communication.* 15, 110-125.

Dowden, P. A., & Marriner, N. A. (1995). Augmentative and alternative communication: Treatment principles and strategies. *Seminars in Speech and Language*, 16(2), 140-157.

Downing, J. E. (1999). *Teaching communication skills to students with severe disabilities.* Baltimore, MD: Paul H. Brookes Publishing Company.

Drager, K. D., Light, J., Speltz, J. C., Fallon, K. A. & Jeffries, L. Z. (2003). The performance of typically developing 2 ½ year olds on dynamic display AAC technologies with different system layouts and language organizations. *Journal of Speech, Language, and Hearing Research.* 46, 298-312.

Duchan, J. F. (1999). Views of facilitated communication: What's the point? *Language, Speech, and Hearing Services in Schools.* 30(4), 401-407.

Dunn, M. L. (1982). *Pre-sign language motor skills: Skill starters for motor development.* Tucson, AZ: Communication Skill Builders.

Durand, V. M. & Merges, E. (2001). Functional communication training: A contemporary analytic intervention for problem behaviors. *Focus on Autism and Other Developmental Disabilities.* 16(2), 110-119, 136.

Elder, P., & Goossens', C. (1994). *Engineering training environments for interactive, augmentative communication: Strategies for adolescents and adults who are moderately / severely developmentally delayed.* Birmingham, AL: Southeast Augmentative Communication Conference Publications.

Elder, P., & Goossens', C. (1996). *Communication overlays for engineering training environments, Books I-IV (for adolescents and adults).* Birmingham, AL: Southeast Augmentative Communication Conference Publications.

Ely, S. (2000). *What is assistive technology: A basic guide for individuals with disabilities and their families (Rev. ed.).* Bloomington, IN: Indiana Institute on Disability and Community.

Erickson, K., Koppenhaver, D., & Yoder, D. (2003). *Waves of words: Augmented communicators read and write.* Toronto, Canada: International Society for Augmentative and Alternative Communication.

Fried-Oken, M. & Bersani, H. A. (2000). *Speaking up and spelling it out: Personal essays on augmentative and alternative communication.* Baltimore, MD: Paul H. Brookes Publishing Company.

Frost, L. A., & Bondy, A. S. (1994). *PECS, the Picture Exchange Communication System: Training manual.* Cherry Hill, NJ: Pyramid Educational Consultants, Inc.

Frost, L., & Bondy, A. (1998). *An introduction to PECS: The Picture Exchange Communication System.* [video recording]. Newark, DE: Pyramid Educational Consultants.

Glennen, S., & DeCoste, D. (1997). *The handbook of augmentative and alternative communication.* San Diego, CA: Singular Publishing Group.

Goossens', C., Crain, S., & Elder, P. (1992). *Engineering the preschool environment for interactive symbol communication: 18 months to 5 years developmentally.* Birmingham, AL: Southeast Augmentative Communication Conference Publications.

Goossens', C., Crain, S., & Elder, P. (1994). *Communication displays for engineered preschool environments, Books I-II.* Birmingham, AL: Southeast Augmentative Communication Conference Publications.

Granlund, M. & Olsson, C. (1999). Efficacy of communication intervention for presymbolic communicators. *AAC: Augmentative and Alternative Communication.* 15, 25-37.

Hodgdon, J. (1995). *Visual strategies for improving communication (Vol. 1): Practical supports for school and home.* Troy, MI: QuickRoberts Publishing.

Hodgdon, J. (1999). *Solving behavior problems in autism: Improving communication with visual strategies.* Troy, MI: QuickRoberts Publishing.

Hunt, P., Soto, G., Maier, J., Muller, E., & Goetz, L. (2002). Collaborative teaming to support students with AAC communication needs in general education classrooms. *AAC: Augmentative and Alternative Communication.* 18(1), 20-35.

Johnson, J. M., Baumgart, D., Helmstetter, E., & Curry, C. (1996). *Augmenting basic communication in natural contexts.* Baltimore, MD: Paul H. Brookes Publishing Company.

Johnston, S. S., Reichle, J. & Evans, J. (2004). Supporting augmentative and alternative communication use by beginning communicators with severe disabilities. *American Journal of Speech-Language Pathology.* 13, 20-30.

Kangas, K., & Lloyd, L. (1988). Early cognitive skills as prerequisites to augmentative and alternative communication use: What are we waiting for? *AAC: Augmentative and Alternative Communication,* 4(3), 211-221.

Koul. R. K., Schlosser, R. W. & Sancibrian, S. (2001). Effects of symbol, referent, and instructional variables on the acquisition of aided and unaided symbols by individuals with autism spectrum disorders. *Focus on Autism and Other Developmental Disabilities.* 16(3), 162-169.

Lane, L. G. (1990). *The Gallaudet survival guide to signing. (2nd ed.).* Washington, DC: Gallaudet Press.

Light, J. (1997). "Communication is the essence of human life": Reflections on communicative competence. *AAC: Augmentative and Alternative Communication,* 13(2), 61-70.

Light, J. C., & Binger, C. (1998). *Building communicative competence with individuals who use augmentative and alternative communication.* Baltimore, MD: Paul H. Brookes Publishing Company.

Light, J., DaHilo, J., English, J., Gutierrez, L., & Hartz, J. (1992). Instructing facilitators to support the communication of people who use augmentative communication systems. *Journal of Speech and Hearing Research,* 35(4), 865-875.

Lloyd, L., Fuller, D., & Arvidson, H. (Eds.). (1997). *Augmentative and alternative communication: A handbook of principles and practices.* Needham Heights, MA: Allyn & Bacon.

McCarthy, C. F., McLean, L., Miller, J., Paul-Brown, D, Romski, M.A., Rourk, J. D., & Yoder, D. E. (1998). *Communication supports checklist for serving individuals with severe disabilities.* Baltimore, MD: Paul Brookes Publishing.

McLean, J., McLean, L., Brady, N., & Etter, R. (1991). Communication profiles of two types of gestures using nonverbal persons with severe to profound mental retardation. *Journal of Speech and Hearing Research,* 34(2), 294-308.

McLean, J., Sack, S., McLean, L., O'Connor, A., & Simmons, S. (1990). *Developing communicative interactions* [training videos and manuals]. Parsons, KS: University of Kansas, Bureau of Child Research.

Mirenda, P. (1985). Designing pictorial communication systems for physically able bodied students with severe handicaps. *AAC: Augmentative and Alternative Communication,* 1(1), 58-64.

Mirenda, P. (1992). School to post school transition planning for augmentative and alternative communication users. *Seminars in Speech and Language,* 13(2), 130-142.

Mirenda, P. (1997). Supporting individuals with challenging behaviors through functional communication training and AAC: Research review. *AAC: Augmentative and Alternative Communication,* 13(4), 207-225.

Mirenda, P. (2001). Autism, augmentative communication, and assistive technology: What do we really know? *Focus on Autism and Other Developmental Disabilities.* 16(3), 141-151.

Mirenda, P. (2003). Toward functional augmentative and alternative communication for students with autism: Manual signs, graphic symbols, and voice output communication aids. *Language, Speech, and Hearing Services in Schools.* 34, 203-216.

Montgomery, J. (Ed.). (1987). Applications of augmentative communication in schools and clinics [Topical issue]. *Seminars in Speech and Language, 8(2).*

Mostert, M.P. (2001). Facilitated communication since 1995: A review of published studies. *Journal of Autism and Developmental Disorders.* 31(3), 287- 313.

Musselwhite, C. (1991). *Mini-grants and volunteers: Developing support for augmentative communication programs.* Birmingham, AL: Southeast Augmentative Communication Conference Publications.

National Center to Improve Practice. (1994). *Welcome to my preschool: Communicating with technology.* [video recording]. Newton, MA: Author.

Nigam, R. (2001). Dynamic assessment of graphic symbol combinations by children with autism. *Focus on Autism and Other Developmental Disabilities.* 16(3), 190-197.

Oxley, J. D., & Norris, J. A. (2000). Children's use of memory strategies: Relevance to voice output communication aid use. *AAC: Augmentative and Alternative Communication,* 16(2), 79-94.

Paul, R. (1997). Facilitating transitions in language development for children using AAC. *AAC: Augmentative and Alternative Communication,* 13(3), 141-148.

Reichle, J., Beukelman, D. R., & Light, J. C. (Eds.). (2002). *Exemplary practices for beginning communicators: Implications for AAC.* Baltimore, MD: Paul H. Brookes Publishing Company.

Reichle, J., York, J., & Eynon, D. (1989). Influence of indicating preferences for initiating, maintaining, and terminating interactions. In F. Brown & D. Lehr (Eds.), *Persons with profound disabilities: Issues and practices* (pp. 191-211). Baltimore, MD: Paul H. Brookes Publishing.

Romski, M. A., & Sevick, R. A. (1996). *Breaking the speech barrier: Language development through augmented means.* Baltimore, MD: Paul H. Brookes Publishing Company.

Rouse, C., & Katera (1997). *How to set up your home to help the nonverbal child.* [video recording]. Solana Beach, CA: Mayer-Johnson Company.

Rouse, C., & Katera. (1997). *Quick and easy: Ideas and materials to help the nonverbal child "talk" at home.* Solana Beach, CA: Mayer-Johnson Company.

Rouse, C., & Katera. (1999). *Ideas for using classroom materials to teach academics to nonverbal children.* Solana Beach, CA: Mayer-Johnson Company.

Rowland, C., & Schweigert, P. (1996). *Tangible symbol systems* [video recording]. San Antonio, TX: Communication Skill Builders.

Rowland, C., & Schweigert, P. (2000). Tangible symbols, tangible outcomes. *AAC: Augmentative and Alternative Communication,* 16(2), 61-78.

Savner, J. (1996). *Visual supports in the classroom.* [video recording]. Shawnee Mission, KS: Autism/ Asperger Syndrome Publishing Company.

Schlosser, R. W. & Blischak, D. (2001). Is there a role for speech output in interventions for persons with autism? A review. *Focus on Autism and Other Developmental Disabilities.* 16(3), 170-178.

Schlosser, R. W. (2003). *The efficacy of augmentative and alternative communication: Toward an evidence-based practice.* San Diego, CA: Academic Press.

Siegel-Causey, E., & Guess, D. (1989). *Enhancing nonsymbolic communication interactions among learners with severe disabilities.* Baltimore, MD: Paul H. Brookes Publishing Company.

Sigafoos, J. & Drasgow, E. (2001), Conditional use of aided and unaided AAC: A review and clinical case demonstration. *Focus on Autism and Other Developmental Disabilities.* 16(3), 152-161.

Sigafoos, J. (1999). Creating opportunities for augmentative and alternative communication: Strategies for involving people with developmental disabilities. *AAC: Augmentative and Alternative Communication,* 15(3), 183-190.

Skelly, M. (1979). *Amer-Ind gestural code based on universal American Indian hand talk.* New York, NY: Elsevier.

Spragale, D., & Micueci, D. (1990). Signs of the week: A functional approach to manual sign training. *AAC: Augmentative and Alternative Communication,* 6(1), 29-37.

Stephenson, J., & Linfoot, K. (1996). Pictures as communication symbols for students with severe intellectual disability. *AAC: Augmentative and Alternative Communication,* 12(4), 244-255.

Sturm, J. M. & Clendon, S. A. (2004). Augmentative and alternative communication, language, and literacy: Fostering the relationship. *Topics in Language Disorders.* 24(1), 76-91.

Tennant, R. A., & Brown, M.G. (1998). *The American sign language handshape dictionary.* Washington, DC: Gallaudet Press.

Trepagnier, C. (1995). Design goals for augmentative communication. *Communication Outlook,* 17(1), 12-21.

Twachtman-Cullen, D. (1997). *A passion to believe: Autism and facilitated communication.* Boulder, CO: Westview Press.

Vicker, B. (1996). *Using tangible symbols for communication purposes: An optional step in building the two-way communication process.* Bloomington, IN: Indiana University, Indiana Institute on Disability and Community.

Weitz, C. R. & DeCoste, D. C. (2001). *AAC in the schools: From consideration to implementation.* [video recording and manual]. Rockville, MD: American Speech-Language-Hearing Association.

8
Mobile Phone and Mobile Computing

Mobile Phone

A mobile or cellular telephone is a long-range, portable electronic device for personal telecommunications over long distances.

Background

Most current mobile phones connect to a cellular network of base stations (cell sites), which is in turn interconnected to the public switched telephone network (PSTN) (the exception are satellite phones). Fully automatic cellular networks were first introduced in the early to mid 1980s (the 1G generation). The first fully automatic cell phone system was the Nordic Mobile Telephone (NMT) system, introduced in 1981.

Prior mobile telephones (the so-called 0G generation), such as Mobile Telephone Service, date back to 1945. These were not categorized as cellular phones, since they did not support handover, i.e. automatic change of channel frequency in the middle of a call, when the user moved from one cell (base station coverage area) to another.

Until the mid to late 1980s, most mobile phones were sufficiently large that they were permanently installed in vehicles as car phones. With the advance of miniaturization, currently the vast majority of mobile phones are handheld. In addition to the standard voice function of a telephone, a mobile phone can support many additional services such as SMS for text messaging, email, packet switching for access to the Internet, and MMS for sending and receiving photos and video.

Mobile phone manufacturers include Apple Inc., Audiovox, Benefon, BenQ-Siemens, High Tech Computer Corporation, Fujitsu, Kyocera, 3G, LG, Motorola, NEC, i-mate, Nokia, Panasonic (Matsushita Electric), Pantech Curitel, Philips, Sagem, Samsung, Sanyo, Sharp, Siemens, SK Teletech, Sony Ericsson, T&A Alcatel, and Toshiba.

There are also specialist communication systems related to, but distinct from mobile phones, such as Professional Mobile Radio. Mobile phones are also distinct from cordless telephones, which generally operate only within a limited range of a specific base station. Technically, the term *mobile phone* includes such devices as satellite phones and pre-cellular mobile phones such as those operating via MTS which do not have a cellular network, whereas the related term *cell(ular) phone* does not. In practice, the two terms are used nearly interchangeably, with the preferred term varying by location. There are many different networks on mobile phones. Some are pay as you go, where top-ups can be purchased and added to a phone unit, so there is no monthly bill. Many are "pay monthly", where a bill is issued every month for the amount of calls and text messages made.

The concept of using hexagonal cells for mobile phone base stations was invented in 1947 by Bell Labs engineers at AT&T (see History of mobile phones) and was further developed by Bell Labs during the 1960s. In 1970 Amos Joel of Bell Labs invented "call handoff" that allowed a mobile phone user to travel through several cells during the same conversation. Martin Cooper of Motorola is widely considered to be the inventor of the first practical cell phone for handheld use in a non-vehicle setting. Using a modern, if somewhat heavy portable handset, Cooper made the first call on a handheld cell phone on April 3, 1973. At the time he made his call, Cooper was working as Motorola's General Manager of its Communications Division.

Radiophones have a long and varied history that stretches back to the 1950s, with hand-held cellular radio devices being available since 1983. Due to their low establishment costs and rapid deployment, mobile phone networks have since spread rapidly throughout the world, outstripping the growth of fixed telephony.

Luxembourg has the highest mobile phone penetration rate in the world, at 164% in December 2005. In Hong Kong the penetration rate reached 117% of population in September 2004. The total number of mobile phone subscribers in the world was estimated at 2.14 billion in 2005. Around 80% of world's population have mobile phone coverage as of 2006. This figure is expected to increase to 90% by the year 2010.

At present, Africa has the largest growth rate of cellular subscribers in the world. African markets are expanding nearly twice as fast as Asian markets. The availability of Prepaid or pay as you go services, where the subscriber does not have to commit to a long term contract, has helped fuel this growth on a monumental scale, not only in Africa but on other continents as well.

All European nations and most Asian and African nations have adopted GSM. In other countries, such as the United States, Australia, Japan, and South Korea, legislation does not require any particular standard, and GSM coexists with other standards, such as CDMA and iDEN.

Brain Cancer Controversy

There have been claims over a period of years that mobile phone use may cause brain cancer. The latest studies from the National Cancer Institute and researchers at the Danish Institute of Cancer Epidemiology in Copenhagen claim that there is no connection between the two.

Mobile-Phone Culture and Customs

In fewer than twenty years, mobile phones have gone from being rare and expensive pieces of equipment used primarily by the business elite, to a pervasive low-cost personal item. In many countries, mobile phones now outnumber land-line telephones, with most adults and many children now owning mobile phones. In the United States, 50% of children own mobile phones. It is not uncommon for young adults to simply own a mobile phone instead of a land-line for their residence. In some developing countries, where there is little existing fixed-line infrastructure, the mobile phone has become widespread. According to the CIA World Factbook the U.K. now has more mobile phones than people.

With high levels of mobile telephone penetration, a mobile culture has evolved, where the phone becomes a key social tool, and people rely on their mobile phone address book to keep in touch with their friends. Many people keep in touch using SMS, and a whole culture of "texting" has developed from this. The commercial market in SMS's is growing. Many phones even offer Instant Messenger services to increase the simplicity and ease of texting on phones. Cellular phones in Japan, offering Internet capabilities such as NTT DoCoMo's i-mode, offer text messaging via standard e-mail.

The mobile phone itself has also become a totemic and fashion object, with users decorating, customizing, and accessorizing their mobile phones to reflect their personality. This has emerged as its own industry. The sale of commercial ringtones exceeded $2.5 billion in 2004.

Mobile-Phone Etiquette

Mobile phone etiquette has become an important issue with mobiles ringing at funerals, weddings, cinemas, and plays. Users often speak at increased volume which has led to places like book shops, libraries, movie theatres, doctors' offices, and houses of worship posting signs prohibiting the use of mobile phones, and in some places installing signal-jamming equipment to prevent usage (although in many countries, e.g., the United States, such equipment is currently illegal). Some new buildings such as auditoriums have installed wire mesh in the walls to which prevents any signal getting through, but does not contravene the jamming laws.

Transportation providers, particularly those involving long-distance services, often offer a "quiet car" where phone use is prohibited, much like the designated non-smoking cars in the past. Mobile phone use on aircraft is also prohibited, because of concerns of possible interference with aircraft radio communications, although the airline Emirates have announced plans to allow limited cellular phone usage on some flights. Most schools in the United States have prohibited cell phones in the classroom due to the high amount of class disruptions that result from their use, and due to the possibility of photographing someone (without consent).

Use in Disaster Response

In Japan, cellular phone companies provide immediate notification of earthquakes and other natural disasters to their customers free of charge. In the event of an emergency, disaster response crews can locate trapped or injured people using the signals from their mobile phones; an interactive menu accessible through the phone's Internet browser notifies the company if the user is safe or in distress.

Use by Drivers

Mobile-phone use while driving is common but controversial. While few jurisdictions have banned motorists from using cell phones while driving outright, some have banned or restricted drivers from using hand-held cell phones while exempting phones used by a hand-free method. It is generally agreed that using a mobile phone while driving is a distraction that brings risk of road traffic accidents. However, some studies have found similarly elevated accident rates among drivers using hand-held and hand-free phones, suggesting that the distraction of a telephone conversation itself is the main safety problem.

Use of handheld mobile phones by drivers is illegal in most European countries (except e.g. Sweden). Use of hands-free mobiles is permitted. Similar laws exist in the U.S. states of New York, New Jersey, Connecticut, California, Illinois and the District of Columbia. In the UK it has been an offence since December 2003 and carries a fixed penalty of £30 rising to £1000 if convicted in court.

Mobile Phone Features

Invented in 1997, the camera phone is now 85% of the market. In a recent Weekend America interview on public radio, Philippe Kahn, the inventor of the camera phone, discusses its social impact and how it connects people around the world [2]. Mobile phones also often have features beyond sending text messages and making voice calls—including Internet browsing, music (MP3) playback, memo recording, personal organizers, e-mail, built-in cameras and camcorders, ringtones, games, radio, Push-to-Talk (PTT), infrared and Bluetooth connectivity, call registers, ability to watch streaming video or download video for later viewing, video call and serve as a wireless modem for a PC.

In most countries, including Europe, Japan, India, and Israel the person receiving a cellular phone call pays nothing. However, in Hong Kong, Canada, and the United States, one can be charged per minute. In the United States, a few carriers are beginning to offer unlimited received phone calls. For example as of December 2006, Sprint now has 4 plans under "Sprint Free Incoming Plans" section of their website, although the restriction is the receiving phone must be on the Sprint PCS network. For the Chinese mainland, it was reported that both of its two operators will adopt the caller-pays approach as early as January 2007.

Mobile Phone Forensics and Evidence

The UK appears to be leading the world when in comes to mobile telephone forensics and evidence. Law enforcement globally, though, relies heavily upon mobile telephone evidence. The concerns over terrorism and terrorist use of technology promoted an enquiry by the UK House of Commons Home Affairs Select Committee into the use of evidence from mobile telephone devices, prompting leading mobile telephone forensic specialists to identify forensic techniques available in this area.

Technology

Mobile phones and the network they operate under vary significantly from provider to provider, and nation to nation. However, all of them communicate through electromagnetic microwaves with a cell site base station, the antennas of which are usually mounted on a tower, pole, or building.

The phones have a low-power transceiver that transmits voice and data to the nearest cell sites, usually 5 to 8 miles (approximately 8 to 13 kilometres) away. When the cellular phone or data device is turned on, it registers with the mobile telephone exchange, or switch, with its unique identifiers, and will then be alerted by the mobile switch when there is an incoming telephone call. The handset constantly listens for the strongest signal being received from the surrounding base stations. As the user moves around the network, the mobile device will "handoff" to various cell sites during calls, or while waiting (idle) between calls it will reselect cell sites.

Cell sites have relatively low-power (often only one or two watts) radio transmitters which broadcast their presence and relay communications between the mobile handsets and the switch. The switch in turn connects the call to another subscriber of the same wireless service provider or to the public telephone network, which includes the networks of other wireless carriers. Many of these sites are camouflaged to blend with existing environments, particularly in high-scenery areas.

The dialogue between the handset and the cell site is a stream of digital data that includes digitized audio (except for the first generation analog networks). The technology that achieves this depends on the system which the mobile phone operator has adopted. Some technologies include AMPS for analog, and D-AMPS, CDMA2000, GSM, GPRS, EV-DO, and UMTS for digital communications. Each network operator has a unique radio frequency band.

Terminology

Related Non-Cell-Phone Systems

Cordless phone (portable phone)

Cordless phones are standard telephones with radio handsets. Unlike mobile phones, cordless phones use private base stations that are not shared between subscribers. The base station is connected to a land-line. Increasingly, with wireless local loop technologies, namely DECT, the distinction is blurred.

Professional Mobile Radio

Advanced professional mobile radio systems can be very similar to cell phone systems. Notably, the IDEN standard has been used as both a private trunked radio system as well as the technology for several large public providers. Similar attempts have even been made to use TETRA, the European digital PMR standard, to implement public mobile networks.

Radio Phone

This is a term which covers radios which could connect into the telephone network. These phones may not be mobile; for example, they may require a mains power supply. Also, they may require the assistance of a human operator to set up a PSTN phone call.

Introduction to GSM

GSM Radio Channel Structure

This diagram shows that the GSM system uses a single type of radio channel. Each radio channel in the GSM system has a frequency bandwidth of 200 kHz and a data transmission rate of approximately 270 kbps. This example shows that each radio communication channel is divided into 8 time slots (0 through 7). This diagram shows that a simultaneous two-way voice communication session requires at least one radio channel communicates from the base station to the mobile station (called the forward channel) and one channel communicates from the mobile station to the base station (called the reverse channel). This example also shows that some of the radio channel capacity is used to transfer voice (traffic) information and some of the radio channel capacity is used to transfer control messages.

Normal Burst Structures

This figure shows the field structures of the normal burst used in the GSM system. This diagram shows that the field structure is different for the normal burst, synchronization burst, and the frequency correction bursts. The fields transmitted during the normal burst include initial tail bits (ramp-up time), training sequence, flag bits, user data bits, final tail bits, and guard period. This diagram shows that the first 3 bits of the time slot are dedicated to the gradual increase of transmitter power level (ramp-up). For the normal burst, this is followed by the information (user data) bits. The flag bits indicate if the normal burst has been replaced with FACCH signaling information. This diagram shows that some of the bits in the center of the burst are used as training bits (to allow equalizer training). At the end of the transmitted burst there are tail bits (for error protection) and 3 guard period bits that are used during the gradual reduction of the RF transmitter signal.

Fast Associated Control Channel (FACCH) Signaling

This figure shows that GSM FACCH signaling replaces (steals) speech frames and replaces them with control information. This example shows the FACCH messages is divided and transmitted over 8 sequential channel bursts and that the speech information that would normally be transmitted is discarded. When received, the FACCH message is reassembled into its original message structure.

Introduction to Global System for Mobile Communication (GSM)

GSM Services

- Voice Services
- Data Services
- Multicast Services
- Short Messaging Services
- Location Based Services (LBS)

GSM Products (Mobile Devices)

- Subscriber Identity Module (SIM)
- Mobile Telephones
- PCMCIA Air Cards
- Embedded Radio Modules
- External Radio Modems

GSM Radio

- Frequency Allocation
- Frequency Reuse

— Time Division Multiple Access (TDMA)
— RF Power Control
— Mobile Assisted Handover (MAHO)

Digital Audio and Baseband
— Analog to Digital Conversion (ADC)
— Digital Speech Compression (Speech Coding)
— Channel Coding
— Echo Cancellation

Radio Channels
— Channel Bandwidth
— Modulation
— Duplex Channels
— Radio Channel Structure
— Time Slot Structure
— Frame Structure
— MultiFrame Structure
— Slow Frequency Hopping
— Discontinuous Reception (Sleep Mode)
— Discontinuous Transmission (DTx) Operation
— Dynamic Time Alignment

Logical Channels
— Traffic Channels
— Control Channels
— Dedicated Control Channel Signaling
— Traffic Channel Signaling

GSM Network
— Base Stations
— Repeaters
— Switching Centers
— Network Databases
— Wireless Network System Interconnection
— Customized Applications for Mobile Network Enhanced Logic (CAMEL)

Device Addressing

— Mobile Station ISDN (MSISDN)
— International Mobile Subscriber Identity (IMSI)
— International Mobile Equipment Identifier (IMEI)
— Temporary Mobile Station Identity (TMSI)

GSM System Operation

— Mobile Telephone Initialization
— Updating Location (Registration)
— Waiting for Calls (Idle)
— System Access
— Mobile Call Origination
— Transferring Calls Between Cell Sites (Handover)
— Receiving a Call on a Mobile Telephone
— Conversation Mode
— Connected Mode
— Authentication

GSM Future Evolution

— Enhanced Data for Global Evolution (EDGE)
— Wideband Code Division Multiple Access (WCDMA)

Technical Introduction to GSM Modem Technology

Facts and Applications of GSM/GPRS Modem

The GSM/GPRS Modem comes with a serial interface through which the modem can be controlled using AT command interface. An antenna and a power adapter are provided.

The basic segregation of working of the modem is as under:

- Voice calls
- SMS
- GSM Data calls
- GPRS

Voice calls: Voice calls are not an application area to be targeted. In future if interfaces like a microphone and speaker are provided for some applications then this can be considered.

SMS: SMS is an area where the modem can be used to provide features like:

- Pre-stored SMS transmission
- These SMS can be transmitted on certain trigger events in an automation system
- SMS can also be used in areas where small text information has to be sent. The transmitter can be an automation system or machines like vending machines, collection machines or applications like positioning systems where the navigator keeps on sending SMS at particular time intervals
- SMS can be a solution where GSM data call or GPRS services are not available

GSM Data Calls: Data calls can be made using this modem. Data calls can be made to a normal PSTN modem/phone line also (even received). Data calls are basically made to send/receive data streams between two units either PC's or embedded devices. The advantage of Data calls over SMS is that both parties are capable of sending/receiving data through their terminals.

Some Points to be Remembered in Case of Data Calls

- The data call service doesn't come with a normal SIM which is purchased but has to be requested with the service provider (say Airtel).
- Upon activation of data/fax service you are provided with two separate numbers i.e. the Data call number and the Fax service number.
- Data calls are established using Circuit Switched data connections.
- Right now the speed at which data can be transmitted is 9.6 kbps.
- The modem supports speeds up to 14.4 kbps but the provider give a maximum data rate of 9.6 kbps during GSM data call.
- Technologies like HSCSD (high Speed Circuit Switched Data) will improve drastically the data rates, but still in pipeline.

Applications and Facts About GSM Data Calls

- Devices that have communication on serial port either on PC or in the embedded environment
- Devices that want to communicate with a remote server for data transfer
- This capability of data transfer can help in reducing processing requirements of the device
- The basic aim is to provide a wireless solution keeping the existing firmware intact

- The clients firmware continues to work without any modifications (no changes in the existing software required)
- GSM data calls can be a good solution where data has to be transmitted from a hand-held device to a central server
- The interface on two sides can be between PC's as well as embedded devices
- Calls can be established by the terminals at either side to start data calls
- The Modem remains transparent during data transfer after the call is established.
- Call establishment utility to be provided in case PC terminals
- Call establishment to be automated in case of embedded terminals. GSM converter can be an option where intelligence of establishing calls has to be put in case of embedded devices. Concept of GSM converter is discussed later in this document

Dial-Up Networks Using GSM Data Calls: Dial up networking is a utility available with Windows through a person can dial the Data call number of this modem from any PC and share the file system on either PC's. This can be a good utility where both terminals are PC based. Sharing the file system remotely enables monitoring of devices remotely. Thus the modem can act as a piece of device which acts as a spy in the system. Can be a good debugging utility wherein a person can configure/monitor a remote PC based system and even rectify it. Some companies do sell their products with a GSM modem inside it just for this handy feature which allows them to configure the machines sitting anywhere in the world. Since the connection can have upper layer protocols like TCP/IP in this connection it becomes more reliable and useful.

GSM Converter: GSM converter will be an add-on device to be attached between a terminal which wants data transfer and the GSM modem. This GSM converter will take care of call establishment where the embedded device cannot make a call. The converter will remain transparent through-out the call once call is established. The GSM converter will be a very small piece of hardware possibly embedded inside the cable itself.

GPRS: This modem can be used to make a GPRS connection. Upon connection the modem can be used for internet connectivity of devices.

Key-Points in GPRS

- The PC/Embedded device dials the Service Provider (say Airtel)
- Data is routed through the ISP (Internet Service Provider
- GPRS is basically Packet Oriented service

- Protocols like TCP/IP are inherent characteristics in GPRS
- One has to talk in terms of IP addresses here not phone numbers
- The implementation is more useful where PC's want to communicate over GPRS
- Although data transfer is done from embedded devices too but with reduced features
- Since you are charged either on monthly flat rates or amount of data transfer taking place GPRS is any day a cheaper option as compared to GSM data call. But GPRS services are not available everywhere.
- The data rate rates in GPRS can go upto 40 kbps

Application Areas in GPRS Using this Modem

- Applications where mobile devices want to upload data to a central server
- Monitoring devices that are continuously logged on to the server. Since you are charged for the amount of data transfer hence a continuous connection can be maintained.
- Virtual private networks
- Radius servers

Virtual Private Networks

A virtual private network (VPN) is the extension of a private network that encompasses links across shared or public networks like the Internet. A VPN enables you to send data between two computers across a shared or public internetwork in a manner that emulates the properties of a point-to-point private link. The act of configuring and creating a virtual private network is known as virtual private networking.

To emulate a point-to-point link, data is encapsulated, or wrapped, with a header that provides routing information allowing it to traverse the shared or public transit internetwork to reach its endpoint. To emulate a private link, the data being sent is encrypted for confidentiality. Packets that are intercepted on the shared or public network are indecipherable without the encryption keys. The portion of the connection in which the private data is encapsulated is known as the tunnel. The portion of the connection in which the private data is encrypted is known as the virtual private network (VPN) connection.

VPN connections allow users working at home or on the road to connect in a secure fashion to a remote organization server using the routing infrastructure provided by a public internetwork (such as the Internet). From the user's perspective, the VPN connection is a point-to-point connection between the user's computer and an organization server. The nature of the intermediate internetwork is irrelevant to the user because it appears as if the data is being sent over a dedicated private link.

VPN technology also allows a corporation to connect to branch offices or to other companies over a public internetwork (such as the Internet), while maintaining secure communications. The VPN connection across the Internet logically operates as a wide area network (WAN) link between the sites.

In both of these cases, the secure connection across the internetwork appears to the user as a private network communication—despite the fact that this communication occurs over a public internetwork—hence, the name virtual private network. VPN technology is designed to address issues surrounding the current business trend toward increased telecommuting and widely distributed global operations, where workers must be able to connect to central resources and must be able to communicate with one another.

To provide employees with the ability to connect to organization computing resources, regardless of their location, a corporation must deploy a scalable remote access solution. Typically, corporations choose either a department solution, where an internal information systems department is charged with buying, installing, and maintaining organization modem pools and a private network infrastructure; or they choose a value-added network (VAN) solution, where they pay an outsourced company to buy, install, and maintain modem pools and a telecommunication infrastructure.

Neither of these solutions provides the necessary scalability, in terms of cost, flexible administration, and demand for connections. Therefore, it makes sense to replace the modem pools and private network infrastructure with a less expensive solution based on Internet technology so that the business can focus on its core competencies. With an Internet solution, a few Internet connections through Internet service providers (ISPs) and VPN server computers can serve the remote networking needs of hundreds or thousands of remote clients and branch offices.

Common Uses of VPNs

The next few sections describe the more common VPN configurations in more detail.

Remote Access Over the Internet

VPNs provide remote access to organization resources over the public Internet, while maintaining privacy of information. A VPN connection used to connect a remote access client to an organization intranet. This is known as a remote access VPN connection.

Rather than making a long distance (or 1-800) call to an organization or outsourced network access server (NAS), the user dials a local ISP. Using the connection to the local ISP, the VPN client creates a VPN connection between the remote access computer and the organization VPN server across the Internet.

Connecting Networks Over the Internet

There are two methods for using VPNs to connect local area networks at remote sites:

- Using dedicated lines to connect a branch office to an organization LAN.

For example, rather than using an expensive long-distance dedicated circuit between the branch office and the corporate hub, both the branch office and the corporate hub routers can use a local dedicated circuit and local ISP to connect to the Internet. The VPN software uses the local ISP connections and the Internet to create a virtual private network between the branch office router and corporate hub router.

- Using a dial-up line to connect a branch office to the Internet.

Rather than having a router at the branch office make a long distance (or 1-800) call to a corporate or outsourced NAS, the router at the branch office can call a local ISP. The VPN client uses the connection to the local ISP to create a VPN connection between the branch office router and the corporate hub router across the Internet. This is known as a site-to-site VPN connection. In both cases, the facilities that connect the branch office and corporate offices to the Internet are local. The corporate hub router that acts as a VPN server must be connected to a local ISP with a dedicated line. This VPN server must be listening 24 hours a day for incoming VPN traffic.

Connecting Computers Over an Intranet

In some organization internetworks, the departmental data is so sensitive that the department's LAN is physically disconnected from the rest of the organization internetwork. Although this protects the department's confidential information, it creates information accessibility problems for those users not physically connected to the separate LAN.

VPNs allow the department's LAN to be physically connected to the organization internetwork but separated by a VPN server. The VPN server is not acting as a router between the organization internetwork and the department LAN. A router would connect the two networks, allowing everyone access to the sensitive LAN. By using a VPN server, the network administrator can ensure that only those users on the organization internetwork who have appropriate credentials (based on a need-to-know policy within the company) can establish a VPN connection with the VPN server and gain access to the protected resources of the department. Additionally, all communication across the VPN can be encrypted for data confidentiality. Those users who do not have the proper credentials cannot view the department LAN.

Radius

The Remote Authentication Dial-in User Service (RADIUS) protocol is a popular method for managing remote user authentication and authorization. RADIUS is a lightweight, UDP-based protocol. RADIUS servers can be located anywhere on the Internet and provide authentication (including PPP PAP, CHAP, MS-CHAP, MS-CHAP v2, and EAP) and authorization for access servers such as NASes and VPN servers.

In addition, RADIUS servers can provide a proxy service to forward authentication requests to distant RADIUS servers. For example, many ISPs have agreements to allow roaming subscribers to use local services from the nearest ISP for dial-up access to the Internet. These roaming alliances take advantage of the RADIUS proxy service. If an ISP recognizes a user name as being a subscriber to a remote network, the ISP uses a RADIUS proxy to forward the access request to the appropriate network. Windows Server 2003 includes a RADIUS server and proxy with the Internet Authentication Service (IAS); an optional Windows networking component installed using Control Panel-Network

Multi-Access Systems

An important issue in wireless communication systems is multiple random access: communication links can be activated at any moment while several links can be active simultaneously. As multi-access and random-access are properties mainly determined by the chosen data-communication technique it is important to keep these requirements in mind from the very beginning. Three possible concepts to realize a multi-access communication system are in use:

1. FDMA

Frequency Division Multiple Access, commonly used in conventional telephone systems: every user gets a certain frequency band assigned and can use this part of the spectrum to perform its communication. If only a small number of users is active, not the whole resource (frequency-spectrum) is used. Assignment of the channels can be done centrally or by carrier-sensing in a mobile. The latter possibility enables random-access.

2. TDMA

Time Division Multiple Access, applied nowadays in mobile phone systems: every user is assigned a (set of) time-slots. Transmission of data is only possible during this time-slot, after that the transmitter has to wait until it gets another time-slot. Synchronization of all users is an important issue in this concept. Consequently, there must be a central unit (base-station) that controls the synchronization and the assignment of time-slots. This means that this technique is difficult to apply in random-access systems.

3. CDMA

Code Division Multiple Access (Spread Spectrum). A unique code is assigned to each user. This code is used to "code" the data message. As codes are selected for low cross-correlation properties, all users can transmit simultaneously in the same frequency channel while a receiver is still capable of recovering the desired signal. Synchronization between links is not strictly required and so random-access is possible. A practical application at the moment is the cellular-*cdma* phone system IS-95 [Qua92].

Combinations are also possible, the popular European cellular phone systems *dect* and *gsm* for instance use a combination of *tdma*and *fdma*. There a single transmission-cell is defined by a combination of a frequency channel and a time-slot.

From the above list it is clear that both *fdma*and *cdma* are candidate transmission techniques to enable multiple random access. There are however a number of reasons for choosing *cdma* over *fdma*. The first alternative provides [Sch94, SOSL85a, Dix84]:

- Interference limited operation. In all situations the whole frequency-spectrum is used. As a result the more active users are present, the higher the interference level will be.
- Privacy due to unknown codes. The applied codes are - in principle - unknown to a hostile user. This means that it is hardly possible to detect the message of another user.
- Applying spread spectrum implies the reduction of multi-path effects. By using a wide frequency-band, the influence of narrow-band fades is reduced.
- Random access possibilities. Users can start their transmission at any arbitrary time (no infrastructure required).
- Good anti-jamming performance. Small-band interference is reduced as explained in the next section.

CDMA Techniques

Code Division Multiple Access (*cdma*) is used in spread spectrum systems to enable multiple-access. It is a transmission technique in which the frequency spectrum of a data-signal is spread using a code uncorrelated with that signal and unique to every addressee. As the applied codes are selected for their low cross-correlation values, it is possible to make a distinction between the different signals. An initiator knows the code of the intended addressee and is so capable of activating the desired communication link.

The first applications were in the military field because of the difficulty to jam or detect spread spectrum signals. Nowadays however spread spectrum systems are gaining popularity also in commercial applications (for instance: IS-95 [Qua92]).

If a signal is combined with a code the bandwidth of the original signal increases. The spectrum is "spread" which justifies the name "spread spectrum". At the same time the spectral power density decreases as the total transmitted power stays equal. The ratio of transmission and information bandwidth is therefore an important parameter in spread spectrum systems. This ratio is referred to as "processing gain":

$$G_p = \frac{BW_1}{BW_i} \quad (1)$$

which is the "spreading factor". The processing gain also determines the number of users that can be allowed in a system, the amount of multi-path effect reduction, the difficulty to jam or detect a signal etc. For spread spectrum systems it is advantageous to have a processing gain as high as possible.

Different spread spectrum techniques exist: Direct-Sequence (*ds*), Frequency-Hopping (*fh*), Time-Hopping (*th*) and Multi-Carrier CDMA (*mc-cdma*). It is also possible to make use of combinations. Overviews of the various spread spectrum techniques can be found in [SOSL85a, Hol82, Dix84, PSM82, SH85, YLF94].

We will now concentrate on the two more popular techniques: direct-sequence and frequency-hopping.

Direct Sequence

Direct Sequence is the most popular Spread Spectrum Technique. The data signal is multiplied with a pseudo random bit sequence, often referred to as pseudo random noise code (*pn-code*).

A *pn-code*is a sequence existing of chips valued -1 and 1 (polar) or 0 and 1 (non-polar). Such bit-sequences have noise-like properties like spectral flatness and low cross and auto correlation values, and thus complicate jamming or detection by non-target receivers [Gol67, HdV71, Roe77, Gla92].

Several families of binary *pn-codes*exist: *m*-sequences, Gold-codes and Kasami-codes where the latter two can be created by combining a number of selected *m*-sequences. An usual way to create a *pn-code*is by means of shift-registers with feed-back taps. By putting the feed-back taps at specific positions, the output sequence of a shift register is of "maximum length". The above mentioned code-families [Gol67] have this property.

In the receiver, the received signal is multiplied again with the same (synchronized) *pn-code*. Since a code exists of +1s and -1s, this operation completely removes the code from the signal and the original data-signal is left. Another observation is that the despread operation is the same as the spread operation. The consequence is that a possible jamming or interference signal in the radio channel will be spread before data-detection is performed. In this way jamming effects are reduced.

A large problem with multi-access direct sequence spreading is the so-called near-far effect which is illustrated. This effect is present when a *cdma* interfering transmitter is much closer to the receiver than the intended transmitter. Although the cross-correlation of "code A" and "code B" is low, the correlation of the received signal from the interfering transmitter with "code A" in the receiver can exceed the correlation of the received signal from the intended transmitter and the correct code. As a result proper data detection is hardly possible

Frequency Hopping

When applying frequency hopping, the carrier frequency is "hopping" according to a unique sequence (an *fh-sequence* of length). In this way the bandwidth is increased by a factor N_{FH} (if the channels are non-overlapping):

$$G_P\ (\mathrm{FH}) = N_{FH}. \tag{2}$$

A disadvantage of frequency-hopping compared to direct-sequence is that it is hard to obtain a high processing gain. A frequency synthesizer is required that is capable of rapidly hopping over a set of carrier (*fh*) frequencies. The more *fh*-frequencies, the higher the processing gain and the more demanding the frequency synthesizer becomes.

On the contrary, frequency-hopping is less vulnerable to the near-far effect than direct-sequence. Frequency-hopping sequences have only a limited number of "hits" with each other. This means that if a near-interferer is present, not the whole signal is blocked but only a limited number of "frequency-hops". From the "hops" that are not blocked it should be possible to recover the original data-message, for instance by applying error correcting techniques.

Two types of frequency-hopping techniques can be distinguished. In "fast frequency hopping" the period of a "frequency-hop" is smaller than a data symbol-period while in "slow frequency hopping" the period of a "frequency-hop" is larger than a data symbol-period. Choosing one of those techniques has consequences on the error correcting coding to be applied.

Mobilr Vomputing: Past, Present and Future

Introduction

Mobile voice communication is widely established throughout the world and has had a very rapid increase in the number of subscribers to the various cellular networks over the last few years. An extension of this technology is the ability to send and receive data across these cellular networks. This is the principle of mobile computing.

Mobile data communication has become a very important and rapidly evolving technology as it allows users to transmit data from remote locations to other remote or fixed locations. This proves to be the solution to the biggest problem of business people on the move - mobility.

In this article we give an overview of existing cellular networks and describe in detail the CDPD technology which allows data communications across these networks. Finally, we look at the applications of Mobile Computing in the real world.

Existing Cellular Network Architecture

Mobile telephony took off with the introduction of cellular technology which allowed the efficient utilisation of frequencies enabling the connection of a large number of users. During the 1980's analogue technology was used. Among the most well known systems were the NMT900 and 450 (Nordic Mobile Telephone) and the AMPS (Advanced Mobile Phone Service). In the 1990's the digital cellular technology was introduced with GSM (Global System Mobile) being the most widely accepted system around the world. Other such systems are the DCS1800 (Digital Communication System) and the PCS1900 (Personal Communication System).

A cellular network consists of mobile units linked together to switching equipment, which interconnect the different parts of the network and allow access to the fixed Public Switched Telephone Network (PSTN). The technology is hidden from view; it's incorporated in a number of tranceivers called Base Stations (BS). Every BS is located at a strategically selected place and covers a given area or cell - hence the name cellular communications. A number of adjacent cells grouped together form an area and the corresponding BSs communicate through a so called Mobile Switching Centre (MSC). The MSC is the heart of a cellular radio system. It is responsible for routing, or switching, calls from the originator to the destinator. It can be thought of managing the cell, being responsible for set-up, routing control and termination of the call, for management of inter-MSC hand over and supplementary services, and for collecting charging and accounting information. The MSC may be connected to other MSCs on the same network or to the PSTN.

The frequencies used vary according to the cellular network technology implemented. For GSM, 890 - 915 MHz range is used for transmission and 935 -960 MHz for reception. The DCS techology uses frequencies in the 1800MHz range while PCS in the 1900MHz range.

Each cell has a number of channels associated with it. These are assigned to subscribers on demand. When a Mobile Station (MS) becomes 'active' it registers with the nearest BS. The corresponding MSC stores the information about that MS and its position. This information is used to direct incoming calls to the MS.

If during a call the MS moves to an adjacent cell then a change of frequency will necessarily occur - since adjacent cells never use the same channels. This procedure is called hand over and is the key to Mobile communications. As the MS is approaching the edge of a cell, the BS monitors the decrease in signal power. The strength of the signal is compared with adjacent cells and the call is handed over to the cell with the strongest signal.

During the switch, the line is lost for about 400ms. When the MS is going from one area to another it registers itself to the new MSC. Its location information is updated, thus allowing MSs to be used outside their 'home' areas.

Data Communications

Data Communications is the exchange of data using existing communication networks. The term data covers a wide range of applications including File Transfer (FT), interconnection between Wide-Area-Networks (WAN), facsimile (fax), electronic mail, access to the internet and the World Wide Web (WWW).

Data Communications have been achieved using a variety of networks such as PSTN, leased-lines and more recently ISDN (Integrated Services Data Network) and ATM (Asynchronous Transfer Mode)/Frame Relay. These networks are partly or totally analogue or digital using technologies such as circuit - switching, packet - switching e.t.c.

Circuit switching implies that data from one user (sender) to another (receiver) has to follow a prespecified path. If a link to be used is busy, the message can not be redirected, a property which causes many delays.

Packet switching is an attempt to make better utilisation of the existing network by splitting the message to be sent into packets. Each packet contains information about the sender, the receiver, the position of the packet in the message as well as part of the actual message. There are many protocols defining the way packets can be send from the sender to the receiver. The most widely used are the Virtual Circuit-Switching system, which implies that packets have to be sent through the same path, and the Datagram system which allows packets to be sent at various paths depending on the network availability. Packet switching requires more equipment at the receiver, where reconstruction of the message will have to be done.

The introduction of mobility in data communications required a move from the Public Switched Data Network (PSDN) to other networks like the ones used by mobile phones. PCSI has come up with an idea called CDPD (Cellular Digital Packet Data) technology which uses the existing mobile network (frequencies used for mobile telephony).

Mobility implemented in data communications has a significant difference compared to voice communications. Mobile phones allow the user to move around and talk at the same time; the loss of the connection for 400ms during the hand over is undetectable by the user. When it comes to data, 400ms is not only detectable but causes huge distortion to the message. Therefore data can be transmitted from a mobile station under the assumption that it remains stable or within the same cell.

CDPD Technology: The Hot Cookie

Today, the mobile data communications market is becoming dominated by a technology called CDPD.

There are other alternatives to this technology namely Circuit Switched Cellular, Specialised Mobile Radio and Wireless Data Networks. As can be seen from the table below the CDPD technology is much more advantageous than the others.

	Cellular Digital Packet Data (CDPD)	*Circuit Switched Cellular*	*Specialized Mobile Radio (Extended)*	*Proprietary Wireless Data Networks*
Speed	best	best	good	good
Security	best	better	good	better
Ubiquity	best	best	good	better
Cost of Service	best	better	better	good
Cost of Deployment	best	best	better	good
Mobility	best	good	better	good
Interoperability	best	good	good	better

CDPD's principle lies in the usage of the idle time in between existing voice signals that are being sent across the cellular networks. The major advantage of this system is the fact that the idle time is not chargeable and so the cost of data transmission is very low. This may be regarded as the most important consideration by business individuals.

CDPD networks allow fixed or mobile users to connect to the network across a fixed link and a packet switched system respectively. Fixed users have a fixed physical link to the CDPD network. In the case of a mobile end user, the user can, if CDPD network facilities are non-existent, connect to existing circuit switched networks and transmit data via these networks. This is known as Circuit Switched CDPD (CS-CDPD).

Service coverage is a fundamental element of providing effective wireless solutions to users and using this method achieves this objective. Where CDPD is available data is split into packets and a packet switched network protocol is used to transport the packets across the network. This may be of either Datagram or Virtual Circuit Switching form.

The data packets are inserted on momentarily unoccupied voice frequencies during the idle time on the voice signals. CDPD networks have a network hierarchy with each level of the hierarchy doing its own specified tasks.

Mobile End User Interface

Using a single device such as a Personal Digital Assistant or personal computer which have been connected to a Radio Frequency (RF) Modem which is specially adapted with the antennae required to transmit data on the cellular network, the mobile end user can transmit both data and voice signals. Voice signals are transmitted via a mobile phone connected to the RF Modem Unit. RF Modems transfer data in both forward and reverse channels using Gaussian Minimum Shift Keying (MSK) modulation, a modified form of Frequency Shift Keying (FSK) at modulation index of 0.5.

Mobile Data Base Station (MDBS).

In each cell of the cellular reception area, there is a Mobile Data Base Station (MDBS) which is responsible for detection of idle time in voice channels, for relaying data between the mobile units and the Mobile Data Intermediate Systems (MDIS), sending of packets of data onto the appropriate unoccupied frequencies as well as receiving data packets and passing them to the appropriate Mobile end user within its domain.

- **Detection of Idle Time**

  This is achieved using a scanning receiver (also known as sniffer) housed in the MDBS. The sniffer detects voice traffic by measuring the signal strength on a specific frequency, hence detecting an idle channel.

- Relaying Data Packets Between Mobile Units and Networks

  If the sniffer detects two idle channels then the MDBS establishes two RF air-links between the end user unit and itself. Two channels are required to achieve bidirectional communications. One channel is for forward communication from the MDBS to the mobile units. This channel is unique to each mobile unit and hence contentionless. The reverse channels are shared between a number of Mobile units and as a result, two mobile units sharing a reverse link cannot communicate to each other.

  Reverse channels are accessed using a Digital Sense Multiple Access with Collision Detection (DSMA - CD) protocol which is similar to the protocol used in Ethernet communication which utilises Carrier Sense Multiple Access with Collision Detection (CSMA - CD). This protocol allows the collision of two data packets on a common channel to be detected so that the Mobile unit can be alerted by the MDBS to retry transmission at a later time.

Once a link is established, the MDBS can quickly detect if and when a voice signal is ramping up (requesting) this link and within the 40ms it takes for the voice signal to ramp up and get a link, the MDBS disconnects from the current air-link and finds another idle channel establishing a new link. This is known as channel hopping.

The speed at which the MDBS hops channels ensures that the CDPD network is completely invisible to the existing cellular networks and it doesn't interfere with transmission of existing voice channels.

When the situation occurs that all voice channels are at capacity, then extra frequencies specifically set aside for CDPD data can be utilised. Although this scenario is very unlikely as each cell within the reception area has typically 57 channels, each of which has an average of 25 - 30% of idle time.

Mobile Data Intermediate Systems (MDIS)

Groups of MDBS that control each cell in the cellular network reception area are connected to a higher level entity in the network hierarchy, the Mobile Data Intermediate Systems. Connection is made via a wideband trunk cable. Data packets are then relayed by MDBS to and from mobile end users and MDIS.

These MDIS use a Mobile Network Location Protocol (MNLP) to exchange location information about Mobile end users within their domain. The MDIS maintains a database for each of the M-ES in its serving area. Each mobile unit has a fixed home area but may be located in any area where reception is available. So, if a MDIS unit recieves a data packet addressed to a mobile unit that resides in its domain, it sends the data packet to the appropriate MDBS in its domain which will forward it as required. If the data packet is addressed to a mobile unit in another group of cells, then the MDIS forwards the data packet to the appropriate MDIS using the forward channel. The MDIS units hide all mobility issues from systems in higher levels of the network hierarchy.

In the reverse direction, where messages are from the Mobile end user, packets are routed directly to their destination and not necessarily through the mobile end users home MDIS.

Intermediate Systems (IS)

MDIS are interconnected to these IS which form the backbone of the CDPD system. These systems are unaware of mobility of end-users, as this is hidden by lower levels of the network hierarchy. The ISs are the systems that provide the CDPD interface to the various computer and phone networks.

The IS's relay data between MDIS's and other IS's throughout the network. They can be connected to routers that support Internet and Open Systems Interconnection

Connectionless Network Services (OSI-CLNS), to allow access to other cellular carriers and external land- based networks.

CDPD Network Reliability

There are some actions that are necessary in order to obtain reliability over a network.

User Authentication

The procedure which checks if the identity of the subscriber transferred over the radio path corresponds with the details held in the network.

User Anonymity

Instead of the actual directory telephone number, the International Mobile Subscriber Identity (IMSI) number is used within the network to uniquely identify a mobile subscriber.

Fraud Prevention

Protection against impersonation of authorised users and fraudulent use of the network is required.

Protection of User Data

All the signals within the network are encrypted and the identification key is never transmitted through the air. This ensures maximum network and data security.

The information needed for the above actions are stored in data bases. The Home Location Register (HLR) stores information relating the Mobile Station (MS) to its network. This includes information for each MS on subscription levels, supplementary services and the current or most recently used network and location area. The Authentication Centre (AUC) provides the information to authenticate MSs using the network, in order to guard against possible fraud, stolen subsciber cards, or unpaid bills. The Visitor Location Register (VLR) stores information about subscription levels, supplementary services and location for a subscriber who is currently in, or has very recently been in that area. It may also record whether a subscriber is currently active, thus avoiding delay and unnecessary use of the network in trying to call a switched off terminal.

The data packets are transmitted at speeds of typically 19.2 Kilobits/second to the MDBS, but actual throughput may be as low as 9.6 Kilobits/second due to the extra redundant data that is added to transmitted packets. This information includes sender address, receiver address and in the case of Datagram Switching, a packet ordering number. Check data is also added to allow error correction if bits are incorrectly received. Each data packet is encoded with the check data using a Reed-

Solomon forward error correction code. The encoded sequence is then logically OR'ed with a pseudo-random sequence, to assist the MDBS and mobile units in synchronisation of bits. The transmitted data is also encrypted to maintain system security.

CDPD follows the OSI standard model for packet switched data communications. The CDPD architecture extends across layers one, two and three of the OSI layer model. The mobile end users handle the layer 4 functions (transport) and higher layers of the OSI model such as user interface.

Applications of Mobile Computing

The question that always arises when a business is thinking of buying a mobile computer is "Will it be worth it?"

In many fields of work, the ability to keep on the move is vital in order to utilise time efficiently. Efficient utilisation of resources (ie: staff) can mean substantial savings in transportation costs and other non quantifyable costs such as increased customer attention, impact of on site maintenance and improved intercommunication within the business.

The importance of Mobile Computers has been highlighted in many fields of which a few are described below:

For Estate Agents

Estate agents can work either at home or out in the field. With mobile computers they can be more productive. They can obtain current real estate information by accessing multiple listing services, which they can do from home, office or car when out with clients. They can provide clients with immediate feedback regarding specific homes or neighborhoods, and with faster loan approvals, since applications can be submitted on the spot. Therefore, mobile computers allow them to devote more time to clients.

Emergency Services

Ability to receive information on the move is vital where the emergency services are involved. Information regarding the address, type and other details of an incident can be dispatched quickly, via a CDPD system using mobile computers, to one or several appropriate mobile units which are in the vicinity of the incident.

In Courts

Defense counsels can take mobile computers in court. When the opposing counsel references a case which they are not familiar, they can use the computer to get direct, real-time access to on-line legal database services, where they can gather information on the case and related precedents. Therefore mobile computers allow immediate access to a wealth of information, making people better informed and prepared.

In Companies

Managers can use mobile computers in, say, critical presentations to major customers. They can access the latest market share information. At a small recess, they can revise the presentation to take advantage of this information. They can communicate with the office about possible new offers and call meetings for discussing responds to the new proposals. Therefore, mobile computers can leverage competitive advantages.

Stock Information Collation/Control

In environments where access to stock is very limited ie: factory warehouses. The use of small portable electronic databases accessed via a mobile computer would be ideal.

Data collated could be directly written to a central database, via a CDPD network, which holds all stock information hence the need for transfer of data to the central computer at a later date is not necessary. This ensures that from the time that a stock count is completed, there is no inconsistency between the data input on the portable computers and the central database.

Credit Card Verification

At Point of Sale (POS) terminals in shops and supermarkets, when customers use credit cards for transactions, the intercommunication required between the bank central computer and the POS terminal, in order to effect verification of the card usage, can take place quickly and securely over cellular channels using a mobile computer unit. This can speed up the transaction process and relieve congestion at the POS terminals.

Taxi/Truck Dispatch

Using the idea of a centrally controlled dispatcher with several mobile units (taxis), mobile computing allows the taxis to be given full details of the dispatched job as well as allowing the taxis to communicate information about their whereabouts back to the central dispatch office. This system is also extremely useful in secure deliveries ie: Securicor. This allows a central computer to be able to track and receive status information from all of its mobile secure delivery vans. Again, the security and reliability properties of the CDPD system shine through.

Electronic Mail/Paging

Usage of a mobile unit to send and read emails is a very useful asset for any business individual, as it allows him/her to keep in touch with any colleagues as well as any urgent developments that may affect their work. Access to the Internet, using mobile computing technology, allows the individual to have vast arrays of knowledge at his/her fingertips.

Paging is also achievable here, giving even more intercommunication capability between individuals, using a single mobile computer device.

The Future

With the rapid technological advancements in Artificial Intelligence, Integrated Circuitry and increases in Computer Processor speeds, the future of mobile computing looks increasingly exciting.

With the emphasis increasingly on compact, small mobile computers, it may also be possible to have all the practicality of a mobile computer in the size of a hand held organizer or even smaller.

Use of Artificial Intelligence may allow mobile units to be the ultimate in personal secretaries, which can receive emails and paging messages, understand what they are about, and change the individuals personal schedule according to the message. This can then be checked by the individual to plan his/her day.

The working lifestyle will change, with the majority of people working from home, rather than commuting. This may be beneficial to the environment as less transportation will be utilised. This mobility aspect may be carried further in that, even in social spheres, people will interact via mobile stations, eliminating the need to venture outside of the house.

This scary concept of a world full of inanimate zombies sitting, locked to their mobile stations, accessing every sphere of their lives via the computer screen becomes ever more real as technology, especially in the field of mobile data communications, rapidly improves and, as shown below, trends are very much towards ubiquitous or mobile computing.

Introduction to Mobility Java Technology

To develop applications using wireless Java technology, you'll need to assimilate information from several fields. You'll need to understand something about wireless communications technology, the business of wireless communications, and a lot about the Java platform. Where should you begin? This page contains a high-level overview of wireless Java technology and many links to detailed information about specific subjects.

Overview of Wireless Communications

Wireless communications is a huge field, encompassing everything from radio and television broadcasting through pagers, mobile phones, and satellite communications. The field of mobile phones is expanding very fast at the same time that standards and protocols are being adopted, used, updated, and sometimes discarded. The other rapidly expanding part of the wireless world is that of wireless local area networks (LANs). Driven by widespread acceptance of the IEEE 802.11 standard, wireless local networking for computers and other devices is spreading rapidly.

Although wireless may seem like a special case, it is actually more intuitive and more natural than wired networking. Some day soon the need to plug a laptop into a network physically will seem quaint and antiquated. The notion that you could walk into a room with your cell phone and have it unable to interact with other devices in the room will seem unbelievably primitive. The future will reveal that *wired* networks are the special case.

Conceptually, wireless communications can be split into two types, *local* and *wide area*. A local device is similar to a key fob with a button that unlocks a car, a 900 MHz cordless phone, a radio control toy, or a Bluetooth network. All of these devices operate overshort distances, typically just a few meters.

Wide area wireless devices operate effectively over a much greater area. A pager or mobile phone is a good example; you can talk on your mobile phone to any other phone on the planet. These devices' greater range relieson a trick, however: a more elaborate land-based network. A mobile phone doesn't have that much more radio power than a radio control toy. What it does have is a network of carefully placed radio antennas (cell towers); the phone can continue to operate as long as it is within range of at least one tower. The mobile phone device receives service from a wireless *carrier*, a company that operates the land-based network.

While a number of industry consortia and standard bodies, such as the International Telecommunication Union, are trying to define or foster the development of standards for the wireless world, today's wireless world is still fragmented and complex. If you buy a mobile phone in the U.S. today, it might run on Motorola's iDEN network or Sprint's PCS network. Take it overseas to Europe and you'll be out of luck—your phone will not work with Europe's GSM network, nor will it work with the PDC network or any of the other mobile networks that live in Japan.

More information about wireless communications is available here:

- Making Sense of Cellular gives an introductory overview of the wireless radio spectrum.
- World of Wireless Communications provides a brief overview of wireless communications and the concept of an embedded device.

Overview of the Java 2 Platform

The Java 2 Platform comprises three elements:

1. The *Java programming language* is syntactically similar to C++ but differs fundamentally. While C++ uses unsafe pointers and programmers are responsible for allocating and freeing memory, the Java programming language uses type safe object references, and unused memory is reclaimed automatically. Furthermore, the Java programming language eschews multiple inheritance (a likely source of confusion and lambiguity in C++) in favor of a cleaner construct, *interfaces*.
2. A *virtual machine* forms the foundation of the Java platform. This architecture offers several attractive features: The virtual machine can be implemented to run a top a variety of operating systems and hardware, with binary-compatible Java applications operating consistently across many implementations. In addition, the virtual machine provides tight control of executed binaries, enabling safe execution of untrusted code.
3. Finally, *an extensive set of standard application programming interfaces (APIs)* rounds out the Java platform. These support almost everything you might want your applications to do, from user interface through cryptography, from CORBA connectivity through internationalization.

Taken together, the Java language, Java virtual machine, and Java APIs compose the Java platform. Moreover, the Java platform is designed to encompass a wide range of computer hardware, everything from smart cards through enterprise servers. Therefore, the Java platform comes in three flavors:

- Java 2, Standard Edition (J2SE) is designed for desktop computers. Most often it runs on top of OS X, Linux, Solaris, or Microsoft Windows.
- Java 2, Enterprise Edition (J2EE) is a comprehensive platform for multiuser, enterprise-wide applications. It is based on J2SE and adds APIs for server-side computing.
- Java 2, Micro Edition (J2ME) is a set of technologies and specifications developed for small devices like pagers, mobile phones, and set-topboxes. J2ME uses subsets of J2SE components, such as smaller virtual machines and leaner APIs.

To learn much more about Java technology or the Java platform, visit http://java.sun.com/:

- The New to Java Programming Center offers an excellent entry point into the Java platform, understanding it, getting it installed on your computer, and starting to program.

The Java Community Process (JCP)

Specifications for J2SE, J2EE, and J2ME are developed under the aegis of the Java Community Process (JCP). A specification begins life as a Java Specification Request (JSR). An expert group consisting of representatives from interested companies is formed to create the specification. The JSR then passes through various stages in the JCP before it is finished. Every JSR is assigned a number. J2ME specifications are commonly referred to by their JSR number.

Overview of J2ME

Unlike J2SE, J2ME is not a piece of software, nor is it a single specification. This difference can be confusing, even for developers who are already familiar with J2SE. Instead, J2MEis a platform, a collection of technologies and specifications that are designed for different parts of the small device market. Because J2ME spans such a variety of devices, it wouldn't make sense to try to create a one-size-fits-all solution.

J2ME, therefore, is divided into *configurations*, *profiles*, and *optional packages*. Configurations are specifications that detail a virtual machine and a base set of APIs that can be used with a certain class of device. A configuration, for example, might be designed for devices that have less than 512 KB of memory and an intermittent network connection. The virtual machine is either a full Java Virtual Machine[1] (as described in the specification) or some subset of the full JVM[1]. The set of APIs is customarily a subset of the J2SE APIs.

A profile builds on a configuration but adds more specific APIs to make a complete environment for building applications. While a configuration describes a JVM[1] and a basic set of APIs, it does not by itself specify enough detail to enable you to build complete applications. Profiles usually include APIs for application life cycle, user interface, and persistent storage.

An optional package provides functionality that may not be associated with a specific configuration or profile. One example of an optional package is the Bluetooth API (JSR 82), which provides a standardized API for using Bluetooth networking. This optional package could be implemented alongside virtually any combination of configurations and profiles.

The J2ME Universe Today

The current universe of configurations, profiles and optional packages is shown in the diagram below.

Configurations

JSR 30	CLDC 1.0	Connected, Limited Device Configuration
JSR 139	CLDC 1.1	Connected, Limited Device Configuration 1.1

JSR 36	CDC	Connected Device Configuration
JSR 218	CDC 1.1	Connected Device Configuration 1.1
Profiles		
JSR 37	MIDP 1.0	Mobile Information Device Profile
JSR 118	MIDP 2.0	Mobile Information Device Profile 2.0
JSR 75	PDAP	PDA Profile
JSR 46	FP	Foundation Profile
JSR 219	FP 1.1	Foundation Profile 1.1
JSR 129	PBP	Personal Basis Profile
JSR 217	PBP 1.1	Personal Basis Profile 1.1
JSR 62	PP	Personal Profile
JSR 215	PP 1.1	Personal Profile 1.1
JSR 195	IMP	Information Module Profile
JSR 228	IMP-NG	Information Module Profile - Next Generation
Optional Packages		
JSR 75	PIM	PDA Optional Packages for the J2ME Platform
JSR 82	BTAPI	Java APIs for Bluetooth
JSR 120	WMA	Wireless Messaging API
JSR 205	WMA 2.0	Wireless Messaging API 2.0
JSR 135	MMAPI	Mobile Media API
JSR 164		JAIN SIMPLE Presence
JSR 165		JAIN SIMPLE Instant Messaging
JSR 172		J2ME Web Services
JSR 177	SATSA	Security and Trust Services API for J2ME
JSR 179		Location API for J2ME
JSR 180	SIP	SIP API for J2ME
JSR 184	3D	Mobile 3D Graphics API for J2ME
JSR 186		JAIN Presence
JSR 187		JAIN Instant Messaging
JSR 190		Event Tracking API for J2ME
JSR 209		Advanced Graphics and User Interface Optional Package for J2ME Platform
JSR 211	CHAPI	Content Handling API
JSR 213		Micro WSCI Framework for J2ME

JSR 214	Micro BPSS for J2ME Devices
JSR 226	Scalable 2D Vector Graphics API
JSR 229	Payment API
JSR 230	Data Sync API
JSR 232	Mobile Operational Management
JSR 234	Advanced Multimedia Supplements
JSR 238	Mobile Internationalization API
JSR 239	Java Bindings for OpenGL ES
JSR 246	Device Management API
JSR 253	Mobile Telephony API (MTA)

As the diagram shows, J2ME has two main branches. The first is based on the Connected, Limited Device Configuration (CLDC). This configuration is for small wireless devices with intermittent network connections, like pagers, mobile phones, and Personal Digital Assistants (PDAs). The Mobile Information Device Profile (MIDP), which is based on CLDC, was the first finished profile and thus the first finished J2ME application environment. MIDP-compliant devices are widely available.

The other major branch of the J2ME tree is based on the Connected Device Configuration (CDC). This configuration is for larger devices (in terms of memory and processing power) with robust network connections. Set-top boxes and internet appliances are good examples of CDC devices, although high-end PDAs like the Sharp Zaurus also fit this configuration well. The Foundation Profile extends CDC and serves as the basis for several other profiles. It provides fundamental APIs gleaned from J2SE, including classes and interfaces from java.lang, java.io, java.security, java.util, and more. For a list of J2ME terms and definitions, see our glossary.

Optional packages bubble like a froth above the CLDC and CDC branches of J2ME. These provide all sorts of capabilities ranging from Bluetooth communication through web services and instant messaging.

For a thorough look at J2ME, see:

- A Survey of J2ME Today

The world of wireless Java technology also includes Java Card, for smart cards. For more information on Java Card, see:

- An Introduction to Java Card Technology - Part 1

About Stacks and JSR 185

Devices implement a complete software *stack*, which usually consists of a configuration, a profile, and optional APIs.

Given the plethora of configurations, profiles, and especially optional packages, how does a developer know what to expect on a device? JSR 185, Java Technology for the Wireless Industry, addresses this question by assembling other building blocks into a complete application environment. JSR 185 mandates CLDC 1.0 or 1.1, MIDP 2.0, and WMA. Support for MMAPI is optional. This helps nail things down for developers; on a JTWI device, the developer has a clear understanding of what APIs will be available.

The Scope of Wireless Java Technology

Wireless Java technology is the intersection of two vast worlds, wireless data communications and the Java platform. Wireless Java technology spans parts of Java Card, J2ME, J2SE, and J2EE. That said, some common misconceptions about wireless Java technology need clearing up:

- *Wireless Java technology and J2ME are not the same thing.* On the one hand, J2ME encompasses more than just wireless devices. While some parts of J2ME are expressly designed for wireless devices, other parts are not—CDC devices are likely to have standard Ethernet connections. On the flip side, wireless Javatechnology is not confined to J2ME alone. You could have a laptop or palmtop computer running J2SE applications, connecting to other computers via an 802.11 LAN.
- *MIDP is not all of J2ME.* MIDP is the first finished profile and has the first installed base of devices out in the world, so people sometimes assume that you are talking about MIDP whenever you talk about J2ME. As you can see from the diagram above, though, J2ME has many facets; MIDP just happened to cross the finish line first.
- *MIDP is not all of wireless Java technology.* The Java platform offers plenty of choices for wireless programming: Personal Profile, J2SE on wireless devices, even the PDA Profile.

For other perspectives on wireless Java technology, select:

- Developing Wireless Applications with J2ME Technology (PDF) contains a high-level view of wireless Javatechnology.
- Introduction to Wireless Technologies describes Sun's wireless technologies briefly.

Why Use the Java Platform for Wireless Development?

The Java platform is an excellent choice for wireless development for many reasons. Here are three compelling advantages:

- The Java platform is safe. Java code always executes within the confines of the Java Virtual Machine[1], which provides a safe environment for executing downloaded code. A binary application could freeze a device or crash it (imagine a blue screen on your mobile phone!) By contrast, at worst a Java applications can bring down only the Virtual Machine, not the device itself.
- The Java language encourages robust programming. The garbage collector saves programmers countless hours of hunting down memory leaks. Likewise, the Java language's exception mechanisms encourage programmers to create robust applications.
- Portability is a big win for wireless Java technology. A single executable can run on multiple devices. For example, when you write a MIDlet (a MIDP application) it will run on any device that implements the MIDP specification. Given the dizzying profusion of wireless devices, not having to maintain a plethora of implementations is a big advantage. Even if a Java application makes use of vendor specific APIs, applications written using the Java programming language are inherently easier to modify for another device than applications written in C or C++.

  A second benefit of portability is the ease of delivering applications to a device over the wireless network (sometimes called Over-the-air, or OTA, provisioning). Binary applications can be moved from a server onto a device, too, but not safely. Because Java code runs inside the Java Virtual Machine[1], code that is downloaded from the network can be run safely. Binary code cannot be contained at execution time and is much less safe.

For more information on the motivations for using the Java platform for wireless development, select:

- Why Java Technology for Wireless?

The Market for Wireless Services

The market for wireless applications and services is huge. This market can be divided into two segments:

- The *consumer* segment consists of games, location-based services, productivity applications, and other generally useful applications. In the near term, these applications will be controlled and distributed by wireless carriers.
- The *custom business* segment will require custom development of wireless clients to connect to existing enterprise applications. Many of these will be wireless applications that use middleware to access company databases.

Where to Go Next

Perhaps the best next step toward getting a good grip on wireless Java technology is to create some:

- Wireless Development Tutorial Part I

  Learn how to set up a development environment for building J2ME client applications. You'll install the tools, then build and run a simple MIDlet. This article has all the information you need to get started with J2ME development.

- Wireless Development Tutorial Part II

  In this article, you'll learn how to set up a Java servlet development environment, either Tomcat or the J2EE Reference Implementation server. You'll write a servlet and create a MIDlet that makes a network connection to the servlet.

REFERENCES

Beukelman, D. (Ed.). (1992). [Topical issue]. *Seminars in Speech and Language*, 13(2).

Biklen, D. & Cardinal, D. (1997). *Contested words, contested science: Unraveling the facilitated communication controversy*. New York, NY: Teachers College Press.

Blischak, D. M. (1994). Phonological awareness: Implications for individuals with little or no functional speech. *AAC: Augmentative and Alternative Communication,* 10(4), 245-254.

Bondy, A. & Frost, L. (2002). *A picture's worth: PECS and other visual communication strategies in autism.* Bethesda, MD: Woodbine House.

Bornstein, H., & Saulnier, K. L. (1984). *The signed English starter.* Washington, DC: Gallaudet Press.

Bornstein, H., & Saulnier, K. L. (1987). *The signed English schoolbook.* Washington, DC: Kendall Green Publications.

Bornstein, H., Saulnier, K. L., & Hamilton, L. B. (Eds.). (1983). *Comprehensive signed English dictionary.* Washington, DC: Gallaudet Press.

Calculator, S. (1999). AAC outcomes for children and youths with severe disabilities: When seeing is believing. *AAC: Augmentative and Alternative Communication,* 15(1), 4-12.

Calculator, S. (1999). Look who's pointing now: Cautions related to clinical use of facilitated communication. *Language, Speech, and Hearing Services in Schools.* 30(4), 408-414.

Calculator, S. (2002). Use of enhanced natural gestures to foster interactions between children with Angleman Syndrome and their parents. *American Journal of Speech-Language Pathology.* 11, 340-355.

Calculator, S., & Jorgensen, C. (1991). Integrating AAC instruction into regular education settings: Expounding on best practices. *AAC: Augmentative and Alternative Communication,* 7(3), 204-214.

Capone, N. C. & McGregor, K. K. (2004). Gestural development: A review for clinical and research practices. *Journal of Speech, Language, and Hearing Research.* 47, 173-186.

Collier, B. (2000). *See what we say: Situational vocabulary for adults who use augmentative and alternative communication.* Baltimore, MD: Paul H. Brookes Publishing Company.

Cress, C.(2004). Augmentative and alternative communication and language: Understanding and responding to parents' perspectives. *Topics in Language Disorders.* 24(1), 51-61.

Cumley, G. D. & Swanson, S. (1999). Augmentative and alternative communication options for children with developmental apraxia of speech: Three case studies. *AAC: Augmentative and Alternative Communication.* 15, 110-125.

Dowden, P. A., & Marriner, N. A. (1995). Augmentative and alternative communication: Treatment principles and strategies. *Seminars in Speech and Language*, 16(2), 140-157.

Downing, J. E. (1999). *Teaching communication skills to students with severe disabilities.* Baltimore, MD: Paul H. Brookes Publishing Company.

Drager, K. D., Light, J., Speltz, J. C., Fallon, K. A. & Jeffries, L. Z. (2003). The performance of typically developing 2 ½ year olds on dynamic display AAC technologies with different system layouts and language organizations. *Journal of Speech, Language, and Hearing Research.* 46, 298-312.

Duchan, J. F. (1999). Views of facilitated communication: What's the point? *Language, Speech, and Hearing Services in Schools.* 30(4), 401-407.

Dunn, M. L. (1982). *Pre-sign language motor skills: Skill starters for motor development.* Tucson, AZ: Communication Skill Builders.

Durand, V. M. & Merges, E. (2001). Functional communication training: A contemporary analytic intervention for problem behaviors. *Focus on Autism and Other Developmental Disabilities.* 16(2), 110-119, 136.

Elder, P., & Goossens', C. (1994). *Engineering training environments for interactive, augmentative communication: Strategies for adolescents and adults who are moderately/ severely developmentally delayed.* Birmingham, AL: Southeast Augmentative Communication Conference Publications.

Elder, P., & Goossens', C. (1996). *Communication overlays for engineering training environments, Books I-IV (for adolescents and adults).* Birmingham, AL: Southeast Augmentative Communication Conference Publications.

Ely, S. (2000). *What is assistive technology: A basic guide for individuals with disabilities and their families (Rev. ed.).* Bloomington, IN: Indiana Institute on Disability and Community.

Erickson, K., Koppenhaver, D., & Yoder, D. (2003). *Waves of words: Augmented communicators read and write.* Toronto, Canada: International Society for Augmentative and Alternative Communication.

Fried-Oken, M. & Bersani, H. A. (2000). *Speaking up and spelling it out: Personal essays on augmentative and alternative communication.* Baltimore, MD: Paul H. Brookes Publishing Company.

Frost, L. A., & Bondy, A. S. (1994). *PECS, the Picture Exchange Communication System: Training manual.* Cherry Hill, NJ: Pyramid Educational Consultants, Inc.

Frost, L., & Bondy, A. (1998). *An introduction to PECS: The Picture Exchange Communication System.* [video recording]. Newark, DE: Pyramid Educational Consultants.

Glennen, S., & DeCoste, D. (1997). *The handbook of augmentative and alternative communication.* San Diego, CA: Singular Publishing Group.

Goossens', C., Crain, S., & Elder, P. (1992). *Engineering the preschool environment for interactive symbol communication: 18 months to 5 years developmentally.* Birmingham, AL: Southeast Augmentative Communication Conference Publications.

Granlund, M. & Olsson, C. (1999). Efficacy of communication intervention for presymbolic communicators. *AAC: Augmentative and Alternative Communication.* 15, 25-37.

Hodgdon, J. (1995). *Visual strategies for improving communication (Vol. 1): Practical supports for school and home.* Troy, MI: QuickRoberts Publishing.

Hodgdon, J. (1999). *Solving behavior problems in autism: Improving communication with visual strategies.* Troy, MI: QuickRoberts Publishing.

Hunt, P., Soto, G., Maier, J., Muller, E., & Goetz, L. (2002). Collaborative teaming to support students with AAC communication needs in general education classrooms. *AAC: Augmentative and Alternative Communication.* 18(1), 20-35.

Johnson, J. M., Baumgart, D., Helmstetter, E., & Curry, C. (1996). *Augmenting basic communication in natural contexts.* Baltimore, MD: Paul H. Brookes Publishing Company.

Johnston, S. S., Reichle, J. & Evans, J. (2004). Supporting augmentative and alternative communication use by beginning communicators with severe disabilities. *American Journal of Speech-Language Pathology.* 13, 20-30.

Kangas, K., & Lloyd, L. (1988). Early cognitive skills as prerequisites to augmentative and alternative communication use: What are we waiting for? *AAC: Augmentative and Alternative Communication,* 4(3), 211-221.

Koul. R. K., Schlosser, R. W. & Sancibrian, S. (2001). Effects of symbol, referent, and instructional variables on the acquisition of aided and unaided symbols by individuals with autism spectrum disorders. *Focus on Autism and Other Developmental Disabilities.* 16(3), 162-169.

Lane, L. G. (1990). *The Gallaudet survival guide to signing. (2nd ed.).* Washington, DC: Gallaudet Press.

Light, J. (1997). "Communication is the essence of human life": Reflections on communicative competence. *AAC: Augmentative and Alternative Communication,* 13(2), 61-70.

Light, J. C., & Binger, C. (1998). *Building communicative competence with individuals who use augmentative and alternative communication.* Baltimore, MD: Paul H. Brookes Publishing Company.

Light, J., DaHilo, J., English, J., Gutierrez, L., & Hartz, J. (1992). Instructing facilitators to support the communication of people who use augmentative communication systems. *Journal of Speech and Hearing Research,* 35(4), 865-875.

Lloyd, L., Fuller, D., & Arvidson, H. (Eds.). (1997). *Augmentative and alternative communication: A handbook of principles and practices.* Needham Heights, MA: Allyn & Bacon.

McCarthy, C. F., McLean, L., Miller, J., Paul-Brown, D, Romski, M.A., Rourk, J. D., & Yoder, D. E. (1998). *Communication supports checklist for serving individuals with severe disabilities.* Baltimore, MD: Paul Brookes Publishing.

McLean, J., McLean, L., Brady, N., & Etter, R. (1991). Communication profiles of two types of gestures using nonverbal persons with severe to profound mental retardation. *Journal of Speech and Hearing Research,* 34(2), 294-308.

McLean, J., Sack, S., McLean, L., O'Connor, A., & Simmons, S. (1990). *Developing communicative interactions* [training videos and manuals]. Parsons, KS: University of Kansas, Bureau of Child Research.

Mirenda, P. (1985). Designing pictorial communication systems for physically able bodied students with severe handicaps. *AAC: Augmentative and Alternative Communication,* 1(1), 58-64.

Mirenda, P. (1992). School to post school transition planning for augmentative and alternative communication users. *Seminars in Speech and Language,* 13(2), 130-142.

Mirenda, P. (1997). Supporting individuals with challenging behaviors through functional communication training and AAC: Research review. *AAC: Augmentative and Alternative Communication,* 13(4), 207-225.

Mirenda, P. (2001). Autism, augmentative communication, and assistive technology: What do we really know? *Focus on Autism and Other Developmental Disabilities.* 16(3), 141-151.

Mirenda, P. (2003). Toward functional augmentative and alternative communication for students with autism: Manual signs, graphic symbols, and voice output communication aids. *Language, Speech, and Hearing Services in Schools.* 34, 203-216.

Montgomery, J. (Ed.). (1987). Applications of augmentative communication in schools and clinics [Topical issue]. *Seminars in Speech and Language, 8(2).*

Mostert, M.P. (2001). Facilitated communication since 1995: A review of published studies. *Journal of Autism and Developmental Disorders.* 31(3), 287- 313.

Musselwhite, C. (1991). *Mini-grants and volunteers: Developing support for augmentative communication programs.* Birmingham, AL: Southeast Augmentative Communication Conference Publications.

National Center to Improve Practice. (1994). *Welcome to my preschool: Communicating with technology.* [video recording]. Newton, MA: Author.

Nigam, R. (2001). Dynamic assessment of graphic symbol combinations by children with autism. *Focus on Autism and Other Developmental Disabilities.* 16(3), 190-197.

Oxley, J. D., & Norris, J. A. (2000). Children's use of memory strategies: Relevance to voice output communication aid use. *AAC: Augmentative and Alternative Communication,* 16(2), 79-94.

Paul, R. (1997). Facilitating transitions in language development for children using AAC. *AAC: Augmentative and Alternative Communication,* 13(3), 141-148.

Reichle, J., Beukelman, D. R., & Light, J. C. (Eds.). (2002). *Exemplary practices for beginning communicators: Implications for AAC.* Baltimore, MD: Paul H. Brookes Publishing Company.

Reichle, J., York, J., & Eynon, D. (1989). Influence of indicating preferences for initiating, maintaining, and terminating interactions. In F. Brown & D. Lehr (Eds.), *Persons with profound disabilities: Issues and practices* (pp. 191-211). Baltimore, MD: Paul H. Brookes Publishing.

Romski, M. A., & Sevick, R. A. (1996). *Breaking the speech barrier: Language development through augmented means.* Baltimore, MD: Paul H. Brookes Publishing Company.

Rouse, C., & Katera (1997). *How to set up your home to help the nonverbal child.* [video recording]. Solana Beach, CA: Mayer-Johnson Company.

Rouse, C., & Katera. (1997). *Quick and easy: Ideas and materials to help the nonverbal child "talk" at home.* Solana Beach, CA: Mayer-Johnson Company.

Rouse, C., & Katera. (1999). *Ideas for using classroom materials to teach academics to nonverbal children.* Solana Beach, CA: Mayer-Johnson Company.

Rowland, C., & Schweigert, P. (1996). *Tangible symbol systems* [video recording]. San Antonio, TX: Communication Skill Builders.

Rowland, C., & Schweigert, P. (2000). Tangible symbols, tangible outcomes. *AAC: Augmentative and Alternative Communication,* 16(2), 61-78.

Savner, J. (1996). *Visual supports in the classroom.* [video recording]. Shawnee Mission, KS: Autism/ Asperger Syndrome Publishing Company.

Schlosser, R. W. & Blischak, D. (2001). Is there a role for speech output in interventions for persons with autism? A review. *Focus on Autism and Other Developmental Disabilities.* 16(3), 170-178.

Schlosser, R. W. (2003). *The efficacy of augmentative and alternative communication: Toward an evidence-based practice.* San Diego, CA: Academic Press.

Siegel-Causey, E., & Guess, D. (1989). *Enhancing nonsymbolic communication interactions among learners with severe disabilities.* Baltimore, MD: Paul H. Brookes Publishing Company.

Sigafoos, J. & Drasgow, E. (2001), Conditional use of aided and unaided AAC: A review and clinical case demonstration. *Focus on Autism and Other Developmental Disabilities.* 16(3), 152-161.

Sigafoos, J. (1999). Creating opportunities for augmentative and alternative communication: Strategies for involving people with developmental disabilities. *AAC: Augmentative and Alternative Communication,* 15(3), 183-190.

Skelly, M. (1979). *Amer-Ind gestural code based on universal American Indian hand talk.* New York, NY: Elsevier.

Spragale, D., & Micueci, D. (1990). Signs of the week: A functional approach to manual sign training. *AAC: Augmentative and Alternative Communication,* 6(1), 29-37.

Stephenson, J., & Linfoot, K. (1996). Pictures as communication symbols for students with severe intellectual disability. *AAC: Augmentative and Alternative Communication,* 12(4), 244-255.

Sturm, J. M. & Clendon, S. A. (2004). Augmentative and alternative communication, language, and literacy: Fostering the relationship. *Topics in Language Disorders.* 24(1), 76-91.

Tennant, R. A., & Brown, M.G. (1998). *The American sign language handshape dictionary.* Washington, DC: Gallaudet Press.

9

Speech Recognition Tools and Technologies

Speech

Speech can be described as an act of producing voice through the use of the vocal cords and vocal apparatus or other means, such as sign language, to create linguistic acts in the form of language that communicate information from an initiator to a recipient.

In more colloquial terms, speech can be described in several different ways:

1. A linguistic act designed to convey information.
2. Various types of linguistic acts where the audience consists of more than one individual, including public speaking, oration, and quotation.
3. The physical act of speaking, primarily through the use of vocal cords to produce voice. See phonology and linguistics for more detailed information on the physical act of speaking.

However, speech can also take place inside one's head, known as intrapersonal communication, for example, when one thinks or utters sounds of approval or disapproval. At a deeper level, one could even consider subconscious processes, including dreams where aspects of oneself communicate with each other (see Sigmund Freud), as part of intrapersonal communication, even though most human beings do not seem to have direct access to such communication.

Problems

There are several factors that can affect the quality of speech as such. Among these are:

1. Diseases and disorders of the lungs or the vocal cords, including paralysis, respiratory infections, and cancers of the lungs and throat.
2. Diseases and disorders of the brain, including alogia, aphasias and speech processing disorders, where impaired perception of the message (as opposed to the actual sound) leads to poor speech production.
3. Articulatory problems, such as stuttering, lisping, cleft palate, ataxia, or nerve damage leading to problems in articulation. Tourette syndrome and tics can also affect speech.
4. Problems in the perception of sound and auditory information can affect speech. In addition to aphasias, anomia and certain types of dyslexia can impede the quality of auditory perception, and therefore, expression. Hearing impairments and deafness can be considered to fall into this category.

Thus, it is clear that speech has both expressive and receptive elements. The purpose of speech can be to convey meaning or to increase social bonds between individuals and/or groups (it is often both). For the latter, shallowness is not a problem. The success of a speech act depends on numerous factors, including the presence or absence of a variety of speech disorders, the ability of the speaker to express the intended message, and the ability and willingness of the audience to play the role of recipient.

Glossophobia is the fear of public speaking.

Speech as a Form of Expression

There is a number of definitions of a speech as a form of expression. Take a closer look at the following variations in meaning:

- The faculty or act of speaking (The faculty or act of expressing or describing thoughts, feelings, or perceptions by articulation of words)
- A talk or public address: "The best impromptu speeches are the ones written well in advance" (Ruth Gordon). (A printed copy of such an address).
- One's habitual manner or style of speaking.
- The language or dialect of a nation or region: American speech.
- The study of oral communication, speech sounds, and vocal physiology.
- Archaic. *Rumor.*

A speech is a tool to convert thoughts into utterances carrying out specific meaning that when combined influences the general overview of the problem discussed. First masters of speech were born in first democratic states like Ancient Greece and Rome. The word "forum" we see online dozens of times a day originates from Greek "forum" (a place for public meetings and discussions). This is the place where ancient Greeks used to express their attitudes and opinions in the public. Free speech as we know is the first characteristic feature of democracy.

Speech is a form of art and the last has a history of over a thousand years. The first world known speaker that actually defined the genre was Socrates, an Athenian citizen managing a school of philosophers called sophists. Being a man of extreme wisdom he influenced the minds of Greeks for a decade until was executed for "corrupting the youth of Athens". His famous follower Plato took up the works and developed it into a literature genre with major peculiarities known to us.

Speech is a composite of sciences (phonetics, anatomy, philosophy, psychology etc.) and therefore it is extremely hard to master the skill. Professional speakers undergo continuous training until they become skilled leaders in the society. But returning to the quote of Ruth Gordon "The best impromptu speeches are the ones written well in advance" one has to admit the importance of writing skills. Nowadays it is easy to create and perform a speech; a lot of assistance is offered. Famous politicians, speakers, and other public mind revealers use a team of assistants to work on a single solid piece of text. Editors and writers are professionally maintaining the process of speech writing and only after the speech is fully tailored to the aim and the style of the speaker, it is presented in public.

Animal Speech

A few animals are capable of imitating human speech. The most notable and obvious of these are parrots, although apparently there are some dogs and cats who are able to as well, albeit indistinctly.

Speech Recognition

Speech recognition (in many contexts also known as *'automatic speech recognition'*, computer speech recognition or erroneously as Voice Recognition) is the process of converting a speech signal to a sequence of words, by means of an algorithm implemented as a computer program. Speech recognition applications that have emerged over the last years include voice dialing (e.g., *Call home*), call routing (e.g., *I would like to make a collect call*), simple data entry (e.g., entering a credit card number), and preparation of structured documents (e.g., a radiology report).

Voice recognition or speaker recognition is a related process that attempts to identify the person speaking, as opposed to what is being said.

Speech Recognition Technology

In terms of technology, most of the technical text books nowadays emphasize the use of Hidden Markov Model as the underlying technology. The dynamic programming approach, the neural network-based approach and the knowledge-based learning approach have been studied intensively in the 1980s and 1990s.

Performance of Speech Recognition Systems

The performance of a speech recognition systems is usually specified in terms of accuracy and speed. Accuracy is measured with the word error rate, whereas speed is measured with the real time factor.

Most speech recognition users would tend to agree that dictation machines can achieve very high performance in controlled conditions. Part of the confusion mainly comes from the mixed usage of the term speech recognition and dictation.

Speaker-dependent dictation systems requiring a short period of training can capture continuous speech with a large vocabulary at normal pace with a very high accuracy. Most commercial companies claim that recognition software can achieve between 98% to 99% accuracy (getting one to two words out of one hundred wrong) if operated under optimal conditions. These optimal conditions usually means the test subjects have 1) matching speaker characteristics with the training data, 2) proper speaker adaptation, and 3) clean environment (e.g. office space). (This explains why some users, especially accented, might actually find that the recognition rate could be perceptually much lower than the expected 98% to 99%).

Other, limited vocabulary, systems requiring no training can recognize a small number of words (for instance, the ten digits) from most speakers. Such systems are popular for routing incoming phone calls to their destinations in large organizations.

Noisy Channel Formulation of Statistical Speech Recognition

Many modern approaches such as HMM-based and ANN-based speech recognition are based on noisy channel formulation (See also Alternative formulation of speech recognition). In that view, the task of a speech recognition system is to search for the most likely word sequence given the acoustic signal. In other words, the system is searching for the most likely word sequence among all possible word sequences W^* from the acoustic signal A (what some will call the observation sequence according to the Hidden Markov Model terminology).

Both acoustic modeling and language modeling are important studies in modern statistical speech recognition. In this entry, we will focus on explaining the use of hidden Markov model (HMM) because notably it is very widely used in many systems. (Language modeling has many other applications such as smart keyboard and document classification; please refer to the corresponding entries.)

Approaches of Statistical Speech Recognition

Hidden Markov Model (HMM)-Based Speech Recognition

Modern general-purpose speech recognition systems are generally based on hidden Markov models (HMMs). This is a statistical model which outputs a sequence of symbols or quantities.

One possible reason why HMMs are used in speech recognition is that a speech signal could be viewed as a piece-wise stationary signal or a short-time stationary signal. That is, one could assume in a short-time in the range of 10 milliseconds, speech could be approximated as a stationary process. Speech could thus be thought as a Markov model for many stochastic processes (known as states).

Another reason why HMMs are popular is because they can be trained automatically and are simple and computationally feasible to use. In speech recognition, to give the very simplest setup possible, the hidden Markov model would output a sequence of n-dimensional real-valued vectors with n around, say, 13, outputting one of these every 10 milliseconds. The vectors, again in the very simplest case, would consist of cepstral coefficients, which are obtained by taking a Fourier transform of a short-time window of speech and decorrelating the spectrum using a cosine transform, then taking the first (most significant) coefficients. The hidden Markov model will tend to have, in each state, a statistical distribution called a mixture of diagonal covariance Gaussians which will give a likelihood for each observed vector. Each word, or (for more general speech recognition systems), each phoneme, will have a different output distribution; a hidden Markov model for a sequence of words or phonemes is made by concatenating the individual trained hidden Markov models for the separate words and phonemes.

The above is a very brief introduction to some of the more central aspects of speech recognition. Modern speech recognition systems use a host of standard techniques which it would be too time consuming to properly explain, but just to give a flavor, a typical large-vocabulary continuous system would probably have the following parts. It would need context dependency for the phones (so phones with different left and right context have different realizations); to handle unseen contexts it would need tree clustering of the contexts; it would of course use cepstral normalization to normalize for different recording conditions and depending on the length of time that the system had to adapt on different speakers and conditions it might use cepstral mean and variance normalization for channel differences, vocal tract length normalization (VTLN) for male-female normalization and maximum likelihood linear regression (MLLR) for more general speaker adaptation. The features would have delta and delta-delta coefficients to capture speech dynamics and in addition might use heteroscedastic linear discriminant analysis (HLDA); or might skip the delta and delta-delta coefficients and use LDA followed perhaps by heteroscedastic linear discriminant analysis or a global semitied covariance transform (also known as maximum likelihood linear transform (MLLT)). A serious company with a large amount of training data would probably want to consider discriminative training techniques like maximum mutual information (MMI), MPE, or (for short utterances) MCE, and if a large amount of speaker-specific enrollment data was available a more wholesale speaker adaptation could be done using MAP or, at least, tree-based maximum likelihood linear regression. Decoding of the speech (the term for what happens when the system is presented with a new utterance and must compute the most likely source sentence) would probably use the Viterbi algorithm to find the best path, but there is a choice between dynamically creating combination hidden Markov models which includes both the acoustic and language model information, or combining it statically beforehand (the AT&T approach, for which their FSM toolkit might be useful). Those who value their sanity might consider the AT&T approach, but be warned that it is memory hungry.

Neural Network-Based Speech Recognition

Another approach in acoustic modeling is the use of neural networks. They are capable of solving much more complicated recognition tasks, but do not scale as well as HMMs when it comes to large vocabularies. Rather than being used in general-purpose speech recognition applications they can handle low quality, noisy data and speaker independence. Such systems can achieve greater accuracy than HMM based systems, as long as there is training data and the vocabulary is limited. A more general approach using neural networks is phoneme recognition. This is an active field of research, but generally the results are better than for HMMs. There are also NN-HMM hybrid systems that use the neural network part for phoneme recognition and the hidden markov model part for language modeling.

Dynamic Time Warping (DTW)-Based Speech Recognition

Dynamic time warping is an algorithm for measuring similarity between two sequences which may vary in time or speed. For instance, similarities in walking patterns would be detected, even if in one video the person was walking slowly and if in another they were walking more quickly, or even if there were accelerations and decelerations during the course of one observation. DTW has been applied to video, audio, and graphics — indeed, any data which can be turned into a linear representation can be analysized with DTW.

A well known application has been automatic speech recognition, to cope with different speaking speeds. In general, it is a method that allows a computer to find an optimal match between two given sequences (e.g. time series) with certain restrictions, i.e. the sequences are "warped" non-linearly to match each other. This sequence alignment method is often used in the context of hidden Markov models.

Knowledge-Based Speech Recognition

This method uses a stored data base of commands that compares simple words with ones in the data base.

For Further Information

Popular speech recognition conferences held each year or two include ICASSP, Eurospeech/ICSLP (now named Interspeech) and the IEEE ASRU. Conferences in the field of Natural Language Processing, such as ACL, NAACL, EMNLP, and HLT, are beginning to include papers on speech processing. Important journals include the IEEE Transactions on Speech and Audio Processing (now named IEEE Transactions on Audio, Speech and Language Processing), Computer Speech and Language, and Speech Communication. Books like "Fundamentals of Speech Recognition" by Lawrence Rabiner can be useful to acquire basic knowledge but may not be fully up to date (1993). Another good source can be "Statistical Methods for Speech Recognition" by Frederick Jelinek which is a more up to date book (1998). Keep an eye on government sponsored competitions such as those organised by DARPA (the telephone speech evaluation was most recently known as Rich Transcription). In terms of freely available resources, the HTK book (and the accompanying HTK toolkit) is one place to start to both learn about speech recognition and to start experimenting (if you are very brave). You could also search for Carnegie Mellon University's SPHINX toolkit.

Speaker Recognition

Speaker recognition, or voice recognition is the task of recognizing people from their voices. Such systems extract features from speech, model them and use them to recognize the person from his/her voice.

Note that strictly speaking there is a difference between *speaker recognition* (recognizing who is speaking) and *speech recognition* (recognizing what is being said). Generally these two terms are frequently confused and voice recognition is used as a synonym for speech recognition instead.

Speaker recognition has a history dating back some four decades, where the output of several analog filters was averaged over time for matching. Speaker recognition uses the acoustic features of speech that have been found to differ between individuals. These acoustic patterns reflect both anatomy (e.g., size and shape of the throat and mouth) and learned behavioral patterns (e.g., voice pitch, speaking style). This incorporation of learned patterns into the voice templates (the latter called "*voiceprints*") has earned speaker recognition its classification as a "behavioral biometric."

Verification Versus Identification

Generally, two applications of *speaker recognition* can be distinguished: If the speaker claims to be of a certain identity and the voice is used to verify this claim this is called *speaker verification* or *voice authentication*. Recent evidence from linguistics has raised doubts about the security of using speaker identification as a means of user authentication. On the other hand, *speaker identification* is the task of determining an unknown speaker's identity. In a sense *speaker verification* is a 1:1 match where one speaker's voice is matched to one template (and possibly a general world template) whereas *speaker identification* is a 1:N match where the voice is matched to N templates.

Speaker verification is usually used in applications which require secure access. The systems operate with the user's knowledge and typically require their cooperation. *Speaker identification* systems are more likely to operate covertly without the user's knowledge. This can for example be used to route users to the correct mailbox, identify talkers in a discussion, alert speech recognition systems of speaker changes, check if a user is already enrolled in a system, etc.

Variants of Speaker Recognition

Each *speaker recognition* system has two phases: Enrollment and test. During enrollment the speaker's voice is recorded and typically a number of features are derived to form a *voice print*, *template*, or *model*. In the test phase (also called verification or identification phase) the speaker's voice is matched to the templates or models.

Speaker recognition systems employ three styles of spoken input: text-dependent, text-prompted and text-independent. This relates to the spoken text used during enrollment versus test.

If the text must be the same for enrollment and test this is called text-dependent recognition. It can be divided further into two cases: The highest accuracies can be achieved if the text to be spoken is fixed. This has the advantage that the system designer can devise a text which emphasizes speaker differences. However, since the text is always the same such systems are vulnerable to Impostors. Furthermore, it is not very user friendly if all users have to remember some complex text and in addition it makes the system language dependent.

Another type of text-dependent system uses pass phrases. The user is free to pick a phrase during enrollment but must use the same phrase during test. Most speaker verification applications use this type of text-dependent input. It has the advantage that an impostor must know the pass phrase, which adds a level of security. However, such systems are still vulnerable to tape recorder attacks. To counter this, many systems allow the specification of several pass phrases. Typically, these are answers to questions. During test the system randomly asks the user one of the questions and the user must provide the correct answer. However, the number of different questions is usually rather limited and thus a patient attacker could still attempt a tape recorder attack.

In text-prompted systems the speaker is asked to speak a prompted text. In principle this could be any kind of text. This however complicates the recognition process quite a bit. On the one hand the system knows the text that is being spoken. On the other hand the system must somehow know how this randomly selected text should sound if spoken by a particular speaker. This involves a much more elaborate model than in text-dependent systems where the text is always the same. The typical implementation makes use of digits. During enrollment the speaker is asked to speak a few digit sequences which are carefully selected such that all digits occur equally often. For every digit one speaker-specific model is trained. This has the advantage that only ten such models must be trained. During test a random digit sequence is selected and the corresponding digit models are concatenated into one model per speaker. Since speakers typically do not change languages frequently, such systems can be made language-independent quite easily.

Text-independent systems are most often used for speaker identification as they require very little if any cooperation by the speaker. In this case the text during enrollment and test is different. In fact, the enrollment may happen without the user's knowledge. Some recorded piece of speech may suffice.

Since text-independent systems have no knowledge of the text being spoken only general speaker-specific properties of the speaker's voice can be used. This does limit the accuracy of the recognition. On the other hand, this approach is also completely language independent.

Technology

The various technologies used to process and store *voiceprints* include frequency estimation, Hidden Markov models, pattern matching algorithms, neural networks, matrix representation and decision trees. Some systems also use "anti-speaker" techniques, such as cohort models, and world models.

Ambient noise levels can impede both collection of the initial and subsequent voice samples. Noise reduction algorithms can be employed to improve accuracies. Performance degradation can result from changes in behavioral attributes of the voice and from enrollment using one telephone and verification on another telephone. Voice changes due to aging also need to be addressed by recognition systems. Some systems adapt the speaker models after each successful verification to capture such long-term changes in the voice.

Many companies market speaker recognition engines, often as part of large voice processing, control and switching systems. Capture of the biometric is seen as non-invasive. The technology needs little additional hardware by using existing microphones and voice transmission technology allowing recognition over long distances via ordinary telephones (wired or wireless).

Speaker Identification

In computer science, speaker identification (for another type of speaker recognition see speaker verification) is a type of speaker recognition. It is the problem of *identifying* a person solely by their voice. It can be used for purposes such as police investigations.

It is different from speaker verification in that, as an example, a criminal's voice is cross checked against a database of criminal's voices looking for a match, and ergo the identity. In contrast, speaker verification seeks to verify, as an example that you really are Mary, seeking to take money out of your bank account using a speaker biometric checking ATM.

Speaker identification problems generally fall into two categories:

- Differentiating multiple speakers when a conversation is taking place.
- Identifying an individual's voice based upon previously supplied data regarding that individual's voice.

The latter is in the scope of biometrics.

Speaker identification is based on complex voice processing algorithms. In contrast, speaker verification is based on more simple voice print comparing.

Hearing (Sense)

Hearing, or audition, is one of the traditional five senses and refers to the ability to detect sound.

In vertebrates, including human beings, hearing is performed by the auditory system. Sound is detected by the ear, and transduced into nerve impulses that are perceived by the brain. Many animals use sound in order to communicate with each other, hearing in these species is particularly important for survival and reproduction.

All sounds are not normally audible to animals. Each species has a range of normal hearing for both loudness (amplitude) and pitch (frequency). Human hearing is most sensitive in the so-called "speech frequencies", which range from about 500 to 2000 kHz. In animals that use sound as a primary means of communication, hearing is typically most acute for the range of pitches produced in calls and speech. A common rule of thumb used to describe human sensitivity to pitch is frequency of 20 Hz to 20 kHz, though this varies significantly with age, occupational hearing damage, and gender; some individuals are able to hear pitches up to 22 kHz and perhaps beyond, while others are limited to about 16 kHz. Frequencies capable of being heard by humans are called audio or referred to as sonic. Frequencies higher than audio are referred to as ultrasonic, while frequencies below audio are referred to as infrasonic.

Human beings develop spoken language within the first few years of life, and hearing impairment can not only prevent the ability to talk but also the ability to understand the spoken word. By the time it is apparent that a severely hearing impaired (deaf) child has a hearing deficit, problems with communication may have already caused issues within the family and hindered social skills. In many developed countries, hearing is evaluated during the newborn period in an effort to prevent this. (Morton CC. Nance WE. Newborn hearing screening—a silent revolution. [Review] [47 refs] [Journal Article. Review] New England Journal of Medicine. 354(20):2151-64, 2006 May 18.) Although sign language is a full means of communication, literacy depends on understanding spoken language.

Some organisms are able to hear ultrasound and/or infrasound. Some bats use ultrasound for echo location while in flight. Dogs are able to hear ultrasound, which is the principle of 'silent' dog whistles. Snakes sense infrasound through their bellies, and there is evidence that whales and elephants may use it for communication. See sound for hearing ranges of various organisms.

Hearing can be measured by behavioral tests using an audiometer. Electrophysiologic tests of hearing can provide accurate measurements of hearing thresholds even in unconscious subjects.

Arthur Reber says, 'Explaining hearing adequately has proven a singularly difficult task. One would almost ensure oneself a Nobel prize by presenting a theory explaining satisfactorily no more than the perception of pitch and loudness.' (A.S. & E.S. Reber, *The Penguin Dictionary of Psychology* (3rd Edn., 2001))

Localization of Sound

Humans are able to hear a variety of sound frequencies, from 20Hz to 20kHz. Humans can hear the direction of the source of a sound, sometimes with surprising accuracy. Two mechanisms are known to be used.

- Bushy neurons can resolve time differences as small as the time it takes sound to pass one ear and reach the other (10 milliseconds).
- For high frequencies, frequencies with a wavelength shorter than the listener's head, more sound reaches the nearer ear.

Neither of these mechanisms work as well in water, in which the speed of sound is faster than in air.

The arrival time of a sound to a particular ear is given greater weight when localizing than relative intensity, according to an observation known as the Law of the First Wavefront.

Language Model

A statistical language model assigns a probability to a sequence of words $P(w_{1..n})$ by means of a probability distribution.

Language modeling is used in many natural language processing applications such as speech recognition, machine translation, part-of-speech tagging, parsing and information retrieval. Estimating the probability of sequences can become difficult in corpora, in which phrases or sentences can be arbitrarily long and hence some sequences are not observed during training of the language model (data sparseness problem of overfitting). For that reason these models are often approximated using smoothed N-gram models.

In speech recognition and in data compression, such a model tries to capture the properties of a language, and to predict the next word in a speech sequence.

When used in information retrieval, a language model is associated with a document in a collection. With query Q as input, retrieved documents are ranked based on the probability that the document's language model would generate the terms of the query, $P(Q \mid M_d)$.

REFERENCES

Arons B. Tools for Building Asynchronous Servers to Support Speech and Audio Applications. Proceedings of the ACM Symposium on User Interface Software and Technology, Monterey California, ACM Press, November 15-18, 1992.

Baber C, Noyes JM. Interactive Speech Technology. Taylor and Francis Ltd, Bristol PA, 1993.

Bolt RA, Herranz E. Two-Handed Gesture in Multi-Modal Natural Dialog. Proceedings of the ACM Symposium on User Interface Software and Technology, Monterey California, ACM Press, November 15-18, 1992.

Bradford JH. The Human Factors of Speech-Based Interfaces: A Research Agenda. SIGCHI Bulletin, 27(2):61-67, April 1995.

Buxton B. HCI and the Inadequacies of Direct Manipulation Systems. SIGCHI Bulletin, 25(1):21-22, January 1993.

Carr D, Plaisant C, Hasegawa H. The Design of a Telepathology Workstation: Exploring Remote Images. Technical Report CAR-TR-708, Center for Automation Research, University of Maryland, College Park, MD, May 1994.

Casali S. P., Williges B. H., Dryden R. D. Effects of Recognition Accuracy and Vocabulary Size of a Speech Recognition System on Task Performance and User Acceptance. Human Factors, 32, 2, (1990), pp. 183-196.

Cohen, PR. The Role of Natural Language in a Multimodal Interface. Proceedings of the ACM Symposium on User Interface Software and Technology, Monterey California, ACM Press, November 15-18, 1992.

Cole R et al. The Challenge of Spoken Language Systems: Research Directions for the Nineties. IEEE Transactions on Speech and Audio Processing, 3(1):1-21, January 1995.

Damper, R.I., Tranchant, M. A. Speech versus Keying in Command and Control: Effect of Concurrent Tasking. International Journal of Human-Computer Studies, 45, (1996), pp. 337-348.

DeHaemer MJ, Wright G, Dillon TW. Automated Speech Recognition for Spreadsheet Tasks: Performance Effects for Experts and Novices. International Journal of Human-Computer Interaction 6(3):299-318, 1994.

Dillon TW, Emurian HH. Reports of Visual Fatigue Resulting From Use of a Video Display Unit. Computers in Human Behavior, 11(1):77-84, 1995.

Dillon TW, McDowell D, Norcio AF, DeHaemer MJ. Nursing Acceptance of a Speech-Input Interface: A Preliminary Investigation. Computers in Nursing 12(6):264-271, November/ December 1994.

Dillon TW, Norcio AF, DeHaemer MJ. Spoken Language Interaction: Effects of Vocabulary Size and Experience on User Efficiency and Acceptability. Proceedings of the Fifth International Conference on Human-Computer Interaction, Orlando, Florida, August 8-13, 1993.

Everett SS, Wauchope K, Perez MA. A Natural Language Interface for Virtual Reality Systems. Technical Report AIC-94-046, NCARAI, US Naval Research Laboratory, Washington, DC.

Feldman CA, Stevens D. Pilot Study on the Feasibility of a Computerized Speech Recognition Charting System, Community Dent Oral Epidemiol, 18:213-215, 1990.

Helander M, Moody TS, Joost MG. Systems Design for Automated Speech Recognition. Handbook of Human-Computer Interaction, 301-319, Elsevier Science, North-Holland, 1990.

Hollbrook JA. Generating Medical Documentation Through Voice Input: The Emergency Room, Top Health Rec Manage, 12(3):58-63, 1992.

House D, Spoken-Language Access to Multimedia (SLAM): A Multimodal Interface to the World-Wide Web. Masters Thesis, Dept. of Computer Science and Engineering, Oregon Graduate Institute, 1995.

Ikerira H, Matsumoto T, Iinuma TA, et al. Analysis of Bone Scintigram Data Using Speech Recognition.Reporting System, Radiation Medicine, 8(1):8-12, 1990.

Issacs E, Wulfman CE, Rohn JA, Lane CD, Fagan LM. Graphical Access to Medical Expert System: IV. Experiments to Determine the Role of Spoken Input, Methods Inform Med, 32(1):18-32, 1993.

Jacob RJK, Sibert LE, McFarlane DC, Mullen MP. Integrality and Separability of Input Devices. ACM Transactions on Computer-Human Interaction, 1(1):3-26, March 1994.

Klatt EC. Voice-Activated Dictation for Autopsy Pathology. Comp Biol Med, 21(6):429-433, 1991.

Mahach, K. R., Boehm-Davis, D., Holt, R. The Effects of Mice and Pull-Down Menus Versus Command-Driven Interfaces on Writing. International Journal of Human-Computer Interaction, 7, 3, (1995), pp. 213-234.

Marsh E, Wauchope K, Gurney JO. Human-Machine Dialogue for Multi-Modal Decision Support Systems. Technical Report AIC-94-032, NCARAI, US Naval Research Laboratory, Washington, DC.

Martin P, Kehler A. SpeechActs: A Testbed for Continuous Speech Applications. Technical Report, Sun Microsystems Laboratories, Inc., Chelmsford, MA.

Massey BT, Geenen JE, Hogan WJ. Evaluation of a Voice Recognition System for Generation of Therapeutic ERCP Reports. Gastrointest Endosc, 37(6):617-620, 1991.

McMillan PJ, Harris JG. Datavoice: A Microcomputer-Based General Purpose Voice-Controlled Data-Collection System, Comput Biol Med, 20(6):415-419, 1990.

Molnar, K. K., Kletke, M. G. The Impacts on User Performance and Satisfaction of a Voice-Based Front-End Interface for a Standard Software Tool. International Journal of Human-Computer Studies, 45, (1996), pp. 287-303.

Mynatt ED, Edwards WK. Mapping GUIs to Auditory Interfaces. Proceedings of the ACM Symposium on User Interface Software and Technology, Monterey California, ACM Press, November 15-18, 1992.

Mynatt ED, Johnson E. Multimodal Access to Graphical User Interfaces for People who are Blind. Technical Report, College of Computing, Georgia Institute of Technology, Atlanta, GA.

Mynatt ED, Weber G. Nonvisual Presentation of Graphical User Interfaces: Contrasting Two Approaches. Technical Report, College of Computing, Georgia Institute of Technology, Atlanta, GA.

Mynatt ED. Auditory Presentation of Graphical User Interfaces. Technical Report, College of Computing, Georgia Institute of Technology, Atlanta, GA.

O'Hara SP, Bryant TN, et al . Speech Recognition and the Clinical Microbiology Laboratory. Medical Laboratory Sciences 49:20-26, 1992.

Oviatt S. Predicting Spoken Disfluencies During Human-Computer Interaction. Computer Speech and Language 9(1):19-35, January 1995.

Oviatt SL, Cohen PR, Wang M. Toward Interface Design for Human Language Technology: Modality and Structure as Determinants of Linguistic Complexity. Speech Communication, 15:283-300, 1994.

Oviatt SL, Cohen PR. Discourse Structure and Performance Efficiency in Interactive and Non-Interactive Spoken Modalities. Computer Speech and Language, 5:297-326, 1991.

Oviatt SL, Cohen PR. Spoken Language in Interpreted Telephone Dialogues. Computer Speech and Language, 6:277-302, 1992.

Peacocke RD, Graf DH. An Introduction to Speech and Speaker Recognition, Computer, 23(8):26-33, 1990.

Poon AD, Fagan LM. PEN-Ivory: The Design and Evaluation of a Pen-Based Computer System for Structured Data Entry. Report KSL-94-30, Knowledge Systems Laboratory, Medical Computer Science, Stanford University School of Medicine, Stanford, CA.

Raman TV, Information of the NII is not just for Viewing! Technical Report, Digital Equipment Corp., Cambridge, MA, March 1995.

Schmandt C, Ackerman MS, and Hindus D. Augmenting a Window System with Speech Input, Computer, 23(8):50-56, 1990.

Shneiderman B. Sparks of Innovation in Human-Computer Interaction, Ablex Publishing Corporation, Norwood, NJ, 1993.

Smith NT, Brian RA, Pettus DC, Jones BR, Quinn ML, Sarnat L. Recognition Accuracy with a Voice-Recognition System Designed for Anesthesia Record Keeping, J Clin Monit, 6(4):299-306, 1990.

Streeter LA. Applying Speech Synthesis to User Interfaces. Handbook of Human-Computer Interaction, 321-343, Elsevier Science, North-Holland, 1990.

Tucker P, Jones DM. Voice as Interface: An Overview. International Journal of Human-Computer Interaction 3(2):145-170, 1991.

Wright P, Lickorish A, Milroy R. Remembering While Mousing: The Cognitive Costs of Mouse Clicks. SIGCHI Bulletin, 26(1):41-45, January 1994.

Wulfman CE, Rua M, Lane CD, Shortliffe EH, Fagan LM. Graphical Access to Medical Expert System: V. Integration with Continuous-Speech Recognition, Methods Inform Med, 32(1):33-46, 1993.

Yankelovich N, Baatz E. SpeechActs: A Framework for Building Speech Applications. Technical Report, Sun Microsystems Laboratories, Inc., Chelmsford, MA.

Yankelovich N, Levow GA, Marx M. Designing SpeechActs: Issues in Speech User Interfaces. ACM CHI'95 Conference on Human Factors in Computing Systems, Denver CO, May 7-11, 1995.

Yankelovich N, SpeechActs and the Design of Speech Interfaces. Workshop on the Future of Speech and Audio in the Interface, ACM CHI'94 Conference on Human Factors in Computing Systems, Boston, MA, April 24-28, 1994.

Yankelovich N, Talking vs. Taking: Speech Access to Remote Computers. ACM CHI'94 Conference Companion, Boston, MA, April 24-28, 1994.

Zue V, Research Overview, 1995 Annual Research Summary, Laboratory for Computer Science, Massachusetts Institute of Technology.

Appendix

INFORMATION TECHNOLOGY ACT OF INDIA, 2000

An Act to provide legal recognition carried out by means of electronic date interchange and other means of electronic communication, commonly referred to as "electronic commerce" which involve the use of alternative to paper-based methods of communication and storage of information, to facilitate electronic filing of documents with the Government agencies and further to amend the Indian Penal Code, the Indian Evidence Act, 1872, the Bankers' Books Evidence Act, 1891 and the Reserve Bank of India Act, 1934 and for matters connected therewith or incidental thereto.

Whereas the General Assembly of the United Nations by resolution A/RES/51/162, dated the 30th January, 1997 has adopted the Model Law on Electronic Commerce adopted by the United Nations Commission on International Trade Law;

And Whereas the said resolution recommends inter alia that all States give favourable consideration to the said Model Law when they enact or revise their laws, in view of the need for uniformity of the law applicable to alternatives to paper-based methods of communication and storage of information;

And Whereas it is considered necessary to give effect to the said resolution and to promote efficient delivery of Government services by means of reliable electronic records.

Be it enacted Parliament in the Fifty-first Year of the Republic of India as follows:

CHAPTER I : PRELIMINARY

1. Short title, extent, commencement and application

(1) This Act may be called the Information Technology Act, 2000.

(2) It shall extend to the whole of India and, save as otherwise provided in this Act, it applies also to any offence or contravention thereunder committed outside India by any person.

(3) It shall come into force on such date as the Central Government may, by notification, appoint and different dates may be appointed provisions of this Act and any reference in any such provision to the commencement of this Act shall be construed as a reference to the commencement of that provision.

(4) Nothing in this Act shall apply to,-

(a) a negotiable instruments as defined in section 13 of the Negotiable Instruments Act, 1881;

(b) a power-of-attorney as defined in section 1A of the Powers -of-Attorney Act, 1882;

(c) a trust as defined in section 3 of the Indian Trusts Act, 1882;

(d) a will as defined in clause (h) of section 2 of the Indian Succession Act, 1925 including any other testamentary disposition by whatever name called;

(e) any contract for the sate of conveyance of immovable property or any interest in such property;

(f) any such class of documents or transactions as may be notified by the Central Government in the Official Gazette.

2. Definition

(1) In this Act, unless the context otherwise requires,-

(a) "access" with its grammatical variations and cognate expression means gaining entry into, instruction or communicating with the logical, arithmetical, or memory function resources of a computer, computer system or computer network;

(b) "addressee" means a person who is intended by the originator to receive the electronic record but does not include any intermediary;

(c) "adjudicating officer" means an adjudicating officer appointed under sub-section (1) of section 46;

(d) "affixing digital signature" with its grammatical variations and cognate expressions means adoption of any methodology or procedure by a person for the purpose of authenticating an electronic record by means of digital signature;

(e) "appropriate Government" means as respects any matter,-

(i) enumerated in List II of the Seventh Schedule to the Constitution;

(ii) relating to any State law enacted under List III of the Seventh Schedule to the Constitution,

the State Government and in any other case, the Central Government;

(f) "asymmetric crypto System" means a system of a secure key pair consisting of a private key for creating a digital signature and a public key to verify the digital signature;

(g) "Certifying Authority" means a person who has been granted a licence to issue a Digital Signature Certificate under section 24;

(h) "certification practice statement" means a statement issued by a Certifying Authority to specify the practices that the Certifying Authority employs in issuing Digital Signature Certificates;

(i) "computer" means any electronic magnetic, optical or other high-speed data processing device or system which performs logical, arithmetic, and memory functions by manipulation of electronic, magnetic or optical impulses, and includes all input, output, processing, storage, computer software, or communication facilities which are connected or related to the computer in a computer system or computer network;

(j) "computer network" means the interconnection of one or more computers through-

   (i) the use of satellite, microwave, terrestrial line or other communication media; and

   (ii) terminals or a complex consisting of two or more interconnected computers whether or not the interconnection is continuously maintained;

(k) "computer resource" means computer, computer system, computer network, date, computer data base or software;

(l) "computer system" means a device or collection of devices, including input and output support devices and excluding calculators which are not programmable and capable of being used in conjunction with external files, which contain computer programmes, electronic instructions, input data and output data, that perform logic, arithmetic, data storage and retrieval, communication control and other functions;

(m) "Controller" means the Controller of Certifying Authority appointed under sub-section (1) of section 17;

(n) "Cyber Appellate Tribunal" means the Cyber Regulations Appellate Tribunal established under sub-section (1) of section 48;

(o) "data" means a representation of information, knowledge, facts, concepts or instructions which are being prepared or have prepared in a formalised manner, and is intended to be processed, is being processed or has been processed in a computer system or computer network, and may be in any form (including computer printouts magnetic or optical storage media, punched cards, punched tapes) or stored internally in the memory of the computer;

(p) "digital signature" means authentication of any electronic record by a subscriber by means of an electronic method or procedure in accordance with the provisions of section 3;

(q) "Digital Signature Certificate" means a Digital Signature Certificate issued under sub-section (4) of section 35;

(r) "electronic form" with reference to information means any information generated, sent, received or stored in media, magnetic, optical, computer memory, micro film, computer generated micro fiche or similar device;

(s) "Electronic Gazette" means the Official Gazette published in the electronic form;

(t) "electronic record" means date, record or data generated, image or sound stored, received or sent in an electronic form or micro film or computer generated micro fiche;

(u) "function", in relation to a computer, includes logic, control, arithmetical process, deletion, storage and retrieval and communication or telecommunication from or within a computer;

(v) "information" includes date, text, images, sound, voice, codes, computer programmes, software and data bases or micro film or computer generated micro fiche;

(w) "intermediary" with respect to any particular electronic message means any person who on behalf of another person receives, stores or transmits that message or provides any service with respect to that message;

(x) "key pair" in an asymmetric crypto system, means a private key and its mathematically related public key, which are so related that the public key can verify a digital signature created by the private key;

(y) "law" includes any Act of Parliament or of a State Legislature, Ordinances promulgated by the President or a Governor, as the case may be, Regulation made by the President under article 240, Bills enacted as President's Act under sub-clause (a) of clause (1) of article 357 of the Constitution and includes rules, regulations, bye-laws and orders issued or made thereunder ;

(z) "licence" means a licence granted to a Certifying Authority under section 24;

(za) "originator" means a person who sends, generates, stores or transmits any electronic message or causes any electronic message to be sent, generated, stored or transmitted to any other person but does not include an intermediary;

(zb) "prescribed" means prescribed by rules made under this Act;

(zc) "private key" means the key of a key pair used to create a digital signature;

(zd) "public key" means the key of a key pair used to verify a digital signature and listed in the Digital Signature Certificate;

(ze) "secure system" means computer hardware, software, and procedure that-

(a) are reasonably secure from unauthorised access and misuse;

(b) provide a reasonable level of reliability and correct operation;

(c) are reasonably suited to performing the intended functions; and

(d) adhere to generally accepted security procedures;

(zf) "security procedure" means the security procedure prescribed under section 16 by the Central Government;

(zg) "subscriber" means a person in whose name the Digital Signature Certificate is issued;

(zh) "verify" in relation to a digital signature, electronic record or public key, with its grammatical variations and cognate expressions means to determine whether-

- (a) the initial electronic record was affixed with the digital signature by the use of private key corresponding to the public key of the subscriber;
- (b) the initial electronic record is retained intact or has been altered since such electronic record was so affixed with the digital signature.

(2) Any reference in this Act to any enactment or any provision thereof shall, in relation to an area in which such enactment or such provision is not in force, be construed as a reference to the corresponding law or the relevant provision of the corresponding law, if any, in force in that area.

CHAPTER II : DIGITAL SIGNATURE

3. Authentication of electronic records

(1) Subject to the provisions of this section any subscriber may authenticate an electronic record by affixing his digital signature.

(2) The authentication of the electronic record shall be effected by the use of asymmetric crypto system and hash function which envelop and transform the initial electronic record into another electronic record.

Explanation- For the purposes of this sub-section, "hash function" means an algorithm mapping or translation of one sequence of bits into another, generally smaller, set known as "hash result" such that an electronic record yields the same hash result

every time the algorithm is executed with the same electronic record as its input making it computationally infeasible-

(a) to derive or reconstruct the original electronic record from the hash result produced by the algorithm;

(b) that two electronic records can produce the same hash result using the algorithm.

(3) Any person by the use of a public key of the subscriber can verify the electronic record.

(4) The private key and the public key are unique to the subscriber and constitute a functioning key pair.

CHAPTER III : ELECTRONIC GOVERNANCE

4. Legal recognition of electronic records

Where any law provides that information or any other matter shall be in writing or in the typewritten or printed form, then, notwithstanding anything contained in such law, such requirement shall be deemed to have satisfied if such information or matter is-

(a) rendered or made available in an electronic form; and

(b) accessible so as to be usable for a subsequent reference.

5. Legal recognition of digital signatures

Where any law provides that information or any other matter shall be authenticated by affixing the signature or any document shall be signed or bear the signature of any person then, notwithstanding anything contained in such law, such requirement shall be deemed to have been satisfied, if such information or matter is authenticated by means of digital signature affixed in such manner as may be prescribed by the Central Government.

Explanation-For the purposes of this section "signed", with the grammatical variations and cognate expressions, shall, with reference to a person, mean affixing of his hand written or any mark on any document and the expression "signature" shall be construed accordingly.

6. Use of electronic records and digital signatures in Government and its agencies

(1) Where any law provides for-

(a) the filing of any form, application or any other document with any office, authority, body or agency owned or controlled by the appropriate Government in a particular manner;

(b) the issue or grant of any licence, permit, sanction or approval by whatever name called in a particular manner;

(c) the receipt or payment of money in a particular manner,

then, notwithstanding anything contained in any other law for the time being in force, such requirement shall be deemed to have been satisfied if such filing, issue, grant, receipt or payment, as the case may be, is effected by means of such electronic form as may be prescribed by the appropriate Government.

(2) The appropriate Government may, for the purposes of sub-section (1), by rules, prescribe-

(a) the manner and format in which such electronic records shall be filed, created or issued;

(b) the manner or method of payment of any fee or charges for filing, creation or issue any electronic record under clause (a).

7. Retention of electronic records

(1) Where any law provides that documents, records or information shall be retained for any specific period, then that requirement shall be deemed to have been satisfied if such documents, records or information are retained in the electronic form, if-

(a) the information contained therein remains accessible so as to be usable for a subsequent reference;

(b) the electronic record is retained in the format in which it was originally generated, sent or received or in a format which can be demonstrated to represent accurately the information originally generated, sent or received;

(c) the details which will facilitate the identification of the origin, destination, date and time of despatch or receipt of such electronic record are available in the electronic record:

Provided that this clause does not apply to any information which is automatically generated solely for the purpose of enabling an electronic record to be despatched or received.

(2) Nothing in this section shall apply to any law that expressly provides for the retention of documents, records or information in the form of electronic records.

8. Publication of rule, regulation, etc., in Electronic Gazette

Where any law provides that any rule, regulation, order, bye-law, notification or any other matter shall be published in the Official Gazette, then, such requirement shall be deemed to have been satisfied if such rule, regulation, order, bye-law, notification or any other matter is published in the Official Gazette or Electronic Gazette :

Provided that where any rule, regulation, order, bye-law, notification or any other matter is published in the Official Gazette or Electronic Gazette, the date of publication shall be deemed to be the date of the Gazette which was first published in any form.

9. Section 6, 7, and 8 not to confer right to insist document should be accepted in electronic form

Nothing contained in sections 6, 7 and 8 shall confer a right upon any person to insist that any Ministry or Department of the Central Government or the State Government or any authority or body established by or under any law or controlled or funded by the Central or State Government should accept, issue, create, retain and preserve any document in the form of electronic records or effect any monetary transaction in the electronic form.

10. Power to make rules by Central Government in respect of digital signature

The Central Government may, for the purposes of this Act, by rules, prescribe-

(a) the type of digital signature;

(b) the manner and format in which the digital signature shall be affixed;

(c) the manner or procedure which facilitates identification of the person affixing the digital signature;

(d) control processes and procedures to ensure adequate integrity, security and confidentiality or electronic records or payments; and

(e) any other matter which is necessary to give legal effect to digital signatures.

CHAPTER IV : ATTRIBUTION, ACKNOWLEDGMENT AND DESPATCH OF ELECTRONIC RECORDS

11. Attribution of electronic records

An electronic record shall be attributed to the originator-

(a) if it was sent by the originator himself;

(b) by a person who had the authority to act on behalf of the originator in respect of that electronic record; or

(c) by an information system programmed by or on behalf of the originator to operate automatically.

12. Acknowledgement of receipt

(1) Where the originator has not agreed with the addressee that the acknowledgement of receipt of electronic record be given in a particular form or by a particular method, an acknowledgment may be given by-

(a) any communication by the addressee, automated or otherwise; or

(b) any conduct of the addressee, sufficient to indicate to the originator that the electronic record has been received.

(2) Where the originator has stipulated that the electronic record shall be binding only on receipt of an acknowledgment or such electronic record by him, then unless acknowledgment has been so received, the electronic record shall be deemed to have been never sent by the originator.

(3) Where the originator has not stipulated that the electronic record shall be binding only on receipt of such acknowledgment, and the acknowledgment has not been received by the originator within the time specified or agreed or, if no time has been specified or agreed to within a reasonable time, then the originator may give notice to the addressee sating that no acknowledgment has been received by him and specifying reasonable time by which the acknowledgment must be received by him and if no acknowledgment is received within the aforesaid time limit he may after giving notice to the addressee, treat the electronic record as though it has never been sent.

13. Time and place of despatch and receipt of electronic record

(1) Save as otherwise agreed to between the originator and the addressee, the despatch of an electronic record occurs when it enters a computer resource outside the control of the originator.

(2) Save as otherwise agreed between the originator and the addressee, the time of receipt of an electronic record shall be determined as follows, namely :-

(a) if the addressee has designated a computer resource for the purpose of receiving electronic records,-

  (i) receipt occurs at the time when the electronic record enters the designated computer resource; or

  (ii) if the electronic records is sent to a computer resource of the addressee that is not the designated computer resource, receipt occurs at the time when the electronic records is retrieved by the addressee;

(b) if the addressee has not designated a computer resource along with specified timing, if any, receipt occurs when the electronic record enters the computer resource of the addressee.

(3) Save as otherwise agreed to between the originator and the addressee, an electronic record is deemed to be despatched at the place where the originator has his place of business, and is deemed to be received at the place where the addressee has his place of business.

(4) The provisions of sub-section (2) shall apply notwithstanding that the place where the computer resource is located may be different from the place where the electronic record is deemed to have been received under sub-section (3)

(5) For the purposes of this section,-

(a) if the originator or the addressee has more than one place of business, the principal place of business, shall be the place of business,

(b) if the originator or the addressee does not have a place of business, his usual place of residence shall be the place of business;

(c) "usual place of residence", in relation to a body corporate, means the place where it is registered.

CHAPTER V : SECURE ELECTRONIC RECORDS AND SECURE DIGITAL SIGNATURES

14. Secure electronic records

Where any security procedure has been applied to an electronic record at a specific point of time, then such record shall be deemed to be a secure electronic record from such point of time to the time of verification.

15. Secure digital signature

If, by application of a security procedure agreed to by the parties concerned, it can be verified that a digital signature, at the time it was affixed, was-

(a) unique to the subscriber affixing it;

(b) capable of identifying such subscriber;

(c) created in a manner or using a means under the exclusive control of the subscriber and is linked to the electronic record to which it relates in such a manner that if the electronic record was altered the digital signature would be invalidated.

then such digital signature shall be deemed to be a secure digital signature.

16. Security procedure

The Central Government shall for the purpose of this Act prescribe the security procedure having regard to commercial circumstances prevailing at the time when the procedure was used, including-

(a) the nature of the transaction;

(b) the level of sophistication of the parties with reference to their technological capacity;

(c) the volume of similar transactions engaged in by other parties;

(d) the availability of alternatives offered to but rejected by any party;

(e) the cost of alternative procedures; and

(f) the procedures in general use for similar types of transactions or communications.

CHAPTER VI : REGULATION CERTIFYING AUTHORITIES

17. Appointment of Controller and other officers

(1) The Central Government may, by notification in the Official Gazette, appoint a Controller of Certifying Authorities for the purpose of this Act and may also by the same or subsequent notification appoint such of Deputy Controllers and Assistant Controllers as it deems fit.

(2) The Controller shall discharge his functions under this Act subject to the general control and directions of the Central Government.

(3) The Deputy Controllers and Assistant Controllers shall perform the functions assigned to them by the Controller under the general superintendence and control of the Controller.

(4) The qualifications, experience and terms and conditions of service of Controller, Deputy Controllers and Assistant Controllers shall be such as may be prescribed by the Central Government.

(5) The Head Office and Branch Office of the office of the Controller shall be at such places as the Central Government may specify, and these may be established at such places as the Central Government may think fit.

(6) There shall be a seal of the Office of the Controller.

18. Functions of Controller

The Controller may perform all or any of the following functions, namely:-

(a) exercising supervision over the activities of the Certifying functions, namely:

(b) certifying public keys of the Certifying Authorities;

(c) laying down the standards to be maintained by the Certifying Authorities;

(d) specifying the qualifications and experience which employees of the Certifying Authority should possess;

(e) specifying the conditions subject to which the Certifying Authorities shall conduct their business;

(f) specifying the contents of written, printed or visual materials and advertisements that may be distributed or used in respect of a Digital Signature Certificate and the public key;

(g) specifying the form and content of a Digital Signature Certificate and the key;

(h) specifying the form and manner in which accounts shall be maintained by the Certifying Authorities;

(i) specifying the terms and conditions subject to which auditors may be appointed and the remuneration to be paid to them;

(j) facilitating the establishment of any electronic system by a Certifying Authority either solely or jointly with other Certifying Authorities and regulation of such systems;

(k) specifying the manner in which the Certifying Authorities shall conduct their dealings with the subscribers;

(l) resolving any conflict of interests between the Certifying Authorities and the subscribers;

(m) laying down the duties of the Certifying Authorities;

(n) maintaining a data base containing the disclosure record of every Certifying Authority containing such particulars as may be specified by regulations, which shall be accessible to public.

19. Recognition of foreign Certifying Authorities

(1) Subject to such conditions and restrictions as may be specified by regulations, the Controller may with the previous approval of the Central Government, and by notification in the Official Gazette, recognise any foreign Certifying Authority as a Certifying Authority for the purpose of this Act.

(2) Where any Certifying Authority is recognised under sub-section (1), the Digital Signature Certificate issued by such Certifying Authority shall be valid for the purposes of this Act.

(3) The Controller may, if he is satisfied that the Certifying Authority has contravened

any of the conditions and restrictions subject to which it was granted recognition under sub-section (1) he may, for reasons to be recorded in writing in the Official Gazette, revoke such recognition.

20. Controller to act as repository

(1) The Controller shall be the repository of all Digital Signature Certificates issued under this Act.

(2) The Controller shall-

(a) make use of hardware, software and procedures that are secure from intrusion and misuse;

(b) observe such other standards as may be prescribed by the Central Government,

to ensure that the secrecy and security of the digital signatures are assured.

(3) The Controller shall maintain a computerised data base of all public keys in such a manner that such data base and the public keys are available to any member of the public.

21. Licence to issue Digital Signature Certificates

(1) Subject to the provisions of sub-section (2), any person may make an application, to the Controller, for a licence to issue Digital Signature Certificates.

(2) No licence shall be issued under sub-section (1), unless the applicant fulfills such requirements with respect to qualification, expertise, manpower, financial resources and other infrastructure facilities, which are necessary to issue Digital signature Certificates as may be prescribed by the Central Government.

(3) A licence granted under this sections shall-

(a) be valid for such period as may be prescribed by the Central Government;

(b) not be transferable or heritable;

(c) be subject to such terms and conditions as may be specified by the regulations.

22. Application for licence

(1) Every application for issue of a licence shall be in such form as may be prescribed by the Central Government.

(2) Every application for issue of a licence shall be accompanied by-

(a) a certification practice statement;

(b) a statement including the procedures with respect to identification of the applicant;

(c) payment of such fees, not exceeding twenty-five thousand rupees as may be prescribed by the Central Government;

(d) such other documents, as may be prescribed by the Central Government.

23. Renewal of licence

An application for renewal of a licence shall be-

(a) in such form;

(b) accompanied by such fees, not exceeding five thousand rupees,

as may be prescribed by the Central Government and shall be made not less than forty-five days before the date of expiry of the period of validity of the licence.

24. Procedure for grant or rejection of licence

The Controller may, on receipt of an application under sub-section (1) of section 21, after considering the documents accompanying the application and such other factors, as he deems fit, grant the licence or reject the application:

Provided that no application shall be rejected under this section unless the applicant has been given a reasonable opportunity of presenting his case.

25. Suspension of licence

(1) The Controller may, if he is satisfied after making such inquiry, as he may think fit, that a Certifying Authority has,-

(a) made a statement in, or in relation to, the application for the issue or renewal of the licence, which is incorrect or false in material particulars;

(b) failed to comply with the terms and conditions subject to which the licence was granted;

(c) failed to maintain the standards specified under clause (b) of sub-section (2) of section 20;

(d) contravened any provisions of this Act, rule, regulation or order made thereunder,

revoke the licence :

Provided that no licence shall be revoked unless the Certifying Authority has been given a reasonable opportunity of showing cause against the proposed revocation.

(2) The Controller may, if he has reasonable cause to believe that there is any ground for revoking a licence under sub-section (1), by order suspend such licence pending the completion of any inquiry ordered by him :

Provided that no licence shall be suspended for a period exceeding ten days unless the Certifying Authority has been given a reasonable opportunity of showing cause against the proposed suspension.

(3) No certifying Authority whose licence has been suspended shall issue any Digital Signature Certificate during such suspension.

26. Notice of suspension or revocation of licence

(1) Where the licence of the Certifying Authority is suspended or revoked, the Controller shall publish notice of such suspension or revocation, as the case may be, in the data base maintained by him.

(2) Where one or more repositories are specified, the Controller shall publish notices of such suspension or revocation, as the case may be, in all such repositories:

Provided that the data base containing the notice of such suspension or revocation, as the case may be, shall be made available through a web site shall be accessible round the clock :

Provided further that the Controller may, if he considers necessary, publicise the contents of data base in such electronic or other media, as he may consider appropriate.

27. Power to delegate

The Controller may, in writing, authorise the Deputy Controller, Assistant Controller or any officer to exercise any of the powers of the Controller under this Chapter.

28. Power to investigate contraventions

(1) The Controller or any officer authorised by him in this behalf shall take up for investigation any contravention of the provisions of this Act, rules or regulations made thereunder.

(2) The Controller or any officer authorised by him in this behalf shall exercise the like powers which are conferred on Income-tax authorities under Chapter XIII of the Income-tax Act, 1961 and shall exercise such powers, subject to such limitation laid down under that Act.

29. Access to computers and data

(1) Without prejudice to the provisions of sub-section (1) of section 69, the Controller

or any person authorised by him shall, if he has reasonable cause to suspect that nay contravention of the provisions of this Act, rules or regulations made thereunder has been committed, have access to any computer system, any apparatus, data or any other material connected with such system, for the purpose of searching or causing a search to be made for obtaining any information or data contained in or available to such computer system.

(2) For the purpose of sub-section (1), the Controller or any person authorised by him may, by order, direct any person incharge of, or otherwise concerned with the operation of, the computer system, data apparatus or material, to provide him with such reasonable technical and other assistance as he may consider necessary.

30. Certifying Authority to follow certain procedures

Every Certifying Authority shall,-

(a) make use of hardware, software and procedures that are secure from intrusion and misuse;

(b) provide a reasonable level of reliability in its services which are reasonably suited to the performance of intended functions;

(c) adhere to security procedures to ensure that the secrecy and privacy of the digital signatures are assured; and

(d) observe such other standards as may be specified by regulations.

31. Certifying Authority to ensure compliance of the Act, etc.

Every Certifying Authority shall ensure that every person employed or otherwise engaged by it complies, in the course of his employment or engagement, with the provisions of this Act, rules, regulations and orders made thereunder.

32. Display of licence

Every Certifying Authority shall display its licence at a conspicuous place of the premises in which it carries on its business.

33. Surrender of licence

(1) Every Certifying Authority whose licence is suspended or revoked shall immediately after such suspension or revocation, surrender the licence to the Controller.

(2) Where any Certifying Authority fails to surrender a licence under sub-section (1), the person in whose favour a licence is issued, shall be guilty of an offence and shall be punished with imprisonment which may extend up to six months or a fine which may extend up to ten thousand rupees or with both.

34. Disclosure

(1) Every Certifying Authority shall disclose in the manner specified by regulations-

(a) its Digital Signature Certificate which contains the public key corresponding to the private key used by that Certifying Authority to digitally sign another Digital Signature Certificate;

(b) any certification practice statement relevant thereto;

(c) notice of the revocation or suspension of its Certifying Authority certificate, if any; and

(d) any other fact that materially and adversely affects either the reliability of a Digital Signature Certificate, which that Authority has issued, or the Authority's ability to perform its services.

(2) Where in the opinion of the Certifying Authority any event has occurred or any situation has arisen which may materially and adversely affect the integrity of its computer system or the conditions subject to which a Digital Signature Certificate was granted, then, the Certifying Authority shall-

(a) use reasonable efforts to notify any person who is likely to be affected by that occurrence; or

(b) act in accordance with the procedure specified in its certification practice statement to deal with such event or situation.

CHAPTER VII : DIGITAL SIGNATURE CERTIFICATES

35. Certifying Authority to issue Digital Signature Certificate

(1) Any person may make an application to the Certifying Authority for the issue of a Digital Signature Certificate in such form as may be prescribed by the Central Government.

(2) Every such application shall be accompanied by such fee not exceeding twenty-five thousand rupees as may be prescribed by the Central Government, to be paid to the Certifying Authority :

Provided that while prescribing fees under sub-section (2) different fees may be prescribed for different classes of applications;

(3) Every such application shall be accompanied by a certification practice statement or where there is no such statement, a statement containing such particulars, as may be specified by regulations.

(4) On receipt of an application under sub-section (1), the Certifying Authority may, after consideration of the Certification practice statement or the other statement under sub-section (3) and after making such enquiries as it may deem fit, grant the Digital Signature Certificate or for reasons to be recorded in writing, reject the application :

Provided that no Digital Certificate shall be granted unless the Certifying Authority is satisfied that-

(a) the application holds the private key corresponding to the public key to be listed in the Digital Signature Certificate;

(b) the applicant holds a private key, which is capable of creating a digital signature;

(c) the public key to be listed in the certificate can be used to verify a digital signature affixed by the private key held by the applicant :

Provided further that no application shall be rejected unless the applicant has been given a reasonable opportunity of showing cause against the proposed rejection.

36. Representation upon issuance of Digital Signature Certificate

A Certifying Authority while issuing a Digital Signature Certificate shall certify that-

(a) it has complied with the provisions of this Act and the rules and regulations made thereunder;

(b) it has published the Digital Signature Certificate or otherwise made it available to such person relying on it and the subscriber has accepted it;

(c) the subscriber holds the private key corresponding to the public key, listed in the Digital Signature Certificate;

(d) the subscriber's public key and private key constitute a functioning key pair;

(e) the information contained in the Digital Signature Certificate is accurate; and

(f) it has no knowledge of any material fact, which if it had been included in the Digital Signature Certificate would adversely affect the reliability of the representations made in clauses (a) to (d).

37. Suspension of Digital Signature Certificate

(1) Subject to the provisions of sub-section (2), the Certifying Authority which has issued a Digital Signature Certificate may suspend such Digital Signature Certificate,-

(a) on receipt of a request to that effect from-

(i) the subscriber listed in the Digital Signature Certificate; or

(ii) any person duly authorised to act on behalf of that subscriber;

(b) if it is of opinion that the Digital Signature Certificate should be suspended in public interest.

(2) A Digital Signature Certificate shall not be suspended for a period exceeding fifteen days unless the subscriber has been given an opportunity of being heard in the matter.

(3) On suspension of a Digital Signature Certificate under this section, the Certifying Authority shall communicate the same to the subscriber.

38. Revocation of Digital Signature Certificate

(1) A Certifying Authority may revoke a Digital Signature Certificate issues by it-

(a) where the subscriber or any other person authorised by him makes a request to that effect; or

(b) upon the death of the subscriber; or

(c) upon the dissolution of the firm or winding up of the company where the subscriber is a firm or a company.

(2) Subject to the provisions of sub-section (3) and without prejudice to the provisions of sub-section (1), a Certifying Authority may revoke a Digital Signature Certificate which has been issued by it at any time, if it is of opinion that-

(a) a material fact represented in the Digital Signature Certificate is false or has been concealed;

(b) a requirement for issuance of the Digital Signature Certificate was not satisfied;

(c) the Certifying Authority's private key or security system was compromised in a manner materially affecting the Digital Signature Certificate's reliability;

(d) the subscriber has been declared insolvent or dead or where a subscriber is a firm or a company, which has been dissolved, wound-up or otherwise ceased to exist.

(3) A Digital Signature Certificate shall not be revoked unless the subscriber has been given an opportunity of being heard in the matter.

(4) On revocation of a Digital Signature Certificate under this section, the Certifying Authority shall communication the same to the subscriber.

39. Notice of suspension or revocation

(1) Where a Digital Signature Certificate is suspended or revoked under section 37 or section 38, the Certifying Authority shall publish a notice of such suspension or revocation, as the case may be, in the repository specified in the Digital Signature Certificate for publication of such notice.

(2) Where one or more repositories are specified, the Certifying Authority shall publish notice of such suspension or revocation, as the case may be, in all such repositories.

CHAPTER VIII : DUTIES OF SUBSCRIBERS

40. Generating key pair

Where any Digital Signature Certificate, the public key of which corresponds to the private key of that subscriber which is to be listed in the Digital Signature Certificate has been accepted by a subscriber, then, the subscriber shall generate the key pair by applying the security procedure.

41. Acceptance of Digital Signature Certificate

(1) A subscriber shall be deemed to have accepted a Digital Signature Certificate if he publishes or authorises the publication of a Digital Signature Certificate-

(a) to one or more persons;
(b) in a repository, or

otherwise demonstrates his approval of the Digital Signature Certificate in any manner,

(2) By accepting a Digital Signature the subscriber certifies to all who reasonable rely on the information contained in the Digital Signature Certificate that-

(a) the subscriber holds the private key corresponding to the public key listed in the Digital Signature Certificate and is entitled to hold the same;

(b) all representations made by the subscriber to the Certifying Authority and all material relevant to the information contained in the Digital Signature Certificate are true.;

(c) all information in the Digital Signature Certificate that is within the knowledge of the subscriber is true.

42 Control of private key

(1) Every subscriber shall exercise shall exercise reasonable care to retain control of the private key corresponding to the public key listed in his Digital Signature Certificate and take all steps to prevent its disclosure to a person not authorised to affix the digital signature of the subscriber.

(2) If the private key corresponding to the public key listed in the Digital Signature Certificate has been compromised, then, the subscriber shall communicate the same without and delay to the Certifying Authority in such manner as may be specified by the regulations.

Explanation- For the removal of doubts, it is hereby declared that the subscriber shall be liable to till he has informed the Certifying Authority that the private key has been compromised.

CHAPTER IX : PENALTIES AND ADJUDICATION

43. Penalty of damage of computer, computer system, etc.

If any person without permission of the owner or any other person who is incharge of a computer, computer or computer network,-

(a) accesses or secures access to such computer, computer system or computer network;

(b) downloads, copies or extracts any data, computer data base or information from such computer, computer system or computer network including information or data held or stored in any removable storage medium;

(c) introduces or causes to be introduced any computer contaminant or computer virus into any computer, computer system or computer network;

(d) damages or causes to be damaged any computer, computer system or computer network, data, computer data base or other programmes residing in such computer, computer system or computer network;

(e) disrupts or causes disruption of any computer, computer system or computer network;

(f) denies or causes the denial of access to any person authorised to access any computer, or computer network by any means ;

(g) provides any assistance to any person to facilitate access to a computer, computer system or computer network in contravention of the provisions of this Act, rules or regulations made thereunder ;

(h) charges the services availed of by a person to the account of another person by tampering with or manipulating any computer, computer system, or computer network,

he shall be liable to pay damages by way of compensation not exceeding one crore rupees to the person so affected.

Explanation.- For the purpose of this section,-

(i) "computer contaminant" means any set of computer instructions that are designed-

(a) to modify, destroy, record, transmit data or programme residing within a computer, computer system or computer network; or

(b) by any means to usurp the normal operation of the computer, computer system, or computer network;

(ii) "computer data base" means a representation of information, knowledge, facts, concepts or instructions in text, image, audio video that are being prepared or have been prepared in a formalised manner or have been produced by a computer, computer system or computer network and are intended for use in a computer, computer system or computer network;

(iii) "computer virus" means any computer instruction, information, data or programme that destroys, damages, degrades or adversely affects the performance of a computer resource or attaches itself to another computer resource and operates when a programme, data or instruction is executed some other event takes place in that computer resource;

(iv) "damage " means to destroy, alter, delete, add, modify or rearrange any computer resource by any means.

44. Penalty for failure to furnish information, return, etc.

If any person who is required under this Act or any rules or regulations made thereunder to-

(a) furnish any document, return or report to the Controller or the Certifying Authority fails to furnish the same, he shall be liable to a penalty not exceeding one lakh and fifty thousand rupees for each such failure;

(b) file any return or furnish any information, books or other documents within the time specified therefor in the regulation fails to file return or furnish the same within the time specified therefor in the regulations, he shall be liable to a penalty not exceeding five thousand rupees for every day during which such failure continues;

(c) maintain books of account or records, fails to maintain the same, he shall be liable to a penalty not exceeding ten thousand rupees for every day during which the failure continues.

45. Residuary penalty

Whoever contravenes any rules or regulations made under this Act, for the contravention of which no penalty has been separately provided, shall be liable to pay a compensation not exceeding twenty-five thousand rupees to the person affected by such contravention or a penalty not exceeding twenty-five thousand rupees.

46. Power to adjudicate

(1) For the purpose of adjudging under this Chapter whether any person has committed a contravention of any of the provisions of this Act or of any rule, regulation, direction or order made thereunder the Central Government shall, subject to the provisions of sub-section (3), appoint any officer not below the rank of a Director to the Government of India or an equivalent officer of a State Government to be an adjudicating officer for holding an inquiry in the manner prescribed by the Central Government.

(2) The adjudicating officer shall, after giving the person referred to in sub-section (1) a reasonable opportunity for making representation in the matter and if, on such inquiry, he is satisfied that the person has committed the contravention, he may impose such penalty or award such compensation as he thinks fit in accordance with the provisions of that section.

(3) No person shall be appointed as an adjudicating officer unless he possesses such experience in the field of Information Technology and legal or judicial experience as may be prescribed by the Central Government.

(4) Where more than one adjudicating officers are appointed, the Central Government shall specify by order the matters and places with respect to which such officers shall exercise their jurisdiction.

(5) Every adjudicating officer shall have the powers of a civil court which are conferred on the Cyber Appellate Tribunal under sub-section (2) of section 58, and-

(a) all proceedings before it shall be deemed to be judicial proceedings within the meaning of sections 193 and 228 of the Indian Penal Code;

(b) shall be deemed to be a civil court for the purpose of section 345 and .46 of the Code of Criminal Procedure, 1973.

47. Factors to be taken into account by the adjudicating officer

While adjudging the quantum of compensation under this Chapter, the adjudicating officer shall have due regard to the following factors, namely :-

(a) the amount of gain of unfair advantage, wherever quantifiable, made as a result of the default;

(b) the amount of loss caused to any person as a result of the default;

(c) the repetitive nature of the default.

CHAPTER X : THE CYBER REGULATIONS APPELLATE TRIBUNAL

48. Establishment of Cyber Appellate Tribunal

(1) The Central Government shall, by notification, establish one or more appellate tribunals to be known as the Cyber Regulations Appellate Tribunal.

(2) The Central Government shall also specify, in the notification referred to in sub-section (1), the matters and places in relation to which the Cyber Appellate Tribunal may exercise jurisdiction.

49. Composition of Cyber Appellate Tribunal

A Cyber Appellate Tribunal shall consist of one person only (hereinafter referred to as the Presiding Officer of the Cyber Appellate Tribunal) to be appointed, by notification, by the Central Government.

50. Qualifications for appointment as Presiding Officer of the Cyber Appellate Tribunal

A person shall not be qualified for appointment as the Presiding Officer of a Cyber Appellate Tribunal unless he-

(a) is, or has been, or is qualified to be, a Judge of a High Court; or

(b) is or has been a member of the Indian Legal Service and is holding or has held a post in Grade I of that Service for at least three years.

51. Term of officer

The Presiding Officer of a Cyber Appellate shall hold office for a term of five years from the date on which he enters upon his office or until he attains the age of sixty-five years, whichever is earlier.

52. Salary, allowances and other terms and conditions of service of Presiding Officer

The salary and allowances payable to, and the other terms and conditions of service including pension, gratuity and other retirement benefits of, the Presiding Officer or a Cyber Appellate Tribunal shall be such as may be prescribed:

Provided that neither the salary and allowances nor the other terms and conditions of service of the Presiding Officer shall be varied to his disadvantage after appointment.

53. Filling up of vacancies

If, for reason other than temporary absence, any vacancy occurs in the office of the Presiding Officer of a Cyber Appellate Tribunal, then the Central Government shall appointment another person in accordance with the provisions of this Act to fill the vacancy and the proceedings may be continued before the Cyber Appellate Tribunal from the stage at which the vacancy is filled.

54. Resignation and removal

(1) The Presiding Officer of a Cyber Appellate Tribunal may, be notice in writing under his hand addressed to the Central Government, resign his office :

Provided that the said Presiding Officer shall, unless he is permitted by the Central Government to relinquish his officer sooner, continue to hod office until expiry of three months from the date of receipt of such notice or until a person duly appointed as his successor enters upon his office or until the expiry of his terms of office, whichever is the earliest.

(2) The Presiding Officer of a Cyber Appellate Tribunal shall not be removed from his officer except by an order by the Central Government on the ground of proved misbehaviour or incapacity after an inquiry made by a Judge of the Supreme Court in which the Presiding Officer concerned has been informed of the charges against him and given a reasonable opportunity of being heard in respect of these charges.

(3) The Central Government may, be rules, regulate the procedure for the investigation of misbehaviour or incapacity of the aforesaid presiding Officer.

55. Orders constituting Appellate Tribunal to be final and not to invalidate its proceedings

No order of the Central Government appointing any person as the Presiding Officer of a Cyber Appellate Tribunal shall be called in question in any manner and no act or proceeding before a Cyber Appellate Tribunal shall be called in question in any manner on the ground merely of any defect in the constitution of a Cyber Appellate Tribunal.

56. Staff of the Cyber Appellate Tribunal

(1) The Central Government shall provide the Cyber Appellate Tribunal with such officer and employees as that Government may think fit.

(2) The officers and employees of the Cyber Appellate Tribunal shall discharge their functions under general superintendence of the Presiding Officer.

(3) The salaries, allowances and other conditions of service of the officers and employees of the Cyber Appellate Tribunal shall be such as may be prescribed by the Central Government.

57. Appeal to Cyber Appellate Tribunal

(1) Save as provided in sub-section (2), any person aggrieved by an order made by Controller or an adjudicating officer under this Act may prefer an appeal to a Cyber Appellate Tribunal jurisdiction in the matter.

(2) No appeal shall lie to the Cyber Appellate Tribunal from an order made by an adjudicating officer with the consent of the parties.

(3) Every appeal under sub-section (1) shall be filed within a period of forty-five days from the date on which a copy of the order made by the Controller or the adjudicating officer is received by the person aggrieved and it shall be in such form and be accompanied by such fee as may be prescribed :

> Provided that the Cyber Appellate Tribunal may entertain an appeal after the expiry of the said period of forty-five days if it is satisfied that there was sufficient cause for not filing it within that period.

(4) On receipt of an appeal under sub-section (1), the Cyber Appellate Tribunal may, after giving the parties to the appeal, an opportunity of being heard, pass such orders thereon as it thinks fit, confirming, modifying or setting aside the order appealed against.

(5) The Cyber Appellate Tribunal shall send a copy or every order made by it to the parties to the appeal and to the concerned Controller or adjudicating officer.

(6) The appeal filed before the Cyber Appellate Tribunal under sub-section (1) shall be dealt with by it as expeditiously as possible and endeavour shall be made by it to dispose of the appeal finally within six months from the date of receipt of the appeal.

58. Procedure and powers of the Cyber Appellate Tribunal

(1) The Cyber Appellate Tribunal shall not be bound by the procedure laid down by the Code of Civil Procedure, 1908 but shall be guided by the principles of natural justice and, subject to the other provisions of this Act and of any rules, the Cyber Appellate Tribunal shall have powers to regulate its own procedure including the place at which it shall have its sitting.

(2) The Cyber Appellate Tribunal shall have, for the purposes of discharging its functions under this Act, the same powers as are vested in a civil court under the Code of Civil Procedure, 1908, while trying a suit, in respect of the following matters, namely : -

(a) summoning and enforcing the attendance of any person and examining him on oath;

(b) requiring the discovery and production of documents or other electronic records;

(c) receiving evidence on affidavits;

(d) issuing commissions for the examination of witnesses of documents;

(e) reviewing its decisions;

(f) dismissing an application for default or deciding it ex parte;

(g) any other matter which may be prescribed.

(3) Every proceeding before the Cyber Appellate Tribunal shall be deemed to be a judicial proceeding within the meaning of sections 193 and 228, and for the purpose of section 196 of the Indian Penal Code and the Cyber Appellate Tribunal shall be deemed to be a civil court for the purposes of section 195 and Chapter XXVI of the Code of Criminal Procedure, 1973.

59. Right to legal representation

The appellant may either appear in person or authorise one or more legal practitioners or any of its officers to present his or its case before the Cyber Appellate Tribunal.

60. Limitation

The provisions of the Limitation Act, 1963, shall, as far as may be, apply to an appeal made to the Cyber Appellate Tribunal.

61. Civil court not to have jurisdiction

No court shall have jurisdictions to entertain any suit or proceeding in respect of any matter which an adjudicating officer appointed under this Act or the Cyber Appellate Tribunal constituted under this Act is empowered by or under this Act to determine and no injunction shall be granted by any court or other authority in respect of any action taken or to be taken in pursuance of any power conferred by or under this Act.

62. Appeal to High Court

Any person aggrieved by any decision or order of the Cyber Appellate Tribunal may file an appeal to the High Court within sixty days from the date of communication of the decision or order of the Cyber Appellate Tribunal to him on any question of fact or law arising out of such order :

Provided that the High Court may, if it is satisfied that the appellant was prevented by sufficient cause from filing the appeal within the said period, allow it to be filed within a further period not exceeding sixty days.

63. Compounding of contraventions

(1) Any contravention under this Chapter may, either before or after the institution of adjudication proceedings, be compounded by the Controller or such other officer as may be specially authorised by him in this behalf or by the adjudicating officer, as the case may be, subject to such conditions as the Controller or such other officer or the adjudicating officer may specify :

Provided that such sum shall not, in any case, exceed the maximum amount of the penalty which may be imposed under this Act for the contravention so compounded.

(2) Nothing in sub-section (1) shall apply to a person who commits the same or similar contravention within a period of three years from the date on which the first contravention, committed by him, was compounded.

Explanation- For the purpose of this sub-section, any second or subsequent contravention committed after the expiry of a period of three years from the date on which the contravention was previously compounded shall be deemed to be a first contravention.

(3) Where any contravention has been compounded under sub-section (1), no proceeding of further proceeding, as the case may be, shall be taken against the person guilty of such contravention in respect of the contravention so compounded.

64. Recovery of penalty

A penalty imposed under this Act, if it is pad, shall be recovered as an arrear or land revenue and the licence or the Digital Signature Certificate, as the case may be, shall be suspended till the penalty is paid.

CHAPTER XI: OFFENCES

65. Tampering with computer source documents

Whoever knowing or intentionally conceals, destroys or alters or intentionally or knowingly causes another to conceal, destroy or alter any computer source code used for a computer, computer Programme, computer system or computer network, when the computer source code is required to be kept or maintained by law for the being time in force, shall be punishable with imprisonment up to three year, or with fine which may extend up to two lakh rupees, or with both.

Explanation.- For the Purpose of this section, "computer source code" means the listing of programmes, computer commands, design and layout and Programme analysis of computer resource in any form..

66. Hacking with computer system

(1) Whoever with the intent to cause or knowing that he is likely to cause wrongful loss r damage to the public or any person destroys or deletes or alters any information residing in a computer resource or diminishes its value or utility or affects it injuriously by any means, commits hacking.

(2) Whoever commits hacking shall be punished with imprisonment up to three years, or with fine which may extend up to two lakh rupees, or with both.

67. Publishing of information which is obscene in electronic form

Whoever publishes or transmits or causes to be published in the electronic form, any material which is lascivious or appeals to the prurient interest or if its effect is such as to tend to deprave and corrupt persons who are likely, having regard to all relevant circumstance, to read see or hear the matter contained or embodied in it, shall be punished on first conviction with imprisonment of either description for a term which may extend to five years and with fine which may extend to one lakh rupees and in the event of a second or subsequent conviction with imprisonment of either description for a term which may extend to ten years and also with fine which may extend to two lakh rupees.

68. Power of Controller to give directions

(1) The Controller may, by order, direct a Certifying Authority or any employee of such Authority to take such measures or cease carrying on such activities as specified in the order if those are necessary to ensure compliance with the provisions of this Act, rules or any regulations made thereunder.

(2) Any person who fails to comply with any order under sub-section (1) shall be guilty of an offence and shall be liable on conviction to imprisonment for a term not exceeding three years or to a fine not exceeding two lakh rupees or to both.

69. Directions of Controller to a subscriber to extend facilitates to decrypt information

(1) If the Controller is satisfied that it is necessary or expedient so to do in the interest of the sovereignty or integrity of India, the security of the State, friendly

relations with foreign States or public order or for preventing incitement to the commission of any cognizable offence; for reasons to be recorded in writing, by order, direct any agency of the Government to intercept any information transmitted through any computer resource.

(2) The subscriber or any person incharge of the computer resource shall, when called upon by any agency which has been directed under sub-section (1), extend all facilities and technical assistance to decrypt the information.

(3) The subscriber or any person who fails to assist the agency referred to in sub-section (2) shall be punished with an imprisonment for a term which may extend to seven years.

70. Protected system

(1) The appropriate Government may, by notification in the Official Gazette, declare that any computer, computer system or computer network to be a protected system.

(2) The appropriate Government may, by order in writing, authorise the persons who are authorised to a access protected systems notified under sub-section (1).

(3) Any person who secures access or attempts to secure access to a protected system in contravention of the provision of this section shall be punished with imprisonment of either description for a term which may extend to ten years and shall also be liable to fine.

71. Penalty for misrepresentation

(1) Whoever makes any misrepresentation to, or suppresses any material fact from, the Controller or the Certifying Authority for obtaining any license or Digital Signature Certificate, as the case may be, shall be punished with imprisonment for a term which may extend to two years, or which fine which may extend to one lakh rupees, or with both.

72. Penalty for breach of confidentiality and privacy

Save as otherwise provide in this Act or any other law for the time being in force, any person who, in pursuance of any of the powers conferred under this Act, rules or regulation made thereunder, has secured assess to any electronic record, book, register, correspondence, information, document or other material without the consent of the person concerned discloses such material to any other person shall be punished with imprisonment for a term which may extend to two years, or with fine which may extend to one lakh rupees, or with both.

73. Penalty for publishing Digital Signature Certificate false in certain particulars

(1) No person shall publish a Digital Signature Certificate or otherwise make it available to any other person with the knowledge that-

(a) the Certifying Authority listed in the certificate has not issued it; or

(b) the subscriber listed in the certificate has not accepted it; or

(c) the certificate has been revoked or suspended,

unless such publication is for the purpose of verifying a digital signature created prior to such suspension or revocation.

(2) Any person who contravenes the provisions of sub-section (1) shall be punished with imprisonment for a term which may extend to two years, or with fine which may extend to one lakh rupees, or with both.

74. Publication for fraudulent purpose

Whoever knowingly creates, publishes or otherwise makes available a Digital Signature Certificate for any fraudulent or unlawful purpose shall be punished with imprisonment for a term which may extend to two years, or with fine which extend to one lakh rupees, or with both.

75. Act to apply for offence or contravention committed outside India

(1) Subject to the provisions of sub-section (2), the provisions of this Act shall apply also to any offence or contravention committed outside India by any person irrespective of his nationality.

(2) For the purposes of sub-section (1), this Act shall apply to an offence or contravention committed outside India by any person if the act or conduct constituting the offence or contravention involves a computer, computer system or computer network located in India.

76. Confiscation

Any computer, computer system, floppies, compact disks, tape drives or any other accessories related thereto, in respect of which any provisions of this Act, rules, orders or regulations made thereunder has been or is being contravened, shall be liable to confiscation :

Provided that where it is established to the satisfaction of the court adjudicating the confiscation that the person in whose possession, power or control of any such computer, computer system, floppies, compact disks, tape drives or any other accessories relating thereto is found is not responsible for the contravention of the provisions of this Act, rules orders or regulations made thereunder, the court may, instead of making an order for confiscation of such computer, computer system, floppies, compact disks, tape drives or any other accessories related thereto, make such other order authorised by this Act against the person contravening of the provisions of this Act, rules, orders or regulations made thereunder as it may think fit.

77. Penalties or confiscation not to interfere with other punishments

No penalty imposed or confiscation made under this Act shall prevent the imposition of any other punishment to which the person affected thereby is liable under any other law for the time being in force.

78. Power to investigate offences

Notwithstanding anything contained in the Code of Criminal Procedure, 1973, a police officer not below the rank of Deputy Superintendent of Police shall investigate any offence under this Act.

CHAPTER XII : NETWORK SERVICE PROVIDERS NOT BE LIABLE IN CERTAIN CASES.

79. Network service providers not to be liable in certain cases

For the removal of doubts, it is hereby declared that no person providing an service as a network service provider shall be liable under this Act, rules or regulations made thereunder for any third party information or data made available by him if he proves that the offence or contravention was committed without his knowledge or that he had exercised all due diligence to prevent the commission of such offence or contravention.

Explanation.- For the purposes of this section,-

(a) "network service provider" means an intermediary;

(b) "third party information" means any information dealt with by a network service provider in his capacity as an intermediary;

CHAPTER XIII : MISCELLANEOUS

80. Power of police officer and other officers to enter, search, etc.

(1) Notwithstanding anything contained in the Code of Criminal Procedure, 1973, any police officer, not below the rank of a Deputy Superintendent of Police, or any other officer of the Central Government or a State Government authorised by the Central Government in this behalf may enter any public place and search and arrest

without warrant any person found therein who is reasonably suspected or having committed or of committing or of being about to commit any offence under this Act.

Explanation.- For the purpose of this sub-section, the expression "public place" includes any public conveyance, any hotel, any shop or any other place intended for use by, or accessible to the public.

(2) Where any person is arrested under sub-section (1) by an officer other than a police officer, such officer shall, without unnecessary delay, take or send the person arrested before a magistrate having jurisdiction in the case or before the officer-in-charge of a police station.

(3) The provisions of the Code of Criminal Procedure, 1973 shall, subject to the provisions of this section, apply, so far as may be, in relation to any entry, search or arrest, made under this section.

81. Act to have overriding effect

The provisions of this Act shall have effect notwithstanding anything inconsistent therewith contained in any other law for the time in force.

82. Controller Deputy Controller and Assistant Controller to by pubic servants

The Presiding Officer and other officers and employees of a Cyber Appellate Tribunal, the Controller, the Deputy Controller and the Assistant Controllers shall be deemed to be public servants within the meaning of section 21 of the Indian Penal Code.

83. Power to give directions

The Central Government may give directions to any State Government as to the carrying into execution in the State of any of the provisions of this Act or of any rule, regulation or order made thereunder.

84. Protection of action taken in good faith

No suit, prosecution or other legal proceeding shall lie against the Central Government, the State Government, the Controller or any person acting on behalf of him, the Presiding Officer, adjudicating officers and the staff of the Cyber Appellate Tribunal for anything which is in good faith done or intended to be done in pursuance of this Act or any rule, regulation or order made thereunder.

85. Offences by companies

(1) Where a person committing a contravention of any of the provisions of this Act or of any rule, direction or order made thereunder is a company, every person who, at

the time the contravention was committed, was in charge of, and was responsible to, the company for the conduct of business of the company as well as the company, shall be guilty of the contravention and shall be liable to be proceeded against and punished accordingly:

Provided that nothing contained in this sub-section shall render any such person liable to punishment if he proves that contravention took place without his knowledge or that he exercised all due diligence to prevent such contravention.

(2) Notwithstanding anything contained in sub-section (1), where a contravention of any of the provisions of this Act or of any rule, direction or order made thereunder has been committed by a company and it is proved that the contravention has taken place with the consent or connivance of, or is attributable to any neglect on the part of, any director, manager, secretary or other officer of the company, such director, manager, secretary or other officer shall also be deemed to be guilty of the contravention and shall be liable to be proceeded against and punished accordingly.

Explanation.- For the purposes of this section.-

(i) "company" means any body corporate and includes a firm or other association of individuals; and

(ii) "director" in relation to a firm, means a partner in the firm.

86. Removal of difficulties

(1) If any difficulty arises in giving effect to provisions of this Act, the Central Government may, by order published in the Official Gazette, make such provisions not inconsistent with the provisions of this Act as appear to it to be necessary or expedient for removing the difficulty :

Provided that no order shall be made under this section after the expiry of a period of two years from the commencement of this Act.

(2) Every order made under this section shall be laid, as soon as may be after it is made, before each House of Parliament.

87. Power of Central Government to make rules

(1) The Central Government may, by notification in the Official Gazette and in the Electronic Gazette make rules to carry out the provisions of this Act.

(2) In particular, and without prejudice to the generality of the foregoing power, such rules any provide for all or any of the following matters, namely :-

(a) the manner in which any information or matter may be authenticated by means of digital signature under section 5;

(b) the electronic form in which filing, issue, grant or payment shall be effected under sub-section (1) of section 6;

(c) the manner and format in which electronic records shall be filed, or issued and the method of payment under sub-section (2) of section 6;

(d) the matters relating to the type of digital signature, manner and format in which it may be affixed under section 10;

(e) the security procedure for the purpose of creating secure electronic record and secure digital signature under section 16;

(f) the qualifications, experience and terms and conditions of service of Controller, Deputy Controller and Assistant Controllers under section 17;

(g) other standards to the observed by the Controller under clause (b) of sub-section (2) of section 20;

(h) the requirements which an applicant must fulfil under sub-section (2) of section 21;

(i) the period of validity of licence granted under clause (a) of sub-section (3) of section 21;

(j) the form in which an application for licence may be made under sub-section (1) of section 22;

(k) the amount of fees payable under clause (c) of sub-section (2) of section 22;

(l) such other documents which shall accompany an application for licence under clause (d) of sub-section (2) of section 22;

(m) the form and the fee for renewal of a licence and the fee payable thereof under section 23;

(n) the form in which application for issue of a Digital Signature Certificate may be made under sub-section (1) of section 35;

(o) the fee to be paid to the Certifying Authority for issue of a Digital Signature Certificate under sub-section (2) of section 35;

(p) the manner in the adjudicating officer shall hold inquiry under sub-section (1) of section 46;

(q) the qualification and experience which the adjudicating officer shall possess under sub-section (3) of section 46;

(r) the salary, allowances and the other terms and conditions of service of the Presiding Officer under section 52;

(s) the procedure for investigation of misbehaviour or incapacity of the Presiding officer under sub-section (3) of section 54;

(t) the salary and allowances and other condition of service of other officer and employees under sub-section (3) of section 56;

(u) the form in which appeal may be filed and the fee thereof sub-section (3) of section 57;

(v) any other power of a civil court required to be prescribed under clause (g) of sub-section (2) of section 58; and

(w) any other matter which is required to be, or may be, prescribed.

(3) Every notification made by the Central Government under clause (f) of sub-section (4) of section 1 and every rule made by it shall be laid, as soon as may be after if is made, before each House of Parliament, while it is in session, for a total period of thirty days which may be comprised in one session or in two or more successive sessions, and if, before the expiry of the session immediately following the session or the successive sessions aforesaid, both House agree in making any modification in the notification or the rule or both House agree that the notification or the rule should not be made, the notification or the rule shall thereafter have effect only in such modified form or be of no effect, as the case may be; so, however, that any such modification or annulment shall be without prejudice to the validity of anything previously done under that notification or rule.

88. Constitution of Advisory Committee

(1) The Central Government shall, as soon as may be after the commencement of this Act, constitute a Committee called the Cyber Regulation Advisory Committee.

(2) The Cyber Regulation Advisory Committee shall consists of a Chairperson and such number of other official and non-official members representing the interests principally affected or having special knowledge of the subject-matter as the Central Government may deem fit.

(3) The Cyber Regulation Advisory Committee shall advise-

(a) the Central Government either generally as regards any rules or for any other purpose connected with this Act;

(b) the controller in framing the regulations under this Act.

(4) There shall be paid to the non-official members of such Committee such travelling and other allowances as the Central Government may fix.

89. Power of Controller to make regulations

(1) The Controller may, after consultation with the Cyber Regulation Advisory Committee and with the previous approval of the Central Government, by notification

in the Official Gazette, make regulations consistent with this Act and the rules made thereunder to carry out the purpose of this Act.

(2) In particular, and without prejudice to the generality of the foregoing power, such regulations may provide for all or any of the following matters, namely :-

(a) the particulars relating to maintenance of data-base containing the disclosure record of every Certifying Authority under clause (m) of section 18;

(b) the conditions and restrictions subject to which the Controller may recognise any foreign Certifying Authority under sub-section (1) of section 19;

(c) the term and conditions subject to which a licence may be granted under clause (c) of sub-section (3) of section 21;

(d) other standards to be observed by a Certifying Authority under clause (d) of section 30;

(e) the manner in which the Certifying Authority shall disclose the matters specified in sub-section (1) of section 34;

(f) the particulars of statement which shall accompany an application under sub-section (3) of section 35;

(g) the manner in which the subscriber shall communicate the compromise of private key to the certifying Authority under sub-section (2) of section 42.

(3) Every regulation made under this Act shall be laid, as soon as may be after it is made, before each House of Parliament, while it is in session, for a total period of thirty days which may be comprised in one session or in two or more successive sessions, and if, before the expiry of the session immediately following the session or the successive sessions aforesaid, both House agree in making any modification in the regulation or both House agree that the regulation should not be made, the regulation shall thereafter have effect only in such modified form or be of no effect, as the case may be; so, however, that any such modification or annulment shall without prejudice to the validity of anything previously done under that regulation.

90. Power of State Government to make rules

(1) The State Government may, by notification in the Official Gazette, make rules to carry out the provisions of this Act.

(2) In particular, and without prejudice to the generality of the foregoing power, such rules may provide for all or any of the following matters, namely :-

(a) the electronic form in which filing, issue, grant receipt or payment shall be effected under sub-section (1) of section 6;

(b) for matters specified in sub-section (2) of section 6;

(c) any other matter which is required to be provided by rules by the State Government.

(3) Every rule made by the State Government under this sections shall be laid, as soon as may be after it is made, before each House of the State Legislature where it consists of two House, or where such Legislature consists of one House, before that House.

91. Amendment of Act 45 of 1860

The Indian Penal Code shall be amendment in the manner specified in the First Schedule to this Act.

92. Amendment of Act 1 of 1872

The Indian Evidence Act, 1872 shall be amended in the manner specified in the Second Schedule to this Act.

93. Amendment of Act 18 of 1891

The Bankers' Books Evidence Act, 1891 shall be amended in the manner specified in the Third Schedule to this Act.

94. Amendment of Act 2 of 1934

The Reserve Bank of India Act, 1934 shall be amended in the manner specified in the Fourth Schedule to this Act.

THE FIRST SCHEDULE : AMENDMENT TO THE INDIAN PENAL CODE

(See section 91)
(45 of 1860]

1. After section 29, the following section shall be inserted, namely :-

"29A. The words "electronic record" shall have the meaning assigned to them in clause (t) of sub-section (1) of section (1) of section 2 of the Information Technology Act, 2000".

2. In section 167, for the words "such public servant, charged with the preparation or translation of any document, frames or translates that document", the words "such public servant, charged with the preparation or translation of any document or electronic record, frames, prepares or translates that document or electronic record" shall be substituted.

3. In section 172, for the words "produce a document in a Court of Justice" the words "produce a document or an electronic record in a Court of Justice" shall be substituted.

4. In section 173, for the words "to produce a document in a court of Justice" the words "to produce a document or electronic record in a Court of Justice" shall be Substituted.

5. In section 175, for the word "document" at the both the places where it occurs, the words "document or electronic record" shall be substituted.

6. In section 192, for the words "makes any false entry in any book or record, or makes any document containing a false statement:, the words "makes any false entry in any book or record, or electronic record or makes any document or electronic record containing a false statement" shall be substituted.

7. In section 204, for the word "document" at both the places where it occurs, the words "document or electronic record" shall be substituted

8. In section 463, for the words "Whoever makes any false documents or part of a document with intent to cause damage or injury", the word "Whoever makes any false documents or false electronic record or part of a document or electronic record, with intent to cause damage or injury" shall be substituted.

9. In section 464,-

(a) for the portion beginning with the words " A person is said to make a false document" and ending with the words "by reason of deception practised upon him, he does not know the contents of the document or the nature of the alteration", the following shall be substituted, namely :-

"A person is said to make a false document or false electronic record-

First- Who dishonestly or fraudulently-

(a) makes, signs, seals or executes a document or part of a document;

(b) makes or transmits any electronic record or part of any electronic record;

(c) affixes any digital signature on any electronic record;

(d) makes any mark denoting the execution of a document or the authenticity of the digital signature,

with the intention of causing it to be believed that such document or part of document, electronic record or digital signature was made, signed, sealed, executed, transmitted or affixed by or by the authority of a person by whom or by whose authority he knows that it was not made, signed, sealed, executed or affixed; or

Secondly- Who, without lawful authority, dishonestly or fraudulently, by cancellation or otherwise, alters a document or an electronic record in any material cancellation or otherwise, alters a document or an electronic record in any material part thereof, after it has been made, executed or affixed with digital signature either by himself or by any other person, whether such person by living or dead at the time of such alteration; or

Thirdly- Who dishonestly or fraudulently causes any person to sign, seal, execute or alter a document or an electronic record or to affix his digital signature on any electronic record knowing that such person by reason or unsoundness of mind or intoxication cannot, or that by reason of deception upon him, he does not know the contents of the document or electronic record or the nature of the alteration.";

(b) after Explanation 2, following Explanation shall be inserted at the end, namely :-

Explanation. 3.- For the purposes of this section, the expression "affixing digital signature" shall have the meaning assigned to it in clause (d) of sub-section (1) of section 2 of the Information Technology Act, 2000.

10. In section 466,-

(a) for the words "Whoever forges a document", the words " Whoever forges a document or an electronic record" shall be substituted;

(b) the following Explanation shall be inserted at the end, namely;

Explanation- For the purpose of this section, "register" includes any list, data or record of any entries maintained in the electronic form as defined in clause (r) of sub-section (1) of section 2 of the Information Technology Act, 2000;

11. In section 468, for the words "document forged" the words "document or electronic record forged" shall be substituted.

12. In section 469, for the words "intending that the document forged" the words "intending that the document or electronic record forged" shall be substituted.

13. In section 470, for the word "document" in both the places where it occurs, the words "document or electronic record" shall be substituted.

14. In section 471, for the word "document" wherever it occurs, the words "document or electronic record" shall be substituted.

15. In section 474, for the portion beginning with the words "Whoever has in his possession any document" and ending with the words " if the document is one of the description mentioned in section 466 of this Code", the following shall be substituted, namely :-

"Whoever has in this possession any document or electronic record, knowing the same to be forged and intending that the same shall fraudulently or dishonestly by used as a genuine, shall, if the document or electronic record is one of the description mentioned in section 466 of this Code.".

16. In section 476, for the words "any document", the words "any document or electronic record" shall be substitute.

17. In section 477A, for the words "book, paper, writing," at both the places where they occur, the words "book, electronic record, paper, writing" shall be substituted.

THE SECOND SCHEDULE : AMENDMENTS TO THE INDIAN EVIDENCE ACT, 1872

(See section 92)

[1 of 1872]

1. In section 3,-

(a) in the definition of "Evidence", for the words "all documents produced for the inspection of the Court", the word "all document including electronic records produced for the inspection of the Court" shall be substituted;

(b) after the definition of "India", the following shall be inserted, namely :-

the expressions; "Certifying Authority", "digital signature", "Digital Signature Certificate", "electronic form", "electronic records". "Information", "secure electronic record", "secure digital signature" and "subscriber" shall have the meanings respectively assigned to them in the Information Technology Act, 2000.;

2. In section 17, for the words "oral or documentary", the words "oral or documentary or contained in electronic form" shall by substituted.

3. After section 22, the following section shall be inserted, namely :-

"22A. When oral admission as to contents of electronic records are relevant.

Oral admissions as to the contents of electronic records are not relevant, unless the genuineness of the electronic record produced is in question."

4. In section 34 for the words "Entries in the books of account", the words "Entries in the books of account, including those maintained in an electronic form" shall be substituted.

5. In section 35, for the word "record" in both the places where it occurs, the words "record or an electronic record" shall be substituted.

6. For section 39, the following section shall be substituted, namely :-

"39. What evidence to be given when statement forms part of a conversation, document, electronic record, book or series of letters or papers.

When any statement of which evidence is given forms part of a longer statement, or of a conversation or part of an isolated document, or is contained in a document which forms part of a book, or is contained in part of electronic record or of a connected series of letters or papers, evidence shall be given of so much and no more of the statement, conversation, document, electronic record, book or series of letters or papers as the Court considers necessary in that particular case to the full understanding of the nature and effect of the statement, and of the circumstances under which it was made.".

7. After section 47, the following sections shall be inserted, namely :-

"47A.Opinion as to digital signature where relevant.

When the Court has to form an opinion as to the digital signature or any person, the opinion of the Certifying Authority which has issued the Digital Signature Certificate is a relevant fact."

8. In section 59, for the words "contents of documents" the words "contents of documents or electronic records" shall be substituted.

9. After section 65, the following sections shall be inserted, namely:-

65A.special provisions as to evidence relating to electronic record.

The contents of electronic records may be proved in accordance with the provisions of section 65B.

65B. Admissibility of electronic records.

(1) Notwithstanding anything contained in this Act, any information contained in an electronic record which is printed on a paper, stored, recorded or copied in optical or magnetic media produced by a computer (hereinafter referred to as the computer output) shall be deemed to be also a document, if the conditions mentioned in this section are satisfied in relation to the information and computer in question and shall be admissible in any proceedings, without further proof or production of the original, as evidence of any contents of the original or of any fact stated therein or which direct evidence would be admissible.

(2) The conditions referred to in sub-section (1) in respect of a computer output shall be the following, namely :-

(a) the computer output containing the information was produced by the computer during the period over which the computer was used regularly to store or process information for the purposes of any activities regularly carried on over that period by the person having lawful control over the use of the computer;

(b) during the said period, information of the kind contained in the electronic record or of the kind from which the information so contained is derived was regularly fed into the computer in the ordinary course of the said activities;

(c) throughout the materiel part of the said period, the computer was operating properly or, if not, then in respect of any period in which it was not operating properly or was out of operation during that part of the period, was not such as to affect the electronic record or the accuracy of its contents; and

(d) the information contained in the electronic record reproduces or is derived from such information fed into the computer in the ordinary course of the said activities.

(3) Where over any period, the functions of storing or processing information for the purposes of any activities of any regularly carried on over that period as mentioned in clause (a) of sub-section (2) was regularly performed by computer, whether-

(a) by a combination of computers operating over that period; or

(b) by different computers operating in succession over that period; or

(c) by different combinations of computers operating in succession over that period; or

(d) in any other manner involving the successive operation over that period, in whatever order, of one or more computers and one or more combinations of computers.

all the computers used for that purpose during that period shall be treated for the purposes of this section as constituting a single computer; and references in this section to a computer shall be construed accordingly.

(4) In any proceedings where it is desired to give a statement in evidence by virtue of this section, a certificate doing any of the following things, that is to say,-

(a) identifying the electronic record containing the statement and describing the manner in which it was produced;

(b) giving such particulars of any device involved in the production of that electronic record as may be appropriate for the purpose of showing that the electronic record was produced by a computer;

(c) dealing with any of the matters to which the conditions mentioned in sub-section (2) relate,

and purporting to be signed by a person occupying a responsible official position in relation to the operation of the relevant device or the management of the relevant activities (whichever is appropriate) shall be evidence of any matter stated in the certificate; and for the purpose of this sub-section it shall be sufficient for a matter to be stated to the best of the knowledge and belief of the person stating it.

5. For the purposes of this section,-

(a) information shall be taken to be supplied to a computer if it is supplied thereto in any appropriate form and whether it is so supplied directly or (with or without human intervention) by means of any appropriate equipment;

(b) whether in the course of activities carried on by any official, information is supplied with a view to its being stored or processed for the purposes of those activities by a computer operated otherwise than in the course of those activities, that information, if duly supplied to that computer, shall be taken to be supplied to it in the course of those activities;

(c) a computer output shall be taken to have been produced by a computer whether it was produced by it directly or (with or without human intervention) by means of any appropriate equipment.

Explanation.- For the purposes of this section any reference to information being derived from other information shall be a reference to its being derived therefrom by calculation, comparison or any other process;

10. After section 67, the following section shall be inserted, namely :-

"67A. Proof as to digital signature.

Except in the case of a secure digital signature, if the digital signature of any subscriber is alleged to have been affixed to an electronic record the fact that such digital signature is the digital signature of the subscriber must be proved;"

11. After section 73, the following section shall be inserted, namely :-

"73A. Proofs as to verification of digital signature.

In order to ascertain whether a digital signature is that of the person by whom it purports to have been affixed, the court may direct-

(a) that person or the Controller or the Certifying Authority to produce the Digital Signature Certificate;

(b) any other person to apply the public key listed in the Digital Signature Certificate and verify the digital signature purported to have been affixed by the person.

Explanation.- For the purpose of this section "Controller" means the Controller appointed under sub-section (1) of section 17 of the Information Technology Act, 2000.

12. After section 81, the following section shall be inserted, namely :-

"81A. Presumption as to Gazettes in electronic forms.

The Court shall presume the genuineness of every electronic record purporting to be the Official Gazette, or purporting to be electronic record directed by any law to be kept by any person, if such electronic record is kept substantially in the form required by law and is produced from proper custody."

13. After section 85, the following sections shall be inserted, namely:-

"85A. Presumption as to electronic agreements.

The Court shall presume that every electronic record purporting to be an agreement containing the digital signature of the parties was so concluded by affixing the digital signature of the parties.

85B. Presumption as to electronic record and digital signatures.

(1) In any proceedings involving a secure electronic record, the Court shall presume unless contrary is proved, that the secure electronic record has not been altered since the point of time to which the secure status relates.

(2) In any proceedings, involving secure digital signature, the Court shall presume unless the contrary is proved that-

(a) the secure digital signature is affixed by subscriber with the intention of signing or approving the electronic record;

(b) except in the case of a secure electronic record or a secure digital signature, nothing in the section shall create any presumption relating to authenticity and integrity of the electronic record or any digital signature.

85C. Presumption as to Digital Signature Certificates.

The Court shall presume, unless contrary is proved, that the information listed in a Digital Signature Certificate is correct, except for information specified as subscriber information which has not been verified, if the certificate was accepted by the subscriber."

14. After section 88, the following section shall be inserted, namely :-

88A. Presumption as to electronic messages.

The Court may presume that an electronic message forwarded by the originator through an electronic mail server to the addressee to whom the message purports to be addressed corresponds with the message as fed into his computer for transmission;

but the Court shall not make any presumption as to the person by whom such message was sent.

Explanation.- For the purposes of this section, the expressions "addressee" and "originator" shall have the same meanings respectively assigned to them in clause (b) and (za) of sub-section (1) of section 2 of the Information Technology Act, 2000;

15. After section 90, the following section shall be inserted, namely :-

"90A. Presumption as to electronic records five year old.

Where any electronic record, purporting or proved to be five years old, is produced from any custody which the Court in the particular case considers proper, the Court may presume that the digital signature which purports to be the digital signature of any particular was so affixed by him or any person authorised by him in this behalf.

Explanation.- Electronic records are said to be in proper custody if they are in the place in which, and under the care of the person with whom, they naturally be; but no custody is improper if it is proved to have had a legitimate origin, or the circumstances of the particular case are such as to render such an origin probable.

This Explanation applies also to section 81A."

16. For section 131, the following section shall be substituted, namely :-

"131. Production of documents or electronic records which another person, having possession, could refuse to produce.

No one shall be compelled to produce documents in his possession or electronic records under his control, which any other person would be entitled to refuse to produce if they were in his possession or control, unless such last-mentioned person consents to their production."

THE THIRD SCHEDULE : AMENDMENTS TO THE BANKERS' BOOKS EVIDENCE ACT, 1891

(See section 93)

[18 of 1891]

1. In section 2-

(a) for clause (3), the following clause shall be substitute namely :-

(3) "bankers books " include ledgers, day-books, cash-books, account-books and all other books used in the ordinary business of a bank whether kept in the written form or as printouts of data stored in a floppy, disc, tape or any other form of electro-magnetic data storage device;

(b) for clause (8), the following clause shall be substituted, namely :-

(8) "certified copy" means when the books of a bank,-

(a) are maintained in written form, a copy of any entry in such books together with a certificate written at the foot of such copy that it is a true copy of such entry, that such entry is contained in one of the ordinary books of the bank and was made in the usual and ordinary course of business and that such books is still in the custody of the bank, and where the copy was obtained by mechanical or other process which in itself ensured the accuracy of the copy, a further certificate to that effect, but where the book from which such copy was prepared has been destroyed in the usual course of the bank's business after the date on which the copy has been so prepared, a further certificate to that effect, each such certificate being dated and subscribed by the principal accountant or manager of the bank with his name and official title; and

(b) consists of printouts of data stored in a floppy, disc, tape or any other electro-magnetic data storage device, a printout of such entry or a copy of such printout together with such statements certified in accordance with the provisions of section 2A;

2. After section 2, the following section shall be inserted, namely :-

"2A. Conditions in the printout.

A printout of entry or a copy of printout referred to in sub-section (8) of section 2 shall be accompanied by the following, namely :-

(a) a certificate to the effect that it is a printout of such entry or a copy of such printout by the principal accountant or branch manager ; and

(b) a certificate by a person in-charge of computer system containing a brief descriptions of the computer system and the particulars of-

(A) the safeguards adopted by the system to ensure that data is entered or any other operation performed only by authorised persons;

(B) the safeguards adopted to prevent and detect unauthorised change of data;

(C) the safeguards available to retrieve data that is lost due to systemic failure or any other reasons;

(D) the manner in which data is transferred from the system to removable media like floppies, discs, tapes or other electro-magnetic data storage devices;

(E) the mode of verification in order to ensure that data has been accurately transferred to such removable media;

(F) the mode of identification of such data storage devices;

(G) the arrangements for the storage and custody of such storage devices;

(H) the safeguards to prevent and detect any tampering with the system; and

(I) any other factor which will vouch for the integrity and accuracy of the system.

(c) a further certificate from the person in-charge of the computer system to the effect that to the best of his knowledge and behalf, such computer system operated properly at the material time, he was provided with all the relevant data and the printout in question represents correctly, or is appropriately derived from, the relevant data".

THE FOURTH SCHEDULE : AMENDMENT TO THE RESERVE BANK OF INDIA ACT, 1934

(See section 94)

[2 of 1934]

In the Reserve Bank of India Act, 1934, in section 58, in sub-section (2), after clause (p), the following clause shall be inserted, namely :-

"(pp) the regulation of fund transfer through electronic means between the banks or between the banks and other financial institutions referred to in clause (c) of section 45-I, including the laying down of the conditions subject to which banks and other financial institutions shall participate in such fund transfers, the manner of such fund transfers and the right and obligations of the participants in such fund transfers. "

Acronyms

AMPS	—	Advanced Mobile Phone Services
ATM	—	Asynchronous Transfer Mode
AUC	—	Authentication Centre
BS	—	Base Station
CDPD	—	Cellular Digital Packet Data
CS-CDPD	—	Circuit Switching Cellular Digital Packet Data
CSMA-CD	—	Carrier Sense Multiple Access with Collision Detection
DCS	—	Digital Communication System
DSMA-CD	—	Digital Sense Multiple Access with Collision Detection
FSK	—	Frequency Shift Keying
GSM	—	Global System Mobile
HLR	—	Home Location Register
IMSI	—	International Mobile Subscriber Identity
IS	—	Intermediate System
ISDN	—	Integrated Services Data Network
MDBS	—	Mobile Data Base Station
MDIS	—	Mobile Data Intermediate Systems
M-ES	—	Mobile End Systems
MNLP	—	Mobile Network Location Protocol
MS	—	Mobile Station
MSC	—	Mobile Switching Centre
MSK	—	Minimum Shift Keying
NMT	—	Nordic Mobile Telephone
OSI-CLNS	—	Open Systems Interconnection - Connectionless Network Services

PCS	—	Personal Communication System
PCSI	—	Pacific Communication Systems Inc.
POS	—	Point of Sale
PSDN	—	Public Switched Data Network
PSTN	—	Public Switched Telephone Network
RF	—	Radio Frequency
VLR	—	Visitor Location Register
WAN	—	Wide Area Network

Glossary

Account: Usually used as a synonym for email address or login ID. (Billing accounts are frequently identified by login IDs.)

Action: A sequence of manipulations that a filter performs on all messages that match the given conditions.

Address: A unique identifier used to determine where to send someone's email. Usually made up of the login ID, the at sign (@), and the name of the company or Internet Service Provider.

AdvTHANKSance: A cute way of saying Thanks In Advance.

AFAIK: Abbreviation for As Far As I Know.

Alias: Same as nickname.

Archie: A search tool for use with FTP that searches an Archie site (a database of filenames) for a specific filename.

ARPANET (Advanced Research Projects Agency Network): The predecessor of the Internet, in use between 1971 and 1990, connecting military and academic institutions. Officially dismantled in 1990.

Article: Message sent to many people. Usenet term; not frequently used to refer to an email message.

BCC: BCC is an abbreviation for Blind Carbon Copy. "Blind" indicates that the receivers can't see who is on the Bcc: list. See also CC.

Body: The part of a message that contains the conversation — as opposed to the part that has information about the message like the time and date, sender, transmission path, and so on. See also header.

Bounce: To be returned as undeliverable. "I tried to send you the summer picnic menu, but the message bounced." Also sometimes used as a noun to refer to a bounced message.

BTW: Abbreviation for By The Way. "BTW, I loved the curried mushrooms and broccoli appetizer!"

Burst: To split a mailing list digest into individual messages.

CC: CC is an abbreviation for Carbon Copy and comes from the days when people had to use carbon paper to make copies. For those of you who are too young to remember, carbon paper used to be one of the only ways to duplicate a document. To make a copy, one had to place a sheet of carbon paper between two pieces of regular paper. Pressure from writing or typing on the top paper would transfer through the carbon paper and leave marks on the bottom paper. While people now rarely use carbon paper for duplicating documents, you can still occasionally see carbon paper in credit card signature slips.

Certificate authority: An organisation that issues digital certificates. A CA is responsible for guaranteeing a certificate holder's identity.

CGI (Common Gateway Interface): A specification for transferring information between a Webserver and a CGI program. The programs cam be written in any language like C, Perl, Visual Basic, Java, as long as it conforms to CGI specifications. CGI makes it possible for Webservers to dynamically interact with users. The most common use of CGI is seen in online forms.

Chat: A real-time textual conversation, often with many participants.

Client: A program that depends upon a program that is running on a different computer. There are now many services available where one program runs on one computer, another runs on a different computer, and they communicate over a network. The program that provides the service is called the server and the program that uses the service is called the client. (The language is a bit imprecise; the respective computers are also frequently called servers and clients.) One good example of a client-server application is the Web. A Web client or browser runs on an individual's personal computer. The browser connects to a Web server, which gives the client the Web page for display. Email is also a client-server application. Messages come to a mailbox on a mail server, where they stay until a mail client retrieves them.

Condition: The piece of the filter that determines whether or not the email software will execute the specified action. Also called criteria by some email programs.

Criteria: Same as conditions in filters.

CRM: Abbreviation for Customer Relationship Management [software].

Customer Relationship: A type of software that tracks interactions with customers,

DHCP (Dynamic Host Configuration Protocol): A protocol used for dynamically assigning IP addresses to clients that request for it. When configuring a DHCP server, a pool or range of IP addresses has to be given. The server then uses DHCP to assign the IP addresses from this pool.

DHTML (Dynamic HTML): Refers to Web pages, that change their contents depending on client requests.

Digest: A collection of messages to a mailing list that are packaged together and sent as one message.

Digital certificate: An attachment sent along with a message for authentication purposes. A digital certificate verifies that the user sending the message is *who* he or she claims to be.

Directory service: A service that stores information on the network in a hierarchical format for easy accessibility. It can store information about applications, equipment, and users on a network.

Discussion group: For practical purposes, same as newsgroup.

Distribution list: Same as mailing list.

DNS (Domain Name System): A system used on the Internet to translate IP addresses into easy to remember names. The service that does this translation is called DNS. DNS servers are connected with each other over the Internet. So, if one DNS server doesn't have an IP address translation in its table, it queries other systems running DNS to find out.

Domain: A group of computers that function under common, rules. On the Internet, it's put as an extension in a host name for identifying the type of host. Various domain types have been identified. These include.com (company/commercial), .edu (educational institutions), .gov (government), .mil (military), .org (organisation). Outside the US, she domain name is a 2-letter country code (.in for India).

Download: To copy a file from a remote machine, for example, with anonymous FTP, or when you want to copy a program from a Website and save it to your hard disk.

ECRM: Abbreviation for Electronic Customer Relationship Management [software]. See Customer Relationship Management.

Email client: A more specific and technical term for a program (like Eudora) that you use to read, organize, send, and store email messages. See also client.

Email ID: Same as login ID.

Emoticon: Cartoon faces "drawn" with text and used to express emotion. Short for "emotional icon."

Envelope information: Also called a message header. See header.

EOM: Abbreviation for End Of Message.

ESP: Abbreviation for Eudora Sharing Protocol.

Eudora Sharing Protocol: A feature of Eudora that lets you synchronize files over email.

FCC: Abbreviation for File Carbon Copy. FCC'd messages are copied to a mailbox. See also CC.

Filter: Filters are tools in an email program that automatically take actions based upon the contents of a message and rules that you define. Note that email filters are different from web filters. Web filters are a form of censorship, designed to prevent people from viewing certain web pages. Web filters might have many different conditions but have only one action: disallow viewing the page. Email filters usually have many possible conditions but also several possible actions. And while web filtering software is designed so that the person browsing the Web can't modify the filters, email filters usually are under the control of the person reading the messages.

Finger: A standard utility that is part of the TCP/IP protocol stack that lets you determine who is a valid user and who is logged into a system you have access to. It's used in UNIX based systems. The syntax is finger username@domain. name, or fingei@host:

Firewall: A system to prevent unauthorised access to a private network. A firewall is used on a network directly connected to the Internet to prevent outside internet users from accessing it.

Flame war: A series of angry or insulting messages between two or more correspondents.

Flame: An angry or insulting message. "I sent a warning to everyone in the company about the Good Tımes virus, and fifty people flamed me for wasting resources!"

Folder: As used by Eudora, a collection of mailboxes. Caution: many other email programs use the term folder where Eudora uses the term mailbox.

Forum: For practical purposes, same as newsgroup.

Forward: To send a copy of a message to a third party. "I hope you don't mind, but your essay about learning how to drive was so funny that I forwarded it to my Aunt Sonia."

Freeware: Software that is distributed free of charge, but often without customer service or much documentation.

FTP (File Transfer Protocol): A simple program to transfer files over a network from one computer to another. Many FT? servers allow you to download files without having an account on the machine, by using anonymous or FTP for a user name and your e-mail address as a password. This is a major means of distributing software and info on the Internet.

FUMLUB: Eudora-specific abbreviation meaning First Unread Message of Last Unread Batch.

FWIW: Abbreviation for For What It's Worth. "I know you're concerned about shaving your head, but FWIW, nobody has ever hassled me about my shaved head."

FYI: Abbreviation for For Your Information. "FYI—someone stole Fred's bicycle this morning, so he's in a bad mood."

Gateway: A device that is connected to the Internet, and allows other machines inside a company's network to access the Internet. In other words, it's the connection point between a LAN and the internet. The device can be a specialised piece of hardware like a router, or it can be software installed on a computer.

GIF (Graphics Interchange Format): A standard graphics image format used on the Internet.

GMTA: Abbreviation for Great Minds Think Alike.

Gopher: A menu-based system for organising and distributing information on the Internet. It's similar to FTP as it lets users browse or download files and directories. A key feature of Gopher is the ability to include menu items that connect the user to other Gopher servers. Gopher is no longer in popular use.

Guest: When you connect to or log onto a remote computer on which you don't have your own account, (perhaps using a special account for guests) you are referred to as a guest or visitor.

Hacker: Originally, this term referred to crackerjack programmers and computer experts and connoted respect. Though this meaning is still in use, this word is now also used (especially by the media) to refer to people who deliberately try to penetrate the security of other computers. The computer user community prefers to call these people crackers.

Header: A piece of information about an email message. Headers typically show who sent the message, who it was addressed to, the date and time that it was sent, and some information about the path that the message took. Header can refer to either the entire set of information or to just one piece (such as the subject or the date). Also called envelope information.

Homepage: An HTML document that serves as the main access point to a company's Website.

HTML: Abbreviation for *HyperText Markup Language*. See *HyperText Markup Language*. A simple and easy to learn programming language that Web documents are written in.

HTTP (HyperText Transfer Protocol): The protocol used on the Internet to transfer HTML documents. All Web browsers use this protocol to read the Web pages.

Hyperlink: Text that, when clicked upon, initiates an action (like retrieving a Web page).

HyperText Markup Language: The language used to create most Web pages.

Hypertext: A new concept for organising information made possible by computers, where keywords or phrases can be used not only to reference additional resources, but also serve as software links to these resources.

IETF: Abbreviation for Internet Engineering Task Force. See Internet Engineering Task Force.

IHAC: Abbreviation for I Have A Customer. "IHAC who says that he broke the cup-holder on his computer."

IMAP: Abbreviation for Internet Messaging Access Protocol. See Internet Messaging Access Protocol.

IMAP4: The Internet Message Access Protocol lets you view your e-mail at the server treating the server mailbox as an extension of your computer. You can view, delete and search for mail on the server, and only download the ones you need to your local machine.

IMHO: Abbreviation for In My Humble Opinion or In My Honest Opinion. "IMHO, Eudora is the best email program available."

IMNSHO: Abbreviation for In My Not-So-Humble Opinion.

Interface: The manner in which a user provides information to a computer program. Some examples are GUI for graphical user interface, and CLI for command line interface.

Internet Engineering: A group that develops standards for Internet technologies,

Internet Messaging Access Protocol: A type of server-based email system. Messages are kept on a server and only temporarily stored on the client. (This is different from Post Office Protocol (POP), where messages are stored on the client and only temporarily stored on the server.) In practical terms, IMAP lets you access your email from two or more computers and it will always look the same. The disadvantage of IMAP is that you need to stay connected to the Internet for the whole time you are working with your email. With POP, the messages are stored on the computer you used to read them. If you go to another computer, you won't see all the messages because some or all are on the first computer. See also Post Office Protocol.

Internet Service: An organization that provides access to the Internet. If you

Internet: The Internet is the Grand Daddy of all networks. It's a collection of computers and computer networks across the world that communicate across dedicated high-speed phone lines using a single protocol family called TCP/ IP.

Intranet: A set of computers that communicate with each other with TCP/IP, can access machines on the Internet, but that can only be accessed by computers that are on the same local network. Machines on an intranet are not supposed to be publicly accessible.

IP address: A unique set of four numbers between 1 and 254 separated by periods, such as 209.194.84.60, used to identify every machine connected to the Internet.

As these numbers are very difficult to remember, they are mapped to an easy to remember name, which is called the host name.

IRC (Internet Relay Chat): A program that allows multiple users to conduct typed conversations in real time over the Internet.

ISO (International Organisation for Standardisation): An international body made up of national standard bodies from over 75 countries. It's engaged indefining Standards. The most popular computer standard defined by ISO was the OSI model.

ISP: Abbreviation for Internet Service Provider. See Internet Service Provider.

ITU (International Telecommunications Union): An international body engaged in defining telecommunication standards.

JPEG (Joint Photographies Expert Group): A standard (compressed) format for color images commonly used on the Internet. They use the JPC or JPEG extensions.

Jughead (Jonzy's universal gopher hierarchy excavation and display): A powerful gopher search tool written by Rhett "Jonzy" Jones.

Kermit: A simple modem protocol for transferring files between Macs and/or PCs, or from these to bigger computers. Since TCP/IP was adopted as the official Internet protocol in 1983, most PC software has abandoned Kermit. However, Kermit and its cousins X-, Y-, and Z-modem are still needed in the absence of an ethernet or SLIP connection.

LDAP (Lightweight Directory Access Protocol): A set of protocols for querying information directories. There are various directory services on the Internet that can be queried for information. LDAP is being used in operating systems like the upcoming Windows 2000 and NetWare for querying their directory services. LDAP is a simpler version of the X.500 directory service standard.

Light mode: A version of Eudora 5 that is free, but with fewer features than Paid mode or Sponsored mode.

List server address: Email address used to communicate with list server software.

List server: A program that automatically administers a mailing list. "If you don't want to get any more messages, don't tell the list, send an unsubscribe message to the list server." Also called a listserv or listbot.

Listbot: Although the name of a particular list server site, this term is frequently used as a generic synonym for list server.

Listname address: The email address that reaches all the subscribers on a mailing list. This is not the same as the list server address, which is used for communicating with the list server software.

Listserv: The name of an early list server software package. Some people now use it to mean a list server or mailing list.

Login ID: The unique identifier used for signing on to a computer or email account. Same as handle, username, email ID, and (sometimes) account.

LOL: Abbreviation for Laughing Out Loud.

Lurker: A person who reads messages on a mailing list or Usenet newsgroup but does not write (post) any messages.

Lynx: A text only Web browser.

Mailbox: A collection of messages.

Mailing list: A free-flowing, many-to-many email conversation with shifting membership. A piece of software (called a list server, listbot, or listserv) will take any messages to a particular email address and re-send them to everybody who has subscribed to that list. Also called distribution list.

Management: Makes using a shared database of knowledge easier, and directs questions to the most appropriate person.

MIME: Abbreviation for Multipart Internet Mail Extensions, an extension to the original email specifications that allows sending messages in essentially any format. (It does not, however, guarantee that the receiver's computer will be able to display any format.)

Mirror site: A site that is the exact replica of another site. This is used by various anonymous FTP sites to reduce bandwidth bottlenecks, so that more users can access it.

MLM: Abbreviation for *Multi-Level Marketing*. See *Multi-Level Marketing*.

MP3(MPEG1 Layer 3): A new format for storing audio information that is becoming very popular on the Internet. It achieves very high compression ratios, and gives high quality playback. Some shareware MP3 players are available on the Internet. There is an upgrade to the Windows Media Player that also supports this standard.

MTA: Abbreviation for *Mail Transport Agent*. See *Mail Transport Agent*.

MUA: Abbreviation for Mail User Agent. See Mail User Agent.

Multi-Level Marketing: A type of pyramid scheme.

Multilink PPP: A protocol that combines the bandwidths of multiple PPP links to give greater throughputs.

Netiquette: The etiquette of communicating over the Internet. The Internet community follows various conventions when transmitting information over the Internet. For example, sending a message in all caps is the equivalent of shouting.

Newbie: A person who is new to the Internet. Depending upon how it is used, it can be derogatory.

Newsgroup: A forum where many people can read and write (post) messages. Once this word only referred to Usenet discussions, but now the word is drifting to include Web-based discussions. "One of the basketball newsgroups had a posting that someone is going to start a second women's professional league."

Nickname: A shortcut for either a single email address or a group of email addresses. For example, you might have a group nickname roses that contains the email addresses of seven people in your rose gardening club. Then if you addressed a message to roses, your email software would send the message to those seven club members. Also called alias, group, or card.

NRN: Abbreviation for No Reply Needed. This is not common, but I would like to see it become common.

NSFNET: The backbone of the Internet since 1990 when ARPANET was dismantled. It originally linked six supercomputers through high-speed phone lines.

Off-Topic: About something that is not directly related to a mailing list's stated purpose.

Online: A standard terminology that indicates whether an Internet connection is live or not.

OT: Common (but by no means universal) abbreviation for Off-Topic.

OTOH: Abbreviation for On The Other Hand. "I think the U.S. president is incompetent. OTOH, her husband is the best politician I've ever seen."

Outbox: A mailbox containing copies of messages that have been sent. "I looked through my outbox for my last message to him, and I sent him the report last Thursday."

Paid mode: A version of Eudora 5 that has all the features and no advertising. See also Sponsored mode and Light mode.

PINE (Pine Is Not Elm): A sophisticated e-mail utility that can send not only text files, but also binary files, such as images and sounds by using MIME.

Ping (Packet Internet Gopher): A utility that checks whether a host on the Internet is accessible or not. It's mostly used to troubleshoot connectivity issues on the Internet.

PNG (Portable Network Graphics): A new graphics format that is becoming popular on the Internet.

Ponzi scheme: A particular type of pyramid scheme.

POP: Abbreviation for Post Office Protocol. See Post Office Protocol.

Port: A 16-bit number used by a server to identify itself to clients. A client connecting to a computer uses an IP address as well as a port number to talk to a particular server.

Post Office Protocol: One specification for how computers must talk to each other to transfer a message from an email server to an email client. Post Office Protocol (commonly abbreviated POP) systems are designed for the user to download, store, and manipulate mail on the user's desktop machine. This is different from IMAP, where the mail is stored and manipulated on a server.

Post: To write a message for a large group. One implication of post instead of write is that the message will be public and not private. "Somebody posted to the Stanford alumni mailing list that they had a job vacancy to fill in floss recycling."

PPP (Point-to-Point Protocol): A protocol that dynamically assigns an IP address to a computer, so that it can access the Internet.

Protocol: A set of rules that computers use to talk to each other. There are many protocols for many purposes, including sending email, transferring email, and sending instant messages.

Provider: Get your email through your company, then your company is your Internet Service Provider.

Public Key Infrastructure (PKI): A technique that uses digital certificates to verify the authenticity of all parties involved in an Internet transaction.

Public/private key encryption: A cryptographic algorithm which uses two keys, one to encrypt and the other to decrypt the data.

Pull technology: The opposite of Push technology in which information is only provided when a client requests for it. The Web functions on pull technology where a browser sends a request to a Website for information. ;

Push technology: A technology being used on the Internet in which a server sends out information to the client without the client requesting for it. The most common use of the technology is seen in subscribing to newsletters, where news is sent to the registered clients without requesting for it.

Pyramid scheme: A scheme where later participants (B) pay money to earlier participants (A) in the hope that even later participants (C) will give them (B) even larger sums of money than they (B) gave to earlier participants (A). This is almost always illegal (except when investing in stock market bubbles).

Redirect: To forward in a manner where the message appears to come directly from the original author, not the person who forwarded it.

Regexp: A way of compactly describing a set of similar text strings. Also known as regular expression.

Reply-to-All: The method of replying where every person in the From: , To: and Cc: headers get the response, not just the person on the From: line. See also Reply-to-Sender.

Reply-to-Sender: The method of replying where only the person in the From: header gets the response, not also any people in the To: and Cc: headers. See also Reply-to-All.

RFC: Abbreviation for Request For Comments, but almost nobody uses the long form. Originally, RFCs were requests for comments. In practice, now RFCs are the rules for how computers talk to each other over the Internet.

RFC822: RFC822 is the name of the original specification for email—before rich text, attachments, and many of the other features of modern email. To say that a message is "RFC822", then, is to say that its formatting is very simple.

RFCs (Request For Comments): The working notes of the committees that develop the protocols and standards of the Internet, including proposed changes. These documents contain a great deal of info about the Net and are maintained by the Internet Activities Board (IAB).

ROTFL: Abbreviation for *Rolling On The Floor Laughing*.

ROTFLMAO: Abbreviation for Rolling On The Floor Laughing (ahem) hard.

Router: A specialized computer that is responsible for sending information onwards towards its final destination.

RSN: Abbreviation for Real Soon Now. This is usually used jokingly when something has been promised (and delayed) for a long time. If you read RSN, you should probably not believe that the item under discussion is going to be ready any time soon.

RTFM: Abbreviation for Read The (ahem) Manual.

Rule: Microsoft's term for filter.

Screen name: One of many email IDs associated with one billing account.

Sendmail: Sendmail is the most common Mail Transport Agent. Sendmail takes a message and sends it on towards its final destination. See also Mail Transport Agent.

Server: Software and/or hardware that provides a service (like Web pages) over a network. See also client

Shareware: Software that is distributed for a small fee. There is a large shareware community that is philosophically opposed to selling software for profit.

Simple Mail Transport Protocol: The protocol (rules) that computers use to talk to each other to send email towards its destination.

SMTP: Abbreviation for Simple Mail Transport Protocol. See Simple Mail Transport Protocol.

Snailmail: Techno-slang for postal (paper) mail.

Socket: A software object that connects a program (process) to a network protocol. A socket allows a software program (process) to converse with other processes over a network. Sockets use different numbers, known as ports to communicate with each other.

Spam: Techno-slang for Unsolicited Commercial Email. It apparently comes from an episode of the Monty Python television show, and is not usually capitalized except at the beginning of sentences. (The words Spam and SPAM are brand names for a particular brand of canned meat.)

Sponsored mode: A version of Eudora 5 that has all the features of Paid mode, but shows you advertisements. See also Paid mode and Light mode.

Subscribe: To join [a mailing list].

Task Force: Including email.

TCP/IP (Transmission Control Protocol/ Internet Protocol): A family of protocols used over the Internet. This family includes protocols for handling data transport (TCP, UDP), routing (IP, ICMP, RIP, OSPF), addresses (ARP, DNS, RARP), user services (BOOTP, FTP, TELNET), gateways (EGP, GGP, IGP), and other services (NFS, NIS, RFC, SMTP, SNMP).

Telnet: A utility to log onto a remote computer.

Thread: A thread is a set of messages on the same topic. Threads usually have the same Subject: or have information in the header that connects a message with the previous message.

Tunneling: A method used to connect two points using the Internet as the channel. VPNs use tunneling to establish connections between different computers. The tunneling is done using various tunneling protocols like PPTP, L2F, IPSec, etc. These protocols encapsulate the data inside the TCP/IP protocol so that it can be sent over the Internet. Some of these protocols like IP Sec also encrypt the data before sending it for security.

Uniform Resource: A Web address, for example http: //www.webfoot.com.

Unsolicited: Fancy name for junk email.

Unsubscribe: To request to be removed [from a mailing list].

URL (Universal Resource Locator): The mechanism used by the Internet to find a particular page, image, or sound. Simply speaking, it's an address for the page.

UseNet (Users' Network): A text-based mechanism that supports discussion groups known as newsgroups, that allow users from anywhere on the Internet to participate. Contrary to the name, it's not actually a network but a service available on the Internet.

Usenet: An application that lets many people write (or post) and read messages (or articles). Articles are distributed by copying them from computer to computer. Usenet is the original Internet discussion forum, but there are now many types.

Veronica (Very Easy Rodent-Oriented Net-wide Index to Computerised Archives): A search tool for use with Gophers (a rodent).

Viral marketing: Viral marketing is a term for any product that encourages (or forces) its customers to advertise the product. For example, many free email services include a mini-ad for their service at the bottom of each message that is sent via the service. This book is another example: if you want to get more readable email, you should convince your correspondents to also read this book.

VPN (Virtual Private Networking): A technology that allows interconnectivity between networks or between mobile users and a network using the Internet backbone as the media for transferring the data.

W3C: The World Wide Web Consortium is an international organisation involved in creating and maintaining most Web-based standards.

WAIS (Wide Area Information Servers): Using keywords supplied by the user, WAIS servers search their databases for any files which contain a match. WAIS goes Beyond Gopher, FTP, and Archie searches, but is somewhat similar to WebCrawler.

Web browser: An application for browsing the Internet. These browsers can read both HTTP and FTP Websites. There are many popular Web browsers around like Netscape Communicator, and Internet Explorer.

Web page: A page written in Hyper-Text Markup Language that's available on the Internet through the HTTP protocol.

Website: A site consisting of various Web pages that can be accesses by anyone connected to the Internet.

Word-wrap: What happens with text where the width of the screen is smaller than the number of characters until a carriage return. If the text is broken into lines at word boundaries, it is word-wrapped. If the text is not broken into lines or is broken in the middle of words, it is not word-wrapped.

WWW (World Wide Web): Now more commonly known as the Web. It's a system that lets users graphically browse through sites on the Internet, and follow pointers (called links or hyperlinks) to other documents that can be anywhere.

X.500: An ISO and ITU standard that defines how a directory service should be structured.

XML (Extensible Markup Language): A new scripting language being developed by the W3C (World Wide Web Consortium) which provides more functionality than HTML.

YMMV: Abbreviation for Your Mileage May Vary, a standard disclaimer in automobile advertisements in the United States. It means, basically, that the author believes his or her statement to be true but recognizes that it might not be a universal truth. "I've never had trouble buying a ticket right before the show starts, but YMMV."

Bibliography

A. Nagasaka and Y. Tanaka. Automatic video indexing and full-video search for object appearances. *Second Working Conference on Visual Database Systems*, pages 119-133, 1991.

A.A. Rodriguez. *Digital Video Compression On Personal Computers: Algorithms And Techniques (San Jose, Ca, February 7-8)*, volume 2187. SPIE, 1994.

A.M. Earnshaw and S.D. Blostein. An error analysis of camera translation direction estimation from optical flow using linear constraints. *IEEE International Conference on Image Processing*, 1995.

Abdullah, Mohammed B. (1991) Speech at the Inauguration of the Folkloric Board of Trustees, NCC Offices, September 12.

Adelman, C. 2000. *A Parallel Postsecondary Universe: The Certification System in Information Technology*. Washington, DC: U.S. Department of Education.

Alberts, D.S., and D.S. Papp, eds. 1997. *The Information Age: An Anthology on Its Impact and Consequences*. Washington, DC: National Defense University.

Allen, T., and M.S. Morton, eds. 1994. *Information Technology and the Corporation of the 1990s*. New York: Oxford University Press.

Alpar, P., and M. Kim. 1991. "A Microeconomic Approach to the Measurement of Information Technology Value." *Journal of Management Information Systems* 7(2): 55–69.

Amegatcher, Andrew. (1990) "Recent Copyright Cases," *Ghana Copyright News*, vol. 2, December, p. 12.

Angus J. Kennedy, *The Internet: The Rough Guide*, London: Rough Guides, 1999, pp. 502.

Ante, S.E., with A. Borrus and R.D. Hof. 2001. "In Search of the Net's Next Big Thing." *Business Week* (March 26): 141.

Anyidoho, Kofi and Tsikata, Fui. (1988) "Copyright and Oral Literature," delivered at the *1st National Conference on Oral Literature*, August 23, Accra.

Asynchronous Tranfer Mode, Solution for Broadband ISDN, Third edition 1993, By Martin de Prycker

Atkinson, R.D., and R.H. Court. 1998. *The New Economy Index: Understanding America's Economic Transformation.* Washington, DC: Progressive Policy Institute.

Attewell, P., and J. Rule. 1994. "Computing and Organizations: What We Know and What We Don't Know." In C. Huff and T. Finholt, eds., *Social Issues in Computing.* New York: McGraw-Hill.

Autor, D., L. Katz, and A. Krueger. 1997. "Computing Inequality: Have Computers Changed the Labor Market?" NBER Working Paper No. 5956. Cambridge, MA: National Bureau of Economic Research.

B. Shahraray. Scene change detection and content-based sampling of video. *SPIE*, 2419:2-13.

B.L. Yeo and B. Liu. Unified approach to temporal segmentation of motion jpeg and mpeg video. *International Conference on Multimedia Computing and Systems*, pages 2-13, 1995.

Badasu, Ambrose. (1988) "Tribute to F.C. Boriginator of Borborbor" *Ghanaian Times*, June 3, p. 4.

Baily, M.N., and A.K. Chakrabarti. 1988. *Innovation and the Productivity Crisis.* Washington, DC: Brookings Institution Press.

Baker, E.L., M. Gearhart, and J.L. Herman. 1994. "Evaluating the Apple Classrooms of Tomorrow." In E.L. Baker and H.F. O'Neil, Jr., eds., *Technology Assessment in Education and Training.* Hillsdale, NJ: Lawrence Erlbaum Associates.

Banker, R.D., R.J. Kauffman, and M.A. Mahmood. 1993. *Strategic Information Technology Management: Perspectives on Organizational Growth and Competitive Advantage.* Harrisburg, PA: Idea Group Publishing.

Berliner, Paul. (1994) *Thinking in Jazz: The Infinite Art of Improvisation*, University of Chicago Press.

Berman, E., J. Bound, and Z. Griliches. 1994. "Changes in the Demand for Skilled Labor Within U.S. Manufacturing: Evidence From the Annual Survey of Manufacturers." *Quarterly Journal of Economics* 109 (May): 367–98.

Berman, H.M., J. Westbrook, Z. Feng, G. Gilliland, T.N. Bhat, H. Weissig, I.N. Shindyalov, and P.E. Bourne. 2000. "The Protein Data Bank." *Nucleic Acids Research* 28(1): 235–42. Available at http://nar.oupjournals.org/cgi/content/full/28/1/235.

Biemiller, L. 1999. "California State U. Adopts New Model to Pay for Journals." *Chronicle of Higher Education* July 16: A26.

Bill Gates, *The Road Ahead*, Viking, 1996, pp.332,.

Blumenstyk, G. 1999a. "Distance Learning at the Open University." *Chronicle of Higher Education* July 23: A35.

Bradley, S.P., J.A. Hausman, and R.L. Nolan. 1993. *Globalization, Technology, and Competition: The Fusion of Computers and Telecommunications in the 1990s.* Boston: Harvard Business School Press.

Bresnahan, T. 1986. "Measuring the Spillovers From Technical Advance: Mainframe Computers in Financial Services." *American Economic Review* 76(4): 742–55.

Brown, B., Geelhoed, E. and Sellen, A., 2001, Music sharing as a computer supported collaborative application. In Proceedings of ECSCW 2001, Bonn, Germany, 179-198.

Brown, J.S., and P. Duguid. 2000. *The Social Life of Information.* Boston: Harvard Business School Press.

Brunnel, D. 2000. *Making the Cisco Connection: The Story Behind the Real Internet Superpower.* New York: John Wiley.

Bull, M., 2000, Sounding Out the City: Personal Stereos and the Management of Everyday Life. Oxford. Berg.

C. Bergeron and E. Dubois. Parametric block estimation of motion and application to temporal interpolation of video sequences. *ICPR-C*, 90:140-146.

C.C.J. Kuo and J. Storer. Guest eds., special issue on still and video image compression. *JVCIR*, 5(4):303-402, 1994.

C.T. Jones and K.D. Sauer. Bayesian approach to segmentation of temporal dynamics in video data. *SPIE*, 1605:522-533.

Campus Computing Project. 2000. "2000 National Survey of Information Technology in Higher Education." Available at http://www.campuscomputing.net/. Accessed September 17, 2001.

Carl R. Nave. Hyperphysics (website)—see About Hyperphysics, Georgia State University, 2003.

Casson, M. 1994. "Economic Perspectives on Business Information." In *Information Acumen: the Understanding and Use of Knowledge in Modern Business,* pp. 136–67. London: Routledge.

Castells, M. 1996. *The Rise of the Network Society.* Cambridge, MA: Basil Blackwell.

Center for Research in Electronic Commerce. 1999. "Internet Economy Indicators." Available at http://www.internetindicators.com/. Accessed August 29, 1999.

Cerf, V.G. 1997. "Computer Networking: Global Infrastructure for the 21st Century." In *Computing Research Association, Computing Research: Driving Information Technology and the Information Industry Forward.* Available at http://www.cs.washington.edu/homes/lazowska/cra/networks.html.

Chandra, J., S.T. March, S. Mukherjee, W. Pape, R. Ramesh, H.R. Rao, and R.O.

Waddoups. 2000. "Information Systems Frontiers." *Communications of the ACM* 43: 71–79.

Charbeneaue, Travis. (1989) "Rehumanize Your Sequence" Pt. 5, *Music Technology*, June, pp. 42-46.

Charles Dodge and Thomas A. Jerse. *Computer Music: Synthesis, Composition, and Performance,* Second Edition. Schrimer Books, New York, 1997.

Childers, T. 1975. *The Information-Poor in America.* Metuchen, NJ: Scarecrow Press.

Chris DiBona et al, *Open Sources: Voices from the Open Source Revolution*, Sebastopol: O'Reilly, 1999, pp.272.

Clemente, P.C. 1998. *State of the Net: The New Frontier.* New York: McGraw-Hill.

C-M. Fan and N.N. Namazi. Estimation of image motion parameters using the em algorithm. *IEEE International Conference on Image Processing*, 1995.

Cohen, S., 1993, Ethnography and Popular Music Studies. In Popular Music 12(2), 123-138.

Collins, John. (1985) *Music Makers of West Africa*, Washington DC: Three Continents Press.

Committee on Issues in the Transborder Flow of Scientific Data, National Research Council. 1997. *Bits of Power: Issues in Global Access to Scientific Data.* Washington, DC: National Academy Press.

Communication Systems, Third edition 1994, By Simon Haykin, pp. 511 - 540

Computer Science and Telecommunications Board (CSTB). 1993. *National Collaboratories: Applying Information Technology for Scientific Research.* Washington, DC: National Academy Press.

Costa, A., and R. Liebmann, eds. 1997. *Supporting the Spirit of Learning: When Process Is Content.* Thousand Oaks, CA: Corwin Press.

Council of Economic Advisers. 2001. *Economic Report of the President Together with the Annual Report of the Council of Economic Advisers.* Washington, DC: U.S. Government Printing Office. Available at http://w3.access.gpo.gov/eop/.

Cron, W.L., and M.G. Sobol. 1983. "The Relationship Between Computerization and Performance: A Strategy for Maximizing the Benefits of Computerization." *Information and Management* 6: 171–81.

Crozier, W. R., 1997, Music and Social Influence. In Hargreaves, D.J. and North, A.C. (Eds) The Social Psychology of Music. Oxford: Oxford University Press.

Cuban, L. 1994. "The Promise of the Computer." In C. Huff and T. Finholt, eds., *Social Issues in Computing.* New York: McGraw-Hill.

Cyert, R., and D. Mowery, eds. 1987. *Technology and Employment: Innovation and Growth in the U.S. Economy.* Washington, DC: National Academy Press.

D. Le Gall. Mpeg: A video compression standard for multimedia applications. *Communications of the ACM*, 34(4), 1991.

D. Swanberg, C.F. Shu, and R. Jain. Knowledge guided parsing in video databases. *SPIE*, 1908, 1993.

Danny Goodman, *Living at Light Speed: your survival guide to life on the information superhighway*, Random House, 1995. pp.244.

Danziger, J.N., and K.L. Kraemer. 1986. *People and Computers: The Impacts of Computing on End Users in Organizations.* New York: Columbia University Press.

David Gauntlett, *Web.Studies: Rewiring media studies for the digital age*, London: Arnold, 2000, pp.250.

David L. Farquhar, *Optimising Windows for Games, Graphics & Multimedia*, Sebastopol, CA: O'Reilly, 2000, pp.278.

David M. Huber and Robert E. Runstein. *Modern Recording Techniques,* Fifth Edition. Focal Press, Boston, 2001.

David, P.A. 1989. *Computer and Dynamo: The Modern Productivity Paradox in a Not-Too-Distant Mirror.* Stanford, CA: Stanford University, Center for Economic Policy Research.

De Nora, T., 1986, How is extra-musical meaning possible: music as a place and space for work. Sociological theory, 4, 84-94.

De Nora, T., 2000, Music in Everyday Life. Cambridge: Cambridge University Press.

Dekutsey, Wilson. (1988) "In Honor of Akpalu," *West Africa*, November 21-27, pp. 2180-2190.

Dewett, T., and G.R. Jones. 2001. "The Role of Information Technology in the Organization: A Review, Model, and Assessment." *Journal of Management* 27: 313–46.

Dickerson, M.D., and J.W. Gentry. 1983. "Characteristics of Adopters and Non-Adopters of Home Computers." *Journal of Consumer Research* 10: 225–35.

Distance Education and Training Council. 1999. "What is the DETC?" Available at http://www.detc.org/. Accessed August 23, 1999.

Downes, L., C. Mui, and N. Negroponte. 1998. *Unleashing the Killer App: Digital Strategies for Market Dominance.* Cambridge, MA: Harvard Business School Press. Available at http://www.killer-apps.com/.

Drew, Rob, 2001, Karaoke Nights: An Ethnographic Rhapsody. Walnut Creek: Altamira.

Drucker, P.F. 1999. "Beyond the Information Revolution." Atlantic Monthly 284 (4/ October): 47–57.

Dutton, W.H., E.M. Rogers, and S.H. Jun. 1987. "The Diffusion and Impacts of Information Technology in Households." In P.I. Zorkoczy, ed., *Oxford Surveys in Information Technology*, p. 4. Oxford, England: Oxford University Press.

E. Chalom and V.M. Bove. Segmentation of frames in a video sequence using motion and other attributes. *SPIE*, 2419:230-241.

E. Touradj, H.H. Chen, and B.G. Haskell. Joint motion estimation and segmentation for very low bit rate video coding. *SPIE*, 2501:787-798.

Educational Testing Service (ETS). 1997. *Computers and Classrooms: The Status of Technology in U.S. Schools, Policy Information Report*. Princeton: Educational Testing Service, Policy Information Center.

Egger, O., and M. Rauterberg. 1996. "Internet Behaviour and Addiction." Available at http://www.ipo.tue.nl/homepages/mrauterb/publications/INTERNET96report.pdf. Accessed March 11, 2002.

ETAN Expert Working Group. (September) 1999. *Transforming European Science through Information and Communication Technologies: Challenges and Opportunities of the Digital Age*. Report prepared for the European Commission, Directorate General for Research. Available at ftp://ftp.cordis.lu/pub/etan/docs/ict-report.pdf.

F. Arman, A. Hsu, and M-Y. Chiu. Image processing on encoded video sequences. *ACM Multimedia Systems*, 1994.

F. Arman, R. Depommier, A. Hsu, and M-Y. Chiu. Content-based browsing of video sequences. *ACM International Conference on Multimedia*, 1994.

F. Dufaux, F. Moscheni, and A. Lippman. Spatio-temporal segmentation based on motion and static segmentation. *IEEE International Conference on Image Processing*, 1995.

F.C.M. Martins and J.M.F. Moura. 3-d video compositing: Towards a compact representation for video sequences. *IEEE International Conference on Image Processing*, 1995.

Fine, C.H., and D.M.G. Raff. 2001. "Automotive Industry: Internet-Driven Innovation and Economic Performance." In Litan, R.E. and A.M. Rivlin eds. *The Economic Payoff from the Internet Revolution*. Washington: Brookings Institution Press, pp. 62–86.

Forester, T. 1989. *Computers in the Human Context: Information Technology, Productivity, and People*. Cambridge, MA: MIT Press.

Forrester Research. 1998. "U.S. On-line Business Trade Will Soar To $1.3 Trillion By 2003, According To Forrester Research." News release. Available at http://www.forrester.com/. Accessed August 29, 1999.

Fountain, J.E. 2001a. *Building the Virtual State: Information Technology and Institutional Change*. Washington, DC: Brookings Institution Press.

Fountain, J.E., with C. Osorio-Urzua. 2001. "The Economic Impact of the Internet on the Government Sector." In Litan, R.E. and A.M. Rivlin eds. *The Economic Payoff from the Internet Revolution.* Washington, DC: Brookings Institution Press.

Freeman, P., and W. Aspray. 1999. *The Supply of Information Technology Workers in the United States.* Washington, DC: Computing Research Association.

Friedlander, A. 1997. *Infrastructure: The Utility of Past as Prologue.* Reston, VA: Corporation for National Research Initiatives.

Friedlander, A., and R.S. Bessette. (January 31) 2001. "The Implications of Information Technology For Scientific Publishing: A Literature Review." Draft report prepared for the Division of Science Resources Studies, Directorate for Social, Behavioral, and Economic Sciences, National Science Foundation. With contributions by J.R. Cooper and R. Love, Esq.

G.K. Wallace. The jpeg still image compression standard. *Communications of the ACM,* 34(4), 1991.

Getz, M. 1997. "Electronic Publishing in Academia: An Economic Perspective." Paper presented at the Scholarly Communication and Technology Conference, Emory University, Atlanta, GA, April 24–25, 1997. Available at http://arl.cni.org/scomm/scat/getz.html. Accessed August 18, 1999.

Giacquinta, J.B., J. Bauer, and J.E. Levin. 1993. *Beyond Technology's Promise: An Examination of Children's Educational Computing at Home.* Cambridge, England: Cambridge University Press.

Glanz, J. 2001a. "Web Archive Opens a New Realm of Research." *New York Times* (on-line) May 1. Available (for fee) at http://www.nytimes.com/.

Goffman, E., 1971, Relations in Public: Microstudies of Public Order. London: Penguin

Gomery, R.E. 1994. "A Ricardo Model with Economies of Scale." *Journal of Economic Theory* 62 (April): 394–419.

Graham, J. 1976. *Making Computers Pay.* New York: John Wiley and Sons.

Griliches, Z. 1997. "Comment on Sichel 'The Productivity Slowdown: Is a Growing Unmeasurable Sector the Culprit?'" *Review of Economics and Statistics* 79 (3/August): 371.

Guernsey, L. 1998. "Distance Education for the Not-So-Distant." *Chronicle of Higher Education* March 27: A29.

Gulliksen, J.E. 2000. "MST vs. MEMS: Where Are We?" *Semiconductor Technology* 1 (10/October). Available at http://www.semi.org/web/wmagazine.nsf/.

Gurstein, P. 1991. "Working at Home and Living at Home: Emerging Scenarios." *Journal of Architectural and Planning Research* 8(2): 164–80.

H. Sawhney, S. Ayer, and M. Gorkani. Dominant and multiple motion estimation for video representation. *IEEE International Conference on Image Processing*, 1995.

H.C. Liu and G.L. Zick. Scene decompostion of mpeg compressed video. *SPIE*, 2419:26-37.

H.J. Zhang, A. Kankanhalli, and S.W. Smoliar. Automatic partitioning of video. *Multimedia Systems*, 1(1):10-28, 1993.

H.J. Zhang, C.Y. Low, and S.W. Smoliar. Video parsing and browsing using compressed data. *Multimedia Tools and Applications*, 1(1):89-111, 1995.

Hargreaves, D.J. and North, A.C., 1997, The Social Psychology of Music. Oxford: Oxford University Press.

Hicks, D.,T. Breitzman, D. Olivastro, and K. Hamilton. 2001. "The Changing Composition of Innovative Activity in the US—a Portrait Based on Patent Analysis." *Research Policy* 30: 681–703.

Hollingsworth, P. 1999. "Web Technology Forces Innovation." *Food Technology* 53 (11): 36.

Howell, D., and E. Wolff. 1993. "Changes in the Information-Intensity of the U.S. Workplace Since 1950: Has Information Technology Made a Difference?" Monograph R.R. #93–08. New York: New York University, C.V. Starr Center for Applied Economics.

Huff, C., and T. Finholt, eds. 1994. *Social Issues in Computing*. New York: McGraw-Hill.

I.K. Sethi and N. Patel. A statistical approach to scene change detection. *SPIE*, 2420:329-338.

Image Compression Survey by Arran Derbyshire(arad@doc.ic.ac.uk) and Chandrarath Kulanthai(ck4@doc.ic.ac.uk)

Interactive Television Survey by Keval Pindoria(khp1@doc.ic.ac.uk) and Gerald Wong Ping Hung(phgw@doc.ic.ac.uk)

International Technology Roadmap for Semiconductors. 2000. "ITRS 2000 Updates." Available at http://public.itrs.net/Files/2000UpdateFinal/2kUdFinal.htm. Accessed July 9, 2001.

Internet Policy Institute. 2001. "Report of the National Workshop on Internet Voting: Issues and Research Agenda." Available at http://www.netvoting.org/. Accessed September 17, 2001.

Interview with Dr Zinonas Ioannou, Mobile Services, Cyprus Telecommunications Authority

Interview with Mr Eleftherios Koudounas, Assistant Commercial Services Manager at Cyprus Telecommunications Authority

J. Meng, Y. Juan, and S.F. Chang. Scene change detection in a mpeg compressed video sequence. *SPIE*, 2419:14-25.

J. Yeh, M. Vetterli, and M. Khansari. Motion compensation of motion vectors. *IEEE International Conference on Image Processing*, 1995.

J.Y. Wang and E.H. Adelson. Spatio-temporal segmentation of video data. *SPIE*, 2182:120-131.

JKatz, L.F. 2000. "Technological Change, Computerization, and the Wage Structure." In E. Brynjolfsson and B. Kahin, eds. *Understanding the Digital Economy*. Cambridge, MA: MIT Press.

Kearsley, G. 2000. "Learning and Teaching in Cyberspace" (version 5/00) Available at http://home.sprynet.com/~Egkearsley/chapts.htm

Kearsley, G., W. Lynch, and D. Wizer. 1995. "Effectiveness and Impact of Computer Conferencing in Graduate Education." *Educational Technology* 35, 37–42.

Lajaoie, S. and Lesgold, A., 1992. "Apprenticeship Training in the Workplace: Computer-Coached Practice Environment as a New Form of Apprenticeship". In J. Farr and M.J. Psotka (eds.), *Intelligent Instruction by Computer: Theory and Practice*. Taylor and Francis: Washington, DC.

Landauer, T.K. 1995. *The Trouble With Computers: Usefulness, Usability, and Productivity*. Cambridge, MA: MIT Press.

Landefeld, J.S., and B.M. Fraumeni. 2001. "Measuring the New Economy." *Survey of Current Business* March: 23–40. Available at http://www.bea.doc.gov/bea/articles/beawide/2001/0301mne.pdf. Accessed September 17, 2001.

Lawrence, S., and L. Giles. 1999. "Accessibility of Information on the Web." *Nature* 400 (July 8): 107–09.

Lesk, M. 1997a. "How Much Information Is There in the World?" Available at http://www.lesk.com/mlesk/ksg97/ksg.html. Accessed August 5, 1999.

Lewis, T. 2000. "Corporate R&D in the Age of E-Commerce." *Research Technology Management* 42 (6/November–December): 16–20.

Library of Congress. 2001. "Fascinating Facts About the Library of Congress." Available at http://www.loc.gov/today/fascinate.html#STATS. Accessed April 17, 2001.

Link, A.N., and J.T. Scott. 1998. "Assessing the Infra-Structural Needs of a Technology-Based Service Sector: A New Approach to Technology Policy Planning." *STI Review* 22 (August).

Litan, R.E., and A.M. Rivlin. 2001. "The Economy and the Internet: What Lies Ahead?" In Litan, R.E., and A.M. Rivlin, eds. *The Economic Payoff from the Internet Revolution*, pp. 1–28. Washington, DC: Brookings Institution Press.

Lyman, P., and H.R. Varian. 2000. "How Much Information?" Available at http://www.sims.berkeley.edu/research/projects/how-much-info/. Accessed March 11, 2002.

M. Cherfaoui and C. Bertin. Temporal segmentation of videos: a new approach. *SPIE*, 2419:38-47.

Machlup, F. 1962. *The Production and Distribution of Knowledge in the United States*. Princeton: Princeton University Press.

Mann, D., C. Shakeshaft, J. Becker, and R. Kottkamp. 1999. *West Virginia's Basic Skills / Computer Education Program: An Analysis of Student Achievement*. Santa Monica, CA: Milken Family Foundation.

Mark Ballora. *Essentials of Music Technology*. Pearson Edition, Upper Saddle River, NJ, 2003.

Marshall, E. 1999. "E-biomed Morphs to E-biosci: Focus Shifts to Reviewed Papers." *Science* 285 (August 6): 810–11.

McQuarrie, E.F. 1989. "The Impact of a Discontinuous Innovation: Outcomes Experienced by Owners of Home Computers." *Computers in Human Behavior* 5: 227–40.

Mesenbourg, T. 2001. "Measuring the Digital Economy". Paper presented at the Netcentric Economy Symposium, University of Maryland, March 30, 2001. Available at https://www.rhsmith.umd.edu/dit/lucas/ditsymp/papers/mesenbourg.pdf. Accessed September 14, 2001.

Mogge, D. 1999. "Seven Years of Tracking Electronic Publishing: The ARL Directory of Electronic Journals, Newsletters, and Academic Discussion Lists." *Library Hi Tech* 17(1): 17–25.

Monaghan, P. 1998. "U. of Washington Professors Decry Governor's Visions for Technology." *Chronicle of Higher Education* June 19: A23.

National Information Infrastructure Advisory Council. 1995. *A Nation of Opportunity: A Final Report of the United States Advisory Council on the National Information Infrastructure*. Available at http://www.benton.org/Library/KickStart/nation.home.html. Accessed September 17, 2001.

National Science and Technology Council, Subcommittee on Computing, Information, and Communications R&D, Committee on Technology. 1999. *High Performance Computing and Communications: Information Technology Frontiers for a New Millennium*. Available at http://www.ccic.gov/pubs/blue00/. Accessed September 17, 2001.

National Science Foundation. 2001a. *The Application and Implications of Information Technologies in the Home: Where are the Data and What Do They Say?* Arlington, VA: National Science Foundation, Division of Science Resources Studies. Available at http://www.nsf.gov/statistics/nsf01313/exec.htm.

National Venture Capital Association. (January 29) 2001. "Venture Capital Investments Achieve Record Levels in 2000, Torid Pace Relaxed in Fourth Quarter." News release. Available at http://www.nvca.org/VEpress01_29_01.htm. Accessed September 17, 2001.

Nemvalts, Kalle. (1988) "Sequence the Swings with Performer," *Electronic Musician 110*, March, pp. 60-69.

Noble, D.F. 1998. "Digital Diploma Mills: The Automation of Higher Education." *First Monday* 3(1). Available at http://www.firstmonday.dk/issues/issue3_1/noble/index.html#author. Accessed September 17, 2001.

Noyelle, T., ed. 1990. *Skills, Wages, and Productivity in the Service Sector*. Boulder, CO: Westview Press.

Odlyzko, A. 1997. "The Economics of Internet Journals." *First Monday* 2(8). Available at http://www.firstmonday.dk/issues/issue2_8/odlyzko/index.html. Accessed September 17, 2001.

Ogburn, W.F. 1964. *On Culture and Social Change: Selected Papers*. O.D. Duncan, ed. Chicago: University of Chicago Press.

Okwesa, Fidelma. (1990) "The Problems of Collecting Data for Dance in Nigeria." Paper delivered at *Audio-Visual Archives Conference*, Falum, Sweden, July.

Oliner, S.D., and D. Sichel. 1994. "Computers and Output Growth Revisited: How Big Is the Puzzle?" *Brookings Papers on Economic Activity* 2: 273–315.

Olson, G.M., and J.S. Olson. 2001. "Distance Matters." *Human Computer Interaction* 15: 139–79. Available at http://intel.si.umich.edu/crew/technical_reports.htm#2001. Accessed March 11, 2002.

Online Computer Library Center (OCLC). 1999. "June Web Statistics." Available at http://wcp.oclc.org/. Accessed September 17, 2001.

R. Zabih, J. Miller, and K. Mai. Feature-based algorithm for detecting and classifying scene breaks. *ACM Multimedia*, 1995.

R.A. Samy and C.A. Bozzo. Dynamic scene analysis and video target tracking. *ICPR*, 84:993-995.

R.I. Taylor and P.H. Lewis. Colour image segmenation using boundary relaxation. *ICPR-C*, 92:721-724.

S. Sullivan, L. Sandford, and J. Ponce. On using geometric distance fits to estimate 3d object shape: Form and deformation from range, ct, and video images. *CVPR*, 93:110-115.

S.A. Rajala and R.L. Stevenson. *Image And Video Processing II (San Jose, Ca, February 7-9)*, volume 2182. SPIE, 1994.

Sichel, D. 1997. *The Computer Revolution: An Economic Perspective.* Washington, DC: Brookings Institution.

Sinclair, B. 1999. "Sequence of Die: Automated Instrumentation for the Genome Era." *The Scientist* 13(8): 18. Available at http://www.the-scientist.com/yr1999/apr/profile1_990412.html.

Solow, R. 1987. "Technological Change and the Aggregate Production Function." *Review of Economics and Statistics* 39 (August): 312–20.

Spiro, R.J. and Jehng, J-C., 1990. "Cognitive Flexibility and Hypertext: Theory and Technology for the Nonlinear and Multidimensional Traversal of Complex Subject Matter". In D. Nix and R. Spiro (eds.), *Cognition, Education, and Multimedia.* Lawrence Erlbaum: Hillsdale, NJ.

Stewart, Michael. (1987) "The Feel Factor: Music with Soul," *Electronic Musician*, October, pp. 57-65.

Stoll, C. 1995. *Silicon Snake Oil: Second Thoughts on the Information Highway.* New York: Doubleday.

TWaterman, Richard. (1952) "African Influence in the Americas," in *Acculturation in the Americas*, (ed.) Sol Tax, University of Chicago Press, pp. 207-218.

Welch, D. 2001. "Can Covisint Climb Out of a Ditch?" *BusinessWeek* May 21: 128B–D.

Williams, M.E. 1985. "Electronic Databases" *Science* 228 (4698/April 26): 445–50, 455–56.

Wilson, E.J. III. 2000. "Closing the Digital Divide: An Initial Review." Washington, DC: Internet Policy Institute. Available at http://www.internetpolicy.org/briefing/ErnestWilson0700.html. Accessed September 17, 2001.

WIPO. (1989) General Introductory Course: *Copyright and Neighboring Rights: Protection of Expressions of Folklore*, Geneva, Switzerland.

Wong, R., and R. Jesty. 2001. "The Wireless Internet: Applications, Technology and Market Strategies." Available at http://www.allnetdevices.com/wireless/opinions/2001/01/10/the_wireless.html. Accessed September 17, 2001.

Woolf, B. and Hall, W., 1995. "Multimedia Pedagogues". *Computer 28*, No. 5, IEEE

World Information Technology and Services Alliance. 1999. *Digital Planet: The Global Information Economy.* Arlington, VA: WITSA.

Wrolstad, J. 2001. "Rising Tide for Wireless Internet." *Wireless NewsFactor* (February 23). Available at http://www.wirelessnewsfactor.com/perl/story/7718.html. Accessed September 17, 2001.

Y. Gong, H. Zen, Y. Ohsawa, and M. Sakauchi. A color video image quantization method with stable and efficient color selection capability. *ICPR-C*, 92:33-36.

Y. Huang and X. Zhuang. Motion-partitioned adaptive block matching for video compression. *IEEE International Conference on Image Processing*, 1995.

Y. Tonomura, A. Akutsu, Y. Taniguchi, and G. Suzuki. Structured video computing. *IEEE Multimedia*, 1(3):34-43, 1994.

Y. Wong. An efficient heuristic-based motion estimation algorithm. *IEEE International Conference on Image Processing*, 1995.

Y.F. Wang, N. Karandikar, and J.K. Aggarwal. Analysis of video image sequences using point and line correspondences. *PR*, 24:1065-1084.

Young, J.R. 1998. "600 Colleges and Universities to Gain Access to a Huge Data Base." *Chronicle of Higher Education* July 3: A20.

Young, Neil. (1992) "Digital is a Huge Rip Off," *Guitar Player*, p. 14, May.

Z. Kui, M. Bober, and J. Kittler. Variable block size video coding with motion prediction and motion segmentation. *SPIE*, 2419:62-70.

Index

D

E